CYBER FORENSICS
A Field Manual for Collecting, Examining, and Preserving Evidence of Computer Crimes

CYBER FORENSICS
A Field Manual for Collecting, Examining, and Preserving Evidence of Computer Crimes

ALBERT J. MARCELLA, Ph.D.
ROBERT S. GREENFIELD

Editors

AUERBACH PUBLICATIONS

A CRC Press Company
Boca Raton   London   New York   Washington, D.C.

Library of Congress Cataloging-in-Publication Data

Cyber forensics : a field manual for collecting, examining, and preserving evidence of computer crimes / Albert J. Marcella, Robert Greenfield, editors.
　　　p. cm.
　　Includes bibliographical references and index.
　　ISBN 0-8493-0955-7 (alk. paper)
　　　1. Computer crimes--Investigation--Handbooks, manuals, etc. I. Marcella, Albert J. II. Greenfield, Robert, 1961-

HV8079.C65 C93 2001
363.25′968--dc21

2001053817

Visit the Auerbach Publications Web site at www.auerbach-publications.com

© 2002 by CRC Press LLC
Auerbach is an imprint of CRC Press LLC

No claim to original U.S. Government works
International Standard Book Number 0-8493-0955-7
Library of Congress Card Number 2001053817
Printed in the United States of America　　2 3 4 5 6 7 8 9 0
Printed on acid-free paper

Editors and Contributors

Albert J. Marcella, Jr., Ph.D., CFSA, COAP, CQA, CSP, CDP, CISA, is an associate professor of Management in the School of Business and Technology, Department of Management, at Webster University, in Saint Louis, Missouri. Dr. Marcella remains the president of Business Automation Consultants, an information technology and management-consulting firm he founded in 1984. Dr. Marcella has completed diverse technical security consulting engagements involving disaster recovery planning, site and systems security, IT, financial and operational audits for an international clientele. He has contributed numerous articles to audit-related publications and has authored and co-authored 18 audit-related texts.

Robert S. Greenfield, MCP, has over 16 years of experience as a programmer/analyst, with the past five years as a systems consultant and software engineer in the consulting field. He has extensive experience designing software in the client/server environment. In addition to mainframe experience on several platforms, his background includes systems analysis, design, and development in client/server GUI and traditional environments. His client/server expertise includes Visual Basic, Access, SQL Server, Sybase, and Oracle 7.3 development. Mr. Greenfield has created intranet Web sites with FrontPage and distributing applications via the Internet. He currently holds professional accreditation as a Microsoft Certified Professional and continues self paced training to achieve MCSE, MCSD, and MCSE/D + Internet ratings.

Abigail Abraham is an Assistant State's Attorney, prosecuting high-technology crimes for the Cook County State's Attorney's Office in Chicago, Illinois. She was awarded her J.D. from The University of Chicago Law School and served as an editor on the law review. Following law school, she clerked for one year for the Honorable Danny J. Boggs, U.S. Court of Appeals for the Sixth Circuit. She is an adjunct law professor at The University of Chicago Law School. In addition, she has designed training for lawyers and for police officers, and lectures around the country on high-technology legal issues.

Brent Deterdeing graduated from the University of Missouri with a degree in computer science and a minor in economics. Brent's involvement with SANS is extensive. He is an author of an upcoming book on firewalls through SANS, as well as chairing the SANS/GIAC Firewalls Advisory Board. He has mentored both small and large classes through SANS/GIAC Security Essentials Training & Certification (GSEC). Brent also authors, revises, and edits SANS courseware, quizzes, and tests. He has earned the SANS/GIAC GSEC (Security Essentials), GCFW (Firewall Analyst — HONORS), GCIA (Intrusion Analyst), and GCIH (Incident Handling) certifications, as well as being a Red Hat Certified Engineer (RHCE). Brent participates in the St. Louis InfraGard chapter.

John W. Rado is a geospatial analyst at National Imagery and Mapping Agency (NIMA) in St. Louis, Missouri. John has worked for NIMA since January of 1991.

William J. Sampias has been involved in the auditing profession for the past decade, with primary emphasis on audits of information systems. Mr. Sampias has published several works in the areas of disaster contingency planning, end-user computing, fraud, effective communications, and security awareness. Mr. Sampias is currently director of a state agency information systems audit group.

Steven Schlarman, CISSP, is a security consultant with PricewaterhouseCoopers. Since joining the firm in 1998, Steve has covered a number of roles, mainly as the lead developer of the Enterprise Security Architecture System and Services. He has published articles on the subject as well as being one of the major thought leaders in the PricewaterhouseCoopers' Enterprise Security Architecture Service line. Prior to joining the firm, Steve had worked on multiple platforms including PC applications, networking, and midrange and mainframe systems. His background includes system security, system maintenance, and application development. Steve has completed numerous technical security consulting engagements involving security architectures, penetration studies ("hacking studies"), network and operating system diagnostic reviews, and computer crime investigation. He has participated in both PC computer forensic analysis and network intrusion management and investigation. Prior to PricewaterhouseCoopers, Steve worked at a U.S. state law enforcement agency in the information systems division.

Carol Stucki is working as a technical producer for PurchasePro.com, a rapidly growing dot.com company that is an application service provider specializing in Internet-based procurement. Carol's past experiences include working with GTE, Perot Systems, and Arthur Andersen as a programmer, system analyst, project manager, and auditor.

Dedication

Erienne, Kristina, and Andy

Michael Jordan said it best, thus, what more can I say...

> I approached practices the same way I approached games. You can't turn it on and off like a faucet. I couldn't dog it during practice and then, when I needed that extra push late in the game, expect it to be there. But that's how a lot of people fail. They sound like they're committed to being the best they can be. They say all the right things, make all the proper appearances. But when it comes right down to it, they're looking for reasons instead of answers. If you're trying to achieve, there will be roadblocks. I've had them; everybody has had them. But obstacles don't have to stop you. If you run into a wall, don't turn around and give up. Figure out how to climb it, go through it, or work around it.

You are each important, special and unique for so many reasons. Always remain close, protect, respect, and love each other. Always know that I love each of you with all my heart.

Thank you Diane, for your constant support and love. My life is a far better one with you in my world. Today, tomorrow, forever...

Al

This book is dedicated to my mother and father who always believed in me, gave me love, guidance, and support in all of my pursuits. A son could not hope for better parents. Thank you both and know that your love gives me strength every day.

To my wife for her patience, and love through it all. And a special thank you goes out to my daughter Hannah, for your understanding, patience, love, wit, and unwavering support.

You are all the best and I love you.

I also would like to recognize Dr. Marcella for giving me this opportunity. Thank you.

Bob

Contents

Disclaimer

As always with texts of this nature, here is the disclaimer....

The information contained within this field manual is intended to be used as a reference, and not as an endorsement of the included providers, vendors, and informational resources. Reference herein to any specific commercial product, process, or service by trade name, trademark, service mark, manufacturer, or otherwise does not constitute or imply endorsement, recommendation, or favoring by the authors or the publisher.

As such, users of this information are advised and encouraged to confirm specific claims for product performance as necessary and appropriate.

The legal/financial materials and information that are available for reference through this manual are not intended as a substitute for legal/financial advice and representation obtained through legal/financial counsel. It is advisable to seek the advice and representation of legal/financial counsel as may be appropriate for any matters to which the legal/financial materials and information may pertain.

Web sites included in this manual are intended to provide current and accurate information; neither the authors, publisher, nor any of its employees, agencies, and officers can warranty the information contained on the sites and shall not be held liable for any losses caused on the reliance of information provided. Relying on information contained on these sites is done at one's own risk. Use of such information is voluntary, and reliance on it should only be undertaken after an independent review of its accuracy, completeness, efficacy, and timeliness.

Throughout this manual, reference links to other Internet addresses have been included. Such external Internet addresses contain information created, published, maintained, or otherwise posted by institutions or organizations independent of the authors and the publisher. The authors and the publisher do not endorse, approve, certify, or control these external Internet addresses and do not guarantee the accuracy, completeness, efficacy, timeliness, or correct sequencing of information located at such addresses. Use of such information is voluntary, and reliance on it should only be undertaken after an independent review of its accuracy, completeness, efficacy, and timeliness.

Acknowledgments

As senior editor for this text, the responsibility to acknowledge and thank all the individuals who have contributed their expertise, time, energies, and efforts to the successful development of this text falls to me. This is no easy task. It is difficult to put into words the appreciation and gratitude I have for each of their efforts and to express appropriately to each of them my sincere thanks for giving their time and themselves to make this text a better product. Simply mentioning each by name here seems a bit inadequate in comparison to their individual and collective contributions.

Given the continual shifting technological landscape in which we all live and work, attempting to harness even for a moment in time, this very technology, and to "look under the hood" so-to-speak, was a daunting assignment. Those professionals whose insights and comments on the critically important field of cyber forensics are included in this text, and deserve substantial credit and our thanks for taking up this challenge and for their spot-on examination and evaluation of key cyber forensics issues.

I wish to formally recognize each contributing author here, although briefly, and have included a more extensive personal profile for each author. To each of you, please know that you have my heartfelt gratitude and personal thanks for your willingness to contribute your talents and expertise to this text.

Thank You:

To my co-editor Bob Greenfield; thank you for contributing your talents in the technical systems arena and for your piece on "The Liturgical Forensic Examination: Tracing Activity on a Windows-Based Desktop."

Thanks to Steve Schlarman, security consultant at PricewaterhouseCoopers, who wrote the chapter on "Network Intrusion Management and Profiling," and to Brent Deterdeing, network security manager, enabling technologies at Solutia, Inc., for insights and comments on "Tools of the Trade: Automated Tools Used to Secure a System Throughout the Stages of a Forensic Investigation."

John Rado, geospatial analyst at National Imagery and Mapping Agency; thank you for sharing your thoughts (and your extensive security/forensics background and library with me), and for developing the focused piece on "Basics of Internet Abuse: What is Possible and Where to Look Under the Hood."

From the Financial and Computer Crime Department of the State Attorney's office of Cook County, Illinois, Attorney Abigail Abraham; thank you for your engaging examination into "Cyber Forensics and the Legal System."

To my long-time colleagues and collaborators Carol Stucki, for your presentations on the "The Goal of the Forensic Investigation" and "How to Begin a Nonliturgical Forensic Examination;" and Bill Sampias for your efforts in developing the areas of guidelines and tools, including the list of critical recommended readings.

Additionally, I would like to thank Carol for all the work she did in compiling the exhaustive reference materials from the Federal Bureau of Investigation, computer examinations library, which appeared in successive issues of the Bureau's *Handbook of Forensic Services*.

Without the contributions of these talented professionals, this text would have been a lesser product.

Last, but by far certainly not the least, I want to acknowledge and thank Christian Kirkpatrick, Acquisitions Editor at Auerbach Publications, for her constant confidence that this text would emerge from a simple concept into a viable product.

Christian, thank you for your steadfast support throughout the lengthy development process that has led to the creation of this viable cyber forensics field manual.

Introduction

As an auditor as well as researcher and author, I realize and value the importance of timely, well-focused, accurate information. It is with this philosophy in mind that the development of this project was undertaken.

To the reader, a note of explanation.... This is not a text, but rather a field manual. It has been written — better yet, compiled — and edited in a manner that will allow you to rapidly access a specific area of interest or concern and not be forced to sequentially wade through an entire text, chapter by chapter, to get to what is important to you.

In the true sense of a field manual, each "chapter" (and we use that term loosely) stands on its own and presents focused, timely information on a specific topic related to cyber forensics. The author of each "chapter" was selected for his or her expertise in a specific area within the very broad field of cyber forensics.

Often a limiting aspect of most projects, especially those written on emerging technical topics, is the inability to cover every aspect of the topic in a single all-inclusive text. This truth befalls this field manual that you are about to use.

Initial research into this growing discipline proved that it would be next to impossible to include all the areas of both interest and importance in the field of cyber forensics that would be needed and required by all potential readers and users in a single text. Thus, this field manual presents specific and selected topics in the discipline of cyber forensics, and addresses critical issues facing the reader who is engaged in or who soon will be (and you will!) engaged in the preservation, identification, extraction, and documentation of computer evidence.

As a user of this field manual, you will see that this manual's strength lies with the inclusion of an exhaustive set of chapters covering a broad variety of forensic subjects. Each chapter was thoroughly investigated; examined for accuracy, completeness, and appropriateness to the study of cyber forensics; reviewed by peers; and then compiled in a comprehensive, concise format to present critical topics of interest to professionals working in the growing field of cyber forensics.

We finally had to select several key areas and put pen to paper, entice several colleagues to share their ideas, and resign ourselves to the fact that we cannot say all that needs to be said in one text, book, or manual. We trust the material we have included will serve as a starting point for the many professionals who are beginning their journey into this exciting discipline.

We begin our journey into the realm of this relatively new discipline by opening with a brief discussion as to the current state of the environment relating to the need for this new field of forensics and then a brief examination of the origins of cyber forensics. Along the way, we will establish several basic definitions designed to assist the reader in moving easily through what could be difficult and confusing terrain.

> Although e-mail is becoming more mission-critical for enterprises, it also has the ability to haunt a company in times of trouble, because records of e-mail messages remain in the company systems after deletion — a feature highlighted during the Microsoft anti-trust trial. The case has featured critical testimony derived from old Microsoft e-mail messages.
>
> — *InfoWorld*, 10/25/99

Background

The ubiquitous use of computers and other electronic devices is creating a rapidly rising wave of new and stored digital information. The massive proliferation of data creates ever-expanding digital information risks for organizations and individuals. Electronic information is easy to create, inexpensive to store, and virtually effortless to replicate. As a result, increasingly vast quantities of digital information reside on mass storage devices located within and without corporate information systems. Information risks associated with this data are many. For example, electronic data can often show — with a high degree of reliability — who said, knew, took, shared, had and did what, and who else might be involved in the saying, knowing, taking, sharing, having, and doing. For the corporation, the free flow of digital information means that the backdoor is potentially always open to loss.

To put the explosive growth of electronic data in perspective, consider that Americans were expected to send and receive approximately 6.8 trillion e-mail messages in 2000 — or about 2.2 billion messages per day.[1] Although some of this e-mail is sent and received by individuals, most of it is being created by and sent from corporate mail servers.

In 2000, the World Wide Web consisted of 21 terabytes of static HTML pages and is growing at a rate of 100 percent per year.[1] There are now about 2.5 billion indexed Web pages, increasing at the rate of 7.3 million pages per day.

Demand for digital storage is expected to grow by more than 1800 percent between 1998 and 2003. A midrange estimate of the amount of data currently stored on magnetic tape is 2.5 exabytes (an exabyte is 1 million terabytes), with another 2.5 exabytes stored on computer hard drives.[1]

Contrasting the growth of paper pages and electronic documents adds additional perspective. The growth of recorded information doubles every three to four years. Over 93 percent of all information produced in 1999 was in digital format. About 80 percent of corporate information currently exists in digital form.

Companies are expected to generate some 17.5 trillion electronic documents by 2005, up from approximately 135 billion in 1995.[2] Some 550 billion documents now exist online.

There is more to this explosive growth than just "documents." Additional forms of electronic data originate from:

- Internet-based electronic commerce, online banking, and stock trading
- Corporate use and storage of phone mail messages and electronic logs
- Personal organizers, such as the Palm Pilot (worldwide PDA sales were expected to total about 6 million units in 2000 rising to 17 million in 2004.)
- Wireless devices such as cell phones and pagers with contacts and task list storage (worldwide mobile phone sales were expected to total about 400 million in 2000, rising to 560 million in 2004[1])
- Digital cameras
- Corporate use and storage of graphic images, audio, and video

These are several of the factors now at work in corporations that increase the risk of litigation and loss of confidential corporate data (from www.fios-inc.com/digital_risk.html, Fios, Inc. (877) 700-3467, 921 S.W. Washington Street, Suite 850, Portland, Oregon 97205)

It is best to state up-front that the emphasis in any cyber forensic examination must be on the forensic element, and it is vital to understand that forensic computing, cyber forensics, or computer forensics is not solely about computers. It is about rules of evidence, legal processes, the integrity and continuity of evidence, the clear and concise reporting of factual information to a court of law, and the provision of expert opinion concerning the provenance of that evidence:

> Companies are very concerned about the notion that anything they write electronically can be used again at any time. If you have to discipline yourself to think, "can this be misconstrued?" that greatly hampers your ability to communicate and introduces a huge level of inefficiency.
>
> — *David Ferris, president of Ferris Research (San Francisco)*

Dimensions of the Problem

Crime: an act committed in violation of the law.

Much of today's computer-related crime is not a violation of formal law. In 1979, the Justice Department defined computer crime as any illegal act for which knowledge of computer technology is essential for its perpetration, investigation, or prosecution.

Criminal law is a crime, which is a wrong against society, typically leading to a conviction, which normally results in jail term or probation. The main purpose is punishment of the offender. Most computer crimes in United States today go unpunished (which weakens deterrence of law).

Evidence must be gathered by law enforcement in accordance with court guidelines governing search and seizure (Fourth Amendment):

> The right of the people to be secure in their persons, houses, papers, and effects, against unreasonable searches and seizures, shall not be violated, and no warrants shall issue, but on probable cause, supported by oath or affirmation, and particularly describing the place to be searched, and the persons or things to be seized.

Computer crime is escalating!

The FBI's caseload is increasing dramatically. In FY 1998, the FBI opened 547 computer intrusion cases; in FY 1999, that jumped to 1154. At the same time, because of opening the National Infrastructure Protection Center (NIPC) in February 1998 and the FBI's improving ability to fight cyber crime, the Bureau closed more cases. In FY 1998, the closed case file increased to 399 intrusion cases; and in FY 1999 it increased to 912 such cases.

However, given the exponential increase in the number of cases opened, cited above, the FBI's actual number of pending cases has increased by 39 percent, from 601 at the end of FY 1998 to 834 at the end of FY 1999. In short, although the FBI has markedly improved its capabilities to fight cyber intrusions, the problem is growing even faster.

The Computer Security Institute released its fifth annual "Computer Crime and Security Survey" for 2001, confirming the alarming facts cited above. Eighty-five percent of respondents detected security breaches over the past 12 months.

At least 64 percent of respondents reported financial losses, including theft of proprietary information, financial fraud, system penetration by outsiders, data or network sabotage, and denial-of-service attacks. Information theft and financial fraud caused the most severe financial losses, put at $151 million and $93 million, respectively. The losses from 186 respondents totaled just over $377 million.

Losses traced to denial-of-service attacks were only $77,000 in 1998, and by 1999 had risen to just $116,250. Further, the new survey reports on numbers taken before the high-profile February 2000 attacks against Yahoo!, Amazon, and eBay. Finally, many companies are experiencing multiple attacks; 19 percent of respondents reported ten or more incidents.

> Attorney Deanne Siemer says she tells judges that digital technology "takes one-third out of the trial time." And that's a huge factor for courts with their enormous backlogs.

> — *Rebecca Ganzel,*
> "Digital Technology in the Courtroom,"
> *Presentations, November 1999*

Computer Forensics

Computer Forensics deals with the preservation, identification, extraction, and documentation of computer evidence. The field is relatively new to the private sector but it has been the mainstay of technology-related investigations and intelligence gathering in law enforcement and military agencies since the mid-1980s.

Like any other forensic science, computer forensics involves the use of sophisticated technology tools and procedures that must be followed to guarantee the accuracy of the preservation of evidence and the accuracy of results concerning computer evidence processing.

What evidence is needed?

- All physical evidence (computer, peripherals, notepads, documentation, etc.)
- Visual output on the monitor
- Printed evidence on a printer
- Printed evidence on a plotter
- Film recorder (magnetic representations)

It is extremely important to realize that evidence must have been gathered in accordance with the Fourth Amendment and the Electronic Communications Privacy Act (ECPA), and that computer-generated evidence is considered "hearsay" with some exclusions. Depending on your role or responsibility in the computer forensics investigation, you may be subject to differing sets of rules and regulations. Internal investigators, for example, are not subject to the Fourth Amendment stipulations; however, they are subject to the ECPA.

Typically, computer forensic tools exist in the form of computer software. Computer forensic specialists guarantee accuracy of evidence processing results through the use of time-tested evidence processing procedures and through the use of multiple software tools, developed by separate and independent developers. The use of different tools that have been developed independently to validate results is important to avoid inaccuracies introduced by potential software design flaws and software bugs.

The introduction of the personal computer in 1981 and the resulting popularity came with a mixed blessing. Society in general benefited, but so did criminals using personal computers in the commission of crimes. Today, personal computers are used in every facet of society to create and share messages, compute financial results, transfer funds, purchase stocks, make airline reservations, and access bank accounts and a wealth of worldwide information on essentially any topic.

Computer forensics is used to identify evidence when personal computers are used in the commission of crimes or in the abuse of company policies. Computer forensic tools and procedures are also used to identify computer security weaknesses and the leakage of sensitive computer data. In the past, documentary evidence was typically stored on paper and copies were made with carbon paper or photocopy machines.

Most documents are now stored on computer hard disk drives, floppy diskettes, Zip disks, and other forms of removable computer storage media. Computer forensics deals with finding, extracting, and documenting this form of "electronic" documentary evidence (www.forensics-intl.com/def4.html).

Along the way, prior to formally pursuing a cyber forensics investigation, several important and critical questions must be asked:

- What is the policy in the organization to report and deal with computer crime? (It may be nonexistent, or it may be not well thought out or tested, or it may even be incompetent.)
- Do you "really" want to prosecute?
- Who do you call in law enforcement and what will be their reaction?

Additional questions that should be considered and appropriate answers well thought out include:

- Can you afford to be without the evidence?
- Are you willing to see this go public?
- Was a thorough investigation conducted?
- Did you violate the ECPA or any privacy issues?
- How will you prove the crime?
- Is there any likelihood of the suspect doing damage prior to arrest? (Dr. Rayford Vaughn, vaughn@cs.msstate.edu)

Obtaining concrete answers to these questions prior to embarking on a cyber forensics audit or investigation is critical. Doing so may help shield the organization (as well as the investigator/auditor/security personnel, etc.) from civil or criminal liabilities.

The material presented in the following pages of this field manual has been selected, developed, and shared with the specific objective of providing the reader with a resource with which to become better prepared to undertake and participate in the cyber forensics audit of a suspect system.

Works Cited

1. University of California at Berkeley, School of Information Management and Systems, October 2000, http://www.sims.berkeley.edu/how-much-info/.
2. *Designing a Document Strategy: Documents…Technology…People.* Craine, K., MC2 Books, 2000.

CYBER FORENSICS 1

Chapter 1

The Goal of the Forensic Investigation

Carol Stucki

Any investigation has a purpose. With this chapter we will start with the reasons why one would need to conduct an investigation involving computers. When we understand the reason why we are conducting the investigation, then we can develop a plan of action on how to conduct that investigation, and where to look for evidence. The information gathered during the investigation can be used for the enforcement of Human Resources (HR) rules for disciplinary action and even legal action. Therefore, the reasons for the investigation are almost as important as the investigation itself.

This chapter reviews several reasons why an investigation is needed and the plan of that investigation, based on those reasons. It also reviews the impact of the action that resulted in the complaint. We first need to determine the impact or feasibility of conducting the investigation. For example, if the cost of the investigation outweighs the benefits, there might not be a reason to conduct the investigation. For the most part, the decision to conduct the investigation is up to management. However, it is the investigators' responsibility to provide the information on which to allow management to base the decision to proceed.

The deliverables from this chapter will be either a recommendation to proceed with the investigation and a plan of action to do so, or to withdraw due to a lack of evidence or justification. With the plan in hand, you will be able to take the steps outlined in the following chapters to implement the investigation. You will actually conduct the investigation and use the tools as described to gather the information and evidence needed to reach a conclusion in your investigation.

0-8493-0955-7/02/$0.00+$1.50
© 2002 by CRC Press LLC

Why Investigate

First we will need to consider the complaint or the initial reason for conducting an investigation. Some typical reasons that may warrant an investigation include but are not limited to:

- Internet usage exceeds norm
- Using e-mail inappropriately
- Use of Internet, e-mail, or PC in a non-work-related manner
- Theft of information
- Violation of security policies or procedures
- Intellectual property infractions
- Electronic tampering

This chapter reviews the typical reasons for investigation and lists some questions to help determine what facts or circumstances surround each reason.

Internet Exceeds Norm

If the complaint is that someone's Internet usage is too high, we should first determine the basis for this complaint. It should also be determined whether the above normal Internet usage was identified through electronic monitoring or by personal observation. It is also appropriate to determine if the usage is out-of-line with company standards for the type of job responsibilities held by the individual under investigation. Equally important is to determine how those standards were determined and developed.

There are different questions to be asked, and answered, in order to investigate the claim, depending on the basis of the complaint.

If the usage was electronically monitored:

1. Did a firewall monitor the usage?
2. Was the usage monitored by Internet Protocol (IP) address or individual identification (ID)?
3. What exactly was monitored? (e.g., time, sites, keywords, etc.)
4. Can more than one person use this personal computer (PC) (or IP address)?
5. Can more than one person use this ID?
6. Can the usage times/dates be correlated to physical access by the individual under investigation? (If monitoring shows access was between 8 a.m. and 10 a.m., was the individual at work during this time?)
7. What was the pattern of access?
8. How does this compare with the individual's work schedule?
9. Could the individual have logged in and then not logged out? (i.e., get to an Internet site and then go to another task on the PC, thus leaving the Internet site up and running?)
10. Are there timeouts set on the Internet access? On the PC login?
11. Are there security cameras, login sheets, key card access logs, or timecards that can verify that it was the individual who accessed the Internet via this PC?
12. Is there a pattern to the usage?

Once you obtain answers to these questions you will begin to see the outlines of a plan of the investigation forming. For example, if Joe Programmer is accused of exceeding Internet norms, based on a report generated from the firewall monitoring system, we can ask some additional questions to validate the concern/complaint.

If the pattern of unusually high utilization was after-hours when Joe was not scheduled to be at work, then there might be a deeper issue that will require further investigating to uncover (i.e., who and how someone was using Joe's ID after-hours). However, if the case is simply that Joe is logging into the Internet first thing in the morning to check the latest news or stock quotes, and not logging out, this is a case where the monitoring or rules might need to be adjusted to account for the high usage. Alternatively, Joe may simply need a refresher course on the company's Internet usage policies.

On the other hand, if the usage concern was based on a person's observation of Joe's actions, there is another, slightly different set of questions to ask, such as:

1. Who made the observation?
2. Are logs available to support the observation? (e.g., login, logout, timecards, firewall access, etc.)
3. Are there other witnesses to support the observation?
4. What exactly was the individual under investigation observed doing?
5. What is the pattern of usage?
6. Are there security cameras, login sheets, time cards, or key card access logs that can verify the individual under investigation had access and was logged on to the Internet?

Again, once you obtain answers to these questions you will begin to formalize a plan of investigation. This plan will differ slightly from the plan based on electronic monitoring. With observation being the basis for a complaint, the ability to verify the usage is more difficult to substantiate — but not impossible.

There are a variety of tools, methods, and techniques outlined in this text that will allow you to substantiate the claim, if there is any evidence. For example, there are several files located on the firewall and the PC that can be retrieved, displayed, and reviewed in order to prove or disprove the above-normal access violation(s).

The above-normal utilization should prompt the investigator and management to inquire about the impact (financial, physical, operational, etc.) of the so-called excessive usage. Several questions to help evaluate the impact include:

1. What damage (if any) did the excessive usage cause?
2. How can the damage be substantiated?
3. How can the damage be quantified?
4. Did the individual under investigation not meet his or her job responsibilities as a result of excessive Internet usage?
5. Did the individual under investigation interfere with another person's job performance as a result of the excessive utilization?
6. Was someone offended by the usage (e.g., inappropriate materials, games being played)?

7. Can you identify this person?
8. Is the person willing to state for the record that he or she she was offended by the usage?
9. Did fraud occur in the form of falsified timesheets — hours of work reported, or any other form, as a result?

The answers to these questions answers will not only help form the plan for this type of investigation, but will also help the investigator and management determine if the investigation should be (can be) pursued.

Inappropriate E-mail

Before performing any investigation on e-mail, you need to ensure that corporate policy allows it. New electronic privacy laws protect the privacy of electronic communications. If corporate policy specifically states that all computers and data stored on them belong to the corporation, then you are probably on safe ground. Be sure that there is such a policy and that the employee under investigation has read the policy before proceeding. Although this is one of the easiest investigations, this type of investigation should be done strictly by the book. If the corporate policy does not contain the rights to the employee's e-mail, then you and your corporation could be subject to a lawsuit for invading the privacy of an employee.

If the reason for an investigation is that there was inappropriate use of e-mail, either through the act of sending offensive material or for personal and non-work-related use, there is yet another set of questions that should be asked. These questions will help determine if there was inappropriate utilization of the company's e-mail systems and if further investigative action is required.

1. What was sent?
2. Can you obtain a copy from the complainant or recipient?
3. Is a copy available from the automated e-mail archive system?
4. Was someone offended? (This could be an harassment issue and require HR involvement.)
5. Who if anyone else received the material?
6. Was the individual under investigation the originator of the e-mail, or was it someone else?
7. How were you able to (or can you) validate this?
8. Could someone else have sent the e-mail, using the ID of the individual under investigation?
9. Are screen-saver passwords used?
10. Could someone else use the PC of the individual under investigation?
11. Was the time that the e-mail was sent during the time the individual under investigation had access to e-mail?
12. Is auto-forwarding of e-mail used? Available? Activated?
13. Was a group list used?
14. Are there patterns or history to the e-mail usage?
15. Have there been previous warnings to the individual under investigation about the e-mail usage?

16. If so, are these warnings documented?
17. What was the intent of the e-mail?

Some of the questions listed in the section on abnormal Internet utilization can also be applied to this type of investigation. The real issue with this type of investigation is to determine whether it is an issue of harassment or a case of violating company e-mail policies/procedures.

Potential exposures to the company, which can result from the lack of a proactive response by management to a harassment complaint, include a lawsuit filed against the company by the complainant, as well as multiple instances of harassment that can lead to multiple lawsuits. Furthermore, to make matters worse, the longer the company waits to investigate, the more likely it is that lawyers will have a field day and turn this into the company not caring, and thus higher rewards to the complainant. To alleviate the appearance of a non-proactive response to harassment complaints, the company should have anti-harassment policies and training programs. This training should be repeated annually for all employees. There should be documentation that is maintained in HR files stating that each employee has attended and signed a statement that he or she has read the company's policies against harassment. This is also documentation that should be gathered during the investigation.

Non-Work-Related Usage of Company Resources

If the reason for the investigation is about non-work-related use of company resources (i.e., PC, e-mail, or access to the Internet), the above questions apply, but there are additional questions that should be asked, including:

1. What exactly occurred? (Was the individual under investigation using his or her PC to engage in "moonlighting" work, e-mail for personal use, etc.?)
2. When did the incident occur?
3. How was it documented?
4. How often or how much does this happen?
5. Is the individual under investigation the only person engaged in this activity, or are there others?
6. How can you determine this?
7. Is the action a widely accepted company practice, albeit a violation of company policy?
8. Did the individual under investigation take the action for personal financial gain?
9. Was the non-work-related usage for personal use?
10. Is there a liability to the company due to the unauthorized use of company property?

These more detailed questions will help frame the direction of the investigation more clearly. Thus, a more appropriate plan of action can be devised and carried out. The main issue with this type of investigation concerns the inappropriate use of company property for personal gain, and whether the inappropriate usage violated any standing company policies.

Theft of Information

The theft of information raises the intensity and seriousness of an investigation to levels that may exceed those established in previously discussed scenarios. The intensity of an investigation into the theft of information will vary, depending on what type of information was stolen, its significance to the company's ability to remain competitive, the nature and sensitivity of the information stolen, and what was done with the stolen information.

Some of the previously mentioned questions can be applied to this type of investigation. However, there are additional questions that relate specifically to the theft of information, including:

1. What type of information was stolen?
2. How has this been (or can this be) verified?
3. How much information was stolen?
4. How was the information stolen?
5. What is the impact or cost of the loss?
6. How can this loss be quantified?
7. How can this be substantiated?
8. Is the cost of the loss tangible or intangible (competitive information can be intangible)?
9. Has the goodwill of the company been damaged as a result of the theft?
10. Has the company lost a competitive edge due to the theft?
11. Was the information totally lost (e.g., copied and then erased or destroyed), or was it copied?
12. Was another company's information, beyond your own, compromised?
13. What was the level of security surrounding the information lost?
14. Who had access to the stolen information?
15. Can this be verified?
16. Are access logs available?
17. Are they free from potential, external tampering?
18. Were there procedures in place for the safe handling/accessing of the lost information?
19. Was the information proprietary, confidential, or restricted?
20. How was this classification determined and communicated?

To determine exactly how the information was stolen, you might need to perform further security and access audits/reviews. For the purpose of planning and investigation, the investigator should develop a sense of how the information was stolen. One reason to quickly determine how the information may have been stolen is an attempt to prevent further information from being stolen in the same manner.

Violation of Security Parameters

Violation of security parameters can vary widely, from an individual simply failing to properly log off when leaving work to covert hacking into secured files. Security parameters are not always those dramatic measures of using guards, secret codes, retinal scanners, and IDs, but they do include the use of security cameras and passwords, and following procedures for handling secure documents.

The violation or misuse of security parameters can lead to the theft or misuse of company information or property, or worse. Violation of security parameter complaints should begin with asking the following questions:

1. What security parameters or measures were violated? *Note*: Care must be exercised in both asking and documenting the response to this question. Some parameters may be proprietary while others may be highly sensitive, and their disclosure might jeopardize the security of entire systems.
2. How were the parameters violated? (See note above.)
3. What was the result of the violation?
4. How can this be substantiated?
5. Were passwords compromised (hacked)?
6. Have new passwords been issued? Reset?
7. Were security measures disabled (e.g., security cameras unplugged, screen savers turned off, etc.)?
8. Were security measures bypassed?
9. If so, how? (See note in question 1 above.)
10. Was information falsified as part of the violation (e.g., fraud — pretending to be someone else)?

The violation of security parameters does not always result in the compromise of company information. However, because the violation of security can lead to the compromise of information, it is important to investigate every violation.

The investigation can lead management to recognize the need to add more security measures or to improve existing measures to both secure and protect the company's information.

Intellectual Property Infraction

Intellectual properties are those ideas, techniques, procedures, or program codes that are considered proprietary and that belong to a specific company. Companies usually have clauses in their employment contracts that state that any intellectual property developed during an employee's employment with the organization belongs to the company and cannot be used outside the organization. Infractions of an organization's intellectual property policies usually involve former employees, contractors, or consultants, using techniques or code that they created (or had access to), who are now at a new employer/competitor.

When investigating this type of infraction, the investigator may wish to begin by asking the following questions:

1. Does the organization require employees involved in or holding specific job responsibilities to sign an intellectual properties agreement/contract?
2. Are signed policies on file?
3. Does the organization have a viable intellectual properties policy?
4. Is it in force?

5. How can this be verified?
6. When was the intellectual property in question first created for the company?
7. How can this be substantiated?
8. Who developed the intellectual property?
9. How can this be verified?
10. When was the intellectual property created or used outside the company, violating the organization's (and previous employee's) intellectual property agreement?
11. Can this be substantiated?
12. Who is the original owner of the intellectual property?
13. Is this merely a case of plagiarism?
14. Are there copyrights involved?
15. Are there patents involved?
16. What proof is there that the intellectual property in question belongs to the company?

With most intellectual property infractions, it is advisable to seek legal counsel in helping to design and plan the investigation. The major concern of management is the impact of the infraction. If the impact is minimal, management may decide that an investigation is not warranted. If, however, the infraction might place the company at a competitive disadvantage, management may wish to proceed with the investigation.

Competent legal counsel may advise that any and all violations of a company's intellectual properties policies be investigated and prosecuted to the fullest extent of the law. Failure to do so (or even to conduct an investigation) might be construed by the courts as indifference, and thus weaken the company's ability to prosecute future cases.

Electronic Tampering

Electronic tampering can involve fraud, mimicking someone or something (i.e., IP spoofing), masking, or masquerading as someone (i.e., social engineering). The intent and result of the tampering is the primary reason to conduct an investigation.

Even if the intent of the tampering involves or can be linked to a noncompetitive prank, there is still reason to investigate. If any tampering can occur, regardless of the reason, then it should be prevented to protect the company's information assets.

When investigating electronic tampering, the following questions provide the investigator with a good starting point. Additionally, the questions listed in the section that addressed the "Violation of Security Parameters" should also be incorporated into the investigation plan.

1. What was tampered with?
2. How can this be verified?
3. Did the tampering result in the perpetration of a fraud?
4. What was the intent of the tampering?

5. How can this be verified?
6. How was the tampering carried out?
7. Who first noticed the tampering?
8. How was the tampering first identified?
9. Could the tampering have been undertaken in more than one way?

Because some forms of tampering can involve theft or fraud, which can be criminal offenses, legal counsel should be involved in planning this type of investigation. To determine exactly how the tampering was performed, it is recommended that the reader examine several of the more technically specific chapters in this book.

We have reviewed some of the questions an investigator can ask and gathered some preliminary information. We now need to review the basis upon which the complaints were formulated, such as a violation of company policies, procedures, or legal statutes.

Establishing a Basis or Justification to Investigate

If there is a justification for a specific complaint or reason to investigate, there should also be rules or a baseline for which the complaint was filed, such as violating a standing company policy or procedure. For example, if company policies and procedures state that employees should only use e-mail for company business, this would be the baseline for a complaint about an individual suspected of using the company's e-mail system for non-work-related activities.

Baselines that guide many complaints (or a justification to investigate) often include a misuse or violation of:

- Company policies and procedures
- Legal statutes
- Mandatory statutes
- Regulatory statutes

The investigator will need to consult these baselines as appropriate and as part of the investigation to determine how the baseline(s) apply and if there are any documented penalties for violation of these baselines. For example, a policy and its associated penalty for sending inappropriate e-mail could result in the loss of employment for the individual found guilty of violating this policy.

First, consult the company's policies and procedures. There are several different policies and procedures within the company that should initially be reviewed. For example, Human Resources, Security, and Employee policies are a good beginning and represent general, most often found standard policy types in force within most organizations.

As part of investigation planning, consider asking the following questions to learn more about the company's current policies and procedures (these are especially relevant to investigation of harassment charges).

1. Are the policies and procedures published and available?
2. Are the policies and procedures current?

3. Are the policies and procedures available in hard or soft copy?
4. Is there mandatory training or orientation to acquaint all employees with these policies and procedures?
5. Are signatures of the employees gathered to verify that all employees have received and reviewed these policies?
6. Have there been audits or reviews to verify compliance with policies and procedures?

There are several additional items of documentation that should be considered for examination, depending on the type of investigation to be undertaken. The investigator should be prepared to ask for and examine:

■ *Contracts*, both with third-party suppliers and with external consultants
■ *Non-disclosure agreements*, with third-party suppliers and with consultants

In addition to company policies and procedures, and contracts, the investigator may find it appropriate to consult legal statutes if criminal activities are involved. Mandatory statutes refer to those contracts that the company has with other companies or entities. Those contracts will also need to be examined in cases of loss of information (data) and the subsequent impact on the organization. Regulatory statutes will need to be examined when the investigation reveals a potential for the loss or disclosure of confidential information (data).

Another reason for consulting the legal, mandatory, and regulatory statutes is to determine the liabilities to the company if no investigation is conducted, when a breach of company security and or policy occurs. For example, if a fraud were to be perpetrated and the company knew about it but does not pursue or report it, the company could be held liable for damages resulting from the fraud. The company could also face penalties for not reporting the fraud.

Determine the Impact of Incident

Once both the reasons for an investigation and the baseline have been determined, we must now determine the impact of the incident. By understanding the impact, we can determine if it is feasible to continue on with the investigation. By their very nature, some incidents, regardless of the impact (financial or otherwise) will need to be investigated.

Some items to keep in mind when determining the impact include, but are not limited to:

■ Benefits to pursue such an investigation
■ Liabilities for not pursuing an investigation
■ Obligations to pursue or not to pursue (goodwill toward public, partners, and other contracts)
■ Resources available (time, people, finances, tools, etc.)

To perform an impact review, you will need to plan your investigation. First, you should review why you are conducting the investigation. For illustration, let us assume that the complaint was that someone was sending inappropriate e-mail. For planning sake, you know you will need to talk to several people; namely, the person who filed the complaint, the person under investigation, the network administrator, the supervisors, and a representative from human resources (HR), as well as your legal department. So, you will need to allot time to speak with each of these individuals. You will need to gather their statements as well as evidence along the way. While speaking with HR and with the supervisors, you will need to gather the company policies and procedures on e-mail, harassment, and any training programs specifically aimed at workplace harassment. You might even need to talk with the auditors to see what kinds of audits they have conducted in the HR department and networking areas to date. (reference audit checklists, list of questions to ask, samples of HR policies).

The second step, now that you have planned interviews and gathered the appropriate documentation, is to draw up a timeline. You should also consider what resources will be available to you in conducting this investigation. Those resources can include personnel in your group and those external to your department/group. In your consideration, you need to know if you have the authority to ask other departments to help you gather information. Having someone gather information for you will save you time and effort. This may, however, compromise the independence of your investigation. Be sure to verify your sources and check with your legal department on the appropriateness of using external third parties for this type of specialized work.

You will also need to consider what tools you can use to gather information. Various tools aimed at providing the auditor with access to erased or "hidden" data will be discussed in subsequent chapters of this text.

As an example, and as a means of further discussing the investigation model, we will operate under the assumption that your organization has (or you have as the auditor/security professional) several of the tools discussed in this text. We will use these tools to help gather evidence that the individual under investigation has sent an offensive e-mail.

Because this example takes a look at e-mail as the source of policy infraction (or worse), we might not need to confiscate any equipment for examination. This is due to the fact that e-mail (for most organizations) runs on network servers and network or operations personnel maintain these servers. You must also keep in mind an important question: How do you determine that the e-mail in question (the one cited as being offensive) was not "planted"? A basic first step for reviewing e-mail includes gathering all the e-mails sent by the individual under investigation (or the e-mails sent during a certain time period).

You might need to trace back several days or weeks, looking at e-mail details to see if there is more than the one e-mail that may have started the complaint. Also, you might need to gather e-mail from and to other persons involved in the incident (if others were involved or affected). You can determine whose e-mail you will need to examine by reviewing a copy of the original e-mail that initiated the complaint. There may be a list of who else was copied on the e-mail. This list is where you start gathering e-mails. How do you gather the e-mails? Ask the network/operations personnel to recover the needed e-mails and have them copied to a file you can access. Most e-mails can be copied to MS Word files in text format.

This step takes a critical "leap of faith" on the part of the auditor/security professional: that the organization does indeed maintain an e-mail log/file and also archives all e-mail traffic. Additionally, the issue of independence is raised here once again. If someone other than the auditor/security professional retrieves these e-mails it is imperative that control be maintained over the retrieval process to ensure accountability and authenticity of the e-mails retrieved from the log file.

Now that you have your list of whom to interview, who will help, and how you plan to gather the evidence, you should be able to put together a timeline with an estimate of hours required for this part of the investigation. The second half of the investigation previously discussed will depend on what you find. This is the ambiguous part, the part where you have to hypothesize, theorize, and even guess at, for planning purposes.

Once again, let us assume the worst-case scenario; you have found one e-mail that contains inappropriate material. Also assume there are several people involved, that one individual initially sent the inappropriate e-mail and several additional individuals passed (e-mailed/forwarded) it around. You will need to review the policies and procedures on the distribution of inappropriate e-mail (if they exist). You will also need to review the personnel files of the people involved (and everyone who forwarded the e-mail(s) in question), and determine if they have been through any company-sponsored harassment training.

The evidence you gathered (for this scenario) will most probably be turned over to HR department personnel so they can follow through on any disciplinary actions (if warranted) or establish new policies, procedures, and controls. Do not forget to plan time to document and summarize your findings. In the worst case, your evidence may be used in a legal case, and not only how you carry out your investigation but also what you document and how you document evidence could be critical.

A major consideration in your documentation efforts is to record who you talked to, when you talked to them, what they said, what evidence you gathered, and how you gathered that evidence; and then to draw your conclusions, all without interjecting personal opinions. Just gather and document the facts.

Summarize your plan. You have your lists of who to talk to, resources to help, and how long it will take. Now you might need to consider the benefits and obligations of conducting or not conducting the investigation. For example, if the investigation will take three weeks with the help of ten people, this is 1200 person-hours. Put this into dollars by multiplying the average wages per hour by the total person-hours. If this amount is more than the consequence of a penalty of $1000 in fines (average wage $20 per hour, total cost $24,000), it might not be cost-effective to conduct this investigation. However, if the consequence has much higher fines, damage to goodwill, or the probability of resulting in a lawsuit (as in the case of the inappropriate e-mail), you may conduct the investigation regardless. Once you have your estimates for the costs and an outline of the benefits of the investigation, you can now formally present this to management for their go/no-go decision to proceed with the investigation.

Who to Call/Contact

Who to call/contact depends on the type investigation that will be conducted (e.g., fraud, misuse of company assets, etc.). In most companies, the department with the most experience in conducting investigations is the internal audit department (although in some organizations an independent fraud investigation unit may be in existence, and can be called upon for assistance). This might be the first contact for help with any investigation. In most cases, you will probably need to contact:

- *Internal audit*: expertise in conducting investigations, past audit results
- *Network/operations*: for tracking IP addresses, e-mails, log files, backup files, monitoring logs, incident reports
- *Data security*: policies and procedures, password usage, security reports, log files, access requests and reports
- *Physical security*: policies and procedures, after-hours logs to work areas, security camera tapes, key card access logs, access requests, incident reports
- *Human resources*: policies and procedures, employee information, complaint reports
- *Legal*: contracts, legal assistance, mandatory, statutory, legal requirements
- *External consultants*: in area of needed expertise

And only after serious reflection and consultation with your legal counsel:

- External law enforcement personnel, agencies, or departments

If You Are the Auditor/Investigator

As the auditor/investigator, you will need to determine the following to conduct an effective investigation:

1. Available resources
2. Authority
3. Obligations/goals
4. Reporting hierarchy
5. Escalation procedures
6. Time frame
7. Procedures to follow
8. Precedence of past investigations
9. Independence

Each of these items is discussed as to its importance in conducting an effective investigation.

Resources

You need to know if you are working alone or with a team. A team might be faster but not warranted for small investigations. With a team you will also need to define who is the leader and who is responsible for each aspect of the investigation.

Authority

You will need to know what your level of authority is in conducting the investigation. Do you have access to the information, areas, and resources (not just personnel) you need to effectively conduct your investigation? Do you have to file requests to gain access? Also, do you have the authority to quarantine files and equipment? You might need to take someone's PC into your possession for investigation so you will need to know if you can take it without impacting ongoing operations. You might also need to know if you have the right to request certain people's time in order to interview them. If the person you wish to interview is an hourly employee, you might need prior permission from his or her supervisor.

Obligations/Goals

You need to know what your obligation is, both ethically and professionally, in this company and with this investigation. If you find that your superior is the individual under investigation, you will need to know how to handle this investigation. You will need to consider what to do if you uncover some illegal activity/action that involves the company, something that if made public could damage the company's reputation, but if not reported could hurt someone else (as well as being illegal and misrepresentative). Hopefully, you will not find yourself in an Erin Brokovich "situation."

Reporting Hierarchy

You will need to identify to whom you must report your findings to, and how to report them. This reporting hierarchy is important in obtaining the go/no-go decision to conduct the investigation. Also, you might need to know who to ask for help in getting the cooperation needed to conduct your investigation.

Escalation Procedures

If you have problems obtaining cooperation or in reporting findings of an urgent matter, you will need to know the escalation procedures for your investigation.

Time Frame

For proper planning purposes, you will need to determine when you expect to complete your investigation and any milestones management expects you to adhere to for your investigation. These milestones might include status reports, for example.

Procedures

If you are the auditor or investigator, you may wish consider following these steps:

1. Review the filed complaint (i.e., the reason for conducting investigation).
2. Determine the legitimacy of the complaint.
3. Review policies and procedures, and appropriate legal statutes.
4. Plan how to conduct the investigation.
5. Determine the impact/feasibility of conducting investigation, or of not conducting one.
6. Obtain management's approval to proceed with the investigation.
7. Contact departments involved and those who will need to help.
8. Gather evidence.
9. Document evidence.
10. Present evidence to management.

Precedence

You will need to determine if there have been other investigations performed, similar to the one and type you are about to investigate. Any past investigations can help with the planning and execution of the current one. Also, prior precedence may have already been set that should be considered and adhered to, such as disciplinary actions previously taken, disclosures made to external third parties, etc.

Independence

Evaluate your ability to act independently. Do you have the authority as well as the authorization to be independent in conducting your investigation? If not, why not?

Good documentation tied to sound processing procedures is essential for success in computer crime cases. Without the ability to reconstruct accurately what has been done, crucial evidence may be subject to question. More important, the qualifications of the expert witness can become an issue if the computer evidence processing was done haphazardly.

— Michael R. Andersen
New Technologies, Inc.
Computer Evidence Processing

Chapter 2

How to Begin a Non-Liturgical Forensic Examination

Carol Stucki

When you have obtained the go-ahead from management to begin an investigation, you will find the steps and procedures for many types of investigations in this chapter. The most common and main type of investigation that this chapter discusses is the non-liturgical examination. The non-liturgical investigation is one that is not foreseen to be taken to trial or involve litigation. However, you should always conduct the investigation using the same procedures as if you are going to trial. By conducting an investigation in thi manner, you will have all the evidence you need in the format you need it in to take action in front of company mnagement or in a courtroom.

One of the first things to consider is: Do you need to isolate equipment or files? If yes, you need to move quickly on this in order to preserve any possible evidence. What you preserve and find on the equipment, most likely a PC, will be the basis of your forensic examination. This chapter reviews such topics as the isolation of equipment, isolation of files, tracking of Web sites visited, tracking of log-on duration and times, tracking of illicit software installation and use, and how to correlate the evidence found.

Isolation of Equipment

Should you need to isolate or quarantine equipment as a part of your investigation, you need to take a few steps to (1) ensure the protection of the equipment, (2) isolate and protect data from tampering, and (3) secure the investigation scene.

0-8493-0955-7/02/$0.00+$1.50
© 2002 by CRC Press LLC

First, you need to ensure that you have the authority to take the equipment. If you are taking any equipment, you should first get authorization from management. If you take working equipment, they will need to make arrangements to replace it while you conduct your investigation.

The first thing to do is ensure that the PC you are about to take as part of your investigation is the correct unit, the one actually used in the illegal activity, used by the employee under investigation. This can be done by checking the asset records, or the records that are kept in some corporations by the operations department. If you need to take an employee's PC, you need to have a witness and have the employee sign a form stating that you took the PC; record the serial number, make, and model, when you took it, and the reason. If you do not have such forms, ensure that you do record what action was taken, obtain the employee's signature, and secure the suspect equipment.

If you have to take an employee's PC, you must move quickly to ensure that the evidence is preserved intact and not tainted, altered, or even destroyed.

Once you have the PC in your possession, you need to preserve the "chain of evidence." You preserve the chain of evidence by making sure that neither you nor anyone else is left alone with the equipment. You should always record your actions with the equipment. A good way to record all the actions and whereabouts with equipment or any other piece of evidence under investigation is to keep a log. This log should show (1) who has access to the equipment, (2) who retains control over the log, and (3) where the log is stored. Additionally, you should record the when (dates and times), where, and why of your every action, so that every minute you have the equipment or data in your possession is accountable. Even if you put this PC in a locked cabinet or secured area, this needs to be recorded in the log.

One of the first things you should do with the PC is "ghost it." This means that you should back up everything on the PC. This way, you can ensure that you will not lose the data when you conduct your investigation. This also preserves the original data that might be disturbed during the investigation.

It is very important for the backup of any data under investigation that the programs used to perform this backup be independent and have integrity. That is, the programs should not be under the influence or control of any person or other program or system that is outside the investigation team. The integrity of the data and equipment needs to be ensured by the use of programs that will not alter the original data in any way, either intentionally or accidentally.

There are a number of programs used to perform such backups that are independent and have integrity. One such program is SafeBack, and it is freeware that is available on the Web.

Isolation of Files

Not all the data needed for an investigation will reside on a user's PC. Therefore, you need to gain access to the same files and directories that the user has access to. The first thing to do is to disable the user's ID. First, ensure that the administrator verifies what action (or actions) will occur to the user's profile and accounts if the user's ID were to be disabled. Only after verifying that no data will be lost, altered, or destroyed by disabling the ID, should the administrator proceed to disable the user's ID.

You need to have someone with security or administration authority disable the users' ID. Operations personnel or a systems/data security office can do this. The easiest way to disable the user's ID is to change the password; but this is not the most efficient, as the user could regain access if he or she were to guess the new password. Ensure that the administrator disables the ID but does not delete it. In some security setups, deleting a user ID will cause data and files to be deleted as well. Because this is not what you want to happen, disable only the ID.

Once the ID is disabled, the next and most important step is to copy all the files to whcih the user had access. This provides a backup for your investigation, as the data cannot be quarantined. The confiscated data, however, cannot be used by the business for as long as you need to conduct your investigation.

Operations or security personnel should have paper files with access requests, and they can run a report that shows what the user had access to on the system. Make sure the list or report they give you contains the group access and public access files for the user. You need to investigate all of the places a user could have copied or hidden data. For the investigation, you might be able to ignore those files with read-only access, but it is always best to be sure and get it all.

Now that you know what the user had access to, request that operations personnel copy the files into a secure location that only you and your team have access to. Copy the file structure as well — all directories and sub-directories. Make two copies of the data: one as a backup and one for you to use in the investigation. This is similar to taking a picture of the crime scene before you start moving things around.

Now that you have a copy of the data to use, the following sections in this chapter provide various examples of potential investigative areas, and demonstrate how you can use the data collected as part of your investigation.

Tracking of Web Sites Visited

If your investigation requires that you track what Web sites have been visited by an employee, you need to begin by reviewing the following items

- Cookies
- Bookmarks
- History buffer
- Cache
- Temporary Internet files

Here we briefly define each of these items, where to find them, how to capture the findings, and how to evaluate what you have found.

Cookies

Cookies are messages given to a Web browser by a Web server. The browser stores the message in a text file called ***cookie.txt***. The message is then sent back to the server each time the browser requests a page from the server.

The main purposes of cookies are to identify users and possibly prepare customized Web pages for them. When you enter a Web site that uses cookies, you may be asked to fill out a form providing such information as your name and interests. This information is packaged into a cookie file and sent to your Web browser, which stores it for later use. The next time you go to the same Web site, your browser will send the cookie to the Web server. The server can use this information to present you with custom Web pages. Thus, for example, instead of seeing just a generic welcome page, you might see a welcome page with your name on it.

The name *cookie* evolved from UNIX objects called *magic cookies.* These are tokens that are attached to a user's ID or program and change depending on the areas entered by the user's ID or program. Cookies are also sometimes called *persistent cookies* because they typically stay in the browser for long periods of time.

You will find cookies on the PC's hard drive, usually the C: drive, under the Windows directory. Cookies is a sub-directory under the Windows directory. The best way to access the Cookies sub-directory and subsequent files stored there is via MS Windows Explorer (see Exhibit 1).

When you open this directory using Windows Explorer, you will find a listing of the Cookies for those Web sites that you have visited. If there are no files under this directory, they have been deleted. If there are files under this directory, you can view the dates and times they were last accessed. You will also see the ID that was used to access these sites on this PC.

Cookies can be deleted in several ways. One way is manually. The user can access the cookies folder and delete all information from the folder. If the deletion was done manually, one place to look for cookies is in the Recycle Bin. There is a Disk Cleanup program that comes with Windows 98 and higher that deletes the information in the following folders: Cookies, Temporary Internet, Download-able Program Files, Recycle Bin, Old ScanDisk Files, and Temporary Files. See Exhibit 2 for a look at the Disk Cleanup program. The Disk Cleanup program does not leave any place to look for deleted files. There are also Cookie Manager programs that will automatically delete old or expired cookies from your cookie folders. These programs allow users to set their own expiration and archive dates. For example, the user can set the Cookie Manager to delete or archive all cookies more than five days old. Some of these manager programs put the deleted cookies into the Recycle Bin and some put them in a temporary archive folder. To find these archive folders, you would have to research the program and find the archive files.

For your investigation, you need to determine where each cookie takes you. Cookies can be named many things (see Exhibit 1); so by exploring and recording where each cookie takes you, you can determine what the user had been doing on the Web sites where the cookies came from. Note the date and time of each cookie; this is when they were created or accessed by the user for the first time for this site. However, some cookies are generated without a user having to actually access a particular site. These "magic cookies," which are generated without a user having to actually access a particular site, are often marketing gimmicks or ploys to get the user to go to their Web site. To determine where a user actually visited, you need to compare the cookies files to the history files. History files are described later in this chapter.

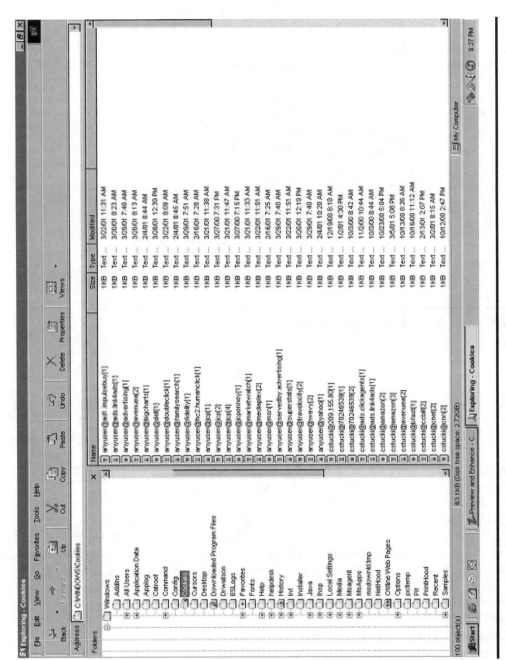

Exhibit 1. Cookies Sub-Directory File Contents

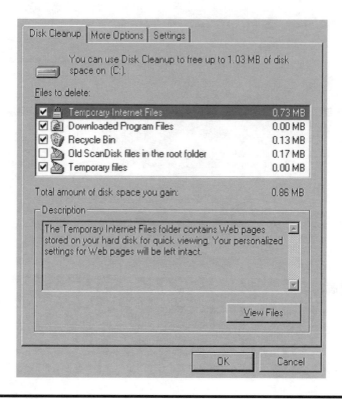

Exhibit 2.   Disk Cleanup Program from Windows 98

Bookmarks

A bookmark is a marker or address that identifies a document or a specific place in a document. Bookmarks are Internet shortcuts that users can save on the Web browser. Thus, users do not have to remember or write down the URL or location of Web sites they might like to revisit in the future. Nearly all Web browsers support a bookmarking feature that lets users save the address (URL) of a Web page so that they can easily revisit the page at a later time.

There are two places bookmarks or favorites are stored. One is in the Web browser under Favorites (see Exhibit 3). Another is on the C:, or hard, drive under the Windows folder, in the sub-folder called Favorites (see Exhibit 4).

The bookmarks or favorites are stored under the users' desired names. However, by clicking on these, you can visit each Web site the user has marked. Because bookmark names can be changed by the user, by sure to examine each one carefully. Be sure that you do not casually skip over a seemingly "tame" bookmark name simply because it does not look like it would be pointing to an unauthorized Web site (e.g., PrettyFlowers@Home). There is no real way to hide a bookmark, but users can bury a bookmark in a folder they create in the bookmark area. So be sure to open the folders you see in the bookmarks listing.

There is an added advantage to seeing the favorites listing from the user's C: drive view. You can see the dates and times when the bookmarks were created or modified. However, this does not provide you with a listing of times when the sites were actually visited, or how frequently.

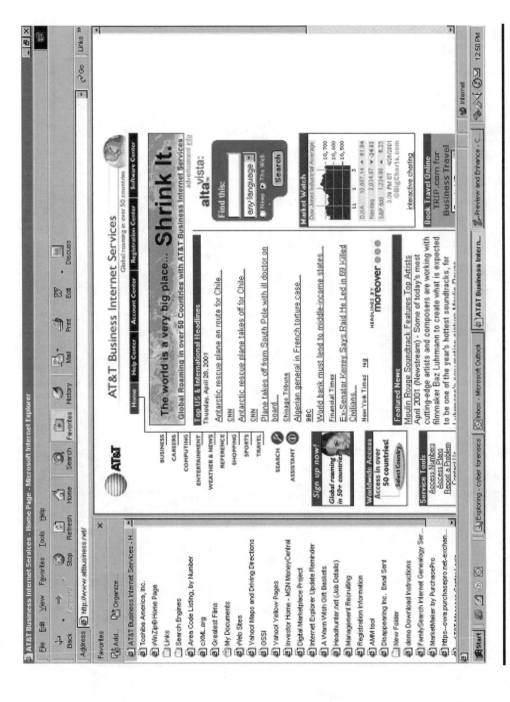

Exhibit 3. Favorites from Web Browser (Explorer)

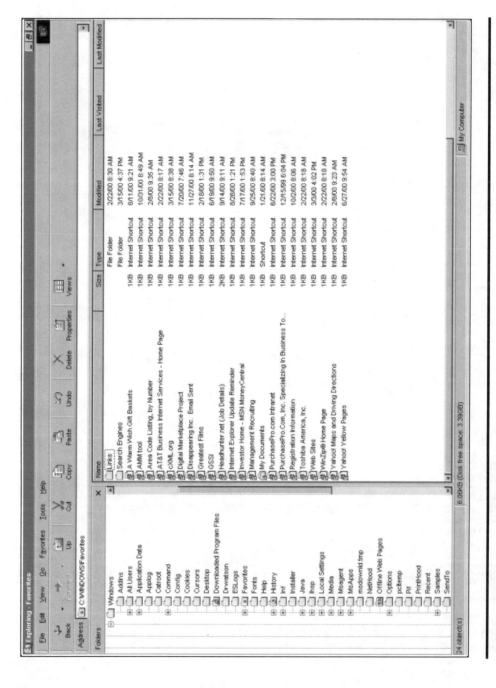

Exhibit 4. Bookmarks from Hard Drive View

History Buffer

A buffer is a temporary storage area, usually in RAM. The purpose of most buffers is to act as a holding area, enabling the CPU to manipulate data before transferring it to a device (e.g., a printer, external device, etc.).

Because the processes of reading and writing data to a disk are relatively slow, many programs keep track of data changes in a buffer and then copy the buffer to a disk. For example, word processors employ a buffer to keep track of changes to files. Then when you *save* the file, the word processor updates the disk file with the contents of the buffer. This is much more efficient than accessing the file on the disk each time you make a change to the file.

Note that because your changes are initially stored in a buffer, not on the disk, all changes will be lost if the computer fails during an editing session. For this reason, it is a good idea to save your file periodically. Most word processors automatically save files at regular intervals.

On the other hand, a history buffer is a storage area on the Web browser of URL sites. What the history buffer shows you, from the Web Browser's point of view, is what URLs or sites have been visited by day and what screens have been opened under each URL (see Exhibit 5).

To get to the history buffer, go to the Web browser. On the tool bar there is an icon or button called History (see Exhibit 5).

The history buffer can be cleared out by the user by simply highlighting and deleting the items in the list. The deleted contents from this list are not stored anywhere else in the browser, but they still exist in the hard drive history buffer.

The view of the history buffer from the hard drive point-of-view is a little different (see Exhibit 6). This view is found via the path Windows, History. Here you see the days of the week that the user actually accessed the Web. By opening one of the days of the week sub-folders, you can see the actual listings of the URLs visited by the user, and the time and dates the sites were last visited. By combining each day's lists, you can derive a pattern of visitation (and browser utilization) to each Web site.

Such information may document/prove that an employee (or at least the individual who sat at the particular PC under review) was accessing the Web: (1) in violation of company policy; (2) during working hours instead of only during predetermined allowable times (i.e., lunch breaks); (3) on weekends or during other off-schedule, non-normal times when employees or other personnel should not be in the building/office; or (4) visiting unapproved or unauthorized sites.

Cache

Cache can be either a reserved section of main memory or an independent high-speed storage device. Two types of caching are commonly used in personal computers: memory caching and disk caching. A memory cache, sometimes called a cache store or RAM cache, is a portion of memory made of high-speed static RAM (SRAM) instead of the slower and cheaper dynamic RAM (DRAM) used for main memory. Memory caching is effective because most programs access the same data or instructions over and over. By keeping as much of this information as possible in SRAM, the computer avoids accessing the slower DRAM.

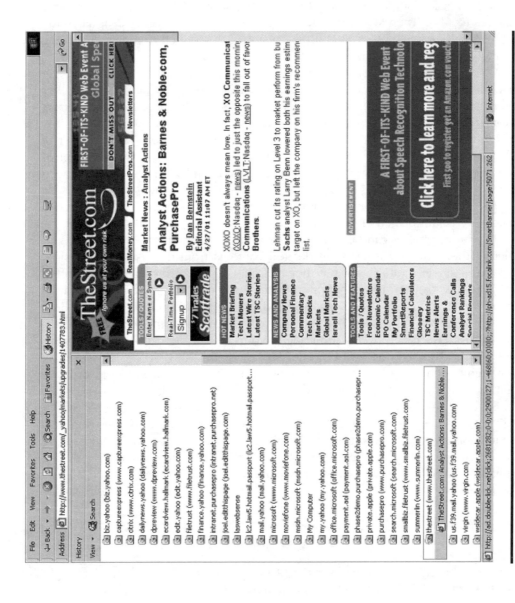

Exhibit 5.   History Buffer from Web Browser

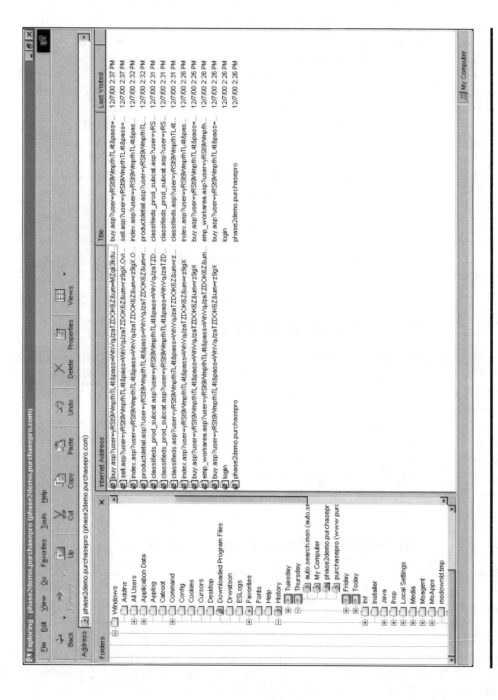

Exhibit 6.   **History Buffer from Hard Drive View**

Some memory caches are built into the architecture of microprocessors. The Intel 80486 microprocessor, for example, contains an 8K memory cache, and the Pentium has a 16K cache. Such internal caches are often called Level 1 (L1) caches. Most modern PCs also come with external cache memory, called Level 2 (L2) caches. These caches sit between the CPU and the DRAM. Like L1 caches, L2 caches are composed of SRAM but are much larger.

Disk caching works under the same principle as memory caching; but instead of using high-speed SRAM, a disk cache uses conventional main memory. The most recently accessed data from the disk (as well as adjacent sectors) is stored in a memory buffer. When a program needs to access data from the disk, it first checks the disk cache to see if the data is there. Disk caching can dramatically improve the performance of applications because accessing a byte of data in RAM can be thousands of times faster than accessing the same byte on a hard disk.

When data is found in the cache, it is called a cache hit, and the effectiveness of a cache is judged by its hit rate. Many cache systems use a technique known as smart caching, in which the system can recognize certain types of frequently used data.

How is cache important to computer forensics? You can get the last set of instructions or data that was saved in the cache. This might be evidence you need to collect in your investigation. Unfortunately, capturing the cache information is tricky and can only be done with special programs.

Temporary Internet Files

Temporary Internet Files are those files that are "image captures" of each screen/site that you visit when you access the Internet or an intranet (see Exhibit 7). Temporary Internet Files is a sub-folder under the Windows folder on the C: drive or hard drive of the PC.

The advantage of looking at the Temporary Internet Files over any other files is that this shows you the address of the site, and when it was last modified, last accessed, and last checked. This can be very useful when gathering evidence of too much Internet access, or inappropriate Internet access. These can also be useful in proving a pattern of logon and duration times.

Tracking of Logon Duration and Times

If you need to review logon duration and times for a given user, you should contact the organization's network operations group (or similarly named/empowered department). This group can provide reports on any given IP address, user ID, and the times that the IP address and ID was logged into the network. Some of these reports can actually tell what addresses the user accessed and when. The most basic report should be able to tell when the ID was logged into the system and when it logged off. With some of the current system architecture, the reports track and log all user activity down to the keystroke. However, this detailed logging does pull down the performance of the servers, so the logging is not always done to this level of detail. You must ask your network operations personnel what type of reporting and subsequent information is available.

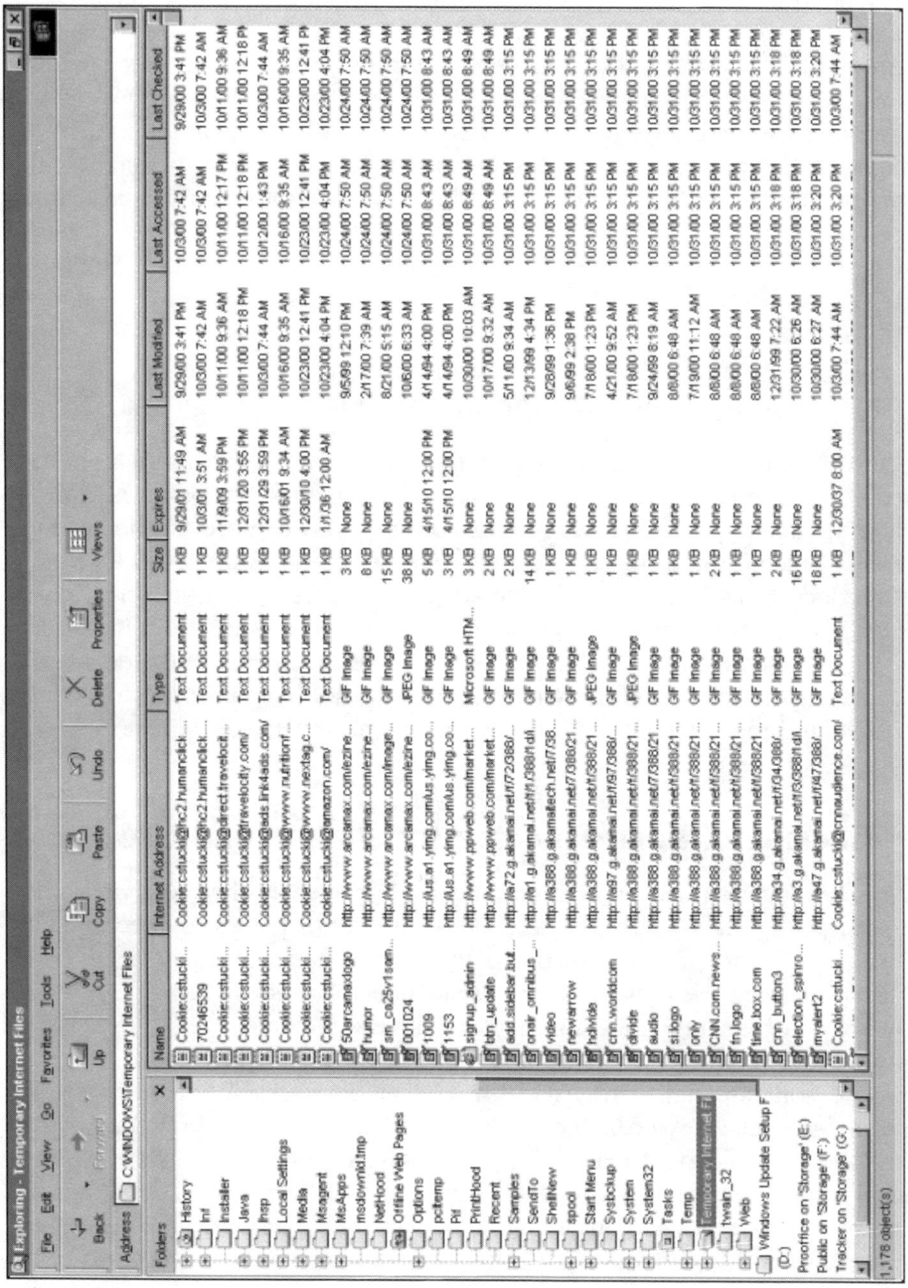

Exhibit 7. Temporary Internet Files

Ask for the entire detail report and see what they record; do not just ask for the basics; you might save time and effort if you ask for everything up front. What you ask for should include not only the activity but also the server monitor reports that pertain to the user, traffic monitoring, and site click-through reports. You want any report that exists that might show what a given user was doing at any moment. You might be surprised just how much information is available and how eager the operations staff personnel are to use their expertise.

Some of the evidence you can gather to help determine logon and duration times can be derived from the Temporary Internet Files and Recent Documents list. These files can help establish and support patterns of use. Although a smart user might clean up these files frequently using the disk cleanup utilities that Windows provides, it is always good to check to see what information is available. The cleanup utilities are in the Start Menu, Programs, Accessories, Disk Cleanup. This utility erases the Internet files, temporary files, and most cookies. See prior sections of this chapter on how to find and access Temporary Files.

Recent Documents List

The recent documents list can show you the latest documents that a user has accessed. There are two ways to see this list of documents, but only one shows you when the items on the list were accessed. First, you can see the documents from the Start menu, under the Documents "tab"/selection. You can click on any one of the documents listed and the document is brought up on the screen (see Exhibit 8). You can also access the same list, via the Recent sub-folder under the Windows folder (see Exhibit 9). This view will give you the name of the document and when each was last modified. Windows 95 does not have this directory; only Windows 98 and more recent copies of Windows have a Recent directory.

Tracking of Illicit Software Installation and Use

If you are investigating a user who may be loading illegal, illicit, or non-work-related software on his or her PC, there are a number of places to check within the PC in question to prove or disprove these unauthorized (and maybe even illegal) actions. Some of these key places include the System Registry, System Information, and by simply viewing the hard drive's contents.

Before you begin this part of an investigation, you must first get a listing of all approved software that can reside on a given PC. This list most probably contains things such as Word, Excel, Microsoft Office, and other work-related software. There should be a master list (i.e., database) of what software resides on every PC that Operations maintains. However, with some site license agreements most of the software might be on a checklist, which Operations personnel use to set up new PCs. Not all these software programs might be on every PC.

The company policies and procedures should have an outline of the software that is not permitted to be loaded on a company-owned PC. The most recognizable programs that are usually not work related are games. When looking for these types of programs, look carefully at the names of the files; users often change the names to avoid detection. To double-check the programs' legitimacy, actually

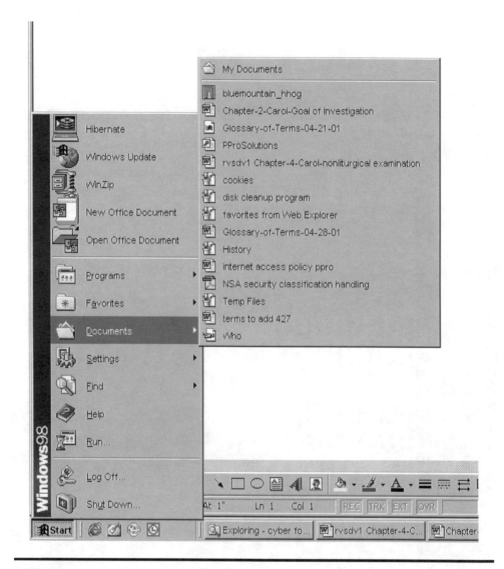

Exhibit 8.   Recent Document List from Start Menu

launch all *.Exe* files to ensure that you get accurate information about what is actually behind the file's name and residing on the PC. Remember: this procedure should be carried out on the mirror imaged, working copy data, and not on the original PC — both to avoid corrupting seized data as well as disrupting networked services or other legitimate data that may reside on the PC in question.

As you are checking the software list, you should also note all the serial numbers and registration numbers of all software that resides on the PC. These numbers should be compared to the software licenses held by the company to ensure that the loaded software is both legal and authorized. For example, a user might have MS Access on his or her PC, but the company might not have authorized or actually loaded this on that user's PC. The user might have obtained certain software packages in some manner, however, not complying with company procedures and thus it has been illegally installed on the PC. This is the most common type of illegally installed software on company equipment today. This

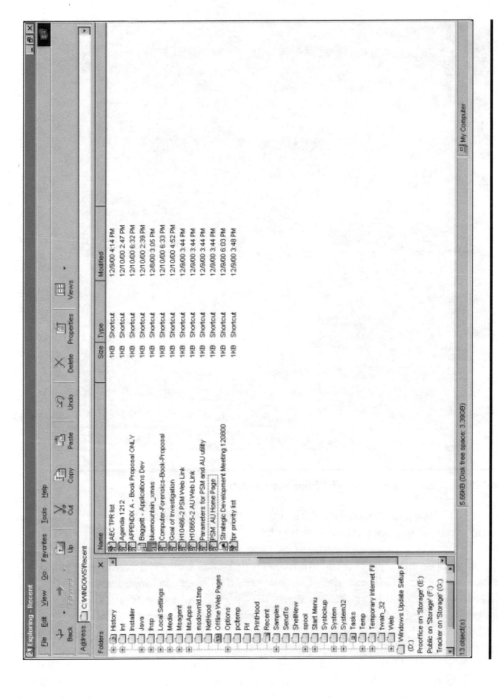

Exhibit 9. Recent Documents List Hard Drive View

is most risky to a company because software license infringement can be expensive to a company if it is discovered and not corrected.

Okay, how do you actually begin to search for this evidence? First, you need your lists of what can be on any given PC and what is registered to be on the specific PC you are investigating. You are also looking for a list of all information that pertains to the PC under review; specifically, information such as verification of assignment of the PC to a specific employee and, if available, all software licensed for the given PC. You should then check and compare the information on these lists against the master list maintained by Operations.

Next, you need to list all the programs that currently reside on the PC. There are several ways to accomplish this. One method is to use the System Registry files; we refer to this as the System Review. Another method is to review all files via the PC directories (i.e., Explorer); we refer to this as the Manual Review. Both methods are discussed briefly in the following paragraphs.

The System Review

The system review can be conducted using some automated methods. One of these methods is to use the System Registry files. There are several System Registries. We discuss the two primary Microsoft registry files. One is a list of all software loaded on the PC; the other is a more comprehensive list of what is loaded, when it was loaded and how it is configured. Both can be used to verify that illegal or non-work-related software or hardware was loaded onto a given PC.

The more simple list of what has been loaded can be viewed by accessing the path from the Control Panel, to the Add/Remove Programs icon (see Exhibit 10).

A more comprehensive list of software and hardware that have been loaded onto a PC can be obtained via the Microsoft System Information panels. The following path can access these: Start, Programs, Accessories, System Tools, System Information (see Exhibit 11). This screen shows the basic system information of the PC being investigated. The most useful information about a PC can be found under the Components directory. This is where you will find some history — when things were loaded and last modified (see Exhibit 12).

There are three levels of information shown on this screen: Basic, Advanced, and History. All three can provide needed information in an investigation, depending on what you are looking to prove.

The Components/System/Basic Information can help determine if illegal or non-work-related software was loaded onto a PC (see Exhibit 12). To determine if there is illegal software or non-work-related software on the PC using this list, first you need a list of all legal software that should be on the machine, along with any serial or license numbers for the software. This list should be available from the Operations department that distributes and fixes the PCs. Next, take this list and verify what software is on the machine; be sure to check the serial numbers. The Components/System/Basic Information list tells you what software is on the machine and when it was loaded. But the serial numbers will be in the "about" information or start-up screen for the software. If the software is not work related, it will not be on your list from the Operations department. You must check company policies about loading non-work-related software on company PCs.

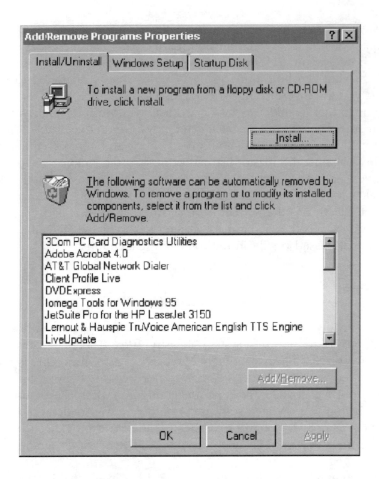

Exhibit 10. Add/Remove Programs Software Listing

Another view to see if software has been loaded onto the PC from the Web is available via Windows Explorer, in the Windows Directory under the Download Program sub-folder (see Exhibit 13).

The Components/System/History information can show when a component (piece of hardware or firmware) was loaded and when it was last modified (see Exhibit 14). However, many components are modified when the user reboots or turns on the computer. The "red herring" items to look for in this history would be things that were not issued with the computer and the user added himself. These might include graphics cards, emulators, or sound cards. The Component/History files are not much different in the information that they provide (see Exhibit 14).

Exhibit 15 shows what has been updated in the last seven days. The Complete History file shows when items were loaded or when they were modified since last being loaded.

The Manual Review

One of the reasons for conducting the Manual Review as well as the System Review is to ensure you have covered all of the bases. What the Manual Review

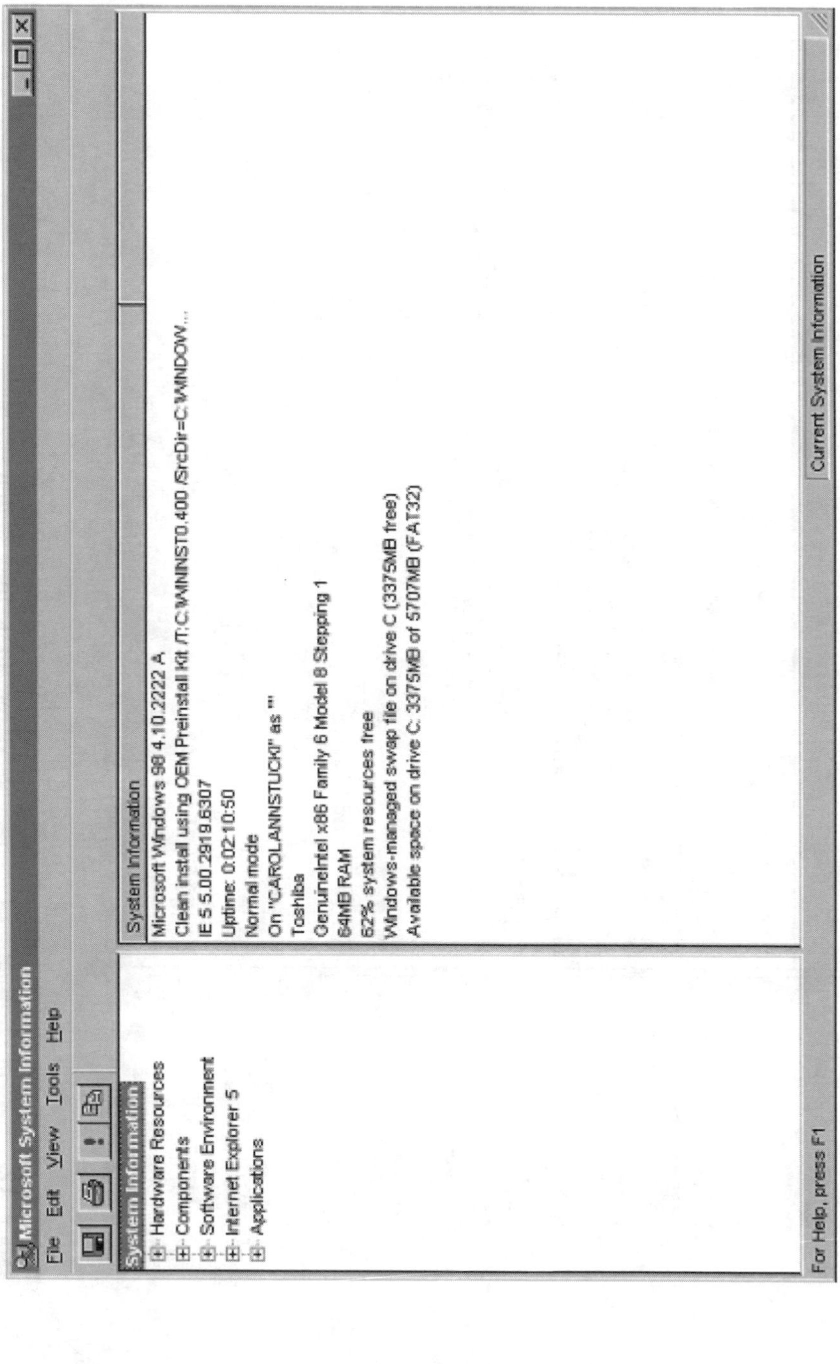

Exhibit 11. System Information Base Screen

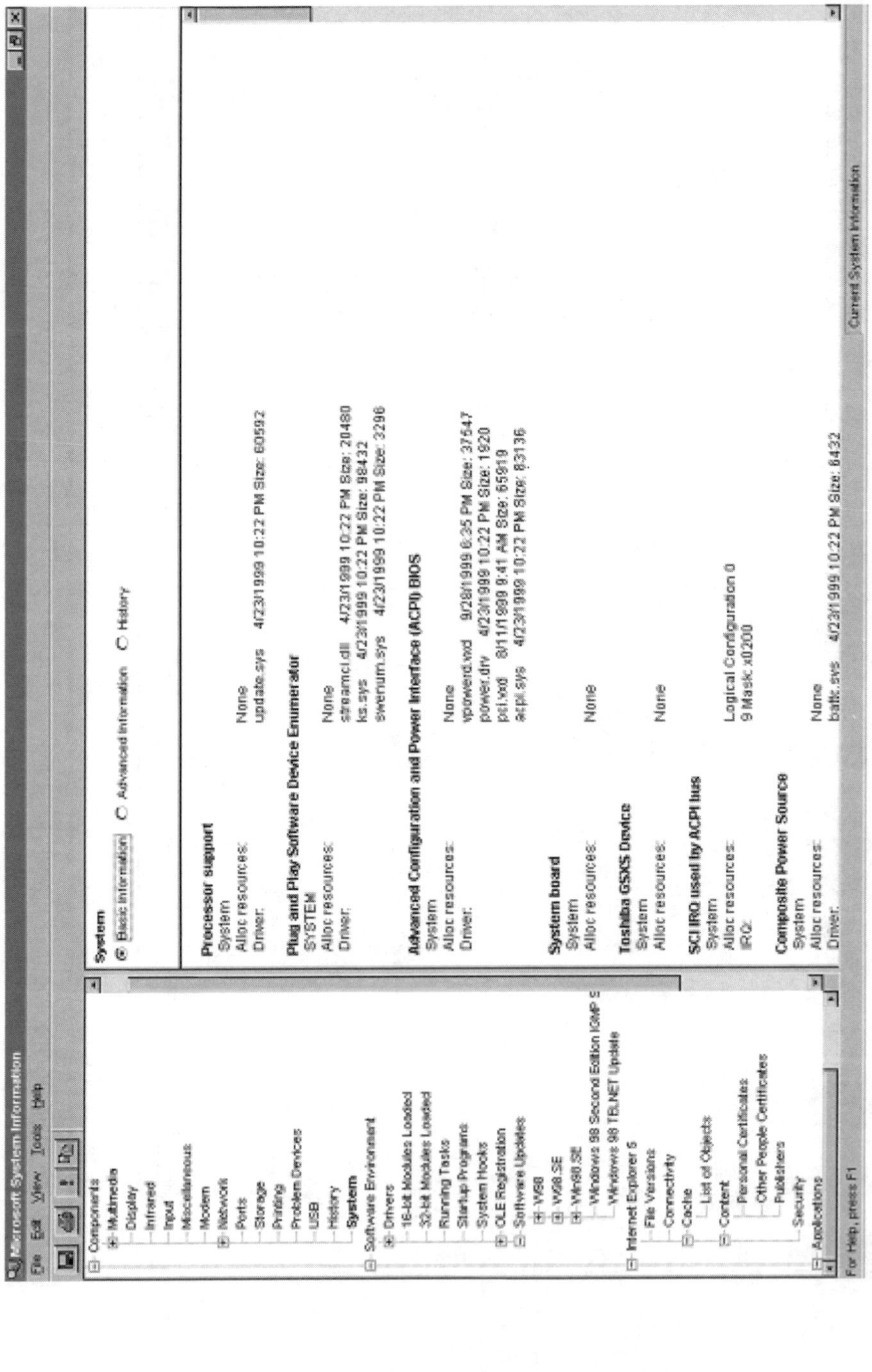

Exhibit 12. System Information/Components/System/Basic Information

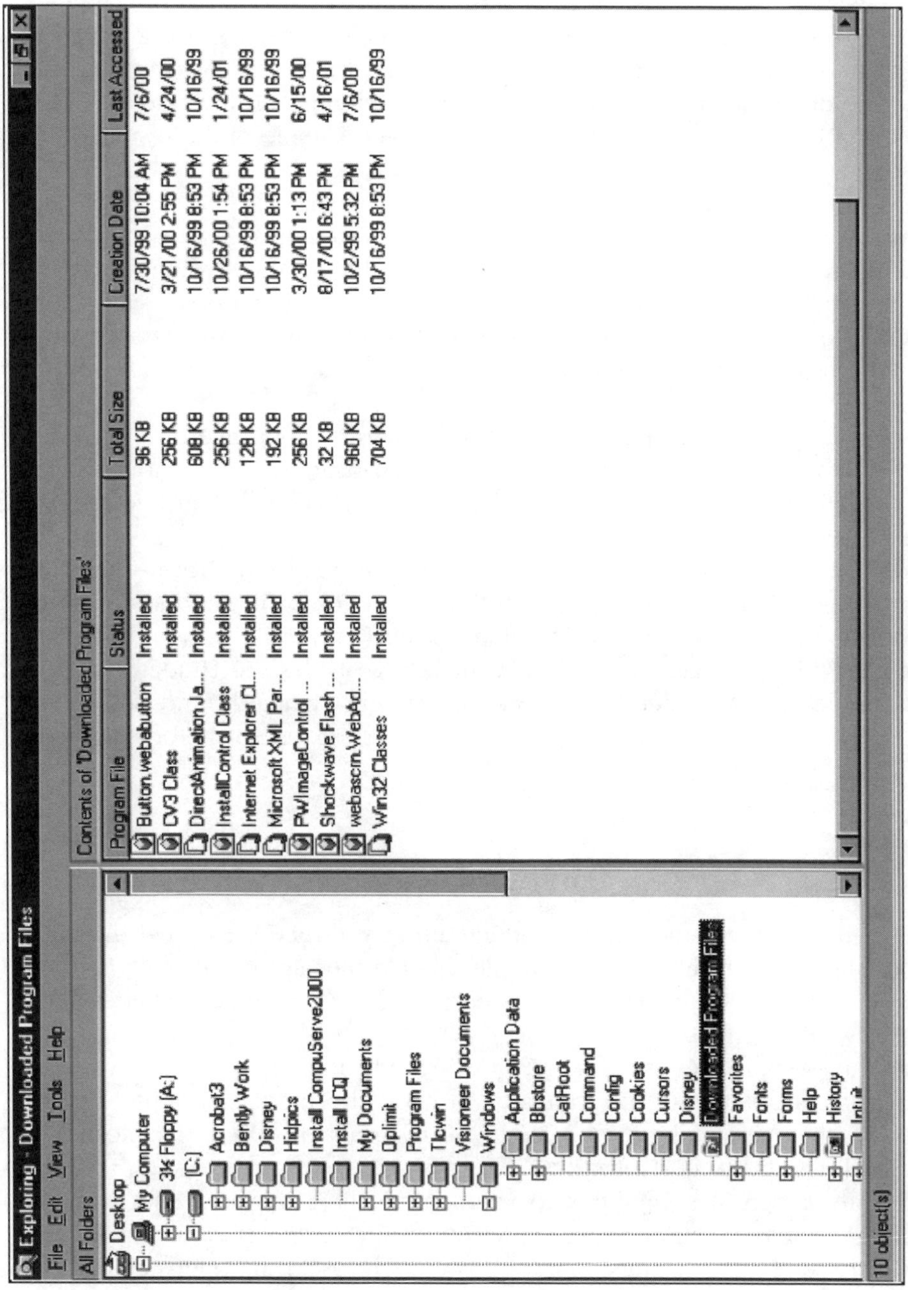

Exhibit 13. Downloaded Programs Viewed from Windows Explorer

will tell you, that the System Review will not, is what actual applications reside on the PC.

The first step in the manual review is to locate all executable programs/ applications on the PC. To do this on the PC, start Explorer — not the Web Browser Internet Explorer, but the Microsoft Explorer. Once there, from the top menu select Tools, Find, Files and Folders. This gives you a pop-up box where you can identify what you want to search for. In this case, we use a wild card query to find all files ending with **.Exe**, or all executable files. Set the "Look in" field to the drive you are investigating; this is usually the C: drive. Select option to look at **all** of the C: drive. See Exhibit 16 for an example of the results of this search.

This can be quite an extensive list. However, you should check each of these references to ensure they do belong to authorized programs. Most unauthorized programs are put under the Programs directory, but do not assume anything; check them all. You can check them by actually launching them. You can do this by clicking on the file from the Find screen. However, to record your findings, it might be best to print this screen and manually check off each item on the list as you verify it.

A quick review of the items in the list might narrow your investigation. If you see icons on the far left that represent something suspicious, you might investigate these first. Suspicious items might include game or playing card icons. See Exhibit 17 for an example of an excerpt of the full list.

Exhibit 17 shows an item on the list with a Playing Card icon — see the freeplus item? This is actually a game, and for most companies and systems may be a violation and should not be installed on the PC.

Another thing to watch out for on your listing of files are Hidden files (see discussion below). You need to check the system standards and settings to determine if the file manager allows you to see these or not before assuming your file list is complete.

Hidden Files

A hidden file is a file with a special hidden attribute turned on so that the file is not normally visible to users. For example, hidden files are not listed when you execute the DOS DIR command. However, most file management utilities allow you to view hidden files.

DOS hides some files, such as MSDOS.SYS and IO.SYS, so that you cannot accidentally corrupt them. You can also turn on the hidden attribute for any normal file, thereby making it invisible to casual snoopers. On a Macintosh, you can hide files with the ResEdit utility.

Why are hidden files important to your investigation? If you do not have the settings on the Folder Options set to allow you to view hidden files, you might miss evidence. To review the settings on the PC you are investigating to ensure that you see hidden files, you need to launch Explorer. From the top menu within Explorer, select View, Folder Options, and the View Tab on the pop-up box (see Exhibit 18).

If the radio buttons are marked so that the hidden files are not to be shown, you will not see all the files. You should reset these so that you can see the hidden files and ensure that you have a complete list.

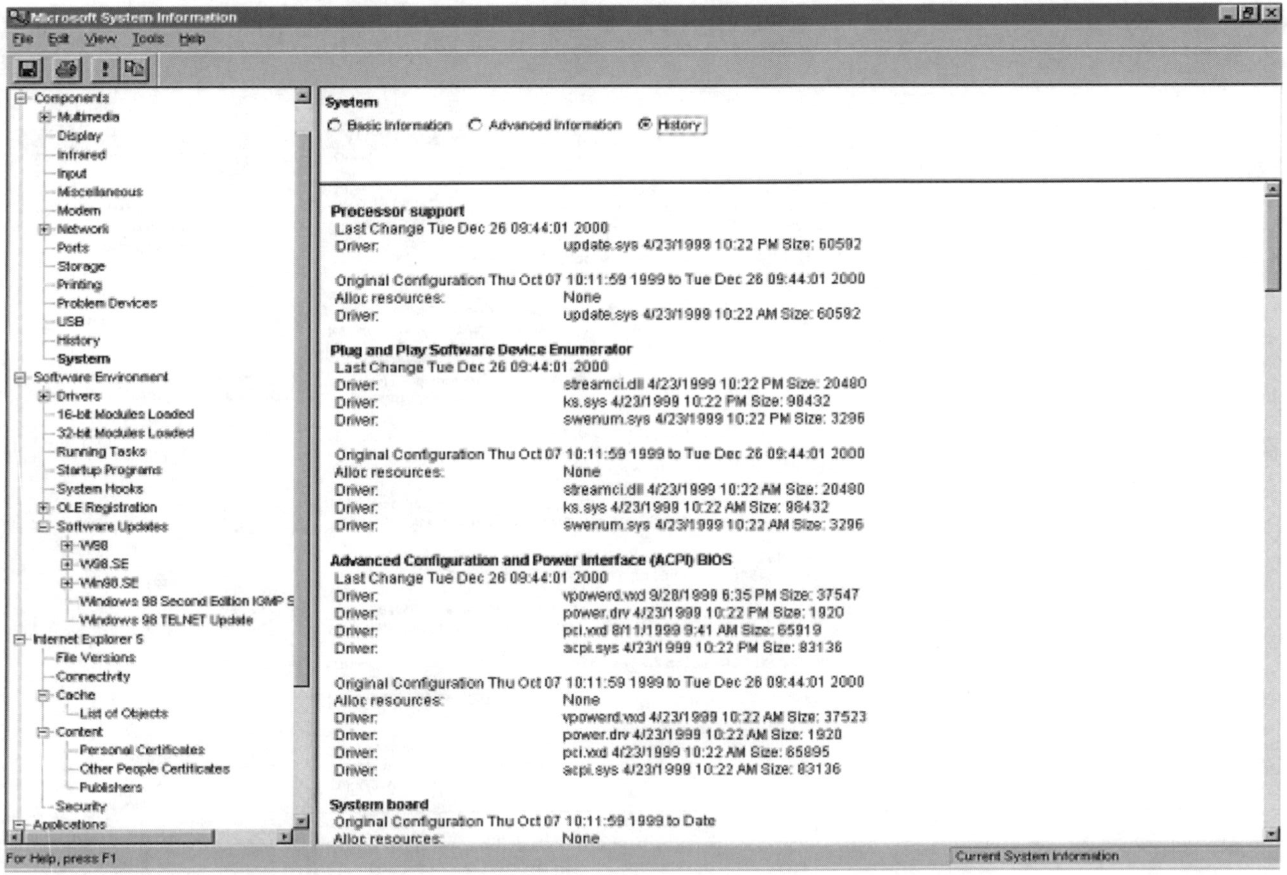

Exhibit 14.   System Information/Components/System/History

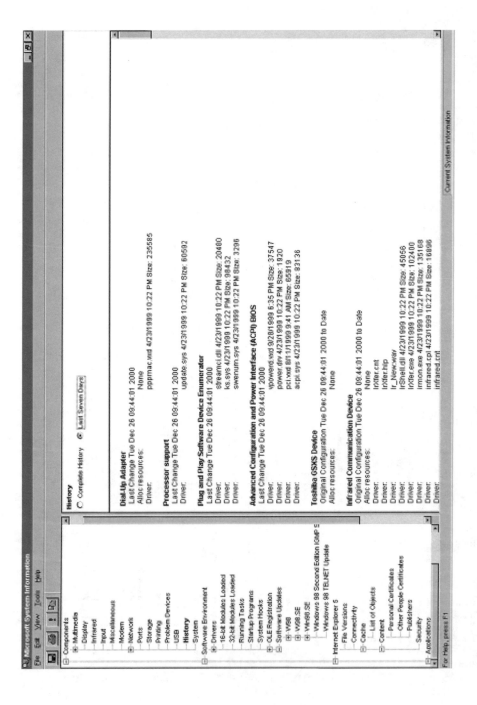

Exhibit 15. System Information/Component/History/Last Seven Days

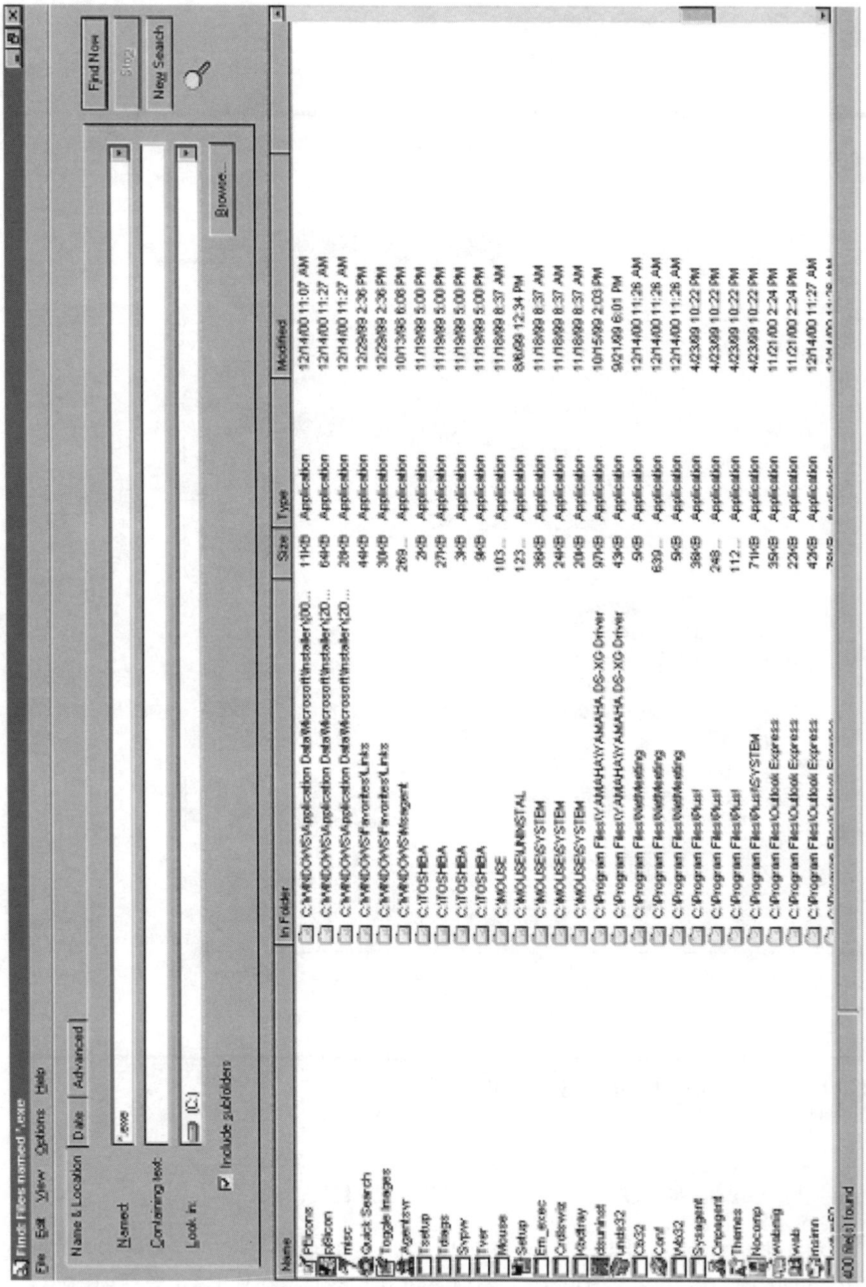

Exhibit 16. Find Files Named: *.exe

Name	In Folder	Size	Type
Network Diagram Wizard	C:\Program Files\Visio\Solutions\Network Diagram	837...	Application
Network Database Wizard	C:\Program Files\Visio\Solutions\Network Diagram	1,0...	Application
Network Equipment Information	C:\Program Files\Visio\Solutions\Network Diagram	69KB	Application
Unwise	C:\Program Files\freeplus	70KB	Application
freeplus	C:\Program Files\freeplus	121...	Application
Imgstart	C:\Program Files\Iomega\Tools	19KB	Application
Iowatch	C:\Program Files\Iomega\Tools	21KB	Application

Exhibit 17.   Find Files Named: *exe Excerpt of List

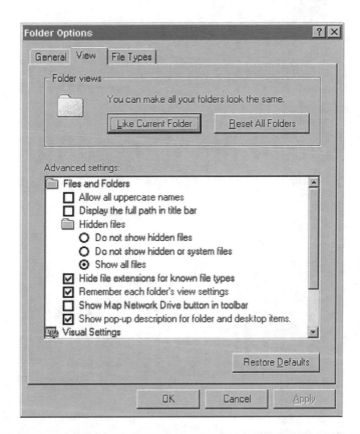

Exhibit 18.   Folder Options to See Hidden Files

How to Correlate the Evidence

Now that you have captured the file evidence and the data, you can graph an access pattern or list the illegal software and when it was loaded. Next, you need to check the access and download dates and times against the timesheets, surveillance, and other witness accounts to ensure that the suspect under investigation actually had the opportunity to engage in unauthorized acts using the PC in question.

In other words, you need to ensure that the employee under investigation actually had access to the equipment on the dates and times listed in the evidence. For example, if the employee had a desktop PC and did not come to work on the date that illegal software was downloaded on his PC, then you might need to look for other supporting evidence (e.g., access logs indicating potential access from an external/remote location). Be advised that the investigator must obtain solid evidence that the employee under investigation actually had an opportunity and was actually using the PC at the time that the unauthorized action took place. Failing to link the employee to the PC and to corroborate and substantiate the evidence, in an irrefutable manner, will result in an inability to hold the employee accountable for his or her actions and further to prosecute the employee via the existing legal system.

When reviewing the evidence you have gathered, you need to follow and show the facts — and only the facts. If you have to make leaps in your logic to get from point A to point B, then you do not have enough evidence to substantiate a claim.

Also, you need to ensure that you can adequately explain how the employee under review was able to commit the offense, illegal act, unauthorized action, etc., and also be able to present evidence/proof of how it was done. This proof should be simple to follow so that there is no doubt that the offense was committed. Someone's career, in addition to their legal freedoms, could be on the line as a result of your findings, as well as the organization's liability (for a wrongful or unsubstantiated accusation). Thus, you want to be sure.

Works Cited

1. Webopedia, www.webopedia.com, Computer Terms and Definitions Web Site.
2. Tinnirello, P., Ed., *Handbook of Systems Development 1999,* Auerbach Publications, Boca Raton, FL, 1999.

Chapter 3

The Liturgical Forensic Examination: Tracing Activity on a Windows-Based Desktop

Robert S. Greenfield, MCP

Gathering Evidence For Prosecution Purposes

One major guideline you need to follow when gathering evidence, whether it be files from a desktop, server, mainframe, or Internet-based external server is to preserve the integrity of the data. This means following careful procedures so you do not contaminate the subject data, and establishing a custodial chain for that evidence so that it is gathered in an approved, supervised, and legal manner for full admissibility in a court of law. Elsewhere in this book, such rules of evidence are covered; thus, we do not take the time here to further elaborate, other than to say that you must be conscientious about the manner in which such data is collected. Keep in mind also that initially you may not intend to prosecute, and are investigating purely for a corporate policy enforcement, and in the process of such investigation may come upon information that you will want to take legal action on. For this reason, it is critical that you treat all data carefully. Realizing too that if you are not in a "right to work" state, you may come under litigation from the targeted individual for an attempted wrongful discharge suit. If this happens, you want to have all your chain of custody and evidence handling procedures outlined and available for review so the courts will not find technical faults with your methods of gathering evidence.

Gathering evidence for prosecution purposes is really the mode you should consider operating in when a forensic examination is needed. For this reason, you should become familiar with the Federal Rules of Evidence, as well as your

0-8493-0955-7/02/$0.00+$1.50
© 2002 by CRC Press LLC

local and state laws pertaining to the admissibility of evidence and what is required to provide "expert witness" testimony should that become necessary. You may not personally qualify as an expert witness in an area, so evidence gathered by you may be disallowed in one or more aspects of your testimony for which expert witness status is required.

The Federal Rules of Evidence are an umbrella under which the subsequent states add their own specific addenda. It is important that you check with your legal department regarding criminal and civil applicability with regard to evidential rules. Get to know the standards that are expected, and obtain if possible, the training to qualify as an expert witness in your state. You should also become knowledgeable as to who you can utilize that would be considered a valid expert witness should you need them. Be prepared with names of companies, individuals, and organizations as part of your overall action plan as you establish it. Make sure you are prepared to deal with possible civil or criminal prosecution needs well ahead of time. Make regular reviews of changes in laws that may require you to make changes in your action plan as well. Developing a corporate response plan to deal with these situations should be a top priority.

Gathering Evidence Without Intent to Prosecute

Of course, you should not let your intention not to prosecute sway your techniques in the gathering of evidence, as discussed in the previous section. However, you may have a situation wherein you are certain you will not have a case for litigation. While it is always preferable to have a complete evidential custody trail, and strict gathering requirements followed, your company may not have the funds, resources, or need to carry through at that level. Proper evidence gathering takes time and can involve a high degree of computer expertise in the more complex cases; so if you take this path, be aware that if you do find some illegal activity going on during the course of your investigation, you will want to immediately stop your activities, and should keep a log of everything you have done to the computer. It goes without saying that you should call the proper law enforcement authorities immediately, naturally. Having the log of activities performed on the computer will also aid in their subsequent investigation. Remember, even if you do not initially intend to prosecute, you may find it necessary in the course of your investigation.

The Microsoft Windows-Based Computer

In a corporate environment, it is best to monitor a computer remotely and trap data that you wish to examine for potential enforcement. This can be facilitated in a number of ways as discussed later. It is also important to remember that there are many areas one can examine on the computer directly. The Windows operating system and the programs that reside on it tend to leave lots of trails in different places that work to our advantage as we audit the computer files.

Depending on which Microsoft operating system is running on the desktop, certain things may be different. These are pointed out as needed where they occur. Some initial background on how things work on a Windows-based computer may be helpful as a primer to look at the items that will be discussed.

Operating Systems Versus Operating Environments

The Windows operating system under Windows 3.1, Windows 95, Windows 98, Windows 98/SE, and even Windows ME are all more technically operating environments. That is to say, they do not necessarily directly talk to your computer's hardware, but instead pass requests for things through the actual operating system, which in the case of the aforementioned platforms is MS-DOS (Microsoft Disk Operating System). Why is this important to know? Glad you asked. It is important because tools designed to work at the DOS level can be employed on these platforms that would not otherwise be available on systems running a true operating system that does not support all of DOS in exactly the same way. Examples of a true operating system would be Windows NT, Windows 2000, Linux, UNIX, and, of course, MS-DOS. All of these have direct communication layers within them that deal with handling memory, storage devices, and external peripherals such as the mouse, a scanner, the monitor, etc. These devices still use little programs called "drivers" that tailor the communications between the device and the operating system for that particular model, but that driver talks to the operating system in a standard way. Think of a driver as an interpreter that tells the operating system what the device can and cannot do, and how to make it do those things.

Storage Versus Memory

Another item that can cause confusion is the difference in storage and memory. You will often hear people not familiar with computers confuse the terms. It is important for you to understand how things are stored on a computer so that you can utilize the tools needed to examine them.

Memory

First and foremost, the term "memory" really refers to the amount of memory physically on computer chips inside the computer itself. If you bought your computer at a store and it came with 128 MB RAM, this means that the computer has 128 megabytes worth of chip memory. A byte is a single character of storage. So, the chip memory in this case could hold approximately 128 million characters of data. Not all of this memory is really available to the user because programs that make the computer run load up in memory when it is powered on. The moment power is cut, or the PC is turned off, regular chip memory is blanked out. This means that it is considered to be "volatile" memory because it does not store anything after you turn the computer off.

Storage

There are two basic kinds of storage: online and offline. Put simply, online storage is that which your computer can get to directly for permanently saving information. A hard disk is a form of online storage because it is always available and not something that can be taken away under normal conditions. As you are probably already suspecting, offline storage is that CD-ROM, DVD, or diskette you use that can be popped in when needed and then taken out of the computer when finished.

Hard disk and floppy storage are subject to exploitation by advanced hackers who may have developed tools to utilize otherwise inaccessible areas of the hard disk for data storage. Techniques can be employed that take advantage of something called "slack space" in hard drive sectors. Basically, slack space is the unused space in a sector on the hard drive. Think of it as if the entire hard drive storage were divided up like the mail slots in a hotel lobby for each of the hotel rooms. When mail comes in (or in this case, a computer file to be stored is saved), it goes into the available mail slot reserved for it. If you have too much mail to fit in the single slot, it may have to overflow into the adjacent slot. The rule for this mailbox, however, is that once a slot contains a file, or part of a file, another file is not normally allowed to be stored in the remaining open portion of that mailbox (or sector in our case) even if there is plenty of room, and the next available mail slot is used. What happens to the potentially empty portion of space in the sector? Well, normally it goes to waste. That is why you can fill a hard drive up with lots of small files that do not add up to the rated storage capacity of the drive. The secret here is that low-level programs can be written to take advantage of these "slack" areas for data storage. Another thing to keep in mind is that data in a slack area may have belonged to an incriminating file prior to its deletion, and a smaller file was subsequently stored on top of it; thus, some of that incriminating information may be left behind in that "slack space." A smart perpetrator can also take advantage of tools that supposedly wipe out information with multiple passes of file writes that write a series of binary 1s and 0s in a series of seven passes over the file area. While recovery of information wiped out in this manner is far more difficult, and in many cases impossible with any meaningful results, some recovery techniques exist that specialists can employ to retrieve some of the data. Factors such as the size of the hard drive, the accuracy of the mechanical system in the drive, the power with which the information was recorded, and even the length of time the information was left on the drive prior to wiping all will have an effect on the probabilities for recovery. Performing such recovery is available from companies that specialize in these tasks, but be advised that it is not inexpensive to have this done.

Detecting these sorts of situations requires a high level of expertise, and normally you will want to bring in a law enforcement agency, or forensic analysis consulting team, to get at that level of data obfuscation.

How Windows Uses Memory and Disk Storage

Windows uses memory in the computer and hard disk storage to run. It loads programs into memory that tell it everything from what kinds of devices are attached to the computer, to how to display a screen and sense and display mouse movement. Windows operating systems and environments are a set of interconnected programs at their low levels, and normally not all of it will want to fit into memory at a given time. This is especially true for things that are "in work," such as a document, browsing the Web where a Web site page needs to be temporarily stored, etc. Windows will use part of the hard drive in a computer to enhance its ability to store data of an intermittent or intermediate nature.

Windows refers to this use of part of the hard disk as virtual memory because it is there to serve as a holding place for things either not yet saved permanently, or things that it uses only during the running of a program but that are not part of the final product.

General Guidelines To Follow

The following tips are important when making a review of a suspect computer and should be followed in any pursuit of suspicious activity, regardless of whether or not you intend to prosecute in a court of law.

Have a corporate action plan. This plan should be in place prior to ever needing to put it to the test. You should make sure you know in advance the various law enforcement agencies, groups, and consultants that can bring expertise to bear if needed. Make sure you have sufficient planning to cover incidents from both the nonskilled perpetrator and the advanced internal hacker. Remember that most corporate security precautions keep out most of the bad guys, that your real external threats will be from advanced hackers, and internal threats abound because those individuals are already behind your external security screens.

Things you should think about as far as advance planning include what tools can be put in place to monitor employee activity if called upon to do so. Some are mentioned in the course of this chapter, but their mention is not to endorse any one company or product over another. There are many companies with many fine products out there. We hope to provide some starting points only. Indeed, the landscape changes far too rapidly to be able to provide an absolute recommendation of any one product in this book because, by the time this is written and goes to press, additional tools from other companies may well be available. It is for this reason that alliances should be formed by you with other corporate auditors to find out what they have done, and are doing. This personal networking of knowledge can lead to your most valuable arsenal of tools, advice, and awareness of services being provided by other firms.

Document everything you do. As an auditor looking for information, you may be called upon to testify as to your processes and procedures. Make sure that you keep a log with date, time, activity performed, and outcome of that activity. This log will come in handy as you proceed through your analysis. You should develop a standardized procedure that works for you in these cases, in accordance with your training and expertise in a given area, and then follow that as the template for your log of activities. This assures a consistent and thorough approach.

Leave ego at the door and do not overstep your training level. If you feel that the investigation will require someone with forensic analysis experience in computers, seek out a forensic analysis firm or your local law enforcement agency to assist. People with a high degree of understanding and technical know-how today can perform criminal activity on computers. Even your local company computer expert is not necessarily equipped to deal with this. Information is presented in this section relating to how data can be hidden, but such information should be looked upon as information that provides a better base of understanding; it is not a substitute for training in these areas of analysis.

Always assume that you are going to run into something of an illegal nature, and follow the rules laid out in the Federal Rules of Evidence. These rules exist to make adjudication rulings against a victimized person or company less likely. Be aware that when you, or a company brought in to do the forensic analysis, fail to follow these Federal Rules of Evidence, you run the risk of having the case tossed out of court. Solid cases have been compromised on technicalities due to lack of adherence to these rules.

Always, ALWAYS assume that a computer has been set up by a potential perpetrator to destroy evidence if the computer is used in a "normal" manner. Programs called Trojans (as in Trojan horse lore) can be put in place that would activate upon start-up of the computer in a regular mode that could wipe out, or otherwise damage potential evidence. A Trojan horse is a program that masquerades as a legitimate program but is really sitting in wait to be activated by the unwary.

Always work only from backups of the data sources on a computer. This means bitstream backups of the hard drive, floppy diskettes, etc. Never work directly on the computer itself (other than to make the initial backups) because any potential damage that is done either by you, or by the booby trap of a perpetrator, could ruin your one and only chance of getting the goods on him or her.

Once you have made a backup of the data, make a backup of your backup and work only from that working copy of your backup. That way, you can re-retrieve information from your primary, protected backup should it become necessary.

When you make a backup, use a product that does a bitstream backup. Standard file copy or file backup programs will not perform these kinds of backups. It is critical that a bitstream backup be used so that data hidden in places on the hard drive can be preserved. A clever perpetrator may actually try to hide files in areas on the hard drive marked as bad when they are not. Files can also be encrypted, and you may only have ghosts of the original file in areas of the computer's file system that are marked as deleted, when in fact they still physically exist. A bitstream backup will make an exact 100 percent mirror-image copy. Tools to do this were originally made for network administrators for the purposes of creating online backups and for distribution of mass installations of software throughout a corporate enterprise. These tools have been vastly improved over the years, and one of the standard tools in use by the FBI and other law enforcement agencies is called SafeBack; it is available from New Technologies, Inc. (www.forensics-intl.com) to authorized personnel. Other tools for making image backups exist from well-known companies such as PowerQuest Corporation (www.powerquest.com), which makes DriveImage Pro. This utility can make exact partition backups as well. Regardless of the product selected, and there are many other products from various vendors out there, you should *learn* how to use them long before you ever *have* to use them. The time to learn is not when you have a crisis and need to employ the tool. Always practice making backups with the tool and know its features. Questions about a product should not go unanswered. The only stupid question is an unasked one. Do not be afraid of asking anything of the appropriate support people. Some companies offer training in the use of their products, and even provide consulting services. While this book is a guide for the auditor wanting to investigate issues of compliance forensically, it is not a substitute for training and the use of experienced individuals, especially if criminal activity is involved. You may wish to bring in a forensics expert and work side-by-side with him or her through your first few incidents. In the corporate environment, you should not work in isolation if at all possible. This gives you the support you will need at first, and it will add to the verifiability of activities performed.

If activity of an illegal nature is suspect, or if activity is suspected that is not in compliance with corporate computer use policy (if such a policy exists), and you want to maintain surveillance on the employee's computer use to further build a case, you must use caution when obtaining information so that the employee does not suspect any evidence gathering activity. Fortunately, especially in a network environment, tools exist today that allow such covert monitoring to be easily facilitated. Some of these tools are discussed later. In the case where a network is not present, or where technical expertise or finances to bring in such expertise is limited, you may need to examine files from the machine by first-hand inspection. This means that you will have to visit the machine and gather the evidence directly. When you do this, you will have to be very careful that you do not alter the files on the machine itself.

One of the tools this author recommends, if you do not have a network, is an external CD-RW or Iomega Zip or Jaz drive that connects to the computer via a USB connection. Most computers now have USB ports. If the suspect computer is running Windows 95 Revision B or later, support for this technology is already embedded in the operating system. These devices allow you to plug into the PC using the USB port, and then unplug, without having to reboot the computer. This is even truer of Windows 2000 machines, for which the USB support is exceptional. An external CD-RW drive is preferable because you are recording to a medium that does not provide for on-media alteration of a given file provided you are using CD-R media. CD-R media are blank CDs that allow you to write once and read many. The fact that you cannot erase them afterward, or rewrite files already placed on the CD, makes them excellent for preserving evidence that you may need to present in litigation. You should make your bitstream backups to the CD-RW drive.

The driver support for Iomega Zip drives is already native in Windows 95 Revision B or later, so you will not need to install additional drivers. Support of the external CD-RW drive may require installation of drivers. If this is needed, the author recommends that you make it a companywide project to install the drivers for it on each and every PC. The reason for this is twofold: (1) it will be readily available to anyone who needs to make a backup of something important; and (2) it will make it easier to perform covert archiving in the future. Making it part of the corporate standard on the desktop for computers not connected to the network also masks the fact that you may be interested in just a particular individual and in obtaining records from just one specific machine at the moment.

Adopting a corporate standard such as the CD-RW device drivers, and therefore requiring your company computers to be updated, also provides a window of opportunity for the installation of other software to aid in monitoring activity. Some of these monitoring products perform their surveillance over the corporate network; others do it on the machine itself; and others support a combination of these environments. One such monitoring product even allows for the covert e-mailing of screen captures and activity logs.

Let us examine some of the areas that are valuable to know about on a Windows-based computer. There are many different areas that the computer uses on a PC to store data, either permanently or temporarily, which can be of use as you conduct a review of activities that have taken place on a given computer. We examine the following kinds of files and file areas on the computer that can provide insight: cookies, bookmarks (a.k.a. Favorites), history buffers, cache storage, temporary Internet files, the system registry, recent documents list, and hidden files. We look at each of these in turn, tell you about their purpose, and how you can exploit their existence for your benefit as an investigator. In the absence of a covert observation tool, it can be very handy to know about all of these areas. We also discuss how some of the covert observation tools work and how you can employ them.

Cookies

This is a term you have no doubt heard bandied about for quite some time. There has been a lot of information, both good and bad, as to what these files are and what they can do. Hopefully, this section will clear up that vague and often-misunderstood file type.

First, what exactly is a cookie? Simply put, a cookie is a file that usually holds things such as a user name and password for a given Web site, any custom settings that may have been put in place for a given Web site, and other data that the Web site may track with regard to the user's visit there. It could contain anything that the Web site has been programmed to store there. It may have, for example, the date and time of the user's last visit, how many visits the user made, and if the user likes to view the Web site with background music on or off. One of the things that cookies normally do not have in them is a complete history of where the user has surfed to on the Web before going to that site. It is possible, however, for it to have information about what site the user was at just prior to visiting the one the cookie is attached to. Other information that can be recorded is the IP address of the computer, and where, once the user was on the site, what pages were visited. Normally, cookies are used to enhance the visitor experience by allowing the site being visited to better customize the viewing experience and tailor it to the visitor. Privacy concerns with regard to the use of cookies are valid to the extent of how much the user wants to reveal to a Web site, and what that Web site has in the way of a privacy policy stating the terms of use. There are utilities out there that will allow the user to control the use of cookies on a computer, and the user can also determine, in the Web browser settings, whether or not to even allow the use of cookies.

From an auditing perspective, the presence of cookies can be great. Adult Web sites often use cookies for the capture of information and customization of site settings. As a result, one usually finds a cookie file for most popular adult Web sites. It should be noted that care should be used when implying that an employee is intentionally visiting adult Web sites on a corporate computer. For example, an employee may have wanted to go to the White House Web site and typed in www.whitehouse.com instead of www.whitehouse.gov. The address ending in .com is an adult Web site; the address ending in .gov is the official Web site of the White House in Washington, D.C. Corporate policies usually address the accidental visiting of a site such as the one mentioned above. By examining cookies, one can determine how often such "mistakes" are made, and thus reveal if there is a pattern. Someone who visits such a site and immediately backs out of that site is probably not intentionally going to it; but someone with an established pattern of visits for any length of time may very well be abusing the resources of the company.

Cookies are stored within a Web browser's file area, and on systems that provide user-by-user security and preference settings (Windows NT, 2000, and XP), they will be within the individual profile for that user within that user's cookies folder. For example, Exhibit 1 is what it would look like on a Windows NT or Windows 2000 machine if one were to display this using Windows Explorer.

Notice that the file extensions on the cookie files are *.txt.* That means that they are text files and that they can be opened using the Notepad application to examine the contents. While this sounds great, often doing so reveals little because the data is usually not directly readable in a meaningful manner. The reason is the way computers store numbers, and also the way those the numbers are subsequently displayed. Many times, the characters coming up mean very little except for the occasional cleartext message sometimes embedded. If there is an AOL cookie on a computer, for example, it may say inside it that the user needs to keep the cookie because the user has saved settings specific to his or her user identity. If the user opens one of these cookies using notepad, Exhibit 2 is what he or she might see.

As seen in Exhibit 2, not much is readable other than the URL from the Web site that placed it there. Utility programs are available that will allow the user to open and view the contents of a cookie in a somewhat more organized fashion, but for our purposes with auditing, the presence of the cookie and the Web site it is connected with is the most valuable portion. It proves that a visit to the site took place. Even if one of the available utilities is used, chances are that the individual other numbers stored in the cookie will have little meaning to anyone other than the Web site that created it. There is no fixed format requirement for a cookie, so it is difficult to obtain consistently useful information from cookies other than the originating URL and the creation date-time stamp, which indicates when the site had been visited initially. If the cookie gets updated or accessed, it may either get a new date-time stamp or it may have a new "modification" date. Using Windows Explorer, right-click on a cookie file and click on the Properties option that shows up. Under the "General" tab, the user will see something similar to Exhibit 3.

Notice toward the bottom of the window in Exhibit 3 the date created, the date it was last modified, and finally, the date it was last accessed on the computer. Be careful when checking this so as not to double-click on the file in question, but simply **right-mouse-click only** and bring up this property page. If you do accidentally double-click on the file, it will alter the Accessed: date. Be advised that the Accessed: date can also be modified if you perform a backup or copy of files from the system. See the suggestions for isolating the computer equipment from changes prior to performing any file operations.

Copy the files to your CD-RW drive to archive them. Another added advantage to the cookies is that they are named with the user ID of the person logged on at the time they were created. This is true of Windows NT, Windows 2000, and later computers as they provide the security by individual logon ID. On older Windows 95 or Windows 98 machines, the cookie files may not have any such identification, so you will have to correlate their creation and update dates with the individual's opportunity to imply a connection.

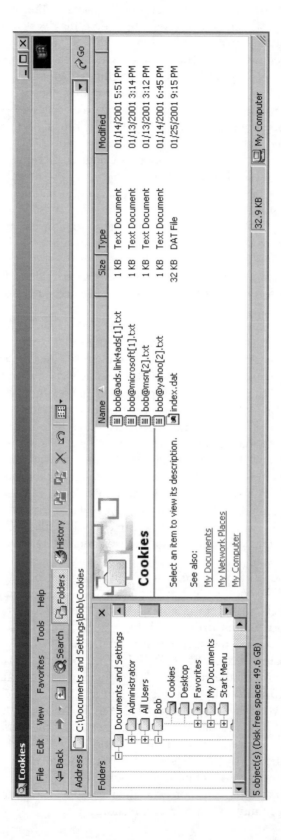

Exhibit 1.   Windows Explorer Cookies Folder

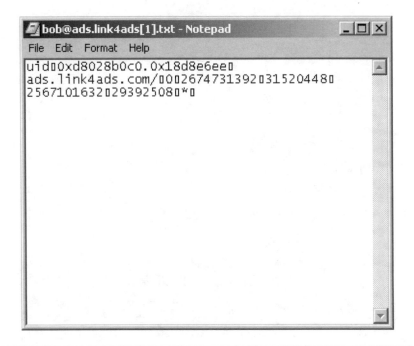

Exhibit 2. Adverstisement Site Cookie

Bookmarks/Favorites

Depending on the configuration of the computer, it may have Microsoft's Internet Explorer (MSIE) Web browser or the Netscape browser. These are the two most common on corporate computers running Windows, although there are other browsers out there, such as Opera, or even some shareware or freeware Web-browsing tool. We will speak to the MSIE or Netscape tools in this book because they are prevalent.

A bookmark (the Netscape term) is the same thing as a Favorite (the Microsoft term). It is a record of the URL (uniform resource locator) that is the address on the Web of a given Web site. These URLs are held in special locations in each of these browsers and, in the case of Microsoft's Favorites, also become available in many other applications as well.

Netscape will have the bookmarks stored as part of a file (by default, it is called "bookmark.htm"). This file is actually stored in the same way as a Web page is written. You can look at the file to find out what places the individual likes to visit. When you are looking for these bookmark files, keep in mind that the user can customize several bookmark files under different names, and open them manually to get at the bookmarks. Also keep in mind that the user may be trying to hide the file by setting its file attribute to "Hidden," or calling it something other than "Bookmark." On Windows NT and 2000 machines, this file may reside in the individual's account area on the computer, but you should look for bookmark files in all areas on the computer.

The Microsoft Favorites present a different issue. They are stored differently and can be customized at different levels. First, on Windows 95- and 98-based

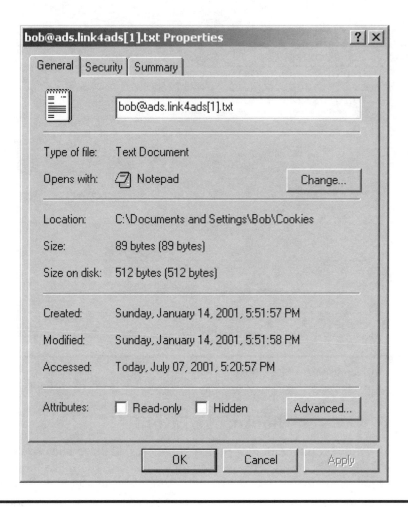

Exhibit 3.   Windows Explorer File Properties

systems, there will be a folder on the computer called Favorites. Within this folder, you may find sub-folders that could be named for whatever the user wanted (category, topic, company name, etc.). And then within these sub-folders there may be additional sub-folders or actual files called Shortcuts, which are files that hold the URL information. On systems supporting multiple users (primarily, these will be Windows NT and Windows 2000 systems), you may have a Favorites folder under an All Users account, which are Favorites that will be available regardless of who is logged on. Under normal conditions, if the user does not have administrative rights (assuming this is a Windows NT or Windows 2000 machine), he or she will not be able to change the All Users folder contents, including the Favorites sub-folder. If this is a Windows 95 or Windows 98 machine, and a user wants to alter an All Users, Favorites folder contents, there is nothing to prevent its alteration. Make sure to examine each Favorites folder for its contents, and check the sub-folders all the way down the line. Keep in mind that individual files and folders could have the Hidden file attribute turned on. You will want to make sure that you use the Windows Explorer with its settings enabled to show hidden and system files. Also remember that you will need to be logged on to that machine as the administrator (in the case of Windows NT and Windows 2000 systems) to be able to traverse across all the folders wherever they may be.

Internet Explorer's History Buffer

One advantage of the Microsoft Internet Explorer is that it keeps a history of where someone has surfed. By default, this option is enabled on Internet Explorer. The individual user can change the time span with which it will track this Web site visitation history, so you may not reap as much benefit from it, depending on how far back it is set to track. It will, however, track all sites visited. So, if a URL was typed into the browser's address bar, clicked from a Favorite entry, or clicked from a hyperlink on a Web page, it will be recorded in the history if it is enabled. Be aware that it is possible to set the history level to record 0 days of history, and to automatically clear all the browser cache upon exit. It is also possible for the user to manually clear the history by clicking on the option in the Internet Options dialog box within either Internet Explorer, or under Internet Options in the Start, Settings, Control Panel, Internet Options area, which brings up the same dialog.

If the contents of the history buffer are available, you hopefully will have a record of repeated use of the Internet in whatever form your company may consider to be abusive (surfing pornography, slacking off by excessive surfing, surfing non-business-related Web sites, etc.). You should look at the history buffer, either from a fresh restore or before you check out the other items in the Favorites list, because any new visits will generate additional entries into the history buffer.

Temporary Storage on the Hard Drive

Let's say you were typing a document in Microsoft Word. Very long documents with lots of pictures may not all fit into the available chip memory, so Windows uses the hard drive to fool the program into thinking you have more memory than you really do. Now, let's say you are working on a critical document. You cannot afford to lose the work being putting into it, so you have turned on the Auto Save feature of Microsoft Word. At a given interval, it will "flush" what it has in memory and virtual memory to a file on the hard drive in a temporary location. Microsoft Excel and Microsoft Word have these automatic save options. It is something to keep in mind in examing a system for files because some of these image files may be left over and could be examined.

When a document is being written, or a spreadsheet is being worked on, often times a file is created by the application making the document in what is called a "temp" area. This "temp" area is just that: a temporary area where files are located while they are being worked on and prior to being formally saved in some folder of the user's choice. On Windows-based computers, the area that is used by default is determined by settings stored in the computer. These settings are held in memory as a reference to where these temporary files should go. The memory reference is labeled with a variable name and is part of the environment within which the computer operates. The two environment variables involved here are the TMP and TEMP variables. They are set to point at some given location on the computer. By default, on Windows 3.1, 95, 98, 98/SE, and ME systems, both will point to the location of *C:\Windows\Temp* or *C:\Temp,* depending on which operating system you are working with. On Windows NT/2000 platform machines, the values set for the TMP and TEMP environment variables will be set to a path sensitive to what user is logged on, so you would have to either try logging on as the individual, or, preferably, as that computer's administrator user and then locate the TEMP folders for the suspect user ID. To be sure where these variables are pointing, click the Start button, usually located in the lower left corner of the screen, and then click on Programs. Find the item in the menu labeled MS-DOS Prompt. Click on it and it will bring up a window that looks like the following:

In the window at the C:/> Prompt, type the word Set and hit Return. The system will show you information about what is stored in the computer's Environment Variables. Make note of where the TMP and TEMP variables point as this directory (also known as a folder), holds residual files at times that may aid in the process of detecting use of the computer for illicit purposes.

On Windows NT/2000 systems, you can click on the Start button, then Run, and enter the word CMD into the Run window. It will bring up a box as shown in Exhibit 4. In the box, simply enter the commands SET TMP and hit the Enter button and SET TEMP and hit the button again. This will show the setting of these two Environment Variables. Exhibit 5 shows the values when logged on as the Administrative user on Windows 2000.

Temporary Internet Files

Just as with a Word or Excel document, a Web browser also uses a temporary location to hold all those graphics and other information on a Web site when you visit a particular location on the Web. In the case of Web browsers, they store data in temporary areas referred to as cache. This cache storage is functionally the same as the TEMP space described previously, but kept separate for the purposes of the Web browser's exclusive use. The idea here is that that if you have visited a particular Web page, downloaded that page, and gone to a subsequent page, it is faster, should you hit the Back button on the browser, to reload the page from hard drive than to download everything again. From an auditing perspective, this can be very useful because, if this area is not cleaned off, you can have the complete trail of what that person saw and downloaded on the Web and save copies of it for evidence. While the savvy Internet user may know to clean these off, or have the Web browser set to remove the files automatically, it is still an opportunity area that should not be overlooked. Most of the files that will be in this area will be HTML documents, graphics files, or perhaps some other Web-based scripting languages or programs. After archiving these files for safekeeping, you can make subsequent copies of them and view them using your own Web browser on your machine to open the HTML files directly and display the pages that were downloaded. Again, it is important to preserve the copies you made of the suspect machine intact and only work from subsequent copies so you do not alter or contaminate the evidence. It is also

Exhibit 4.   W2K Command Window

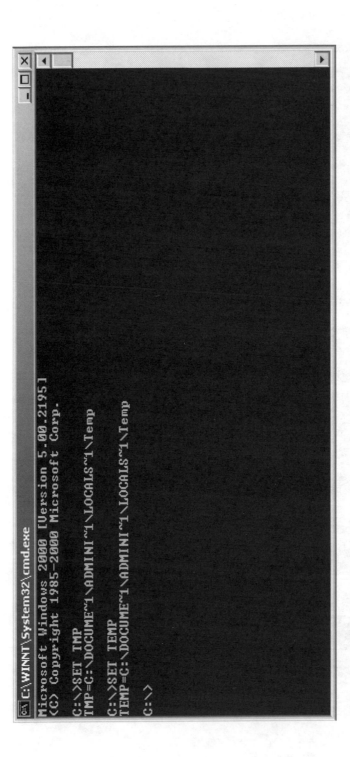

```
C:\WINNT\System32\cmd.exe

Microsoft Windows 2000 [Version 5.00.2195]
(C) Copyright 1985-2000 Microsoft Corp.

C:\>SET TMP
TMP=C:\DOCUME~1\ADMINI~1\LOCALS~1\Temp

C:\>SET TEMP
TEMP=C:\DOCUME~1\ADMINI~1\LOCALS~1\Temp

C:\>
```

Exhibit 5.   W2K Command Window

valuable to note the date-time stamp on these files and correlate them with the individual's use of the computer to further enhance the evidence chain.

Another consideration you may have to deal with is a multi-lingual suspect. Internet Explorer is particularly advanced in its ability to handle multiple language sets. Netscape provides this as well, although at the current time not to the same level as Internet Explorer. If the saved Web page appears to be unreadable and you bring up the HTML page using a program like Notepad, for example, it may be that the non-HTML portions of the page are in an alphabet other than English. You should therefore use the browser to examine the HTML files. Because you are working off of a bitstream backup, whatever languages were supported will be similarly supported in the computer you are using to examine the files. You may have to get a translator involved if you do not speak the language. Do not assume that the page being examined is of no consequence just because it is in Russian, Chinese, or Greek. Cybercrime now spans the globe, and the Internet facilitates it instantaneously. The larger a company grows, the greater the likelihood of having to deal with a multi-lingual situation. If your company hires people from abroad, you may well have to deal with languages from any of those countries because the suspect may well be conversing with people in his or her homeland via e-mail, or surfing to a Web site there, etc. The key here is to be prepared and assume nothing. This author once worked in a firm that brought in people from India, became good friends with a number of them, and learned that in just that group of people there were 15 different dialects of the same native language represented. And, to further complicate matters, some of these dialects were so divergent from one another that the only language that they could all consistently communicate in and be properly understood was English. Subtleties like this are things you may have to cope with. If you are dealing with someone as a suspect from abroad, it may not necessarily be enough to have someone familiar with just the general countries language, but be versed in the specific region's dialect as well.

System Registry

The system registry is a key set of files that allows the computer to track and make available certain key aspects of computer applications system level files. A registry entry may contain, for example, the path and filename of a particular file, and its version number. A program with such an entry can use that registry entry to check to see if maybe a system level file was changed over what it expected to see on the computer. Things such as the individual support components of a program, the program itself, and data pertaining to registration, licensing, use, and features of that application also may reside in the system registry. For example, your individual copy of Microsoft Word, Microsoft Excel, or some other piece of software, may put its registration information directly into the system registry and correlate this with a licensing monitoring program in your corporate structure.

What you as an auditor would be looking for in the system registry would be programs that may have been illegally installed on the computer, legitimate copies of software that may have been illegally installed on more than one computer, or other bootleg software that may open the company to litigation if licensing is not obtained from the vendor.

Exhibit 6.   W2K Run Command from Start

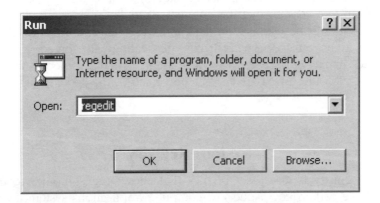

Exhibit 7.   W2K Run Command Regedit

A computer-savvy perpetrator can use the system registry to hide or alter registration, or other information as well.

There are tools you can use to scan the system registry, many of which are shareware tools, but there is already a handy tool provided by Microsoft. It is called Regedit.exe (which is short for Registry Editor). You do not normally see it but it is there. If you left-mouse-click on your Windows Start button, you will see the pop-up menu appear (Exhibit 6). At the bottom of this menu is an icon that says Run beside it. When you click it, it will bring up a prompt for a command to run (Exhibit 7). Type in the word "regedit" and hit return or click the OK command button. This will bring up the Regedit program. It is very important that you work carefully so that you do not accidentally change a registry setting.

This program is designed for you to be able to actually look at registry entry settings, and, if you are knowledgeable, change settings. For our purposes, we utilize this merely as a tool to view what things are stored in the registry. The screen for the Regedit program looks like the one in Exhibit 8.

The left half of the window that appears shows the section of the registry you are viewing, and the portion on the right is the specific entry or entries that pertain to that section. The Regedit window works in a manner similar to the Windows Explorer, with a folder-based architecture. This architecture serves to compartmentalize entries in the registry based on function and applicability within that function. Registries can be huge, and you should be prepared to spend time sifting through this. You do not want to skip through something because that something you skip may well be an area that someone has hid something.

The best way to systematically go through the system registry is to print it out and scour the hardcopy. This way, you can check off each entry as you examine it. It is tedious, but this ensures that you have covered all your bases and it can further be utilized as an exhibit in court, provided the proper rules of evidence and chain of custody are observed. To print the registry, click the Registry menu item in the upper left corner to bring up the drop-down menu (see Exhibit 9). On the menu you will see the entry for Print…. This will let you print the entire registry, or just the selected branch of that registry if you are highlighting just an individual portion of it.

Remember, registries are sometimes huge. So, when you are printing this, have patience and lots of paper on hand. I would recommend that you have a high-speed laser printer for this, due to the resulting print job size, but any Windows-based printer will do. As you scan through the printout, keep in mind that you are looking for something that is abnormal, hidden, or possibly look legitimate but pertain to a bootlegged piece of software. Remember also that a savvy computer user may have altered an entry to appear completely legal. You may need to correlate the software information you find with the licensing distribution database (if you have one), which should list who has what software, and what release levels and serial numbers should be present. If your company does not have such a listing, keep in mind that bootlegged software on an employee's machine can subject your company to hefty fines. Fines can be far in excess of the cost of obtaining a valid license.

When you click the Print… option, the panel in Exhibit 10 results. Note the bottom section of the central panel. This is where you have the option of printing all the registry, or just a portion. If you highlighted just a portion, you would see that branch of the registry in the Selected branch portion. You will want to use the All function, however. Make sure it is selected (as in Exhibit 10) and click the Print button at the bottom of the panel. Keep an eye on your paper supply and ink or toner cartridge so that you get a good, clean, legible copy.

The different top-level branches of the system registry are as follows.

HKEY_CLASSES_ROOT

This is where different file extensions become registered so programs can interact with them. For example, you might see an entry for .bmp. A file with a .bmp file extension would have an entry that designates it as belonging to the image class

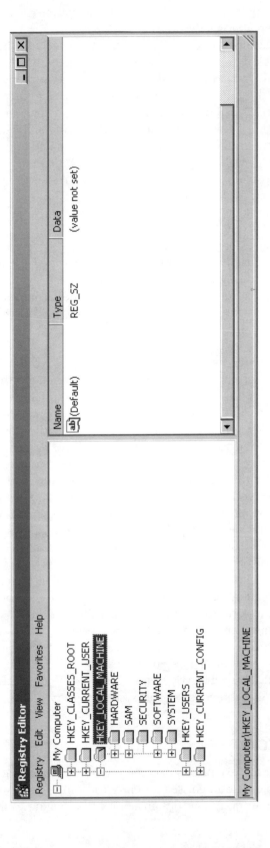

Exhibit 8. Regedit Screen Shot, with Registry Menu

Exhibit 9. Regedit Printing Function

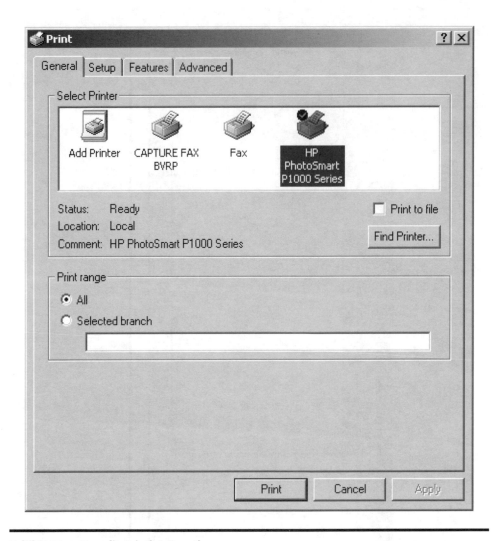

Exhibit 10.   Regedit Printint Function

of objects. You may also see an entry for what program it is supposed to, by default, be opened with. Each known file extension on the system is registered this way. Find the entry for the .doc extension. It belongs to the "application" content type and, by default, is handled by the msword program, which is the file name for Microsoft Word program in the Microsoft Office Suite.

You do not need to become an expert at reading every entry in the registry, and indeed, entire books have been written on just working with the Windows system registry; rather, you should become sufficiently familiar with things so that you can spot if something just does not look right. If you have any doubts about an entry, consult an expert, preferably one versed in forensics and cybernetic sleuthing.

HKEY_CURRENT_USER

Because you are logged on as the administrator (or an administrative level account), this registry branch will contain the settings that were based on the preferences set up for that ID. This holds information such as what image is on the Windows background (a.k.a. wallpaper), what font is set as the users preference, etc. This is one entry that you can probably skip, but scan through it anyway, just in case someone made a new entry in there that may not belong.

HKEY_LOCAL_MACHINE

This is where you may hit some real paydirt. The areas within this branch are for the machine's configuration, including hardware and software loads, security, and other system level settings (see Exhibit 8 for the branch headers).

If bootlegged software or other nonauthorized software was loaded, it will, in all likelihood, show up in here in the Software branch. If the program is very old, it may not utilize the system registry for everything, but may instead depend on text files to retain setting information. These text files were referred to as .ini files (pronounced eye-en-eye), which stands for initialization files. This was the common form of program preferences recording and setup information in the early days of Windows 3.x and was still actively used well into the use of Windows 95. Most current programs do not use the .ini file concept, but work with the system registry due to it being the encouraged standard from Microsoft. It is for this reason also that you should look for these .ini files wherever they may be on the computer. Use the search function available from the Windows Start menu and search for all the files ending in .ini. While most programs do not use them for their system settings, some programs do still have them for backward compatibility, or because the developers of the software did not want, or perhaps did not need, the sophistication of the system registry to support their application in some areas.

HKEY_USERS

Under normal conditions, this portion of the system registry holds unique identifying information on various identities registered on the system. These entries are normally generated by the computer and do not normally contain information generated by the user directly. The information contained in this area will look very cryptic. This is also a potential hiding spot for things, so be on the lookout. It is difficult to say what a clever perpetrator might hide in here. Perhaps the perpetrator will keep a record of unique system identifiers so he can spoof things. Perhaps he will not even use the registry for this, but it is always a possibility that should not be ignored.

HKEY_CURRENT_CONFIG

Again, this area is generated by the computer and holds information about the current configuration of various system level elements of the computer. Among these system elements you may find certain switches for Microsoft products and Internet connections and options.

The author's advice is to look at system registry entries on corporate standard desktops that you know have not been compromised. Become acquainted with what looks normal. Buy a good book on the system registry and read up on its usage and parts. You do not have to become a programmer by any means, but use the book as a guide for what is and is not supposed to be in an area. It will help you understand a lot more about how to spot abnormal entries or subtle changes that may indicate a problem.

Remember: if you are in doubt about an entry, it is best to involve an expert who can assist you. Such an expert should not normally be from within your company information systems group, but rather a person trained in forensic analysis as it pertains to computers. Your local law enforcement agency should be able to either assist, or provide guidance as to whom in your area may be qualified. Do not let ego stand in the way of a successful investigation.

Enabling and Using Auditing via the Windows Operating System

If you are lucky, and the suspect's computer is running either the Windows NT or Windows 2000 operating system, you may well be in luck in tracking activity on the suspect's computer. Part of these operating systems features includes an auditing feature that can be extremely useful.

Before getting too excited, there are some prerequisites and a caveat you should heed. First, setting up auditing properly and securely takes someone trained in the administration and security aspects of the operating system involved. Second, this will only work on the two operating systems if the suspect's computer is storing data on the hard drive where the hard drive is partitioned using the NTFS file system. It is possible that the suspect's computer could be running the same file system as Windows 95, Windows 98, or Windows ME, in which case no security would be available. The non-secure file system (FAT16 and FAT32) was never designed to store security attributes about a file or the users on the computer. On the Windows 95, 98, and ME operating systems, you could establish a "Windows Password," but all it does is store desktop preferences such as wallpaper and fonts, etc. A user can blast right past those logon screens by simply clicking the Cancel button on the logon prompt and have full access to everything on that computer. The only protection a file has on FAT16 or FAT32 includes the Read Only, Hidden, and System file attributes that could protect it a little from prying eyes. While this may be great for you as an auditor examining someone's computer running one of these computers, it is a gaping corporate security hole and does not afford any level of real protection, or auditing capability. Tools that people can buy that supposedly "lock down" the Windows 95, 98, or ME desktops are not really a deterrent. Those computers can still be booted from a floppy diskette and then full access to the hard drive is possible. Their methods of securely storing data usually involves setting up a series of Trojan files that redirect requests through a program to where the real file is located, usually with an altered name and file extension, and sometimes with altered file attributes to further try to hide the files.

As corporate policy, those computers capable of having the NTFS file system used on them should be switched over to them. New computer installations should use this when initially configured, and existing systems that do not yet have it should be switched over. There are tools available that will allow you to easily change the partition file system without losing existing data or programs (although a thorough backup should always be done before such a switch) from companies such as PowerQuest Corporation (www.powerquest.com). Their product, Partition Magic, is one of the best in the industry and is the only one currently available that lets you switch both up to NTFS and back to FAT16 or FAT32, with data in place.

The NTFS file was designed to be secure. This file system also tends to be more resistant to file fragmentation. Remember the discussion of how the areas on a hard drive are like the hotel lobby mailbox system? Well, say you have a lot of mail (i.e., a huge file), and the available areas in the mailbox system (free places on the hard drive) are not contiguous in nature, meaning they have a spot free here and there scattered throughout the filing system. What happens to the file to be stored? Well, as you might have already guessed, it gets split up. It will become fragmented into as many pieces as needed, and the file system will keep track of where each piece is. The more fragmented a file becomes, the longer it takes to retrieve. This is often the cause of computer performance degradation over time. What makes NTFS resistant to fragmentation is that the file system management portion of the operating system will look at the size of the file to be stored and try to find the largest available contiguous block of space it can to put it. While it is not going to prevent fragmentation entirely, the degree of fragmentation is lower because of this more intelligent handling. The FAT16 or FAT32 file systems simply start storing at the first empty spot and work forward to store the file.

Fragmentation can make low-level data recovery efforts more difficult because of the need to track down all the pieces. This is yet another reason to be using the more secure and more intelligently managed NTFS file system in your organization.

One other feature available only on the Windows 2000 operating system is something called Folder Redirection. This feature lets you have a hard drive folder, or even an entire hard drive, located somewhere other than the user's local computer. This feature can be made transparent to the user and is best used on desktop systems. Laptops that are potentially undocked and redocked (or repeatedly disconnected and reconnected to the network) are not suitable for this entire drive redirection because the location of the drive, not being local, would require synchronizing the files back to the laptop over the network before undocking, and again once it was docked. The time involved to do this level of synchronization is impractical. It is recommended, however, that you consider redirecting the section of the system that contains the Event Logs so that the logs for a computer are actually stored on a secure, remote server. This prevents tampering and provides an easier way to make ongoing examinations of a given system. Setting this up will require some expert administration skills; the details of this setup are beyond the scope of this text. Be aware, however, of the capabilities and look into implementing this audit tracking and remote storage of the logs if at all possible.

When you enable auditing, you cause entries to be made to an event log. On Windows NT and Windows 2000, the Event Log Viewer (see Exhibit 11) is used to observe the entries made by the auditing of activities. Event Logs are divided into three or four sections: System Messages, Application Messages,

Event Viewer

Action View

Tree

Event Viewer (Local)
- Application Log
- Security Log
- System Log
- IExplore

Security Log 1,587 event(s)

Type	Date	Time	Source	Category	Event	User	Computer
Success Audit	07/08/2001	9:37:31 AM	Security	Object Access	562	SYSTEM	TBJ36E1IZP93QS7
Success Audit	07/08/2001	9:37:31 AM	Security	Object Access	562	SYSTEM	TBJ36E1IZP93QS7
Success Audit	07/08/2001	9:37:31 AM	Security	Object Access	562	SYSTEM	TBJ36E1IZP93QS7
Success Audit	07/08/2001	9:37:31 AM	Security	Object Access	560	SYSTEM	TBJ36E1IZP93QS7
Success Audit	07/08/2001	9:37:31 AM	Security	Object Access	560	SYSTEM	TBJ36E1IZP93QS7
Success Audit	07/08/2001	9:37:31 AM	Security	Object Access	560	SYSTEM	TBJ36E1IZP93QS7
Success Audit	07/08/2001	9:37:31 AM	Security	Detailed Tracking	593	SYSTEM	TBJ36E1IZP93QS7
Success Audit	07/08/2001	9:37:31 AM	Security	Privilege Use	577	SYSTEM	TBJ36E1IZP93QS7
Success Audit	07/08/2001	9:37:31 AM	Security	System Event	515	SYSTEM	TBJ36E1IZP93QS7
Success Audit	07/08/2001	9:37:31 AM	Security	Detailed Tracking	592	SYSTEM	TBJ36E1IZP93QS7
Success Audit	07/08/2001	9:37:31 AM	Security	Privilege Use	576	Karen	TBJ36E1IZP93QS7
Success Audit	07/08/2001	9:37:31 AM	Security	Logon/Logoff	528	Karen	TBJ36E1IZP93QS7
Success Audit	07/08/2001	9:37:15 AM	Security	Account Logon	680	SYSTEM	TBJ36E1IZP93QS7
Success Audit	07/08/2001	8:33:16 AM	Security	Detailed Tracking	593	SYSTEM	TBJ36E1IZP93QS7
Success Audit	07/08/2001	8:32:00 AM	Security	Detailed Tracking	593	SYSTEM	TBJ36E1IZP93QS7
Success Audit	07/08/2001	8:31:44 AM	Security	Detailed Tracking	592	SYSTEM	TBJ36E1IZP93QS7
Success Audit	07/08/2001	8:30:29 AM	Security	Detailed Tracking	593	SYSTEM	TBJ36E1IZP93QS7
Success Audit	07/08/2001	8:30:13 AM	Security	Detailed Tracking	593	SYSTEM	TBJ36E1IZP93QS7
Success Audit	07/08/2001	8:28:58 AM	Security	Detailed Tracking	592	SYSTEM	TBJ36E1IZP93QS7

Exhibit 11. Event Log Viewer General Screen

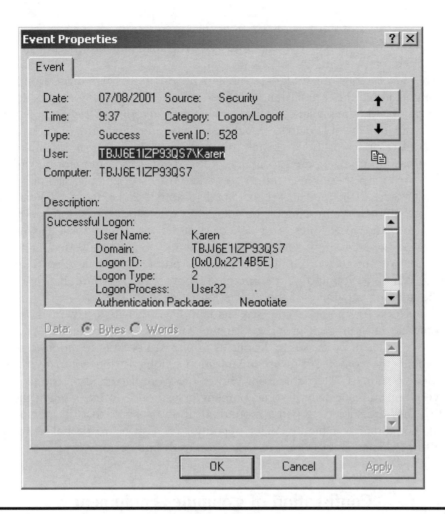

Exhibit 12.   Event Log Viewer Logon Item Details

Security Logs, and possibly IExplore (which contains auditing information on Internet Explorer Events). The event viewer program is used by an administrator-level account on either Windows NT or Windows 2000 to bring up these logs. The event viewer is split into two panes, with the logging areas and the individual events listed. The amount of time an event log is kept depends on the settings for the logs, which tell the computer when to overwrite the oldest entries. If you are going to be monitoring someone over an extensive time frame, you may need to make this a fairly large value.

As you can see from the screen capture of a sample system in Exhibit 12, the auditing function can capture as high or as low a degree of event granularity as you wish. Specific file and application access can be audited, as well as logon and logoff times and other user activities. The entry highlighted in Exhibit 11 shows a logon on event for a user on the computer. If you want to view the exact contents of that event, you simply double-click to get more information about it and the detail view will appear for that entry.

As seen in Exhibit 12, this particular entry shows a successful logon of the user under the account shown. You can view the details of any event regardless of which portion of the logs they are in. If you are auditing the use of a given application, for example, you can find out who invoked the program, when it was started, etc.

The success of your auditing will depend on the expert invocation of the auditing feature, the establishment of proper security configurations in your organization, and the vigilance with which such monitoring of a suspect is carried out. Do not limit event logs to too small a size when tracking someone for possible infractions of policy or the law. Such trespasses may not occur on a daily or even weekly basis, so be prepared to maintain logs over a long monitoring duration. Do not forget that these logs need to be backed up also. Separate backups should be made onto CD-R media and that media should be kept tucked away in a secure, controlled environment with full chain of custody provisions as per the federal and other local Rules of Evidence. Most default settings for logs will make them overwrite after a few days or a week. The idea behind most default auditing is not that of enforcement, but of debugging problems with a given computer system. It is up to you and your corporate security team to ensure that monitoring via the auditing capability of the events log is made efficacious.

More food for thought. You may actually have to initiate covert monitoring of someone in your own group or on the corporate security team. Make sure you have sufficient processes and policies in place to be able to monitor anyone. Remember: the computers in an organization belong to the company and are corporate resources. The rights to privacy in the workplace and on the computer are very limited, especially if your company gives notice to users when they log on that they are subject to being monitored. If you suspect that the person who needs monitoring is a highly skilled security expert, you are probably going to have to get expert help from an outside forensics and security firm.

Confiscation of Computer Equipment

When you confiscate a computer, you should keep in mind all factors relating to Rules of Evidence and establishing a custodial chain. From an evidential perspective, you will want to have the computer isolated and secured as quickly as possible. There are a number of factors to consider when impounding the equipment. First and foremost, make sure that when you impound it that you have a secure location to bring it to. All your hard work will be for naught if it can be intimated in court that unauthorized persons gained access to the computer and might have tampered with it.

Make certain you document the original state of the computer. This can and should include taking date/time stamped photographs of the computer and its attached peripherals from all angles. If the system is powered up when you arrive, photograph the screen. Make sure that you do this quickly, as a password protected screen-saver may come on that will inhibit your ability to make a proper shutdown of the system. Shut down the system following the normal Windows shutdown process. Keep in mind that a clever individual may have put a Trojan horse program in place to destroy parts of the system or evidence. This is another reason to have employed covert monitoring ahead of time.

A sudden power down can be potentially damaging to the computer due to the loss of data from the memory buffer that was not committed to the hard drive. Normally, a Windows shutdown writes all unsaved buffer and disk cache to the hard drive as part of its shutdown process. Once the computer is powered down, leave it off until you have made your bitstream backups. You should work only from a similar computer that you set up from the restored bitstream backups made from the suspect computer. Leave the suspect computer off if at all possible. If damage is to occur, it will happen to the computer you are working off of, and that system can be restored again from the bitstream backups if need be.

Tag all connections into the computer and even draw a diagram of the connections so that the system can be put back together identically in the secure location. You will want to tag not only the wire leading into the computer, but also the socket it goes into. Photographing the connection is also a good idea once the tags are in place.

Make sure you protect the floppy diskette or other media drives. It is important that the read/write heads of the floppy drive or other media not be misaligned due to handling damage. Many diskette drives come packaged from their manufacturers with a cardboard insert, especially on older drives, to protect the heads. If possible, use one for the floppy drive. If not, make sure the computer is wrapped carefully (after fingerprints are taken if necessary), with shock-absorbent foam padding or thickly wrapped in bubble wrap on all sides, prior to transport.

Make sure all personnel handling the equipment ground themselves first before touching the chassis, components, and media. They should wear rubber-soled shoes and not wear any clothing made of synthetic materials that can attract, or even generate, static electricity.

Remember that transporting the computer equipment is a prime area where the chain of custody must be properly maintained. Transport should be performed by more than one person, and should be direct from the suspect's site to the secure storage location. No single part of the equipment should be let out of the sight and possession of at least two trusted and duly trained and authorized people for even a moment. If you intend to go to court, you have to be able to prove that no opportunity existed for the tampering, damage, or substitution of the evidence.

Make sure that once the equipment is brought to the secure location, that it is kept secure. Tampering and damage prevention are critical, and the physical security of the lockup area must be maintained. Video surveillance of the lockup area is recommended and should be in use while your examination of the system is performed. This will help ensure that the defendant can perpetrate no claims of poor process control or other bungling. If such surveillance is not feasible, then having an expert witness present during your examination to cross-check your findings is also a valuable resource.

Once your examination of the suspect's system is completed using the parallel computer, you should fire up the suspect's computer and cross-check your results as a further point of evidence.

Other Methods of Covert Monitoring

Many computer programs exist that can spy on every keystroke, every window brought up, and every e-mail sent, all without the knowledge of the person operating the computer. Such utilities work at various levels and have a wide range of prices. One of the newest entries into the fray for this is a program called SpectorSoft, made by SpectorSoft, Inc. (www.spectorsoft.com). The program, which costs less than under $100 as of this writing, takes intermittent snapshots of what is being done on a computer. It maintains these logs of activity in great detail. One version of this company's software will even covertly e-mail out the logs to an account you designate on a regular basis. While it is not 100 percent unbreakable in terms of finding it, one would have to know exactly when it was installed to be able to find it, and even then, it would be quite a chore to locate. It is just one more weapon to consider in your arsenal of analysis and monitoring for illicit or illegal activity.

Other tools exist to monitor usage profiles of everything from Web browsing habits to e-mail. Another vulnerability that new programs are also taking into account in their monitoring capabilities is that of anonymous e-mail services available via the Web. Someone with a Hotmail or Yahoo! e-mail account could send company-sensitive data out using these services and until now, there was no good way to easily track and prosecute that. This is changing, thanks to these new tools. It is difficult to block the use of Web-based e-mail due to the fact that many of the uses for such e-mail systems are perfectly legitimate. A contractor might use such an e-mail account to keep in touch with his or her company, for example. Such communications may be of a sensitive nature between that individual and the company, and using a service such as Yahoo! or Hotmail keeps their mail off the company's servers, reducing corporate workload and keeping corporate privacy intact.

While your corporate firewall may not allow it, many companies do not block the protocols or ports in the firewall to disallow communications via a chat program like AOL's Instant Messenger, Yahoo! Messenger, ICQ, MSN Messenger, PowWow, IRC chat clients, or NetMeeting sessions. If your company allows such messaging services to pass through the corporate firewall, remember that a file can be sent out or received directly through these tools and it will bypass your e-mail scanning protections. Corporate secrets could be revealed very quickly using these tools, and because it is done without e-mail, yet a typed message is sent, it is easier to covertly send out messages like this, but can be just as damaging as if someone picked up the phone and told it to the recipient directly. A program that can capture keystrokes and screen shots will capture evidence of activity like this, and can further enhance your stack of evidence. It should be used in conjunction with the other tools mentioned, such as auditing through the operating system.

One other tool exists that can capture all data in or out of a computer. That tool is called a sniffer. A sniffer can trap data packets as they are sent out from the computer and as they are received. It is literally an intercept of the information traveling down the network wire, although it does not prevent the transmission of such data in either direction. While it will not capture purely locally stored information (information that never leaves the confines of the PC itself), anything that goes out of or into the computer will be caught. Windows 2000 Server and Windows NT Server come with a program that can remotely monitor any computer address and trap the data to and from it. While designed as a tool for performance and trouble monitoring, it can be put into play for such monitoring tasks. All that is needed is the Internet Protocol address (i.e., IP address) of the computer to be monitored. Check with a trained Windows NT or Windows 2000 Administrator about information on this tool and its use. It comes with the Server versions of both Windows NT and Windows 2000.

Advanced spy equipment also exists that can monitor the minute electromagnetic fluxes coming from the keyboard or the communications port of the computer. Such equipment, when used properly, is another way to trap all data going into or coming out of a computer. This kind of equipment is not inexpensive, and it will not work against computers hardened against electronic eavesdropping (the government refers to this as an equipment's Tempest rating). But your average computer will send out tons of impulses that can be captured from the wires and keypad buttons on the keyboard and mouse, to the fluxes in the monitor screen and wires leading from the graphics port of the computer.

An awareness of the tools available for the purposes of monitoring and collecting data is half the battle of getting up and running effectively. Hopefully, this chapter was of aid in bringing about such awareness and helping guide you to a successful implementation of your forensic detection and investigation skills.

Chapter 4

Basics of Internet Abuse: What is Possible and Where to Look Under the Hood

John W. Rado

The following material was developed with a specific objective: to assist an investigator, auditor, security professional, or law enforcement professional in finding clues about a suspect's Internet activities. This chapter does not attempt to be all-encompassing, but instead was developed to assist the novice (as well as the seasoned professional) in becoming more aware of where to look in, on, and around a computer for information and evidence.

Terms

We begin with the introduction of several key terms and their definitions. It is important for all professionals working in this emerging field of cyber forensics to have a working and functioning lexicon of terms that are uniformly applied throughout the profession and industry.

- *Bookmarks:* A quick way to revisit a Web site.
- *Cookies:* Cookies are a way that computers identify users. These cookies can change, based on user direction and how Web sites are built. There are ways to defeat cookies, as discussed later. A cookie is a text file that can be read only by the originating Web site, unless several Web sites form an association whereby sites within the association can read the others' cookie files. Cookies are stored on a computers hard drive. If you disable cookies, then every time you visit a Web site, you will be asked to reregister as though that was your first time at that site. If you have

Internet Explorer as a browser, the Cookie Alert tracks which sites have left cookies on your hard drive. Cookies are unique for each Web site.

- *DNS:* Domain Name Server. Converts your request for information from an URL to an IP address and tells your computer how to assemble Web page information. An URL is really a collection of facts. Each fact is really a Web hit. The DNS tells the Web server application how to send the URL (collection of facts) back to your computer and how your computer should reassemble that information into the same format as seen on the Web page.
- *History files:* Show the titles of Universal Resource Locators (URLs) that someone has visited. To view one, simply double-click on an URL in the History file of interest and the computer will automatically drive to that Web location.
- *IP address:* Internet Protocol address. A numerical address by which computers interact on the Internet. The IP address is made up of two parts: the identification number of the host and the identification of the client.
- *ISP:* Internet service provider. A company that gives you access to the Internet.
- *Logfile:* A history of Web activity.
- *TCP/IP:* Transmission Control Protocol/Internet Protocol. Ensures that data sent from one computer is sent correctly and notifies both sender and receiver if information is incorrect. It is the basis of communication between computers everywhere.
- *URL:* Universal Resource Locator. This is the fancy name of a Web site. The URL name is designed for people to recognize its source easier than by its IP address.
- *Webhit:* A request for an item on a Web page. This value is tracked to verify the usefulness or popularity of a Web site.

Types of Users

One type of user only requests data and does not give personal data to a Web site. This kind of user can only be tracked with regard to where that user went and how times that user went back. A second type of user enters personal data at a Web site. The user's data is sent to the Web server where it is analyzed and sends back information it thinks is pertinent to you.

E-Mail Tracking

E-mails can be deleted but are not erased from the hard drive until the computer overwrites the exact space that that file filled. Software tools exist that can reassemble this data and other deleted files if the space has not been overwritten.

IP Address Construction

Finding who owns an IP or Web address is relatively easy. IP addresses originate from one of three Internet registry databases. Remember that IP addresses are a series of numbers.

The Internet Assigned Numbers Authority contacts the American Registry of Internet Numbers (ARIN, www.arin.net). ARIN distributes IP addresses in North and South America, the Caribbean, and Sub-Saharan Africa. You can register your IP address with them. You can also find information about IP addresses, not only where they are located but also who owns specific IPs. This is done through their Web site and clicking on their link of "Whois." From there, you can search for owners of IP addresses.

The other two registry databases are (1) the Asia Pacific Network Information Center (APNIC, www.apnic.net) and (2) the Reseaux IP Europeans (RIPE, www.ripe.net).

Browser Tattoos

Both Netscape and Internet Explorer track user movements one way or another. Internet Explorer 5.0 alerts Web sites when a page is bookmarked. This function cannot be turned off. However, when Internet Explorer searches Explorer, Explorer sends the search to Microsoft and then Microsoft sends the search out to the search engines. The response of the search is routed back through Microsoft and then back to your computer. Microsoft can cull the tattoos from your computer for its use. Some versions of 4.0 even go so far as to reveal the user's name.

Netscape tracks user surfing by Smart Browsing (Exhibit 1) and "What's Related." (Exhibit 2).

How an Internet Search works

Users type in a URL on the location bar. The user's PC contacts his ISP, who then searches the Web. The request goes to a server, which based on the coding of the Web page (i.e., HTML [Hyper Text Markup Language]), tells the server how to encode the Web page to the requesting computer. Text and photos are sent separately to the requester's computer, in the form of packets (of information) and reconstructed into a whole document at the requester's computer. The server application tells how the Web site should send the information. The ISP tells the Web server which ISP and which computer (the IP address) to send to. The server application tracks these requests in a log file. These files can be examined at the ISP's site.

Netscape

What to look for: URLs — see bookmarks or location bar image files, files with .gif, or .jpg extensions on the HD location bar (see Exhibit 3). The HD location bar stores all URLs that are manually typed in, but not those from searches.

If someone used a search engine, you can view the History file for a History Files (Exhibit 4). CTRL H brings up the history window (Exhibit 5). Any URL of interest, regardless of how long ago it was visited, can be re-seen simply by double-clicking on the URL in question.

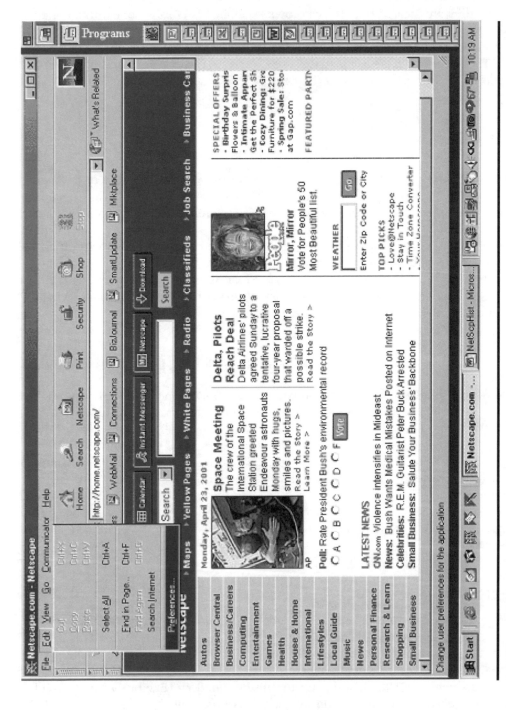

Exhibit 1.   Smart Browsing

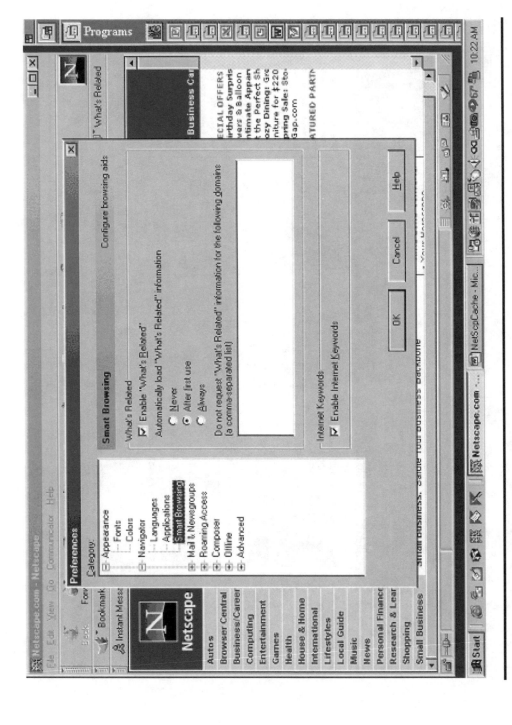

Exhibit 2.   Tracking "What's Related"

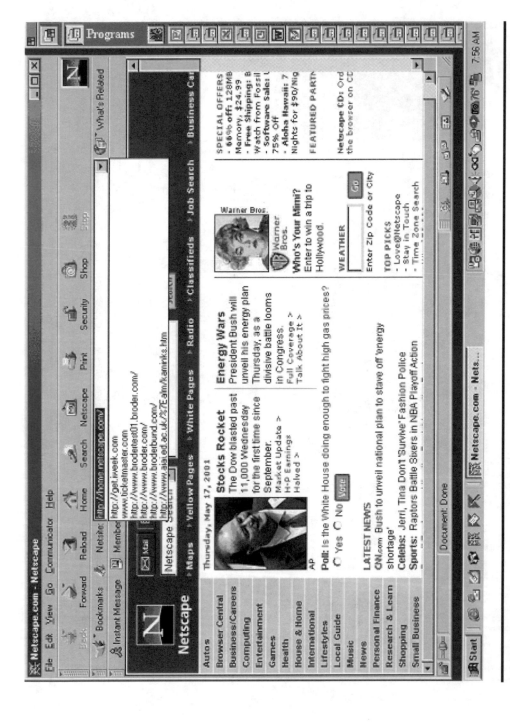

Exhibit 3.   The Hard Drive Location Bar

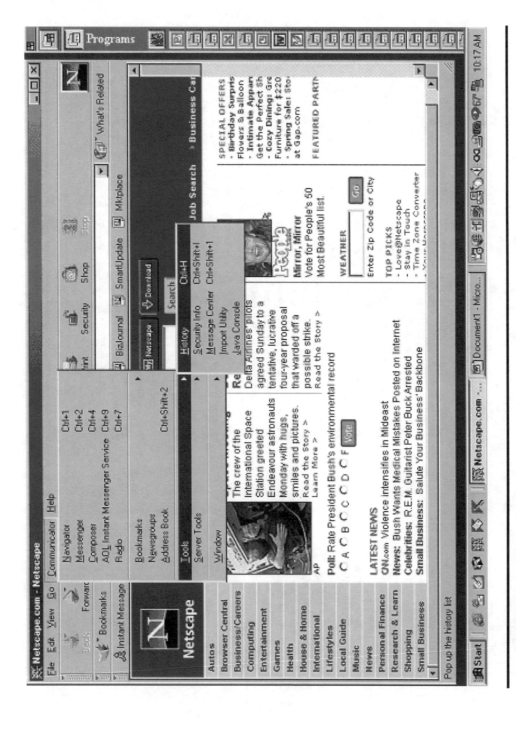

Exhibit 4.   Opening the History File

Title	Location	First Visited	Last Visited	Expiration	
Tower Records - New Christian Series - Classic ...	http://www.towerrecords.com/product.asp...	2 days ago	2 days ago	5/28/2001 3:34 ...	1
Tower Records - Mormon Tabernacle Choir - Lor...	http://www.towerrecords.com/product.asp...	2 days ago	2 days ago	5/28/2001 3:33 ...	1
Tower Records - John Nilsen - Above Me	http://www.towerrecords.com/product.asp...	2 days ago	2 days ago	5/28/2001 3:32 ...	1
Tower Records - Hymnscapes - Vol. 1: Assurance	http://www.towerrecords.com/product.asp...	2 days ago	2 days ago	5/28/2001 3:32 ...	1
Tower Records - Hymnscapes Discography	http://www.towerrecords.com/discography...	2 days ago	2 days ago	5/28/2001 3:32 ...	1
Tower Records - Edward Gerhard - Christmas	http://www.towerrecords.com/product.asp...	2 days ago	2 days ago	5/28/2001 3:31 ...	1
Tower Records - American Boychoir - Hymn	http://www.towerrecords.com/product.asp...	2 days ago	2 days ago	5/28/2001 3:30 ...	1
Tower Records - Music, Video, DVD and More	http://www.towerrecords.com/	2 days ago	2 days ago	5/28/2001 3:30 ...	2
Tower Records - Search	http://www.towerrecords.com/searchresult...	2 days ago	2 days ago	5/28/2001 3:30 ...	2
Tower Records - The Frank & Walters Discogra...	http://www.towerrecords.com/discography...	2 days ago	2 days ago	5/28/2001 3:29 ...	1
A Canoes By Mohawk	http://www.mohawkcanoes.com/	5 days ago	5 days ago	5/25/2001 4:05 ...	6
PADDLERS PAGE	http://www.mohawkcanoes.com/padpag....	5 days ago	5 days ago	5/25/2001 4:05 ...	2
howto	http://www.mohawkcanoes.com/how%20t...	5 days ago	5 days ago	5/25/2001 4:05 ...	2
flatwater order form	http://www.mohawkcanoes.com/fworder....	5 days ago	5 days ago	5/25/2001 4:04 ...	1
LookSmart / Search Results for "mohawk cano...	http://www.looksmart.com/r_search?l&sea...	5 days ago	5 days ago	5/25/2001 4:02 ...	2
tandem canoes	http://www.mohawkcanoes.com/tandem%...	5 days ago	5 days ago	5/25/2001 4:02 ...	7
canoe paddling tips	http://www.mohawkcanoes.com/canoe%...	5 days ago	5 days ago	5/25/2001 4:01 ...	1
canoe paddles	http://www.mohawkcanoes.com/canoe%...	5 days ago	5 days ago	5/25/2001 4:00 ...	1
faq	http://www.mohawkcanoes.com/faq.htm	5 days ago	5 days ago	5/25/2001 3:52 ...	1
acc1	http://www.mohawkcanoes.com/acc1.HTM	5 days ago	5 days ago	5/25/2001 3:34 ...	2
acc2	http://www.mohawkcanoes.com/acc2.htm	5 days ago	5 days ago	5/25/2001 3:32 ...	1
video	http://www.mohawkcanoes.com/video.htm	5 days ago	5 days ago	5/25/2001 3:29 ...	1
The Info Zone	http://home.netscape.com/infozone....	5 days ago	5 days ago	5/25/2001 3:27 ...	1
whitewater canoes	http://www.mohawkcanoes.com/whitewat...	5 days ago	5 days ago	5/25/2001 3:25 ...	1
Canoes for Kids	http://www.mohawkcanoes.com/kids%20...	5 days ago	5 days ago	5/25/2001 3:23 ...	1
Net Search Page - Looksmart	http://home.netscape.com/escapes/searc...	5 days ago	5 days ago	5/25/2001 3:21 ...	1
Net Search	http://home.netscape.com/escapes/intern...	5 days ago	5 days ago	5/25/2001 3:21 ...	1
Redirect Net Search	http://home.netscape.com/bookmark/4_5...	5 days ago	5 days ago	5/25/2001 3:21 ...	1
Historic log cabin	http://members.aol.com/gunflnt/bwa/histo...	6 days ago	6 days ago	5/25/2001 12:08 ...	1
Homepage	http://members.aol.com/gunflnt/bwa/inde...	6 days ago	6 days ago	5/25/2001 12:08 ...	2
Activities	http://members.aol.com/gunflnt/bwa/activ...	6 days ago	6 days ago	5/25/2001 12:07 ...	1
rates	http://members.aol.com/gunflnt/bwa/rates...	6 days ago	6 days ago	5/25/2001 12:04 ...	1

History — File Edit View Communicator Help

Netscape

Exhibit 5. The History File

Cache is a storage area on the hard drive (HD). To access, simply type in "about:cache" in the location bar. A great deal of information resides here. Click on a link shown to see pictures; click again to see the image itself. It is tedious at best to scroll through the entire cache.

Another way to access the cache is to go to the Cache folder, through Find Files. In the Cache folder are numerous files with unknown file names. Netscape randomly renames these vignettes of pages with its own naming system and there is no rhyme or reason to it. The files in the cache can be viewed by their size. Look for the .gif and .jpg files; they are what you are after. Ideally, image sizes over 100 Kb should be viewed.

The simplest way to get to the Cache file is through Start, Find, Files or Folders. After selecting Files or Folders, a window will appear; type "Cache" in the white block and hit Return. After the computer searches the hard drive, a list will appear. This list contains every entry with Cache in it.

You are looking for a Cache Folder. When you double-click on the folder, a file will open and look much like the window shown in Exhibit 6. In the lower left-hand corner, you will see an annotation of how many objects are in that file and the total size of all the objects in that file. To select an individual file, simply move your mouse to whichever file is of interest. In doing so, the size of the selected file will appear in the lower left hand corner. From here, you can select all images that you wish and not only see the size of the file, but also exactly what that file is.

Internet Explorer

Long Method: Location bar: Show Internet Explorer main page
History: Click on sundial (see Exhibit 7)
Short Method: View button atop history window and select "By Site"
Cache: in Internet Explorer, this is called "Temporary Files." To get more out of the Temporary Files: go to the Tools menu and select Internet Options (Exhibit 8), select "General" (Exhibit 9), and click on "Temporary Internet Files" (Exhibit 10). If you click "Delete Files…," that will wipe out any information of interest. Click on "Settings" to view the files (see Exhibit 11); this can be in the thousands.

Through Windows Explorer

Start button, Programs, Windows Explorer, View menu, select Details. This divides the display to show file sizes, types, and dates, and the left side shows the folders. Make sure that the "C" drive is open. Go to Windows folder, Temp Internet Folder, All Files. All Files in the Temp folder show up on the right-hand side of the screen and also the Cookie files will show there. Look for large-size .jpg and .gif extended files.

Swap Files

A special notepad is available when additional memory is needed in Windows 95/98. In Windows NT, these are known as Page files. They can be 20 to 200 Mb

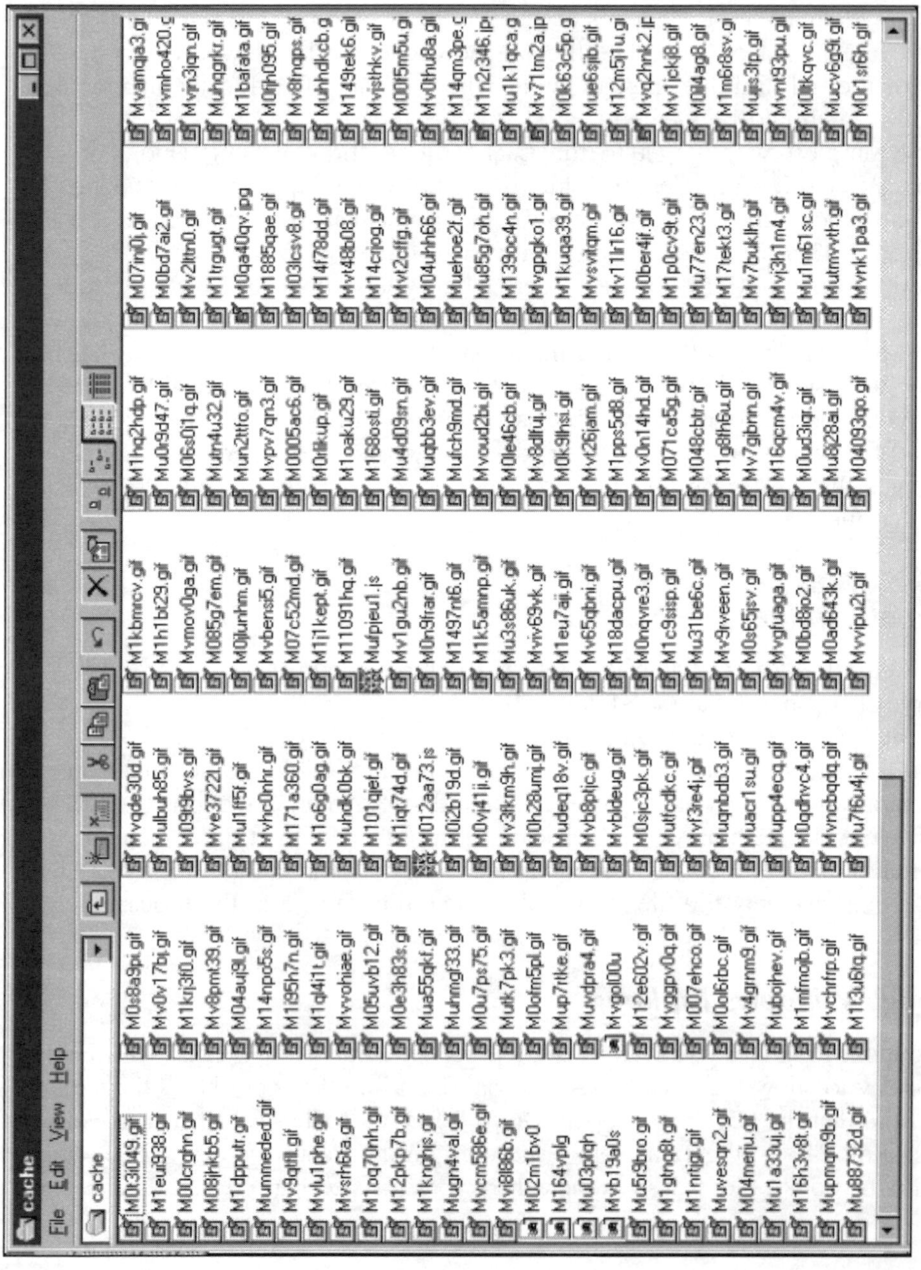

Exhibit 6. The Cache Folder

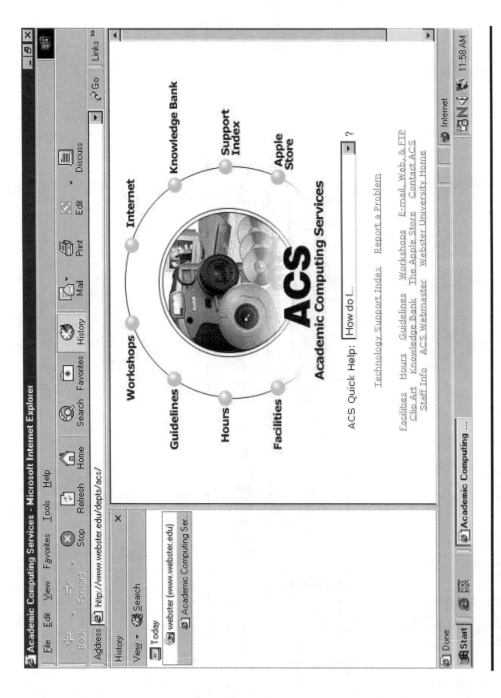

Exhibit 7.   History by Site with Internet Explorer

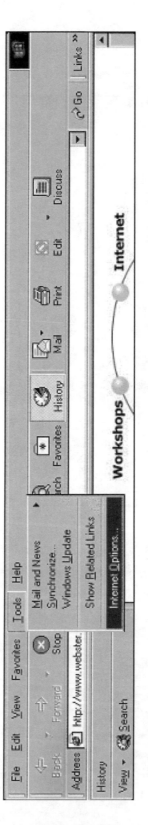

Exhibit 8.   Internet Options

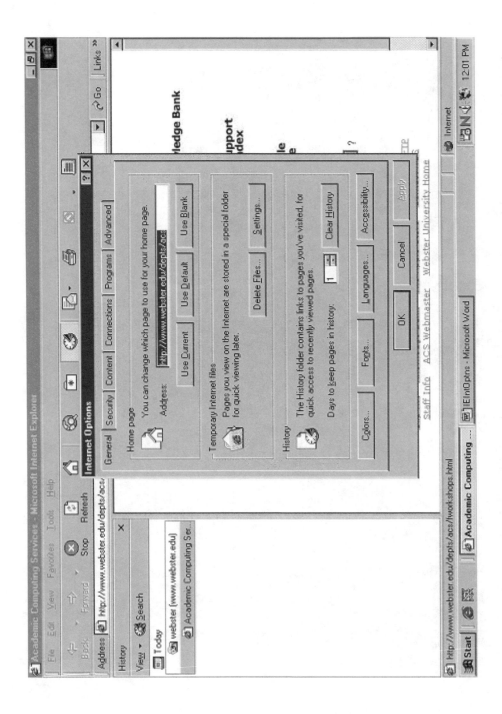

Exhibit 9.   The "General" Tab

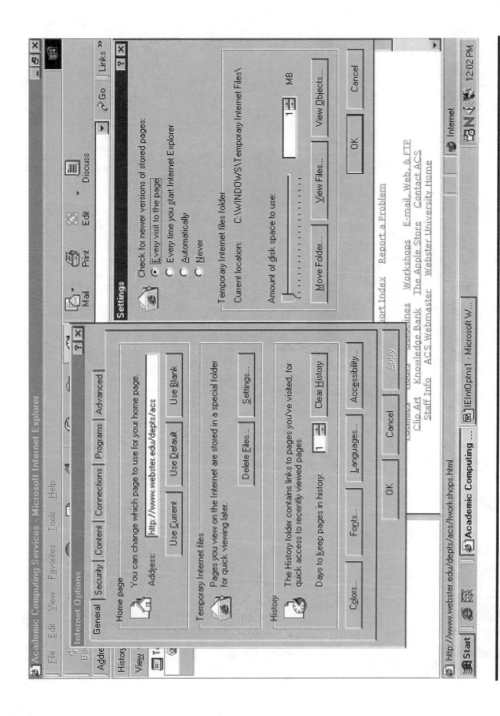

Exhibit 10.   Temporary Internet Files Settings

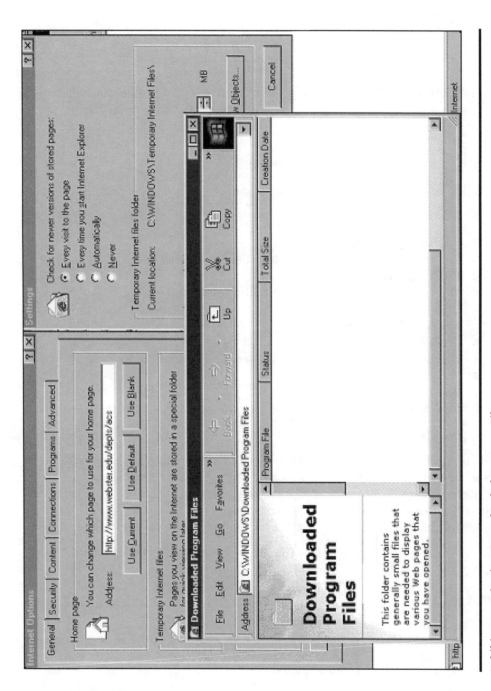

Exhibit 11. Viewing Downloaded Program Files

or more in size. Remnants of word documents, e-mail, Internet surfing, and just about anything else resides here. Swap files uses part of the hard drive for memory. This file can be temporary or permanent and is set by the user. The swap file in Windows95/98 is "win386.swp." This is also in the Root directory of the Virtual Memory dialog box.

ISPs

The ISP server (ISPS) keeps track of when you got on the Internet, where you went, how long you stayed, and how many times you have been back.

Servers

Webmasters can program an application to generate a report detailing the following information from your computer:

- Your computer's IP address
- The number assigned to a specific user and the password
- URL or graphics accessed
- Whether or not the page requested was received
- How much data was sent from the requester's computer and compared to how much was sent back
- Other URLs visited
- User's ISP and the browser type (Netscape or Internet Explorer)
- Cookie filenames
- Your computer's operating system
- How long you visited a site and how many times you have been back

If you are a registered user, the server can reveal your password and will probably make a guess as to the users demographics and suggest advertisement channelled to the user based on its knowledge of those demographics.

Server snooping software includes Little Brother, Surf Watch, Checkpoint Firewall 1, Internet Manager, and Cyber Snoop.

Keylogger records every keystroke made by a user on a computer having such installed on it.

Works Cited

1. Anderson, Heidi, Gathering Information: Techniques for Learning More about Who Is Viewing a Website, *PC Today,* Nov. 97, Vol. 11, Issue 11. http://www.smartcomputing. com/editorial/ar...day/goingonline/971137b.html&guid+1lhmvh50
2. Dichter, Mark S. and Michael S. Burkhardt, *Electronic Interaction in the Workplace: Monitoring, Retrieving and Storing Employee Communications in the Internet Age.* Morgan Lewis.
3. http://www.morganlewis.com/art61499.htm.
4. "How Do They Spy on You," wysiwyg://30/http://netsecurity.ab...urity/library/ weekly/aa082100b.htm

5. Trumble, Chris, Understanding IP Addresses, *PC Privacy,* Apr. 2000, Vol. 8, Issue 4. http://www.smartcomputing.com/editorial/…earchtype = 0&WordList = %22 tracking +URLs%

6. Levine, Diane E., All-Knowing Numbers: Computer Mechanisms Reveal Users' Private Data, *Smart Computing,* Sept. 99, Vol. 10, Issue 9. http://www.smartcomputing.com/editorial/…earchtype = 0&WordList = %22tracking+URLs%

7. Mann, Richard, Find Out What Your Kids Are Doing on the Internet, 8 Aug 00. wysiwyg://6/http://www.themestream…gsp?c_id = 46807&id_list = &cookied = T

8. Mann, Richard, Checking up on Netscape Navigator Users, 8 Aug 00. wysiwyg:// 8/http://www.themestream.com/articles/46815.html

9. Mann, Richard, Checking up on Microsoft Internet Explorer Users, 8 Aug 00. wysiwyg://11/http://www.themestream.com/articles/16873.html

10. Windows Swap File Defined, New Technologies Inc., http://www.forensics-intl. com/def7.html

11. Phelps, Alan, Address Bar, *Learning Series, Internet Tools,* Feb. 00, Vol. 6, Issue 2, http://www.smartcomputing.com/editorial/…3rlf0&searchtype = 0&WordList = URL +Tracki.

12. Sherman, Chris, How to Make History, Wysiwyg://9/http://websearch.about.com/ i…tm?iam = dpile&terms = %2B%22URL+tracking%

13. Nelson, Michelle, Web Tracking is Watching You: Log Files and Cookies Record Your Actions and Anticipate Your Interests, *Smart Computing, Reference Series, How Computers Work,* Nov. 99, Vol. 3, Issue 4. http://www.smartcomputing.com/editorial/…3rlr0&searchtype = 0&WordList = URL+Tracki

14. Nelson, Michelle, Web Tracking Is Watching You: Log Files and Cookies Record Your Actions and Anticipate Your Interests, *Smart Computing, Guide Series, PC Privacy,* Apr. 00, Vol. 8 Issue 4. http://www.smartcomputing.com/editorial/ …3rlr0&searchtype = 0&WordList = URL = Tracki

15. Nelson, Michelle, Web Tracking Is Watching You: Log Files and Cookies Record Your Actions and Anticipate Your Interests, *Smart Computing, Reference Series, How the Internet Works,* Part I, Feb. 01, Vol. 5, Issue 1. http://www.smartcomputing.com/editorial/…3rlr0&searchtype = 0&WordList = URL = Tracki

Chapter 5

Tools of the Trade: Automated Tools Used to Secure a System Throughout the Stages of a Forensic Investigation

Brent Deterdeing

This chapter addresses, discusses, and examines the tools used to secure a system throughout all stages of an incident. It also analyzes and groups these tools into three distinct groups: detection, protection, and analysis tools. Detection tools are used before and after an incident to identify risk, while protection tools are used to mitigate that risk, and analysis tools are used to measure risk.

So what is the risk? Security professionals utilize the following risk model in assessing risk:

$$[(\text{Criticality} + \text{Lethality}) -$$
$$(\text{Network countermeasures} + \text{Host-based countermeasures})]$$

The entire methodology of risk assessment will be best left for another text. However, several good examples of texts dealing with risk assessment can be found in Appendix B. Keep this model in mind as the risks that both systems and networks face are discussed.

Detection Tools

Detection tools are used to identify risks. The analysis of detection tools begins with network-based tools. Network-based tools evaluate one host from another host using the network. There several are unique issues when dealing with network tools; however, this chapter investigates these in terms of one such tool — **Nmap**. Nmap is the most widely used tool for such network analysis.

Of the network tools available to users, by far the most useful, versatile, and common is nmap. Nmap is such a commonly used and widespread tool that in-depth coverage of this tool is warranted here, as are some of the issues surrounding it.

Nmap (available at www.insecure.org) is the commonly accepted authority in information-gathering tools. It is the first tool that both an attacker and a defender reaches for, and for good reason. It is an extremely versatile and useful information-gathering tool that yields much of the necessary information about a machine and its possible weaknesses. However, care must be taken when using Nmap, as we shall see.

Nmap began as a port scanner, intended to aid in the mapping (identifying) of possible security holes on a system or set of systems. According to www.insecure.org:

> Nmap is a utility for port scanning large networks, although it works fine for single hosts. Sometimes you need speed, other times you may need stealth. In some cases, bypassing firewalls may be required. Not to mention the fact that you may want to scan different protocols (UDP, TCP, ICMP, etc.).

Nmap can specify a machine or set of machines via IP address, DNS name, or network number, and can connect to those machine(s) via TCP connect, TCP SYN, TCP FIN, TCP Xmas, TCP NULL, TCP bounce, TCP ACK, UDP ICMP, ICMP, TCP, and direct RPC. Nmap can fragment packets in several timing schemes to further thwart firewalls that may count the number of packets over a given time period.

One of Nmap's signature features is operating system (OS) detection. OS detection is accomplished through TCP/IP fingerprinting. TCP/IP fingerprinting works by sending a series of nonstandard packets to an operating system and then seeing what is returned. This fingerprint is matched to a database that ships with Nmap and contains several hundred operating system "fingerprints." Nmap also supports features such as dynamic ttl times, parallel scanning and pinging, flexible target and port specification, decoy scanning, and output to text or machine-readable formats.

Nmap is an open-source project, meaning that its source code is freely available to look at, modify, and use at one's will. Nmap is available on many operating systems simply because users of those operating systems took the code and ported it to the OS of their choice. Being open-source, Nmap is, of course, free. Although free, it offers more functionality and better performance than its pricey brethren. Nmap is in wide use by anyone needing information on a system, be they the system administrators or someone attempting to attack or otherwise compromise a system.

Fyodor, a self-proclaimed hacker, wrote Nmap as a port scanning tool, as described above. Fyodor recently gave an interview to SecurityFocus.com (www.securityfocus.com/>Audio/Visual->Interviews->Fyodor). In this interview,

Fyodor stated one use of Nmap that he found most gratifying was its use to find proxies to bypass censorship, as was experienced and the case in China several years ago. Nmap, however, has many other uses, which include both (arguably) "good" and "bad" uses. Fyodor also mentioned in this interview that Nmap can develop into a full-blown, commercially available vulnerability scanning utility, while keeping the existing features in the free tool. Also discussed in the interview was a version for Windows NT, which recently became available from Eeye Security, and can be found at www.eeye.com/html/Databases/Softwar e/ nmapnt.html. Fyodor will gladly accept an NT port for Nmap, although he will not develop it himself. Again, from www.insecure.org:

> All my programming work is for UNIX as I believe Windows 98/NT is still too primitive for power users. I also believe that Microsoft intentionally engages in anti-competitive and ethically challenged actions, which can have devastating results for the industry and consumers.

SecurityFocus.com asked Fyodor if he was concerned about a rumor stating that Nmap could be banned by the government. The possibility has been discussed in mailing lists and open forums. However, Fyodor commented that he saw no need to worry over this perceived threat, as he does not believe that Nmap could be banned, due to its large dissipation and the fact that it is open-sourced code.

Fyodor's vision of a hacker is a person with a passion for technology and exploring its limits. This would apply to those who find and publish security holes (gray-hats), as well as those hackers who commit crimes using the information (black-hats), although they are not hackers because they committed crimes, but because of the skills they used to commit them.

Fyodor has a distinct dislike for "script kiddies." It has been argued that tool authors such as Fyodor are responsible for script kiddies having the success that do. However, system administrators (white-hats) need security scanners, despite the fact that attackers can use those same tools to uncover security holes. Is it better to expose security holes until they get fixed or to not have tools such as Nmap available, thus making holes harder to find? It is commonly accepted that security through obscurity is really no security at all. Fyodor agrees with this assessment, and went on to state that he thinks script kiddies have actually helped the security field, as they are constantly scanning networks and finding holes.

This constant scanning reveals holes that are occasionally exploited, typically with the consequence of a company's public embarrassment. However, these holes are often quickly fixed, leaving them closed for other potentially more dangerous attackers such as corporate espionage or malicious intruders. This also increases the likelihood of other holes being discovered by both the victim company and other companies/organizations before they can be exploited.

Although security through obscurity is no security at all, there is an argument that the large volume of exploits made known does more to harm security then it does to help it. Fyodor argued that it is this large volume of exploits that has brought a higher understanding and concern of security issues. He pointed out the state of affairs several years ago: when compared to today, we are much more secure. That is, companies are taking more responsibility to make their products more secure. For example, consider Microsoft. Compare the security offered in Windows 95 vs. the security offered in Windows NT.

Clearly, steps have been taken in the right direction in the past several years. In future versions of Nmap, expect to see socks proxy bounce scanning, IP ID scanning, traceroute support, more input and output forms, faster scans, Solaris binaries (à la RPMs), an improved front end, a default configuration file (.nmaprc), and making Nmap a shared library.

Nmap is, without dispute, a very powerful tool that has many uses for the white-, gray-, and black-hats of the security community. There are, however, several important factors to consider before using Nmap to scan a single machine or a large network. Although port scanning is legal (in the United States), it is not "nice." Scans from unauthorized sources can be deemed as an invasion with unpredictable results.

A recent experience with Nmap can be used as an example. The task was to scan a class B network to see what could be found. Not having much experience with Nmap nor with data retrieval, several precautions were taken to preserve data on the production-level system.

Permission to conduct the Nmap test was obtained from the networking supervisor, as well as from the chief security officer, whose responsibilities included network scanning. The option selected for this test was to perform a full scan with TCP SYN packets on the default timing.

The scan was run three times per week and the results were used to gather any useful information. Several illegal ftp sites were shut down and some OS accounting information was gathered. However, several people noticed the scan, which had come unannounced to them. Management was aware of the scan, the security officer knew, but no one else did. Better care should have been taken to publish the scan to those who would notice it (such as, "We will be scanning you sometime this month."). Although useful information was gained, it was less than well received by clients and the test organization as a whole.

A well-documented, narrow scan should have been performed, as opposed to a full "scan everything" approach. The scan resulted in several unpredictable events. Many people had personal firewalls in place and saw the test scans as an attack. Not only did users flood the security officer with demands for a cease to the scan test, but they also retaliated.

No one did anything very malicious, but they let the tester know that they got in and did not appreciate the test scans. Another nasty side effect of the scan using Nmap was that some older machines crashed as a direct result of their being scanned. The crashed machines were later fixed, but the scan interrupted batch jobs on several servers.

Thus, seemingly innocuous scans had wide-ranging implications that impacted many people and did little to foster a positive image of general security within the test organization. Overall, some useful information was gleaned from the scans, but no more than could be gained from a simple scan that is much less invasive. Scanning is a job that any security officer should perform on a routine basis. However, care should be taken not to adversely affect anyone and to acquire prior written authorization. In this manner, scanning can yield many benefits without having any adverse effects on operations or personnel.

Previously, it was mentioned that Nmap arguably has both good and bad uses. The good uses of Nmap are apparent. Nmap is a very powerful information-gathering tool that helps many security professionals on a daily basis. However, it can also be argued that Nmap has features that provide for bad uses. In this context, a bad use is one that holds benefit for attackers and nothing but detriment for defenders. One such feature that could be argued to provide a bad use is the ability of Nmap to fragment packets, coupled with timings that send very few packets spread over a long period of time.

When packets are fragmented and very seldom come through, a firewall or intrusion-detection device is unlikely to notice anything suspicious. The slow timing ensures that no alarms go off by having a large number of packets, a large amount of data, or connections to many ports of a single device or port in a given period of time. Fragmenting the packets allows an attacker to possibly sneak packets through a firewall by confusing/bypassing packet filters.

Because packet filters only look at the first fragment of a packet, attackers can conceal data with overlapping fragments and headers. This can be useful for a distributed denial-of-service (DDoS) attack. Another feature of Nmap, which falls under the bad use category, is Nmap's ability to generate many false scans, which divert attention from the true scan. These bad uses certainly benefit the attacker community, but do they help the good guys? Is this not security through obscurity? To a point, yes it is. Yet, if fragmentation were not incorporated into Nmap, would it leave a security hole open? Perhaps it would.

Of what use is decoy scanning to a defender? There is no good use of decoy scanning to a defender. So perhaps fragmentation is a good thing; it makes us prepare for the real-world possibility of dealing with fragmentation and seal a possible security hole. However, some would argue that decoy scanning is a feature that Nmap does not need, as it only serves to benefit the attacker and be a detriment to the defender. There are other such features in Nmap that are not mentioned here. These two examples were chosen to help illustrate that some features in Nmap, which may appear to be harmful, may actually be a good feature after all (e.g., fragmentation), while other aspects of Nmap such as decoy scanning may continue to be regarded as undesirable features to include in such a product as Nmap.

Exhibit 1 shows that Nmap has a very functional front end and offers the user many options for scanning. One sees the many options for scanning that Nmap presents, as well as some standard output. Nmap documentation is excellent and provides clear and concise explanations for both scanning options and output formats.

Nmap, however wonderful it may be, is not a panacea. A free, open-sourced tool that runs under Linux complements Nmap extremely well. It is called Nessus (see Exhibit 2) and is available at www.nessus.org/. Nessus scans a host for specific exploits that may be present on the machine. Nessus is a vulnerability scanner that is superior to most, if not all, commercial products. It operates as a client/server model and has an excellent graphical user interface (GUI).

Exhibit 2 provides a portion of the type of exploits that Nessus looks for. One of Nessus' greatest strengths is in its ability to do both technical and executive reporting that rivals other commercial products. A typical Nessus report would look like the one in Exhibit 3.

Nessus is a wonderful general-purpose vulnerability scanner. Windows-based alternatives exist, but can run upward of $12,000 per year. Another excellent scanner is Retina by eEye Securities and can be found at www.eeye.com/. At times, a more specific tool is used for a specific host. For example, if auditing a

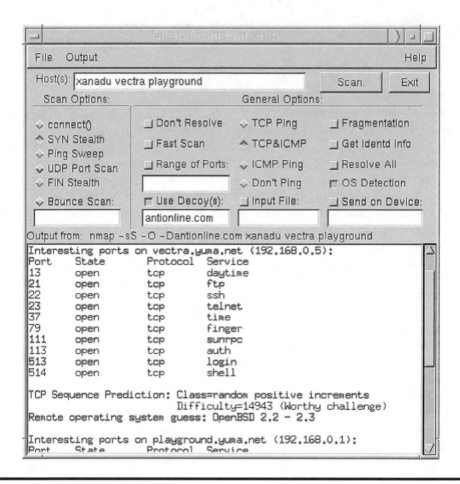

Exhibit 1. Nmap

Web server for vulnerabilities, one may first run Nmap, then Nessus, and follow up with a scan from whisker (www.wiretrip.net/rfp/p/doc.asp?id = 21&iface = 2). Whisker is an excellent scanner written by Rain Forest Puppy that looks specifically for cgi vulnerabilities. It does not have a Windows-based equivalent, although many vulnerability scanners duplicate some of its functionality.

Another specific tool that is frequently used is Firewalk. Firewalk, available at http://packetfactory.net/Projects/Firewalk/, employs traceroute-like techniques to analyze IP packet responses to determine gateway ACL filters and map networks. In essence, it sends packets at a system behind a firewall with incrementing ttl values to determine what ports on a packet-filtering device are open. Firewalk does not have a Windows-based equivalent. It does have a fairly easy-to-use GUI, as seen in Exhibit 4.

The above four tools are extremely capable tools and are used by both attackers and defenders for the same purpose: to discover what vulnerabilities exist on a system that may be exploited. However, the defenders have another avenue not typically available to attackers: the ability to work on the system. It is this avenue that must be pursued by security-conscious system and security administrators to protect their systems. These tools that run directly on a system are referred to as host-based tools.

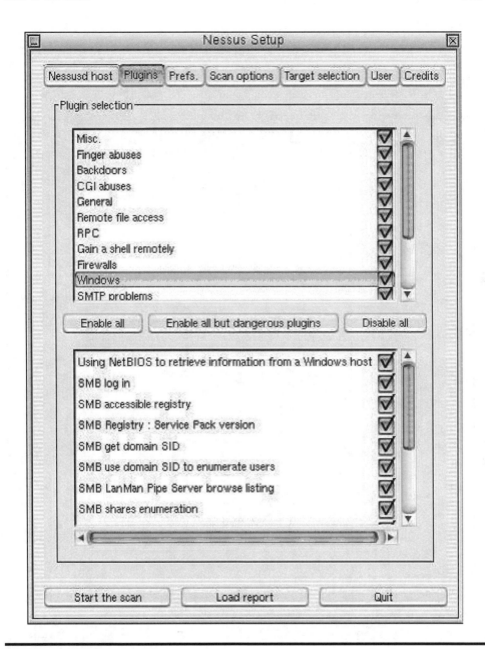

Exhibit 2. Nessus

Tripwire is a file and directory integrity checker available at http://www.trip-wire.com <http://tripwire.com/>. It runs in both UNIX, Linux, and Windows-based environments. The free version for Linux is available at www.tripwire.org. It is a tool that aids system administrators and users in monitoring a designated set of files for any changes. Used with system files on a regular (read: daily) basis, Tripwire can notify system administrators of corrupted or tampered files. Tripwire is one of the first things that should be run on a "clean" install. Tripwire gets an MD5 hash of all system files and stores it in a database. This database can be compared to a previous database to identify modified files. The commercial version provides a method of managing multiple hosts from a central station.

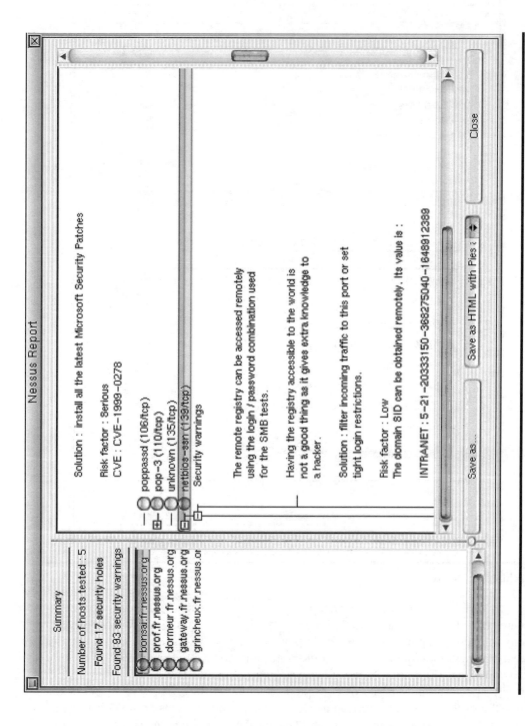

Exhibit 3. Nessus Report

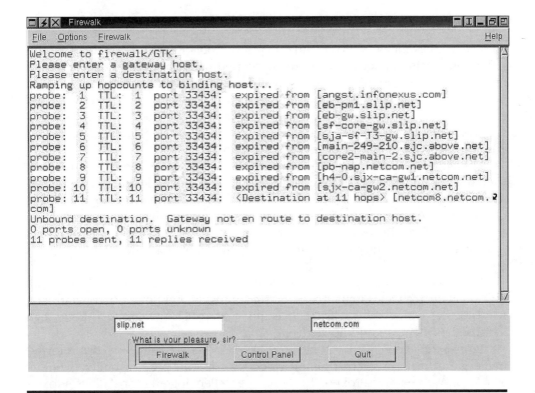

Exhibit 4.   Firewalk

An alternate approach to the detection of malicious activity directed at a UNIX/ Linux machine is found in scanlogd (available from <http://openwall.com/scan-logd/>). Scanlogd identifies port scans directed against a machine and logs them. As pointed out for nmap, port scans are the first step an attacker takes. A scanlogd alert has the following format:

saddr[:**sport**] to **daddr** [and others,] ports **port**[, **port**...], ..., **flags**[, TOS **TOS**][, TTL **TTL**] **@HH:MM:SS**

A tool frequently overlooked by system administrators and security personnel alike is the simple lsof command. The lsof command can be used to list open files and open sockets as well, and includes the associated process in its output. This greatly helps to identify what process is responsible for a given port's activity. Lsof is included on most Linux and UNIX distributions. A useful command is the following (performed on a RedHat 7.0 machine):

```
lsof -i +M
```

This command will list all open Internet sockets. To reduce this list to just the daemons:

```
lsof -i +M | grep '^c' | cut -b2-20 | sort -u
```

There are more tools available, but these are among the most common and useful the author has found.

Protection Tools

Protection tools mitigate the risk that detection tools identify. They mitigate this risk by increasing either network- or host-based countermeasures accounted for in the initial risk formula. Once again, the analysis begins with network-based tools; more specifically, tools that are used to boost network countermeasures. An important concept comes into play here: defense in-depth. Network security is like an onion; once one layer is peeled away, another reveals itself. To this end, one layer of network security is not adequate.

Routers are the devices that pass traffic to the correct location. They typically form the first line of defense for a network. Routers can and should be configured to not route certain types of traffic. They act as a noise filter by stopping some of the more common malicious traffic. By filtering this traffic, they mitigate risk.

Firewalls form the second layer of defense in a secured network. They mitigate risk by acting as a sentry for a network and only allowing traffic through that is specifically permitted.

Intrusion detection systems (IDSs) function as burglar alarms for a network by identifying malicious traffic based on signatures. Without them, an organization may not even know if it has been compromised. They mitigate risk through increased awareness and knowledge.

Proxies function as an insurance policy of sorts by validating that allowed traffic is not malicious. For example, Web proxies can prevent buffer overflow attacks on Web servers. Proxies also provide excellent logging capabilities. Proxies mitigate risk by stopping malicious traffic for a specific type of traffic and by maintaining excellent logs. Network countermeasures are complemented by host-based countermeasures, and host-based countermeasures are more easily and more rapidly deployed.

Snort is an open-sourced IDS that can be used to monitor a network or a specific host for intrusions. It runs on both Windows and UNIX/Linux platforms and can be found at www.snort.org.

Personal firewalls function in the same way as network firewalls. UNIX/Linux machines can employ ipchains or iptables rule-sets to function as firewalls. Windows-based machines can make use of products such as BlackICE Defender, found at www. networkice.com/products/blackice_defender.html. BlackICE is easily configured and maintained, and has excellent reporting capability, as seen in Exhibit 5.

Along the same lines as proxies, tcpwrappers for UNIX/Linux hosts come into play. If an ipchains or iptables firewall allows only port 80 through for a Web server, tcpwrappers can be configured to only respond to specific hosts. Tcp-wrappers come default with UNIX/Linux and can be configured using/etc/hosts (see Exhibit 6).

As a common-sense entry, SSH (or Secure Shell) is an absolutely vital tool. SSH is the secure replacement for Telnet. Any remote administration should be done using SSH due to its encryption properties. OpenSSH is a free alternative for SSH and is available at www.openssh.com. It can be configured with/etc/ssh-config (see Exhibit 7).

Logs are only valuable if they are watched. To help with this process on UNIX/Linux hosts, swatch (available from www. stanford.edu/~atkins/swatch/)

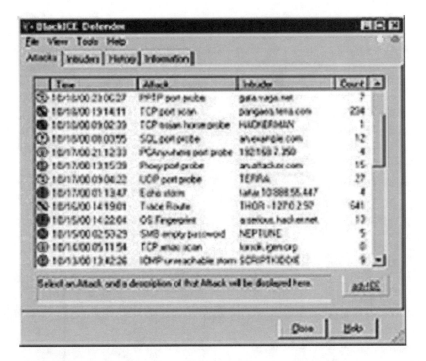

Exhibit 5. BlackICE

was built. Swatch will follow system logs and alert via several methods if pre-configured events occur. Swatch, in conjunction with tcpwrappers or snort, can be an extremely effective monitoring device. Swatch is run with the following command:

```
swatch [ — config-file file] [ — restart-time time]
[ — input-record-separator regex] [[ — examine
file_to_examine] | [ — read-pipe program_to_pipe_from]
| [ — tail file_to_tail]] [ — daemon]
```

As another common-sense entry along the same lines as SSH, PGP comes into play. PGP, which stands for Pretty Good Privacy, is freely available for both Windows and UNIX/Linux hosts. It provides a means by which to encrypt and sign e-mail and files and is absolutely vital when transmitting secure information across the Internet. PGP can be found at www.pgp.com/ and interacts with many popular e-mail programs, as seen in Exhibit 8.

Protection tools can be implemented on both the host and the network. Network-based tools/countermeasures are more expensive, more complex, and take longer to implement than individual host-based tools. However, they are absolutely vital to the security of a network. Furthermore, if they are not configured properly, it can lead to a false sense of security. Both network- and host-based tools should only be managed by someone properly trained in how to do so. Assuming the worst, however, one can now examine some of the tools used to analyze a machine after it has been compromised.

```
allow and /etc/hosts. deny.
#
# hosts. Allow  This file describes the names of the hosts which are
#                 allowed to use the local INET services, as decided
#                 by the `/usr/sbin/tcpd' server.

ALL: 192. 168. 1. 0, 127. 0. 0. 1

#
# hosts. Deny   This file describes the names of the hosts which are
#                 *not* allowed to use the local INET services, as
#                 decided by the `/usr/sbin/tcpd' server.
#
# The portmap line is redundant, but it is left to remind you that
# the new secure portmap uses hosts. deny and hosts. allow. In
# particular you should know that NFS uses portmap!

ALL: ALL
```

Exhibit 6.   Configuring TCPWrappers Using/etc/hosts

Analysis Tools

Analysis tools are used to measure risk. They measure risk by assessing what an incident did, how it was done, and what the consequences were. There are several steps to the analysis of any incident, no matter how big or small. They are to prepare, identify, contain, eradicate, recover, and follow-up, and are self-explanatory. The network-based tools used in preparation are the same as those used in detection: Nmap, Nessus, Whisker, and Firewalk. To this list one can generically add logs from the network-based tools referenced in Chapter 5 on protection tools, such as firewalls, IDSs, routers and proxies. We will primarily look at two toolkits to analyze a machine. These toolkits are categorized as forensics toolkits. The Coroners toolkit runs under *NIX and EnCase is a toolkit that runs under Windows.

The importance of a very strong technical ability to use these toolkits cannot be overemphasized. If one does not thoroughly understand the following requirements, a system can be left far worse than when initially compromised from a forensic viewpoint. Just as a traffic cop should not investigate a murder scene, an inexperienced and untrained person should not attempt cyber forensics. When dealing with cyber forensics, some requirements must be met. These include a technical awareness through knowledge of the technical implication of actions, an understanding of how data can be modified, cleverness, open-mindedness, deviousness, a high standard of ethics, continuing education, and the use of redundant data sources. Some concepts must also be known and understood; these include knowing the importance and implications of speed, knowledge that everything done to a system changes it, a strong distrust of the system itself, consideration of policies, accepting of failures, and preparation for surprise.

The Coroners toolkit (TCT) combines many highly useful tools into one package and is freely available at www.fish.com/tct. It is a collection of tools designed to assist in the forensic examination of a computer. It is primarily designed for UNIX systems, but does have limited functionality when dealing with non-UNIX media. TCT is not to be used for the first time in an emergency; familiarity with the tools and their uses is necessary to use it correctly. Go to www.fish.com/tct and read everything on the site before attempting to use TCT. If you are not an experienced UNIX system administrator, you will most likely cause more damage than good attempting to use it.

EnCase is a forensics toolkit available at www.encase.com from Encase, Inc. It provides a user-friendly interface and much the same functionality as TCT and can be used by someone with far less technical ability. EnCase provides a familiar Windows Explorer style view to work from (See Exhibit 9). This view displays files without altering them in any way, including free space that contains deleted files. This view also has a preview pane, which can be quite helpful when sorting through many files.

One particular feature that is lacking in other similar packages is the Report view, where an analyst can actually build a case as they proceed (see Exhibit 10).

EnCase supports FAT12, FAT16, FAT32, NTFS, CDFS, and EXT2. EnCase allows point-and-click file hashing as well, an invaluable tool to authenticate files later (see Exhibit 11).

```
# This is ssh server systemwide configuration file.

Port 22
Protocol 2,1
ListenAddress 0. 0. 0. 0
#ListenAddress ::
HostKey /etc/ssh/ssh_host_key
ServerKeyBits 768
LoginGraceTime 600
KeyRegenerationInterval 3600
PermitRootLogin yes
#
# Don't read ~/. rhosts and ~/. shosts files
IgnoreRhosts yes
# Uncomment if you don't trust ~/. ssh/known_hosts for RhostsRSAAuthentication
#IgnoreUserKnownHosts yes
StrictModes yes
X11Forwarding yes
X11DisplayOffset 10
PrintMotd yes
KeepAlive yes

# Logging
SyslogFacility AUTHPRIV
LogLevel INFO
#obsoletes QuietMode and FascistLogging
```

```
RhostsAuthentication no
#
# For this to work you will also need host keys in /etc/ssh/ssh_known_hosts
RhostsRSAAuthentication no
#
RSAAuthentication yes

# To disable tunneled clear text passwords, change to no here!
PasswordAuthentication yes
PermitEmptyPasswords no
# Uncomment to disable s/key passwords
#SkeyAuthentication no
KbdInteractiveAuthentication yes

# To change Kerberos options
#KerberosAuthentication no
#KerberosOrLocalPasswd yes
#AFSTokenPassing no
#KerberosTicketCleanup no

# Kerberos TGT Passing does only work with the AFS kaserver
#KerberosTgtPassing yes

CheckMail no
#UseLogin no

# Uncomment if you want to enable sftp
Subsystem     sftp   /usr/libexec/openssh/sftp-server
MaxStartups 10:30:60
```

Exhibit 7.   Configuring OpenSSH with/etc/ssh-config

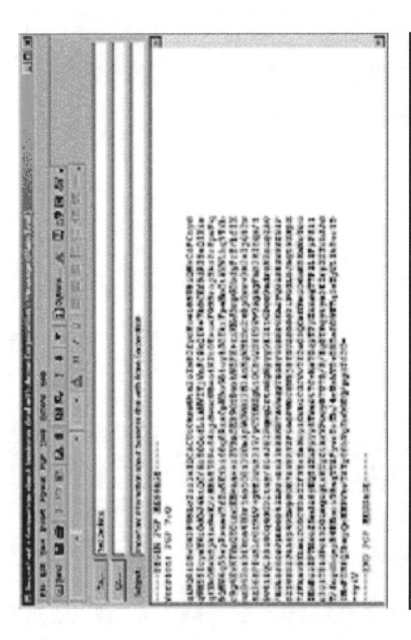

Exhibit 8. PGP Interacting with E-Mail Program

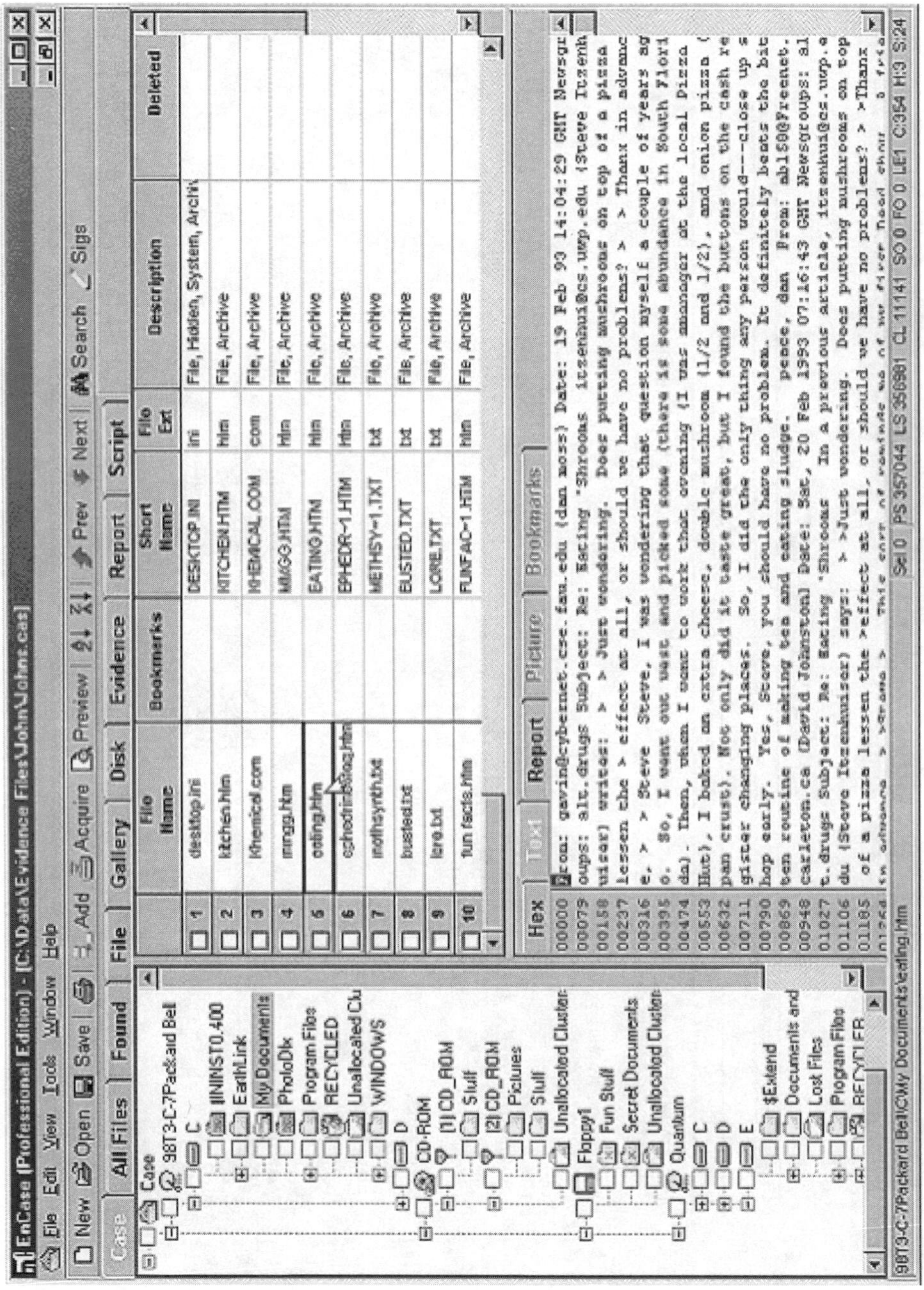

Exhibit 9.   EnCase

EnCase (Professional Edition) - [C:\Data\Evidence Files\John\Hatch Investigation.cas]

File   Edit   View   Tools   Window   Help

New | Open | Save | | Add | Acquire | Preview | Disk | Zoom In | Zoom Out | Export... | Prev | Next | Search | S

Case | All Files | Found | File | Gallery | Disk | Evidence | Report | Script |

EnCase Report

Case: Hatch Investigation   Page 1

Evidence Number "2000-8-2"   Alias "Quantum"

File "C:\Data\Evidence Files\John\Quantum.E01" was acquired by Sheldon at 05/09/00 06:48:06PM.
The computer system clock read: 05/09/00 06:48:06PM.

Acquisition Notes:
Copyright 2000 Guidance Software, Inc...

File Integrity:
Completely Verified, 0 Errors.
Acquisition Hash: 228D6DB0637024AF7A666D4FAFE8FC70
Verification Hash: 228D6DB0637024AF7A665D4FAFE8FC70

Drive Geometry:
Total Size   1.2GB (2503872 sectors)
Cylinders: 621
Heads: 64
Sectors: 63

Partition Table:

Code	Type	Start Sector	Total Sectors	Size
06	BIGDOS	0	717696	350.4MB
07	NTFS	830592	1669248	815.1MB
06	BIGDOS	717696	112896	55.1MB

QuantumMaster Boot Record 0-62   Sel 0 PS 0 SO 0 FO 0 LE 1 CO 1 HO 0 S:1

Exhibit 10.   Report View in EnCase

EnCase (Professional Edition) - [C:\Data\Evidence Files\John\Hatch Investigation.cas]

File Edit View Tools Window Help

New | Open | Save | Add | Acquire | Preview | Disk | Evidence | Report | Script | Prev | Next | Search | Sigs

Case | All Files | Found | File | Gallery | Disk | Evidence | Report | Script

	File Name	Full Path	Hash Value	Hash Set	Hash Category	Signature
179	cis.scp	Quantum\E\WINNT\system32\ras\c	dc0310f3c8f4386c1a13f3c0f96b3143	Z00003	Corel Office		No Mismatch
180	PIPELINE.DLL	Quantum\C\PhotoDlx\RegFiles\PPE	8caac7f91af71a447c90d2aa32f51af6	Z00003	Corel Office		No Mismatch
181	12520850.CPX	Quantum\C\WINDOWS\SYSTEM\	d69ee057cd82d0dee7d311809ebefb2e	Z00004	Office 97 in		No Mismatch
182	12520850.cpx	Quantum\E\WINNT\system32\t1252	d69ee057cd82d0dee7d311809ebefb2e	Z00004	Office 97 in		No Mismatch
183	12520437.CPX	Quantum\C\WINDOWS\SYSTEM\	0a0fcb9eb28bdc8cd835716343b003b14	Z00004	Office 97 in		No Mismatch
184	12520437.cpx	Quantum\E\WINNT\system32\t1252	0a0fcb9eb28bdc8cd835716343b003b14	Z00004	Office 97 in		No Mismatch
185	script.fon	Quantum\E\WINNT\Fonts\script.for	dc1e71d27bf49ca161de0d1945bfb4a2	Z00005	DOS 6-22 &	Known	No Mismatch
186	roman.fon	Quantum\E\WINNT\Fonts\roman.fo	12a5fd4ca67a9a1c0cc35e9ea38c3d6b	Z00005	DOS 6-22 &	Known	No Mismatch
187	modern.fon	Quantum\E\WINNT\Fonts\modern.f	a26dc0b54eb93d917far4074dc125ad94	Z00005	DOS 6-22 &	Known	No Mismatch
188	mciwave.drv	Quantum\E\WINNT\system32\mciw	e05ee70699e3ccd5399B4cf15ac8328581	Z00005	DOS 6-22 &	Known	No Mismatch
189	mciseq.drv	Quantum\E\WINNT\system32\mciss	28c71zefbc949B4cde27ebe9cb5395a3	Z00005	DOS 6-22 &	Known	No Mismatch
190	graphics.pro	Quantum\E\WINNT\system32\graph	bc33ae525d6a807f7186273B6df78426	Z00005	DOS 6-22 &	Known	No Mismatch
191	serife.fon	Quantum\E\WINNT\Fonts\serife.for	7036de1a2c57dae02665090S5a5a328bx	Z00005	DOS 6-22 &	Known	No Mismatch
192	loadfix.com	Quantum\C\WINDOWS\SYSTEM\	53646050f7b20be0103d7bee8111028c1	Z00005	DOS 6-22 &	Known	No Mismatch

Hex | Text | Report | Picture | Bookmarks

```
0000  Windows Latin 1(1252)/850 [Multilingual-Latin 1)  111  130:44  131:159  132:44  133:95  134:253  135:252  137:37
0109  138:83  139:60  140:79  145:96  146:39  147:34  148:34  150:45  151:95  154:115  155:62  156:111  159:89  1
0218  60:32  161:173  162:109  163:156  164:207  165:190  166:221  167:245  168:249  169:184  170:166  171:174  172
0327  :170  173:240  174:169  175:238  176:248  177:241  178:253  179:252  180:239  181:230  182:244  183:250  184:
0436  247  185:251  186:167  188:172  189:171  190:243  191:168  192:183  193:181  194:182  195:199  196:1
0545  42  197:143  198:146  199:128  200:212  201:144  202:210  203:211  204:222  205:214  206:215  207:216  208:20
0654  9  209:165  210:227  211:224  212:226  213:229  214:153  215:158  216:157  217:235  218:233  219:234  220:154
0763  221:237  222:232  223:225  224:133  225:160  226:131  227:198  228:132  229:134  230:145  231:135  232:138
0872  233:130  234:136  235:137  236:141  237:161  238:140  239:139  240:208  241:164  242:149  243:162  244:147
0981  245:228  246:148  247:246  248:185  249:151  250:163  251:160  252:129  253:236  254:231  255:182  /  18:164
```

Quantum\C\WINDOWS\SYSTEM\12520850.CPX

Set 0 PS 75600 LS 75537 CL 4699 SO 0 FO 0 LE1 C18 H48 S1

Exhibit 11.   Point-and-Click File Hashing with EnCase

EnCase is a superb tool that is easy to use, even for those who are not technically strong. Training is highly recommended. The downside to EnCase over TCT is the price; EnCase costs well over $1000.

Analysis tools can be implemented on both the host and the network. Network-based tools/countermeasures are more expensive, more complex, and take longer to implement than individual host-based tools. However, they are absolutely vital to the security of a network. Furthermore, if they are not configured properly, it can lead to a false sense of security. Both network- and host-based tools should only be managed by someone properly trained in how to do so. This point cannot be overemphasized.

This brings us to the conclusion of this examination of basic forensic tools of the trade. There are more complex and sophisticated tools available, most for a fee; however, there are many that are free (see Chapter 17). As one begins to use these tools more frequently, one will undoubtedly want to increase one's audit and examination prowess and seek out these other tools. As always, evaluate each tool for "an appropriateness of fit" and its ability to assist in uncovering the information one seeks, in order to minimize the risks and exposures resulting from the misuse or abuse of information technology.

Chapter 6

Network Intrusion Management and Profiling

Steven Schlarman, CISSP

Computer forensics covers a wide range of technical areas. One of the most complex types of computer forensics activities is the investigation of a network intrusion. A network intrusion is the compromise of a networked computer. This is popularly known as the hacking case. Although this type of security incident seems straightforward — a computer has been broken into — the ensuing response and investigation is a complicated exercise. With the proliferation of networks, both public and private, connectivity is growing every day. There are also several famous hacking cases, such as the Kevin Mitnick case and the Phonemasters investigation. These incidents turned into complex investigations that spanned a number of systems, multiple organizations, and various jurisdictions. One of the major tasks during an investigation of this type is to properly manage the activities during the investigation while maintaining consistency and integrity of any forensic evidence.

To manage a network intrusion, several activities need to be addressed. This chapter is designed provide a guide for developing an intrusion management strategy within the Computer Emergency Response Team (CERT) function.

The areas covered within this chapter are:

- Common intrusion scenarios
- Intrusion profiling
- Intrusion investigation management

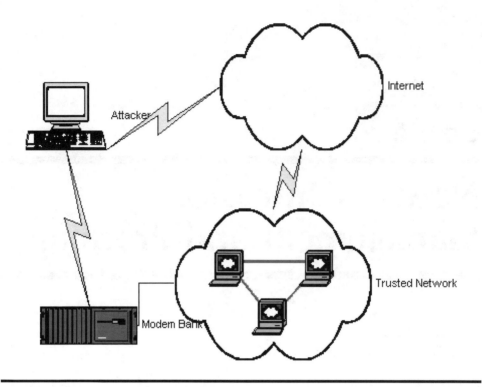

Exhibit 1.   External Attacks

Common Intrusion Scenarios

Network intrusions can come in a variety of different scenarios. These include both external (Exhibit 1) and internal (Exhibit 2) intrusions. An external intrusion is an intrusion outside the normal network trust zone, such as from the Internet or via dial-up modem. Internal intrusions would be attacks from systems within the trusted zone, that is, the corporate network. Internal intrusions might be part of a larger compromise — the intruder has compromised a system from an external connection and is now targeting internal systems — or a legitimate insider could be targeting internal systems.

The sequence of network intrusions usually follows a pattern.

- Information gathering
- Network and system reconnaissance
- System vulnerability exploitation

Forensic evidence can be gathered and analyzed from each stage, depending on the level of auditing and system monitoring enabled on the target system. Listed below each phase are some ideas for forensic evidence locations. Much of this evidence will depend on how well the system is configured to log network or system usage. The use of logging on systems is highly recommended but realistically all events cannot be logged. The logs would then become too large to determine any real substantial information from them. However, knowing basic intrusion techniques should allow one to communicate certain standards on

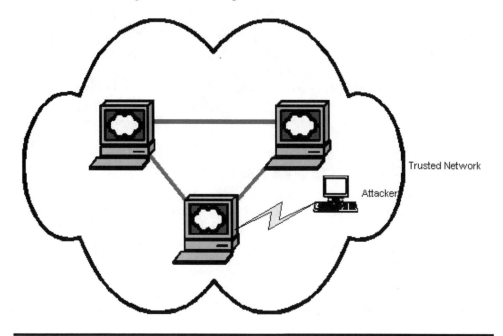

Exhibit 2.   Internal Attacks

logging to the system administrators and provide them with some guidance on what to log.

Information Gathering

Network intruders usually begin by gathering information regarding targets. This information will assist the intruder in compiling extraneous information regarding the company, personnel, or data. Some of these activities could include social engineering, Web site mirroring, and Dumpster diving. These activities are focused on gathering nontechnical information but can provide key pieces of data for use during a network intrusion. Kevin Mitnick and other crackers are famous for using some of these techniques.

Examples include:

- *Social engineering.* Social engineering is the use of social skills to ascertain information. This would include phoning internal employees and posing as customers, internal employees, recruiters, or internal information system personnel. Targeted information may be key systems personnel, username and passwords, system names, phone numbers, or security-related processes (such as the method help desk personnel use to reset passwords, or default passwords for new users).
- *Web site mirroring.* Pulling down an entire Web site of a corporation is a technique that assists in gathering information about every page on that Web site. Also included in this information may be employee names, e-mail addresses, system names, employee IDs, and other corporate data that can be used. Web crawlers and tools that effectively walk down every link in a Web site are freely available for this. Tools include Sam Spade (www.samspade.org) and Httrack (www.httrack.com).

■ *Dumpster diving.* This is the age-old technique of lurking about trash Dumpsters and looking for discarded information. A cleaner technique could be as simple as going to the site and walking around the work areas. Vital information can be found in this manner, such as phone books, organizational charts or the proprietary information one is trying to protect in the first place. However, this discussion is outside the scope of this book.

Forensic Evidence

Technical forensic information for these types of activities is limited. For Web site mirroring, one may find evidence in http logs or firewall logs. It would appear as a large number of hits from one source in a limited time. The other information-gathering techniques — social engineering and Dumpster diving — utilize non-technical methods.

Network and System Reconnaissance

Before an intruder can target a specific system for compromise, the network and system must be analyzed to either find targets or determine services open for attack on systems. Network reconnaissance focuses on the network layer to identify operational systems or valid network addresses. System reconnaissance focuses on a range of hosts or a specific host to determine system information. These activities can be combined or separated, based on target or level of stealth.

Examples include:

■ *Network reconnaissance.* Network reconnaissance is the process of determining live hosts on a network segment. This will include activities such as ping sweeps, DNS querying, sniffing, and router table analysis. The objective is to find the active hosts in a network address range.

■ *System reconnaissance.* System reconnaissance is the process of determining active services, operating system versions, and basic system information for a specific host. Port scanning and MIB/SNMP queries are examples. Port scanning will test a range of network ports to identify which network services are active, such as Telnet, ftp, http, NetBios, and rpc. SNMP queries can also be used to discover system information.

Some of the tools available that support these activities are:

■ Nmap (www.insecure.org/nmap/)
■ Cheops (www.marko.net/cheops/)
■ NetScan Tools (www.nwpsw.com/)
■ Nessus (www.nessus.org)

Forensic Evidence

Network reconnaissance is most likely to be found in router logs if logging is turned on to an appropriate level. Reconnaissance activity, such as ping sweeps,

Exhibit 3. Hidden Directories

Hidden directories are directories that are not initially evident in the directory listing. In UNIX, any directory name starting with a period (.) will not be listed in a normal directory listing. One must issue an ls, a directory listing to see hidden directories. In Windows 9x, NT, or 2000, directories can be created with the Hidden attribute. One must issue a dir/a command to see the hidden directories.

will appear as ICMP packets on a large range of destination addresses with the same source address. Also, DNS servers may show some DNS query activity. From an external perspective, firewalls should log much of the network and system reconnaissance. However, it is not uncommon to see this type of activity from the Internet. As many tools as there are available, there are many more people willing to test these tools. Therefore, any static Internet connection is frequently hit by some type of reconnaissance traffic.

From system reconnaissance, information can be collected from many system logs. In UNIX, the system log is a source of much information. Also, httpd or tcp-wrapper logs can provide connection information.

System Vulnerability Exploitation

The types of system vulnerabilities that can be exploited are as numerous as the types of systems deployed. Each operating system, application, network service, and implementation has known vulnerabilities. Determining the vulnerability used can be a difficult task, especially if the intruder has wiped system log records, installed a rootkit, or destroyed or damaged the system. The vulnerability can be as simple as guessing the password of an account or as complex as IP spoofing. The types of exploits are beyond the scope of this book. However, there is certain evidence that can be pieced together to determine the vulnerability exploited.

Forensic Evidence

Forensic evidence on the exploit is varied. To determine *how* the intruder broke into the system may be difficult. It may be a matter of piecing together various bits of information or being lucky and finding the actual exploit code. The following are some ideas on where to look for evidence.

- *System logs.* Any log the system generates should be thoroughly examined. This includes all system, security, and application logs.
- *Temporary or hidden directories.* Intruders will often compile, store, or create their code (or working files) in a temporary directory or a hidden directory (see Exhibit 3).
- *User home directories.* Information on user activities can be found in home directories. In UNIX, many systems are configured to record users' commands to a history file. This file should be searched for commands issued by the user.

Forensic evidence gathering from a large networked system can be challenging. If the host is a production-level server, it could host thousands of users, multiple applications, many databases, and be essential to the operation of the company. Therefore, the normal forensic procedure of seizing the entire computer is unrealistic. Certain steps must be taken to ensure the integrity of the evidence.

Some rules of thumb:

1. *Document every interaction with the host.* This includes documenting the host one is logging in from, the accounts used, the date/time, all commands issued, all files touched, etc. It is essential to maintain detailed documentation to conduct an investigation. In the course of the investigation, one may want to correlate accounts and login times. If the investigation team has not documented what logins and accounts are theirs, there may be confusion on what the intruder had done. User command history files may also become confusing if one has not documented commands issued.

2. *Copy all system logs and files from the machine to a secure location before analyzing.* The action of looking at the logs may in and of itself trigger a log event. Therefore, do not analyze the logs until they have been copied from the host. Also, before any analysis, copy this information to read-only media, such as a CD-ROM. As stated, some hosts may be too large to copy the entire system for analysis. Therefore, one may have to focus on what files to copy. An initial collection would include all system logs and user login history, all user home directories and files, and all temporary directories and files. Then, based on the directory listing gathered in Step 3, one may wish to copy more files from the host. Also, there are several tools that assist an intruder in destroying or modifying system logs. Therefore, logs cannot be considered 100 percent correct.

3. *Collect as much system information as possible.* This includes an entire directory listing of the machine. (For example, in Solaris, one could issue `ls -alcR > dir.txt` to recursively list all files [including hidden files] sorted by last modification date and capture that to a file. In Windows 2000, one can issue a `dir/a/s/o-d > dir.txt` to capture a similar listing.) One should use this list to identify all files modified during the period of compromise. Other things to document include operating system and patch/service pack level, applications present on the host, and general host information.

The next step in analyzing a network intrusion may be creating a profile of the intrusion. Intrusion profiling can assist in determining the motive and scope of the intrusion, as well as providing a basis to manage the intrusion investigation.

Intrusion Profiling

The Concept of Criminal Profiling

Criminal profiling is a tool primarily used by law enforcement for violent crimes — rape, serial murder, and other like crimes. With a few twists, this concept can also be applied to computer intrusions. This concept not only has significant applications in the investigative side of the incident, but also has applications in other areas relating to the incident. The process of creating the profile involves seeing the intrusion in context, relating the activities to the threat to business functions and needs, and making educated guesses based on probability, experience, and clues.

There are several factors included in creating the criminal profile of a hacker. The intrusion activities can be analyzed to compile the necessary facts needed to begin the profile. This profile can assist in not only tracking the intruder, but also identifying future targets within a system, signatures of the attacks, possible past intrusion locations and the risk or threat of the hacker. This chapter is not meant as an instruction on gathering evidence from a system intrusion, but as a method of analyzing the evidence or providing ways to look at the intrusion to glean more information than may be readily apparent.

The concept of criminal profiling hinges on taking the entire incident in context. Implications and educated guesses can be made from certain pieces of the crime. In violent crimes, criminal profiling is used to determine, among other things, the possible age, sex, motivation, and social status of the suspect. In digital crime, the possible motive, technical abilities, and geographic location are some of the items that the evidence may reveal. The information surrounding the incident must be taken as a whole and pieced together to complete the puzzle.

Things To Do

One of the helpful tasks in this process is to create a timeline of activities. The timeline can begin as a rough estimate of the incident; but as the investigation unfolds, it will grow in its conciseness and completeness. Information from access logs, system logs, and phone logs will construct the timeline. From that point, the different systems and activities will be added so that the penetration becomes a sequence of definable processes.

Another task that must be done is the organization, documentation, and securing of the evidential records. Network intrusions generate a multitude of information; the system logs themselves can create more information than is manageable. Part of the evidential process is to gather all the evidence in its natural form; for example, copies of the entire system log files. It may be helpful for the investigative process to reduce this information to only relevant material. This process should be documented and organized to support the findings.

The relationship between the business data and systems and the intrusion must be determined. This involves gathering a concise description of all of the compromised systems and their place in the business, including input from data owners, information systems personnel, or upper management to pull this information together. Once the information is compiled, then any correlation between the data and the business must be contemplated. That is, the compromised systems must be taken as a whole to decide if there is a business link between them. This will help determine if there is the possibility of a corporate espionage scenario.

Creating the Profile

Several facts are needed to begin the profiling. Log files, a list of accessed files and systems, entry points and, the method of penetration are some of the things needed. The more specific and accurate the information, the better the profile. This is one good reason for active monitoring and logging of systems. Even if only one system has been identified as being penetrated, the activity on that one host can be used to begin the profile. The profile might identify other points of the environment that need to be examined, just as the criminal profile in real-world crimes might indicate possible future or past victims. A full review of the data for the profile is necessary.

One of the major tasks involved in any investigation is information management. The review of log files is a major undertaking on some systems. Information must be whittled down to just the pertinent facts. This may be time-consuming on large systems, but it is necessary to identify the full extent of the intrusion, gather only appropriate evidence, and set the stage for the criminal profiling of the attacker. The information pulled from the log files should be confined to activity on the system during that time of the attack. A list of all files read or written during the time should be compiled. This may not be feasible if the attack has been ongoing or is not detected early on. This is another reason for active security monitoring.

The sooner investigators can get to the evidence, the more information the evidence will reveal. This is true in real-world crimes as well as cyber crimes. A lot of the facts needed are the same as any other investigation. One needs to be able to answer the basic questions of all investigations: When? What? Where? and How? The investigation itself is geared to answer the ultimate question — Who? The criminal profile may answer the question "Why?" and give other information that can be useful in other areas.

The necessary information includes:

- Time of intrusion (When?)
- Source of attack and list of systems penetrated (Where?)
- Method of penetration (How?)
- List of files accessed, including written/read files, files created during intrusion/activities during the penetration (What?). The accessed files should be separated by function: system files, files created for the penetration, data files, etc. The activities that have been logged should also be categorized. This is discussed later.

Once this information is compiled and organized, then the profiling can begin. The profile will begin to bring the information together to create an organized picture of who the intruder might be. This will assist greatly during the investigation and clean-up of the incident. Knowing the type of information needed can also assist in determining evidence collection and activity monitoring during active or ongoing intrusions. We address each piece of information and glean information from each one.

Pieces of the Puzzle

Time of Intrusion: When?

The time of the intrusion will give some information about the possible physical location of the intruder. The typical view is that hackers work only at night. This is not always true, but when one begins to look at the incident as a whole, the time of attack is important. If attacks happen during business hours at the location, then time zones eight to twelve hours ahead or behind the system locations are possibilities. The other possibilities of daytime attacks are local competitors and local users/insiders. Nighttime attacks are different. The attacks perhaps have two different implications. Either the intruder is local or somewhat local (i.e., a time zone within four hours), or the intruder is aware of the location of the system or the downtime of administrators.

The last two possibilities — knowing the location or knowing the low periods of administrator activity — have several interesting implications. First, if the intruder is aware of the physical location of the system, then it is possible the system has been targeted or has been penetrated before and the intruder has had time to determine the physical location. The implication that the intruder knows when system administrators are not present or active is that the intruder has insider ties, either a local user or someone with access to company practices. Nighttime attacks then imply that the attacker is aware of the system location. This may be as simple as the intruder has looked at the system time and determined when the best time to penetrate the system. Regardless, the intruder has gathered some information about the systems and is using low system time to attack the system.

Source of Intrusion: Where?

This fact is, for the most part, straightforward. If the access appears local (i.e., no evidence of dial-in or external network addresses [Internet or business connections]), then the intrusion is an internal employee or person — or there is a need to take a look at your physical security environment. Access from external networks or dial-in access points only point to outside locations. It does not rule out the possibility that the intruder is a local user. Other information may lead to exclude local users but an external source of the attack does not. It only provides a lead to other systems that need to be contacted and followed. If the attack is from a dial-in access point, then possibly the intruder is internal (i.e., the intruder knows the dial-in number) or war-dialing activity has identified your dial-in point.

The access point should be looked at with regard to possible suspects. All persons that supervise the source intrusion device should be questioned. This will identify any user errors or testing that appear to be intrusion activities. It will also lead to other information about the mode of entry and may point to possible suspects, including disgruntled past and present employees. At this time also, the points of proper evidential procedures can be addressed.

List of Systems Accessed: Where?

This list of systems will provide information on possible motives. Targeted systems or limited intrusions indicate that the intruder is looking for specific data. A host is considered targeted if once access to the main system or network is achieved, the host is then singled out for attack and consequently focused on. The intruder may run several attacks against the host and ignore other possible hosts. If the intrusion is limited (i.e., the intrusion has been contained to a collection of hosts) then similarities between the hosts should be analyzed. The penetration may be limited due to system connectivity or tighter controls that constricted the activity. If the hosts are similar in the type of data or business function (accounting, research and development, payroll, etc.), then the intruder may be targeting specific information and data. This points again to an organized, focused attempt against the systems.

Method of Penetration: How?

This information may or may not give evidence as to the technical level of the intruder. It can also provide other implications that should be considered. If the attack is a very technical attack (e.g., IP spoofing or attack source code compiling) then one is dealing with a technically advanced hacker. This cannot be taken too far because scripts and instructions on compiling source code attacks are prevalent in the cracker underground. This only points out that the intruder does have some knowledge of cracking techniques. Access through an easier method (e.g., brute forcing, default accounts, social engineering, etc.) does not exclude technical ability. It only shows that the intruder does have knowledge of intrusion techniques and started with the easier attacks. The penetration may not have needed to be very technical to gain access.

Any compromised account should be checked for the presence of, or lack of, a password. If there is a password, it should be run through a password cracking program to identify the password. It should also be investigated to see if the password was changed. Knowing the password of the compromised account provides insight into pieces of knowledge that the intruder had. If the account had no password, or a very obvious password (username = password), then the results are inconclusive. If the password is not readily apparent, then the attacker had some knowledge about the account. This may include insider knowledge of the account or prior acquisition of the password file. Part of this process can include looking at the password on the account from backup tapes to determine if the attacker changed the password.

List of Files Accessed/Activities During the Penetration: What?

This information is crucial to the investigation and the profile of the intruder. The more granular the logs and the more specific the information, the better the activity can be documented and analyzed. For example, the type of files accessed may indicate the particular data the intruder is looking for. Searching or accessing system directories (/etc or /bin on UNIX, \winnt on NT, for example) may indicate two things: the intruder is either unfamiliar with the system type or is just "playing" with the system. Someone playing with the system implies more of the technically curious hacker. Other indications of a curious hacker include searching user directories, reading mail, and looking for games. Searching or accessing data directories that contain business data indicates a different motive. If specific business-related information is accessed, read, or written, then the intruder does have a more business focus. It may be as simple as looking for a good trophy. Or it may indicate deeper motives. This is where an analysis of the data itself is important. Data owners or users can give information on where the data fits in the business side of the organization. Also, this information can be sharpened to determine a fuller motive.

If the data access is organizationwide — everything from the company Christmas party plans to accounting files to research developments — then the intruder was just grabbing everything. This indicates less penetration organization, less knowledge of the company, and a more haphazard approach. Similar information accessed or collected will indicate more penetration organization, a better sense of the organization or business functions in general, and a focused information type. Good penetration organization and information focus indicate that the intruder is actively attacking a company for a specific reason. These implications lead to a more corporate espionage angle on the attack.

Furthermore, the method of data searching and the time the intruder takes in browsing for information are important. If the intruder appears to know where information is, then insider connections are likely. Unless an intruder penetrates a system, looks at a directory list, and sees the "juicy company secrets" directory, it should take an outsider some time to identify crucial or interesting business-related information. If the intruder does any text searches, and one is lucky enough to find traces of this (possibly in the form of simple scripts or deleted output files), the strings in the search criteria will indicate what the intruder is looking for. This again depends on the level of evidence that is collected. On typical systems, this activity may not be logged but evidence should be searched for this information. Some of this information may be contained in the history files for compromised accounts.

A brief summary of certain intrusion traits and some of the possible conclusions is displayed in Exhibit 4.

Intrusion Management and Response

Intrusion management techniques include many of the techniques used in other types of investigations. At times, it will be necessary to utilize interviewing methods, documentation skills, technical expertise, and other means of gathering information. However, the key point in managing a network intrusion is to gather the right team to support the investigation. Another key point is to have a documented incident response policy and procedure manual.

Intrusion Management Team

Managing and investigating an intrusion must be a team effort. There are many different facets of the investigation, each drawing upon specific skills and

Exhibit 4.   Intrusion Traits and Conclusions

Trait	Method of Identification	Possible Conclusions
When? *(time of intrusion)*		
Daytime	Access times through logs	Physical location of attacker; time zone 8–12 hours away
Nighttime	Access times through logs	Physical location is local; attacker knows location of site
Where? *(source of intrusion)*		
Local network addresses	System logs/connection locations	Local user/user on the premises
Dial-in	System logs/connection locations	User with knowledge of dialin access points; dial-in access point identified through war dialing
Internet/external network	System logs/connection locations	Inconclusive; some activities may indicate inside knowledge
Where? *(compromised hosts)*		
Targeted hosts	Concentrated effort toward particular hosts (i.e., repeated attempts using different methods, subject of attacks such as scanners, etc.)	Host function or data is known; insider knowledge
How? *(method of penetration)*		
Simple method of penetration (i.e., lack of passwords, poor password [username = password])	Identified compromised accounts	Inconclusive
Not readily apparent password	Running the current, or possibly past, password of the compromised account through a password cracker	Knowledge of the account; prior acquisition of the password file
Technical attack (i.e., IP spoofing, source code compiling/modifying		Advanced attacker or attacker with knowledge of cracking techniques
What? *(activities during intrusion)*		
Methodical probing/ scanning of network	Evidence of port scans/ scanning software in system logs across an IP range or network segment	Attacker has knowledge of how to survey network; planned, methodical attack

Exhibit 4. Intrusion Traits and Conclusions (Continued)

Trait	Method of Identification	Possible Conclusions
Haphazard approach	Analysis of activity pattern (i.e., jumping from system to system in a random fashion)	Unorganized, potentially inexperienced, attacker; little knowledge of internal network structure
Searching through system directories	History files for compromised accounts	Technically "curious" attacker; cracker not familiar with operating system; cracker searching for opportunity to place Trojan horse program
Targeting systems with a common business role	List of attacked machines	Directed attack on business information

experiences. Ideally, the incident management team should be identified, organized, and deployed as a working group within the organization. For intrusions, some of the key roles can be laid out as follows:

- *Intrusion management leader (IML)* — A leader should be identified for every computer incident response team (CIRT). The IML should be responsible for overall management of the investigation. Experience in investigation techniques is essential, as is a firm grasp of the technical elements. The IML will then:
  — Coordinate the incident response effort
  — Act as a point of contact for the team
  — Act as a liaison between incident response team and management, legal and law enforcement
  — Delegate and organize efforts
- *Technical intrusion management (TIM)*. TIM members should be identified for key technical platforms. Therefore, the Computer Incident Response Team may have a list of TIM members for different technologies. These members are deployed, depending on the technical needs of the investigation. TIM is responsible for:
  — Performing technical analysis and support
  — Performing technical tasks, including all analysis of logs and collection of technical information
  — Technical incident interpretation
  — Gathering technical evidence
  — Coordinating technical efforts with system administrators
  — Coordinating recovery efforts
- *Management Representative (MR)*. MR should also be part of the intrusion management team. It is very important to have someone from management who understands the situation, the business risk, and can determine the impact of the intrusion on the overall environment. The MR will:
  — Provide management support and guidance in response efforts
  — Direct or authorize funding

— Decide level to contact law enforcement or if information security should proceed with pursuit
— Communicate incident to other management

■ *Incident Librarian (IL).* An IL should be identified to record all activities of the intrusion management team. The librarian is responsible for recording, documenting, and organizing information from any intrusion. The IL should:

— Document all intrusion activity discovered
— Document all response activities
— Coordinate documentation methods to all system administrators for consistency
— Document time spent on intrusion, along with any monetary losses (calculate loss due to man-hours for all incidents)
— Coordinate collection of system logs, records, etc., with person responsible for securing evidence
— Maintain summary reports of all incidents for historical documentation

There are supporting members of the intrusion management team as well. These members should be identified and consulted when appropriate.

■ *Business analyst.* Key business unit leaders or analysts should be identified to assist with critical or business-threatening incidents. They can provide information when a critical or emergency situation involves a high risk to company assets. If a threat, or potential threat, has been identified to specific systems, data or processes, a business analyst should be consulted to assist in quantifying the risk in business terms. This will aid in the management of the incident and also provide insight into damage or recovery costs.

■ *Legal counsel.* Legal counsel should be provided for incidents through the General Counsel. A representative of the General Counsel should be identified to assist in computer-related incidents. This legal analyst should be familiar with local, state, and federal computer crime statutes, electronic evidence standards, investigative procedures, and civil and criminal litigation processes.

Intrusion Management Policies and Procedures

One of the fundamental components of any security program is the Security Policy and Standards. Supporting these policies are the specific procedures that are documented to provide operational details. Intrusion management is no different. As part of the overall security policy of an organization, there must be a documented incident response policy. This policy should outline how the organization handles any and all security incidents. As a part of this overall security incident management policy, a section should be devoted to system intrusions.

A policy, by nature, is high level and does not contain many details. The objective of a policy is to communicate the acceptable environment as determined by management. However, it is important to expand on these policies to provide more information to the general population. This information can assist the organization in identifying intrusions and will provide a framework upon which to build intrusion management procedures.

An intrusion management policy should include the following:

- A description of the overall security incident management process
- An official incident classification scheme (i.e., a scheme to identify the severity and threat level of a specific incident)
- Contact information to report any suspected incident
- Documented roles and responsibilities for both the general population (how and when to report an incident) and the incident management team
- Overall standards the incident management team will follow

The next level of documentation that should be developed is the intrusion management and investigation procedures. These procedures will vary, based on the size of the organization, the technical environment, and other factors. However, there are some fundamental standards that should be met when detailing intrusion management and investigative procedures.

Documented evidential procedures should be developed for all technical platforms within the organization. Although these procedures may not be used each time, it is essential to document and strictly follow evidential procedures. A scripted set of procedures customized for the operating system provides a consistent forensic process. The procedures should match the organization's implementation of the technology, the operating system auditing capabilities, the command set, and system recovery and backup procedures. For example, if the organization has determined what logging capabilities are to be implemented, then the evidential collection procedures should expect that information to be logged. Alternatively, the overall system auditing and logging standards of the organization should support the level of evidence on which the investigative procedures depend. There is no use looking for logs that are not turned on in the first place; and no reason to turn on logging functions that are not necessary. These procedures are crucial for investigation of intrusions, but also provide a consistent method of creating the technical profile of the computer during the incident.

Therefore, a sound technical step in creating incident investigation procedures is to interview system administrators or technology representatives and determine the logging and auditing technologies used in the current implementations. From this, one can determine what evidence is being collected on a daily operational level. If this operational data collection will not support a detailed evidential investigation, then changes should be made at the system level. In this manner, both the system administrators and technical investigation members of the intrusion management team will understand the current technical environment.

Another good element of intrusion management procedures is documentation standards. It is fairly straightforward to create an incident management documentation template to use when investigating incidents. A simple form can provide much documentation support during and after the incident. Forms can be developed for both nontechnical and technical investigation activities.

A technical investigation activity form should include all system-relevant information and the activity performed. A good practice is to create a profile of the system prior to any investigation activity. This can include a physical profile (physical location, hardware serial numbers, etc.) and a logical profile (file system layout, user database, etc.). Then, during the investigation, a log should be captured of all activities performed on that specific system.

A nontechnical investigation activity form might include activities such as interviews, non-system evidence, or other nontechnical activities. A form to capture all information collected during any interviews with system administrators, human resources, legal, or other personnel will help build a solid documentation file.

Conclusion

Managing network intrusions is a complex facet of the computer forensics field. Any large-scale compromise of a network will involve a heavy dose of analysis, investigative procedures, and evidence collection. By having a documented process, detailed investigative procedures, and a trained team, the response and management of an intrusion can be streamlined and be made much more efficient. Understanding common intrusion scenarios is the first step in determining the proper response activities.

Techniques such as intrusion profiling can be instrumental during the investigation. In the end, the profile is designed to provide a better understanding of the intruder. By taking the intrusion in context, putting facts together in an organized fashion, and analyzing the business threat, decisions can be made to manage the intrusion. The management of the intrusion can take into consideration the profile of the intruder — not just technical facts — in the decision process. These factors will lead to better management of the threat. As a final statement, the profiling activity is not an exact science. It is based on certain assumptions that may or may not apply. The main premise of profiling is taking the intrusion in its full context to provide insight into and understanding of the situation.

Finally, putting the right team in place with the right guiding policies is extremely important. The skills needed for a technical investigation are varied. Combining the right skills into the right team is crucial to providing an organization with a sound intrusion management strategy. Developing a fundamental policy, and then driving down the policy into detailed technical and investigative procedures, is the final step toward a strong operational intrusion management team.

Chapter 7

Cyber Forensics and the Legal System

Abigail Abraham

This chapter was developed to assist the reader in understanding and identifying where there may be problems in handling information to build a case, whether that information is committed to paper, recorded on electronic media, or retained in a person's memory. If you find yourself involved in litigation, work with the attorney as much as you need to be comfortable with the intersection of the IT world and the law. The information here should provide some perspective on that intersection and also provide some basic legal vocabulary so you can feel more comfortable from the outset. Learn from the illustrations provided herein, and adapt them to situations as they arise in your work.

To put the legal perspective of this chapter into context, a short overview of the U.S. legal system is in order. The U.S. federal system consists of the federal government, the 50 states, and untold political subdivisions. The laws, therefore, are quite fractured. In general, examples or procedures provided here refer to the federal system because many state requirements follow the Federal Rules of Evidence — some more loosely than others. It is impossible to provide information that is state specific, or even specific to the federal system.

How the System Works

The U.S. legal system is more than what we lawyers call "black letter law." It includes common law, which is the study of case law: judicial opinions, deciding matters in controversy, and reported publicly. Furthermore, while a good lawyer or researcher might be able to tell what the law is in well-settled areas, one small change in the facts as told to the lawyer may alter the analysis. Similarly, one small change in the evidence admitted at trial can change the outcome. Handling

0-8493-0955-7/02/$0.00+$1.50

information that might form the underpinnings of litigation, and full and complete disclosure of facts to your attorney, are critical indeed.

The trial court applies the law as it (the court) sees it. The trier of fact, whether judge or jury, makes factual determinations and assesses the credibility of witnesses. In evidentiary issues, judges perform gate-keeping functions. They determine whether something can be admitted into evidence. The trier of fact then decides the weight (believability) accorded the evidence.

Objections to a judge's rulings must be timely made at trial to preserve them for the appeal process. What this means is that lawyers must always be aware of the record; they need to ensure a clean record of their own conduct at trial and also ensure that any objections they may have to opposing counsel's actions are voiced contemporaneously with the event they are disputing. If a party wants a piece of evidence barred from the trial, the attorney must object to the attempted introduction of that piece of evidence at the time the opposing counsel tries to admit it (or beforehand in motions, if appropriate). Should the attorney not object to the introduction of a specific piece of evidence, but, instead, at the end of trial decide in retrospect that the evidence should not have been admitted, the complaint will almost certainly not be heard.

Litigation is zero sum. The outcome of any trial will leave one party, if not both, unhappy. A party that has lost usually has the right to appeal.[1] But an appeal is taken only after the time, expense, and angst of the whole trial. Even if the trial is rife with problems, the unhappy attorney or party will not get an opportunity to appeal in the midst of the proceeding or following an unfavorable ruling. The right to appeal arises only when there is a final adjudication in the trial court, for until then there is no decision to appeal. Furthermore, there is no review of the witnesses' credibility, and many of the trial judge's decisions are given great deference. In other words, it is important that potential evidence be handled appropriately, and that lawyers and witnesses be well prepared for trial, because there is little opportunity to "correct" trial errors.

If the appeal is successful and the court mandates a new trial, the entire process must be started again. If there is a second trial, the witness testimony must be substantially the same or the witness risks impeachment by his or her testimony at the first trial. Therefore, it is difficult to overestimate the importance of trial preparation, and cooperation between the attorney and the witnesses who are prepared for trial.[2] Although trial preparation is important for the initial trial, it is vital if the witness testimony at the retrial is to be consistent with the first.

Thus, it is the trial court that is, for all practical purposes, the arbiter of disputes. Good lawyering is extremely important, but recognize that the practice of law is an art, not a science. There are circumstances in which an attorney may opt for a particular tactic that, in hindsight, was not the best choice despite the fact that it was well thought out. Judgment calls by an attorney or a judge in admitting evidence, the need to property present evidence, the need to properly preserve the record so that the dispute is alive for an appeal, all occurring simultaneously in a dynamic process, are all part of what makes litigation so interesting — and yet so uncertain.

A final note about the differences between civil and criminal trials. The burden of proof is different in the two systems. In a civil trial, the plaintiff must prove his or her case to a preponderance of the evidence (more than 50 percent) standard; in a criminal trial, the government must prove its case beyond a reasonable doubt. A defendant in a criminal case has a right not to testify; a defendant in a civil case enjoys no such immunity. In situations in which there are pending criminal and civil matters on the same issue, the civil matter is usually held in abeyance until the criminal matter is litigated.

Issues of Evidence

Any information is, theoretically, admissible in court if it is relevant and its probative value outweighs its prejudicial effect. That is, it must first bear on some issue in the case, it must help the trier of fact believe a given assertion is true or not true, and the help that it provides or its meaning to the case must outweigh any prejudice someone might experience from hearing or seeing the information. An example of prejudicial effect outweighing the probative value of evidence might arise in a murder prosecution. Certain, unusually gruesome photographs may be held inadmissible if they do not illustrate some point better than a less gruesome photograph and would therefore only tend to needlessly inflame the passions of the trier of fact such that his or her decision might be clouded.

In addition to the requirements of relevance and the balancing of probative value and prejudicial effect, there must be guarantees of trustworthiness of the information, or an opportunity to examine the information proffered. Commonly, that examination is conducted by having witnesses offer the information in live testimony and affording the opponent of the information the opportunity to cross-examine the witness. The guarantee of trustworthiness rests on the facts that the person has taken an oath; that the person is subject to cross-examination; and that the trier of fact (either judge or jury) has the opportunity to examine each witness's demeanor, delivery, and all else involved in the testimony. The trier of fact also chooses whom to believe in the event there are conflicts in the testimony.

The U.S. legal system has several techniques through which it tries to ensure the reliability of testimony and evidence. There are three summarized here: foundation, prohibition on hearsay, and chain of custody. These are what one needs to be aware of when helping a lawyer prepare a case.

Foundation

To ensure a context for information elicited at trial, certain foundational requirements must be met. Those requirements differ with different kinds of evidence. For example, in those rare circumstances in which an out-of-court statement is admissible, the person testifying must provide the proper foundation in response to questions from the proponent of the evidence. The proper foundation for a conversation includes stating who was present for the conversation, where and when it occurred, and whether it was in-person or on the telephone. By contrast, the foundation for a photograph is generally the witness's testimony concerning what the photograph depicts, and that it is a true and accurate representation of what it purports to be at the relevant time. Other forms of evidence have other requirements. Failure by the attorney to elicit this foundational information from the witness may trigger a sustainable objection from opposing counsel. If the attorney/proponent is unable to elicit the necessary foundational information from the witness, the evidence or testimony will be inadmissible.

Hearsay

The U.S. legal system also has a general prohibition against hearsay, although there are many exceptions. Hearsay is defined as an out-of-court statement used to prove the truth of the matter asserted. Hearsay could be testimony by Jane that Mark said he saw the blue Chevrolet Impala cause the accident. The legal system requires that Mark testify, not that Jane testify about what Mark said. The reasons for that requirement are, in part, that opposing counsel cannot cross-examine Jane about Mark's ability to remember or to observe, the trier of fact is unable to assess Mark's credibility, and there are no assurances of the trustworthiness of the testimony. However, there are a number of exceptions to the general rule against admission of hearsay testimony. The exceptions of interest here concern an allowance for business records and the related exceptions. What constitutes a business record and why there is an exception to the rule against hearsay in the case of business records are explored shortly.

Chain of Custody

The third, and last, technique designed to ensure the reliability of evidence is the chain of custody. The U.S. legal system seeks to ensure that the proponent of evidence can demonstrate an unbroken chain of custody for certain items he or she wants to have admitted. Once again, the objective is to show that the evidence has sufficient guarantees of trustworthiness that the item is what it is purported to be, and has not been tampered with or altered.

Often there is agreement between the parties to admit some piece of evidence without requiring testimony to prove the foundational elements. That is most commonly the case on business records when the opponent of the evidence knows that the testimony is easily elicited. Such an agreement is called a stipulation. Stipulations move trials along more expeditiously and make them less boring. Stipulations do not have to be accepted, however. Sometimes, the proponent of the evidence believes that the information will have greater impact on the trier of fact (usually a jury, not a judge) if it comes from testimony rather than from a dryly read stipulation. A refusal to accept a stipulation is more likely on issues involving injuries in a personal injury suit or a criminal case than on issues involving the production of bank records. A stipulation may not even be offered if the opponent of the evidence believes there is a defect, like a break in the chain of custody, or if the opponent believes that there is some other way to block the information from the trial.

There are a variety of issues concerning recovery, preservation, generation, and presentation of information in the information technology (IT) arena that may be of evidentiary value. To provide a framework for the discourse, consider the following scenario. It is one that could trigger either civil or criminal litigation. It sets the scene for an all-too-common problem in business and allows us to look at some of the rules surrounding information and its use in court.[3]

Hacker, Cracker, or Saboteur

Setting the Scene

Mr. Sneak works for Victim, Inc. Sneak has decided to go to work for Competitor, Inc. Sneak is annoyed with Victim's management, believing that Victim did not demonstrate appreciation of his work through adequate recognition, compensation, or promotion. Sneak wants to ensure rapid success at Competitor. In addition, he wants to hurt Victim if possible. Competitor is entirely unaware of Sneak's behavior or intentions, and would not approve.

During the normal course of business, Sneak has access to proprietary information maintained on a computer at Victim, Inc. Sneak has garnered increasing permissions on the system. Victim's IT staff has been less than assiduous about maintaining and looking at audit trails on the system and has been meaning to review policies, but Victim is a small company with trusted employees and this has not been a priority.

In early May, Sneak e-mails two Zipped databases to his personal Web-based account. The firewall at Victim strips off inbound attachments, but not outbound attachments. Even the inbound strip has been causing some problems as people find the need to legitimately electronically transfer documents to staff when on the road. At the end of May, Sneak gives Victim two weeks' notice.

Two days later, Sneak's immediate supervisor, Boss, becomes concerned with Sneak's increasingly hostile behavior. Boss has IT staff lock Sneak out of the network and secure Sneak's office computer and extraneous magnetic media. Sneak summarily quits when his machine is taken from his office.

Boss asks the IT staff to look through Sneak's computer. The IT staff intends to look at the machine, but the following day becomes extremely busy when there is an intrusion to the network and the system crashes. The intruder was able to obtain superuser access. The IT professionals at Victim work to determine what permissions the intruder set for him- or herself and what information he or she may have obtained or corrupted while trying to bring the system back online for the rest of Victim's employees.

To start monitoring its system, Victim's IT staff turns on audit and logging functions that are not routinely enabled. In the meantime, the IT personnel determine when the system was compromised, not just when it crashed. They ultimately restore the system from clean backups, losing some information in the process. They were unable to determine the full extent of the damage and deemed it safer to go to what they believed to be a clean backup and install the patch for the exploit. In the course of the investigation, various documents and computer inquiries were run. Much later, in response to requests from the various attorneys involved in the case, the same inquiries were run at the conclusion of the investigation.

Meanwhile, Boss keeps Sneak's computer in his office for the week it takes for IT staff to believe that they have secured the network and can examine Sneak's computer.

The IT analysis of Sneak's computer shows reason to believe that Sneak illegally e-mailed proprietary information to himself. The investigation also shows that Sneak was spending a remarkable amount of time looking at information that would allow him to exploit Victim's network weaknesses in just the way that it appears the system was attacked the day after Sneak's office computer was secured. After some additional investigation and analysis of records, there is a reasonable belief that Sneak stole proprietary information and was responsible for the computer crash, and that he may have evidence at his home. Victim involves the police. A search warrant is executed at Sneak's house (only available in criminal investigations) and Sneak's computer is seized.

The investigation also reveals Victim's proprietary information on Competitor's computers. Competitor fully cooperates.

There are several legal actions pending, including:

- Victim, Inc. has filed a civil suit against Sneak, seeking a monetary award for damages that Victim alleges were chargeable to Sneak, either direct or collateral.
- Sneak has a civil suit pending against Victim, alleging wrongful and retaliatory discharge.
- Sneak has been criminally charged with theft of the intellectual property and with computer tampering for use of the exploit and the subsequent computer crash.
- None of the cases has come to trial, and some of the looming evidentiary issues are discussed below.

When Boss took control of Sneak's computer, he needed it analyzed.

Issue 1: What happens if Boss contacts the police and asks them to conduct the analysis of Sneak's computer rather than turning it over to IT staff?

Once the police are involved in an investigation, requests the police make to Victim's security staff or employees become requests from the government. Thus, the investigation is bound by the legal framework that pertains to police, the framework of which includes the U.S. Constitution, statutes, and case law.[4] If the matter is under investigation, the police, in cooperation with the prosecutor, may be able to use compulsory process of some sort (subpoenas, search warrants, and the like) to obtain information necessary to the investigation. Because this is way too early in the process for Victim to consider filing a civil suit, Victim could not use compulsory legal process, and will not be able to until such time as it files a civil suit in the matter (even if Sneak is not named as the defendant at that time). If Victim, Inc.'s personnel search Sneak's personal property at Victim, Inc.'s premises at the request of the police, they should likely proceed under the authority of a search warrant. If, however, Victim, Inc.'s personnel search Sneak's personal property before they have involved the police, then a search warrant would not be necessary. If Victim, Inc.'s personnel overstep, Sneak could bring a civil action against Victim, but the evidence would generally be admissible. In addition to the Constitutional constraints, there are some statutes that treat government action and private action differently.[5]

Advantages of involving the police include that certain kinds of legal process and a certain amount of investigative assistance are available. The police will likely take control of the investigation, and will be responsible for securing evidence and ensuring that proper investigative and evidence handling procedures are followed.

Disadvantages of involving the police include that Victim's staff become agents of the police; and that once the police are involved, it is difficult to uninvolve them.

In this example, Boss opted not to involve the police because it was not clear that there was a criminal matter at that point — the threshold for police involvement. Boss took Sneak's computer and kept it in his office for a week, at which point the IT staff said they would have the chance to look at the machine. Unfortunately, while Boss often locks his office when he leaves for the evening, he does not always do this: generally, he leaves his office open from the time he comes in in the morning until the time he leaves at the end of the day, even if he is in meetings for hours at a time during the course of a day.

At the end of the week, the IT staff said they could examine the computer taken from Sneak. The machine was moved to the IT area, and an IT staff member turned the machine on and started to look through the files. The IT staff found information on the computer that made them believe Sneak had sent himself large files. The IT staff also found that Sneak had spent a lot of time on the Web looking at technical computer sites.

Issue 2: Is the information that the IT staff found admissible in court?

There are a number of issues here. Records, whether in hardcopy or recorded electronically, are generally classified as hearsay, but there are many circumstances in which they are admissible. In this case, were are a number of things found by IT staff. As to the theft of proprietary information, the IT staff found that there were e-mails and notes on Sneak's computer and in his electronic diary with cryptic references to dates and times that match what they believe to be the times that Sneak e-mailed the information to himself. That belief is corroborated by the forensic analysis performed by the police on Sneak's home computer. Therefore, it is important to get the entire chain of the transfer of information: Sneak's notes on his computer, logs Victim may have, Sneak's downloads to his personal computer at home, and Sneak's transfer of the files to Competitor's computer.

The records on Sneak's computer might be admissible as admissions. Assuming the information can be attributed to Sneak, out-of-court statements made by parties that are against his penal or pecuniary interest are admissions and are not considered to be hearsay. Therefore, Sneak's computer documents may be admissions.

However, the fact that the information was on Sneak's computer does not mean that it was placed there by Sneak; it is still necessary to put his fingers at the keyboard because there is, as yet, no proof that Sneak himself typed in, worked on, or is otherwise responsible for the information and documents on the computer in his office without more. The "more" that is necessary might include testimony to prove that Sneak is the only one who used the computer, or could include an analysis of the information on the computer to show (circumstantially) that Sneak was the person responsible for the information on the computer. There are several ways to do that. One is to show that the information tends to be that which only Sneak would know. Another way would be to show that Sneak was the only one with dominion and control over the computer. A third way would be to use password control in the event any of the information was created or sent out under an identifiable password connectible to Sneak.

Another issue here is the method by which the IT staff conducted the examination. If they worked on Sneak's computer rather than on an image of the computer media, it will be anywhere from difficult to impossible to get the information admitted at trial. The better practice is to work on an image or to explain, quite clearly, why it was not possible, and then to document all the actions taken while working on the suspect machine.

Proving that Sneak was responsible for the transfer is part and parcel of the effort to get the material admitted, in part because it affects the relevance of the evidence. If the proponent of the evidence cannot show, circumstantially or otherwise, that Sneak was responsible for sending out the computer files, then the fact that the files were sent out is not relevant to Sneak's behavior, and one of the elements of this instance of computer tampering may be impossible to prove.

Issue 3: Was the computer maintained securely enough to ensure the integrity of the information?

This is called chain of custody. The "chain" accounts for the possession or whereabouts of the item or evidence from the time it was gathered or obtained until the time it is offered in court. It shows that there was no opportunity to tamper with or change the contents of or state of the item; thus, it is exactly as it was when obtained and its integrity has been maintained. As a practical matter, if the item sought to be introduced into evidence is fungible,[6] the chain is more closely watched than if the item is unique. For example, one quantity of cocaine looks much like a similar quantity of cocaine; one urine sample taken in a drug test or one vial of blood taken for blood alcohol determination looks much like the next. Therefore, a strict chain of custody must be observed to show there was no opportunity to tamper with the item from the time of seizure to the time of trial.

By contrast, if a gun with an imprinted serial number is seized and held pending trial, and that gun is properly described when seized, a break in the chain is not as damaging as with a fungible item such as drugs. The gun can be identified in other ways at trial because it is a unique item.

If an error or break in the chain occurs and it is brought to the attention of the court, the judge must decide whether the break is so severe as to merit exclusion of the item from the trial (i.e., render the proffered evidence inadmissible). The judge may, however, decide that, while the chain is incomplete or broken, the item nonetheless should be admitted. The defects should affect the weight that the trier of fact accords the evidence at trial. An objection, however, accomplishes several tasks: it might rattle the witness or opposing counsel; it might provide grist for the attorney's closing argument and allow him or her to muddy up more substantive issues; and it might preserve the opposition for appeal so that the opponent of the evidence can raise the issue if he or she loses the trial.

As chain-of-custody issues apply to this scenario, it becomes evident that while a failure to secure the computer pre-analysis could be fatal, it is more likely that the judge would allow the evidence in, and the chain of custody issues would go to weight of the evidence. Think about what could have been done to destroy the integrity of the computer and the information. Ensure that you talk with the lawyer about the possibilities. The reason to do that is to ensure that the lawyer does not get blindsided during the trial in either of two ways. First, the lawyer should know what questions are reasonable that opposing counsel might ask of his witness. If he knows and understands possible questions, he can understand the answers and decide whether he believes cross-examination would hurt his case and determine whether he needs to rehabilitate his witness on redirect. He also knows when to ask the witness open-ended questions on redirect and be confident that the answers his witness gives will help clarify an issue in the case. The second reason to discuss possible defenses with the lawyer is so that the lawyer is prepared to instantly cross-examine defense witnesses.

One of the rules at trial is that all potential witnesses are excluded from the courtroom during the trial so that they cannot hear other witnesses' testimony and possibly tailor their answers accordingly. Unless the lawyer has a computer professional who he does not intend to use as a witness sitting with him at counsel table, the lawyer must understand the computer or IT issues well enough to cross-examine opposing counsel's witnesses.

Possible tampering of the computer equipment taken from Sneak's office could include having someone get into Boss's office and remove Sneak's machine, replacing it with another. If, however, the serial numbers were recorded, that would not have been possible. In such a case, someone would have had to get into Boss's office and swap out the hard drive in the computer. If there was loose media from Sneak's office retained in Boss's office, it is more likely that the loose media (disks or CDs) could have been lost, stolen, or substituted. In general, however, evidence mishandled is the result of carelessness, and not malice with intent to frame someone. Thus, mishandling electronic evidence is most likely to result in the loss of material, and not the creation of inculpatory matter. Mishandling evidence will not put on a disk e-mails by someone sending proprietary information to himself, but it could result in the accidental erasure of the e-mail. Improper forensic technique could result in failure to recover evidence from disk space where Sneak intentionally hid it or where the computer wrote to the disk in the normal course of its operation. Most problematic with improper forensic technique is the alteration of dates on files if an analysis is performed on the suspect media.

The next step in the investigation is that the IT professionals turned on the logging function on the computer system after they discovered that it had been compromised.

Issue 4: Is the logging admissible?

This issue goes to the notion of what constitutes a business record. The general principle is that writings of various descriptions are normally considered hearsay and are inadmissible unless they fall under one (or more) of the exceptions to the hearsay rule. One of those exceptions is that business records are generally admissible.

For something to be considered a business record, it must generally satisfy the following conditions:

1. Made in the normal course of business
2. Relied on by the business

3. Made at or near the occurrence of the act the record purports to record
4. Offered through a competent witness, either the custodian of the record or another who can testify to those issues

The requirements for public and private business records are often different, with those for public records less stringent. For a computerized private business record to be admissible, it may also be necessary to provide testimony about the type of computer on which it was created or is maintained; the reliability of the equipment as well as the personnel involved in these processes; what or where the source data is and how the records are created; what the purpose or use of the record is; what quality checks are in place to ensure the accuracy and reliability of the records; etc. If the equipment involved is not in common usage, there must also be testimony offered as to its acceptance as "standard and efficient equipment." Finally, the record must be identified as that which was described in the supportive testimony. Each of the issues mentioned (and each of those omitted in the name of reader compassion) has been litigated, and there is a body of case law to flesh out what each line means in different situations.

Applying the general principles to this situation is a bit tricky. First, there is reason to believe that the logging, although it could be a function performed in the normal course of business, was not done in this case. The logging was turned on only after a problem was detected. If something is prepared in anticipation of litigation, then the record loses its presumptions of trustworthiness and becomes only one more piece of information that a proponent or party is trying to get into court for his own purposes, and created solely in furtherance of those objectives. Note that it is different if the underlying information was generated or developed in the normal course of business but the record or analysis of that information was prepared in anticipation of litigation. For example, if logging was always enabled but the report distilled out only a small portion of the log, the *report* is prepared in anticipation of litigation but the underlying information gathering was not. There is an argument, however, that turning on the logging function, when it is an automated system on a computer, does not trigger the bias issues normally of concern for records prepared in anticipation of litigation.

In this instance, then, if the judge decides that the logging is done in anticipation of litigation, the logs would not be admissible under the business records exception. Note that there may be some other hearsay exceptions under which counsel might get the documents admitted. Note also that the fact that a document itself is inadmissible does not mean that the information contained in the document is inadmissible as well, or that the conclusions to be drawn are inadmissible. The same situation routinely occurs in court in discussing the content of conversations. Out-of-court conversations are generally inadmissible. However, it is common to hear an exchange such as:

Q: Did you have a conversation with Jane?

A: Yes.

Q: Was the conversation in person or on the telephone?

A: In person.

Q: Who was present?

A: Jane, Mike, and me.

Q: Where and when did the conversation occur?

A: At Jane's home, in mid-July 1999.

Q: Without going into what was said, did you take any action based on that conversation?

A: Yes.

Q: Please describe what you did.

In this exchange, the substance of the conversation is not included and is not part of the testimony (at least from this witness), but it becomes clear that there was action taken as a result of the information gathered in the conversation. Therefore, it is possible to infer some of the substance from the action the witness took after the conversation. Using the same technique, it may be possible to admit some information from the log, although the document itself might not be received into evidence. For example, the witness might testify that after examining the log, he determined that the intrusion had come from a certain Internet Protocol (IP) address, and then describe how he traced the IP address, which led to the defendant's home, and then either a data wiretap or a search warrant and recovery of evidence. The witness has obliquely testified that the result of an examination of the log was to direct the investigation in some way that generated a lead which pointed to the defendant.

Another issue is that the intruder may have obtained superuser status. That, of course, throws the entire accuracy of the logs and the system into doubt. For that reason, additional work may be necessary, or the IT professional will need to explain why he or she believes that the logging function survived without compromise, and therefore it should be believed. Note also that, in this case, even if the logging function had been turned on prior to the event, and even if the system had been copied and all chain-of-custody procedures followed, there would still be an issue as to what the intruder was able to accomplish after obtaining superuser status. If such an intrusion is successful, it can throw doubt on the integrity of the entire system. If an intrusion is at a lesser level than superuser status, the legal issues still exist but are not as severe.

At this juncture, one might be concerned with the question of what constitutes "best evidence."

Issue 5: Is a printout of a computer record of an event "best evidence" for the purposes of the best evidence rule?

The best evidence rules are generally just that; they consider that the original of an item is better than a duplicate, copy, or derivative form, and require that the best evidence be offered at trial. For example, the original document is better evidence than the microfiche copy of the original. Similarly, an original is better than a photocopy. Once again, the purpose of the rule is to ensure the authenticity and accuracy of a document (and its contents), and this is best done through the original. It is easier to detect a forgery or alteration on an original check than it is on the microfiche of a possibly original check.

In the computer arena, and with the ability to produce endless "originals" merely by hitting one key, there is some question as to what constitutes an original. In general, the rules have become that any original printout is as good as any other original printout. Still, however, there will be authentication and verification issues.

Back to the scenario and the computer seized from Sneak's home, which was accidentally left in an open squad room for several weeks after it was analyzed.

Issue 6: Is the information from Sneak's home computer admissible?

At first, this computer was handled in a forensically appropriate manner; when it was seized, it was held securely until such time as the forensic analysis was conducted. The forensic analyst acquired an image of the computer media, which was an exact, bit-for-bit copy of the media seized from Sneak's home.[7] In addition, the analyst ran a hash on the media, both original and image, and confirmed that the image was exact. The analyst then conducted the examination on the image, and secured an image for defense counsel, anticipating that criminal charges would be brought forth. The computer was properly handled forensically for the analysis, but was mishandled after the image was acquired.

The evidence should not be tainted by the inadvertent failure to secure it after the image was acquired. First, if the suspect computer is still functional, it would be possible to again run a hash and check it against the hash originally obtained and the image originally obtained. Second, the computer was secured appropriately through the original acquisition of the image. Therefore, if for some reason the computer is nonfunctional or, more troubling, the hash values are different, the computer itself would likely be inadmissible, but the information obtained from the image should be admissible (to the extent appropriate under the rules). If the image was for some reason inadequate such that the analyst had to return to the original media, and the original media had been left unsecured, the analysis would be similar to that of Sneak's office computer that had been left unsecured in Boss's office for a week.

Litigation is only something undertaken when all else has failed, whether that litigation is civil or criminal. The purpose of civil litigation is to make the plaintiff whole, insofar as the remedies available within the legal system are able to do that. The purpose of criminal litigation is to express society's outrage at the defendant's conduct and exact some penalty, whether it be monetary or a loss of liberty or privileges. If proper steps are taken in handling information, and IT staff and the lawyers exhibit respect for one another and work together for a common goal, the litigation can intrude as little as possible on the day-to-day operations of the company, and have the greatest probability of producing an appropriate result.

Best Practices

1. Secure all information and media that you suspect may be an issue in litigation.
2. Record any steps you may take to copy media, including computer platform, software used, and keystrokes taken. This is particularly important when the original will be unavailable because the original is too voluminous.
3. Do not commingle subjects in written communications, including in e-mails. Written documents may well be discoverable in litigation and may not be redacted so as to ensure the privacy of the information that does not pertain to the matter being litigated.
4. Promote cooperation between IT staff and legal counsel, and between corporate staff and law enforcement professionals, whether police or prosecutors.

Notes

1. The reason I say "**usually** has the right to appeal" is that in criminal matters, the state is not allowed to appeal from a verdict of not guilty.
2. If at any time you have questions about admissibility of evidence, evidence handling, conduct of a trial, or anything else within the purview of the lawyer with whom you are working, be sure to ask, and be sure that you keep inquiring until you receive an answer you understand. As with any profession, there is a profession-specific language. You should understand the lawyer's language well enough to be comfortable with the issues he or she is raising and his or her preparation of you for trial. Similarly, the lawyer should keep asking questions of you until he is able to explain, in layman's terms, the IT or computer issues that will be presented in court.
3. As the scenario develops, at many junctures there will be questions and several answers. Often, there will not be a right or wrong answer. Rather, there will be an analysis of the event, with an explanation as to the consequences of making one decision or another. Those decisions are judgment calls best made on the basis of as much specific information as it is possible to gather at that time; and these decisions — because they are judgment calls — should be re-assessed at every turn.
4. If, of course, the police are not involved, the legal framework remains that for non-police.
5. See, for example, the different requirements for government actors or private actors obtaining subscriber information from Internet service providers under 18 USC § 2703.
6. Fungible: freely exchangable or interchangeable with other goods or substances of the same kind.
7. There are circumstances under which an image is impractical, particularly in the case of an enormous volume of computer information such as discovery proceedings in civil litigation between large companies, or the criminal prosecution of a target business. In those cases, it is absolutely critical for the forensic analyst to be able to explain why the media was handled as it was, and the analyst should document every step taken that the files selected for analysis were copied. IT professionals

are likely to be in this situation on a frequent basis, particularly because they will be asked by their supervisors to check out one problem or another. If there is any reason at all to believe that the work will be the subject of litigation at any time, there should be a complete detailed record kept of all steps taken to analyze media or files.

Acknowledgments

The author gratefully acknowledges the help of Ken Citarella, Andrea Lucci, and Dick Reeve. Their suggestions and encouragement were critical. Any clarity or elegance in the prose can be attributed to them. Any errors are solely the author's.

FEDERAL AND INTERNATIONAL GUIDELINES

Chapter 8

Searching and Seizing Computers and Obtaining Electronic Evidence

Recognizing and Meeting Title III Concerns in Computer Investigations

Robert Strang, U.S.A. Bulletin, *March 2001*

The dramatic increase in crimes involving the Internet, and computer crimes more generally, is well documented. The "2000 CSI/FBI Computer Crime and Security Survey" documented that 90 percent of the 643 respondents (primarily large U.S. corporations and government agencies) detected computer security breaches within the last twelve months, totaling hundreds of millions of dollars in losses. In light of the increased criminal opportunities created by the ever-growing reliance on, and growing interconnectedness between network computers, there can be no doubt that experienced and sophisticated computer criminals pose a substantial challenge to law enforcement.

There has also been a corresponding increase in the difficulty in catching computer criminals. There are a number of reasons why this is so. The anonymity provided by computer communications has long been recognized as one of the major attractions to would-be computer criminal subjects. This difficulty has been heightened by the use and availability of so-called "anonymizers," services that repackage electronic mail and thereby diminish the ability to trace it. In addition, many victims and Internet service providers (ISPs) fail to record, or preserve for a sufficient length of time, historical logs and other records that might otherwise lead to the identification of subjects engaged in wrongdoing. Furthermore, the practice of jumping from compromised network to compromised network, including networks with servers located outside of the United States, can also make tracing the communications back to the initial subject extremely difficult. This is especially true where subjects have made efforts to cover their tracks or where proof of criminal activity, or even their fleeting presence, is lost before it can be secured. Finally, victims may be unaware of criminal activity on their network or, if aware, slow or unwilling to report it due to competitive reasons. For these and other reasons, there are many computer crimes where it will be impossible for law enforcement to identify the perpetrators involved. Therefore, exclusive reliance on historical investigations will allow criminal activity carried out by more experienced and skillful criminals to go undetected and/or unpunished.

Issues Raised by Proactive Investigations

As a result of these limitations, law enforcement is increasingly turning to proactive investigations where undercover agents seek out the individuals who are already engaging in computer crimes — attempting to record, in real-time, computer criminals while they are involved in the criminal act. The proactive approach bypasses some of the investigatory hurdles of anonymity, lack of records, and under-reporting inherent in computer cases. It also has the added benefit of potentially stopping the criminal before the damage is done. Use of real-time monitoring of criminal activity is even advantageous in some historical investigations where a subject returns to, or passes through the same victim's network. As criminals are increasingly adept at avoiding leaving an historic trail, such investigations are the next logical step for law enforcement (and one that is increasingly being taken).

Such undercover operations and recording are also feasible. The very expectation of anonymity that benefits criminals also helps law enforcement undercover agents enter this world without being scrutinized, as long as they can talk the talk. Agents can even use other undercover identities to vouch for themselves. From a technical perspective, so-called "sniffer" computer programs that are capable of recording all keystroke activity on a particular computer network are a well-known and widely available tool for system administrators, hackers, and law enforcement alike.

These types of investigatory techniques often raise legal issues. One of the major issues raised by real-time monitoring is compliance with federal wiretapping statutes. This chapter focuses on the ability to legally and contemporaneously record and identify subjects, and to develop admissible evidence which is central to a successful investigation. Agents and other investigators, some with only limited experience in this area may turn to prosecutors with questions regarding what they can and cannot do in their efforts to use real-time monitoring of criminals during the course of undercover operations. It is critical for prosecutors to be able to identify potential legal issues relating to such recordings by agents, in advance, before problems arise.

Because the current legal road map is largely without judicial markers, it is important to address some of the potential issues raised by the application of the privacy laws to real-time monitoring, as well as some of the statutory exceptions that may permit monitoring to take place absent a court order.

Application of Title III to "Electronic Communications"

In 1986, Congress passed the Electronic Communications Privacy Act ("ECPA"), which, among other things, extended the prohibitions contained in Title III of the Omnibus Crime and Control and Safe Streets Act of 1968 (the "Wiretap Act"), 18 U.S.C. §§ 2510-2521, to electronic communications that are intercepted contemporaneously with their transmission — that is, electronic communications that are in transit between machines and which contain no aural (human voice) component. Thus, communications involving computers, faxes, and pagers (other than "tone-only" pagers) all enjoy the broad protections provided by Title III *unless* one or more of the statutory exceptions to Title III applies. In the computer context, both the government and third parties are prohibited from installing "sniffer" computer software, such as the FBI's Carnivore program, to record keystroke and computer traffic of a specific target unless one of the exceptions is present.

Where the government is seeking to intercept and monitor all electronic communications originating from a target's home or through the e-mail account at the target's ISP, the application of Title III differs little from its historical application to telephone wiretaps. The issues agents and prosecutors are likely to encounter are typically technical, not legal. This is particularly true when law enforcement is dealing with ISPs who may have little or no experience in providing Title III assistance to law enforcement, have technical or manpower difficulties in providing access to the subject's accounts, or show an overall reluctance in working with law enforcement.

Sometimes, however, the potential effect of Title III's restrictions on computer law enforcement can be unexpected. For example, if a hacker breaks into a victim's computer, engages in criminal activity, and uses it to store credit card numbers, common sense would suggest the subject hacker enjoys no reasonable expectation of privacy. Perversely, however, the subject hacker's communications may enjoy statutory protection under Title III, and thus any interception of that illegal activity by a private party (including the victim) or law enforcement must fall within one of the statutory exceptions in order to monitor without a court order. In the above example, the victim's consent is likely to be sufficient to fall within one of Title III's statutory exceptions.

This example, however, becomes more difficult if the subject hacker simply uses the victim's computer as a jump point from which to illegally hop to new downstream victims or to communicate with the hacker's confederates, as is frequently the case. Does a victim have a right to monitor communications that are being made by a subject hacker who is trespassing on their computer, and is no longer seeking to damage it, but rather is passing through on his or her way to commit more mischief? Does the government enjoy the same rights to monitor that communication as the victim? How, if at all, does the analysis change when the government is the primary victim of the hacking activity?

The analysis of these scenarios is currently dependent on how courts interpret the breadth of existing statutory exceptions to Title III that were written to address the interception of simple, two-way telephone conversations. Thus, under current law, a hacker, a trespasser on another party's computer network, an intruder who enjoys no expectation of privacy, may nevertheless receive certain statutory protections under Title III. Prosecutors must therefore consider whether the statutory exceptions to Title III permit any proposed monitoring. The following are three statutory exceptions that appear to offer potential alternatives to the administrative and judicial burdens involved in seeking court-ordered monitoring under Title III.

Consent of a Party "Acting Under Color of Law"

The most commonly used exception to Title III's requirements permits "a person acting under color of law" to intercept an "electronic communication" where "such person is a party to the communication, or one of the parties to the communication has given prior consent to such interception." 18 U.S.C. § 2511(2)(c).

While there are not many judicial decisions in this area, two circuits appear to recognize that the owner of a computer may be considered a "party to the communication" and thus can consent to the government monitoring electronic communications between that computer and a hacker. *See United States v. Mullins*, 992 F.2d 1472, 1478 (9th Cir. 1993); *United States v. Seidlitz*, 589 F.2d 152, 158 (4th Cir. 1978). Thus, this exception appears to permit a victim to monitor and to authorize the government to monitor, hacking activity directly with his or her computer.

By contrast, if the communication merely passes through a victim's computer, a court may consider it a strain to conclude that the victim computer is a "party" to the communication. Technically, the victim's computer is receiving electronic communications and passing them on to downstream victims and/or confederates of the subject hacker. The literal possibility of monitoring this downstream traffic is present, as all the data streams through the victim's computer, but is the victim a "party to the communication" if the communications are simply passing through its system? A court may conclude that the owner is not a "party" capable of giving consent to key stroke monitoring given its pass-through role.

This is more than a metaphysical concern. Hackers regularly seek to pass through the computers of victims they have previously hacked to: (1) cover their trail when they arrive at their next victim or victims; (2) continue to make use of favorable features of a compromised network such as storage space, bandwidth, and processing speed; (3) return to hacking tools they have left there for safe-keeping; or (4) simply as a pattern of passing through old conquests to make sure their previous exploits have not been detected. This situation can arise even when a government computer is the initial victim. From there, the subject may hop (typically Telnet) to the next network without taking the trouble of backing out of the hacked system. It is possible that the downstream network may not even be a true victim, but rather may belong to a system friendly to the subject hacker. In any event, the statutory exception requires that this new victim give "prior consent" to the monitoring, which will be almost an impossibility in the short term where the victim or victims typically cannot be known in advance.

Consent of a Party "Not Acting Under Color of Law"

Title III also permits "a person not acting under color of law" to intercept an "electronic communication" where "such person is a party to the communication, or one of the parties to the communication has given prior consent to such interception." 18 U.S.C. § 2511(2)(d).

In addition to permitting a victim to monitor communications to which he or she is a party before law enforcement gets involved, this exception provides a very powerful tool to law enforcement: obtaining the implied consent of the subject hacker himself or herself through computer "banners."

Computer networks frequently make use of computer banners that appear whenever a person logs onto the network. Each of us, for example, passes through such a banner each day when we log onto the Department of Justice's computer network. A banner is nothing more than a program that is installed to appear whenever a user attempts to enter a network from a designated point of entry known as a "port." Banners vary substantially in wording, but they usually inform the user that: (1) the user is on a private network; and (2) by proceeding, the user is consenting to all forms of monitoring. Government networks already employ such broad-based banners, and we encourage private industry to follow suit. Businesses are often amenable to doing so, although often for non-law enforcement purposes, such as the monitoring of their employees' use of the Internet.

Thus, the subject hacker gives implied consent to monitoring whenever he or she passes through a properly worded banner. A properly worded banner should also result in implied consent by the subject hacker to the monitoring of all downstream activities, thus alleviating Title III concerns in much the same way as telephone monitoring of inmates, based on implied consent, has been upheld by the courts.

Due to their pervasiveness, the presence of banners is unlikely to deter or arouse suspicion in a subject who has already decided to enter a network illegally. In the case where a private network failed to have a sufficiently broad banner to permit monitoring, a later attempt to add a banner between visits may cause suspicion on the part of the hacker. Even in this situation, however, the very nature of the hacking experience frequently involves the constant cat and mouse game between network system administrators, seeking to remove hackers from their systems by terminating a compromised account or by "patching" the vulnerability that permitted the hackers to illegally enter the network, and the hackers attempting to return to the system and overcome and disable its security features. Thus, the addition of a new banner may not concern a dedicated hacker. The subject hacker may not be aware that Title III may prevent law enforcement from monitoring all of the intruder's activities while he or she is connected to the compromised computer network.

Finally, there are technical limitations to the use of banners. Computer systems are designed to have hundreds of ports for different types of uses such as electronic mail, remote log-in, or Telnet. Most of these ports are not in use and remain closed, and can only be opened by a system administrator, or by a hacker who has illegally obtained the same privileges as a system administrator. Due to the technical nature of these ports, which goes beyond the scope of this article, it is not possible to install a banner or other message on a certain percentage of the ports. It is possible for a determined hacker to gain the same privileges (known as "superuser" or "root" status) on a network and open one or more of these ports, perhaps to serve as a future "back door" means of entry. Having once been given notice that the subject has given implied consent to monitoring by making use of a network, however, that consent should be valid for future use whether entry was made through a bannered or a non-bannered port. The only question this possibility raises is whether an affiliated or unaffiliated hacker might use one of these non-bannered ports for entry, and never pass through a banner.

Protection of the Rights and Property of the Provider

Title III also permits providers of a communication service, including an electronic communication service, the right to intercept communications as a "necessary incident to the rendition of his service" or to protect "the rights or property of the provider of that service." 18 U.S.C. § 2511(2)(a)(i).

This exception permits a private party to monitor activities on its system to prevent misuse of the system through damage, fraud, or theft of services. Since computer hacking often involves damage or disabling of a network's computer security system, as well as theft of the network's service, this exception permits a system administrator to monitor the activities of a hacker while on the network.

This exception to Title III has some significant limitations. One important limitation is that the monitoring must be reasonably connected to the protection of the provider's service, and not as a pretext to engage in unrelated monitoring. While no court has explored what this limitation means in the computer context, by way of analogy, one court has held that a telephone company may not monitor all the conversations of a user of an illegal clone phone unrelated to the protection of its service. *See McClelland v. McGrath*, 31 F. Supp.2d 616 (N.D. Ill. 1998).

Furthermore, the right to monitor is justified by the right to protect one's own system from harm. An ISP, for example, may not be able to monitor the activities of one of its customers under this exception for allegedly engaging in hacking activities on other networks. This limitation also makes it harder for a network administrator to justify the monitoring of hacking activities of a subject who has jumped to a new downstream victim. This potential limitation is unfortunate as it becomes more applicable precisely when the consent of a "party to the communication" is also at its weakest.

Another important limitation of this exception is that it does not permit a private provider of the communication service to authorize the government to conduct the monitoring; the monitoring must be done by the provider itself. Thus, where a provider lacks the technical or financial resources, or desire to engage in monitoring itself, it may be difficult for the government to step in to assist. Similarly, in situations where the government becomes aware that an ISP or network system administrator is monitoring illegal activity in order to protect its "rights and property," the government should be careful not to direct or participate in the monitoring, or cause it to be continued, because the provider may be deemed an agent of the government, and the exception may not apply. *Compare United States v. Pervaz*, 118 F.3d 1 (1st Cir. 1997), with *McClelland, infra.*

Even with these limitations, the provider exception can be very useful, particularly when a system administrator aggressively chooses to investigate hacking activity, or when the victim computer network is owned by the government. The technical gap in the use of implied consent described above, the inability to place consent banners on certain ports, can be filled by the use of the provider exception to monitor computer intrusions coming through these ports.

Conclusion

While Title III concerns are only one of the potential issues raised by proactive investigations in the computer context (others may include entrapment or even third-party liability), they are certainly among the most important. When all else fails, the prosecutor can always seek a Title III interception order. While this requires both departmental and judicial approval, there are a few aspects of obtaining such a "datatap" order that may make it less of a burden than obtaining a traditional telephone wiretap order. First, with respect to the interception of electronic communications, law enforcement is not limited to predicate offenses, but rather may seek it for any federal felony (note that some forms of hacking may constitute only a misdemeanor). *See* 18 U.S.C. § 2516(3). Second, with respect to the recording on or through a victim computer, the actual hacking activities typically constitute a federal felony, thus meeting the probable cause standards for seeking the authorization will be simple. *See* 18 U.S.C. § 2518(3)(a).

Third, the method of recording the results of the datatap are not difficult; the information can be obtained using specialized software or commercially available sniffer programs. Finally, minimization presents far less of a problem than it does for the execution of a traditional wiretap. *See* 18 U.S.C. § 2518(5). The burdens encountered and time lost in seeking Title III authorization makes the proper use of the exceptions discussed in this article extremely useful tools in investigating criminal activity. With the aid of proper monitoring, as well as the use of the many tools to obtain historical activities of subject hackers, law enforcement can overcome the potential anonymity provided by a computer, and identify and prosecute those criminals who abuse it to violate the law.

For more information on how Title III applies to the Internet, see Chapter 4 of the Computer Crime and Intellectual Property Section's new manual "Searching and Seizing Computers and Obtaining Electronic Evidence in Criminal Criminal Investigations." It is available at www.cybercrime.gov/searchmanual.htm.

Computer Records and the Federal Rules of Evidence

Orin S. Kerr, Trial Attorney, Computer Crime and Intellectual Property Section, March 2001

This section explains some of the important issues that can arise when the government seeks the admission of computer records under the Federal Rules of Evidence. It is an excerpt of a larger DOJ manual entitled "Searching and Seizing

Computers and Obtaining Electronic Evidence in Criminal Investigations," which is available on the Internet at www.cybercrime.gov/searchmanual.htm.

Most federal courts that have evaluated the admissibility of computer records have focused on computer records as potential hearsay. The courts generally have admitted computer records upon a showing that the records fall within the business records exception, Fed. R. Evid. 803(6):

> **Records of regularly conducted activity**. A memorandum, report, record, or data compilation, in any form, of acts, events, conditions, opinions, or diagnoses, made at or near the time by, or from information transmitted by, a person with knowledge, if kept in the course of a regularly conducted business activity, and if it was the regular practice of that business activity to make the memorandum, report, record, or data compilation, all as shown by the testimony of the custodian or other qualified witness, unless the source of information or the method or circumstances of preparation indicate lack of trustworthiness. The term "business" as used in this paragraph includes business, institution, association, profession, occupation, and calling of every kind, whether or not conducted for profit.

> — *See, e.g., United States v. Cestnik*, 36 F.3d 904, 909-10 (10th Cir. 1994);
> *United States v. Moore, 923 F.2d 910, 914 (1st Cir. 1991);*
> *United States v. Briscoe, 896 F.2d 1476, 1494 (7th Cir. 1990);*
> *United States v. Catabran, 836 F.2d 453, 457 (9th Cir. 1988);*
> *Capital Marine Supply v. M/V Roland Thomas II, 719 F.2d 104, 106*
> *(5th Cir. 1983)*

Applying this test, the courts have indicated that computer records generally can be admitted as business records if they were kept pursuant to a routine procedure for motives that tend to assure their accuracy.

However, the federal courts are likely to move away from this "one size fits all" approach as they become more comfortable and familiar with computer records. Like paper records, computer records are not monolithic: the evidentiary issues raised by their admission should depend on what kind of computer records a proponent seeks to have admitted. For example, computer records that contain text often can be divided into two categories: computer-generated records and records that are merely computer-stored. *See People v. Holowko*, 486 N.E.2d 877, 878-79 (Ill. 1985). The difference hinges upon whether a person or a machine created the records' contents. Computer-stored records refer to documents that contain the writings of some person or persons and happen to be in electronic form. E-mail messages, word processing files, and Internet chat room messages provide common examples. As with any other testimony or documentary evidence containing human statements, computer-stored records must comply with the hearsay rule. If the records are admitted to prove the truth of the matter they assert, the offeror of the records must show circumstances indicating that the human statements contained in the record are reliable and trustworthy, *see* Advisory Committee Notes to Proposed Rule 801 (1972), and the records must be authentic.

In contrast, computer-generated records contain the output of computer programs, untouched by human hands. Log-in records from Internet service providers, telephone records, and ATM receipts tend to be computer-generated records. Unlike computer-stored records, computer-generated records do not contain human "statements," but only the output of a computer program designed to process input following a defined algorithm. Of course, a computer program can direct a computer to generate a record that mimics a human statement: an e-mail program can announce "You've got mail!" when mail arrives in an inbox, and an ATM receipt can state that $100 was deposited in an account at 2:25 pm. However, the fact that a computer, rather than a human being, has created the record alters the evidentiary issues that the computer-generated records present. *See, e.g.,* 2 J. Strong, *McCormick on Evidence* § 294, at 286 (4th ed. 1992). The evidentiary issue is no longer whether a human's out-of-court statement was truthful and accurate (a question of hearsay), but instead whether the computer program that generated the record was functioning properly (a question of authenticity). *See id.*; Richard O. Lempert & Steven A. Saltzburg, *A Modern Approach to Evidence,* 370 (2d ed. 1983); *Holowko,* 486 N.E.2d at 878-79.

Finally, a third category of computer records exists: some computer records are both computer-generated *and* computer-stored. For example, a suspect in a fraud case might use a spreadsheet program to process financial figures relating to the fraudulent scheme. A computer record containing the output of the program would derive from both human statements (the suspect's input to the spreadsheet program) and computer processing (the mathematical operations of the spreadsheet program). Accordingly, the record combines the evidentiary concerns raised by computer-stored and computer-generated records. The party seeking the admission of the record should address both the hearsay issues implicated by the original input and the authenticity issues raised by the computer processing.

As the federal courts develop a more nuanced appreciation of the distinctions to be made between different kinds of computer records, they are likely to see that the admission of computer records generally raises two distinct issues. First, the government must establish the authenticity of all computer records by providing "evidence sufficient to support a finding that the matter in question is what its proponent claims." Fed. R. Evid. 901(a). Second, if the computer records are computer-stored records that contain human statements, the government must show that those human statements are not inadmissible hearsay.

Authentication

Before a party may move for admission of a computer record or any other evidence, the proponent must show that it is authentic. That is, the government must offer evidence "sufficient to support a finding that the [computer record or other evidence] in question is what its proponent claims." Fed. R. Evid. 901(a). *See United States v. Simpson*, 152 F.3d 1241, 1250 (10th Cir. 1998).

The standard for authenticating computer records is the same as for authenticating other records. The degree of authentication does not vary simply because a record happens to be (or has been at one point) in electronic form. *See United States v. DeGeorgia*, 420 F.2d 889, 893 n.11 (9th Cir. 1969); *United States v. Vela*, 673 F.2d 86, 90 (5th Cir. 1982). *But see United States v. Scholle*, 553 F.2d 1109,

1125 (8th Cir. 1977) (stating in dicta that "the complex nature of computer storage calls for a more comprehensive foundation"). For example, witnesses who testify to the authenticity of computer records need not have special qualifications. The witness does not need to have programmed the computer himself, or even need to understand the maintenance and technical operation of the computer. *See United States v. Moore*, 923 F.2d 910, 915 (1st Cir. 1991) (citing cases). Instead, the witness simply must have first-hand knowledge of the relevant facts to which he or she testifies. *See generally United States v. Whitaker*, 127 F.3d 595, 601 (7th Cir. 1997) (FBI agent who was present when the defendant's computer was seized can authenticate seized files); *United States v. Miller*, 771 F.2d 1219, 1237 (9th Cir. 1985) (telephone company billing supervisor can authenticate phone company records); *Moore*, 923 F.2d at 915 (head of bank's consumer loan department can authenticate computerized loan data).

Challenges to the authenticity of computer records often take one of three forms. First, parties may challenge the authenticity of both computer-generated and computer-stored records by questioning whether the records were altered, manipulated, or damaged after they were created. Second, parties may question the authenticity of computer-generated records by challenging the reliability of the computer program that generated the records. Third, parties may challenge the authenticity of computer-stored records by questioning the identity of their author.

Authenticity and the Alteration of Computer Records

Computer records can be altered easily, and opposing parties often allege that computer records lack authenticity because they have been tampered with or changed after they were created. For example, in *United States v. Whitaker*, 127 F.3d 595, 602 (7th Cir. 1997), the government retrieved computer files from the computer of a narcotics dealer named Frost. The files from Frost's computer included detailed records of narcotics sales by three aliases: "Me" (Frost himself, presumably), "Gator" (the nickname of Frost's co-defendant Whitaker), and "Cruz" (the nickname of another dealer). After the government permitted Frost to help retrieve the evidence from his computer and declined to establish a formal chain of custody for the computer at trial, Whitaker argued that the files implicating him through his alias were not properly authenticated. Whitaker argued that "with a few rapid keystrokes, Frost could have easily added Whitaker's alias, 'Gator' to the printouts in order to finger Whitaker and to appear more helpful to the government." *Id.* at 602.

The courts have responded with considerable skepticism to such unsupported claims that computer records have been altered. Absent specific evidence that tampering occurred, the mere possibility of tampering does not affect the authenticity of a computer record. *See Whitaker*, 127 F.3d at 602 (declining to disturb trial judge's ruling that computer records were admissible because allegation of tampering was "almost wild-eyed speculation … [without] evidence to support such a scenario"); *United States v. Bonallo*, 858 F.2d 1427, 1436 (9th Cir. 1988) ("The fact that it is possible to alter data contained in a computer is plainly insufficient to establish untrustworthiness."); *United States v. Glasser*, 773 F.2d 1553, 1559 (11th Cir. 1985) ("The existence of an air-tight security system [to prevent tampering] is not, however, a prerequisite to the admissibility of computer print-outs. If such a prerequisite did exist, it would become virtually impossible to admit computer-generated records; the party opposing admission would have to show only that a better security system was feasible."). *Id.* at 559. This is consistent with the rule used to establish the authenticity of other evidence such as narcotics. *See United States v. Allen*, 106 F.3d 695, 700 (6th Cir. 1997) ("Merely raising the possibility of tampering is insufficient to render evidence inadmissible."). Absent specific evidence of tampering, allegations that computer records have been altered go to their weight, not their admissibility. *See Bonallo*, 858 F.2d at 1436.

Establishing the Reliability of Computer Programs

The authenticity of computer-generated records sometimes implicates the reliability of the computer programs that create the records. For example, a computer-generated record might not be authentic if the program that creates the record contains serious programming errors. If the program's output is inaccurate, the record may not be "what its proponent claims" according to Fed. R. Evid. 901.

Defendants in criminal trials often attempt to challenge the authenticity of computer-generated records by challenging the reliability of the programs. *See, e.g., United States v. Dioguardi*, 428 F.2d 1033, 1038 (2d Cir. 1970); *United States v. Liebert*, 519 F.2d 542, 547-48 (3d Cir. 1975). The courts have indicated that the government can overcome this challenge so long as "the government provides sufficient facts to warrant a finding that the records are trustworthy and the opposing party is afforded an opportunity to inquire into the accuracy thereof[.]" *United States v. Briscoe*, 896 F.2d 1476, 1494 (7th Cir. 1990). *See also Liebert*, 519 F.2d at 547; *DeGeorgia*, 420 F.2d. at 893 n.11. *Compare* Fed. R. Evid. 901(b)(9) (indicating that matters created according to a process or system can be authen-ticated with "[e]vidence describing a process or system used ... and showing that the process or system produces an accurate result"). In most cases, the reliability of a computer program can be established by showing that users of the program actually do rely on it on a regular basis, such as in the ordinary course of business. *See, e.g., United States v. Moore*, 923 F.2d 910, 915 (1st Cir. 1991) ("[T]he ordinary business circumstances described suggest trustworthiness, ... at least where abso-lutely nothing in the record in any way implies the lack thereof.") (computerized tax records held by the IRS); *Briscoe*, 896 F.2d at 1494 (computerized telephone records held by Illinois Bell). When the computer program is not used on a regular basis and the government cannot establish reliability based on reliance in the ordinary course of business, the government may need to disclose "what operations the computer had been instructed to perform [as well as] the precise instruction that had been given" if the opposing party requests. *Dioguardi*, 428 F.2d at 1038. Notably, once a minimum standard of trustworthiness has been established, questions as to the accuracy of computer records "resulting from ... the operation of the computer program" affect only the weight of the evidence, not its admissibility. *United States v. Catabran*, 836 F.2d 453, 458 (9th Cir. 1988).

Prosecutors may note the conceptual overlap between establishing the authen-ticity of a computer-generated record and establishing the trustworthiness of a computer record for the business record exception to the hearsay rule. In fact, federal courts that evaluate the authenticity of computer-generated records often assume that the records contain hearsay, and then apply the business records exception. *See, e.g., UnitedStates v. Linn*, 880 F.2d 209, 216 (9th Cir. 1989) (applying business records exception to telephone records generated "automatically" by a computer); *United States v. Vela*, 673 F.2d 86, 89-90 (5th Cir. 1982) (same). As discussed later in this article, this analysis is technically incorrect in many cases: computer records generated entirely by computers cannot contain hearsay and cannot qualify for the business records exception because they do not contain human "statements." *See* Part B, *infra*. As a practical matter, however, prosecutors who lay a foundation to establish a computer-generated record as a business record will also lay the foundation to establish the record's authenticity. Evidence that a computer program is sufficiently trustworthy so that its results qualify as business records according to Fed. R. Evid. 803(6) also establishes the authenticity of the record. *Compare United States v. Saputski*, 496 F.2d 140, 142 (9th Cir. 1974).

Identifying the Author of Computer-Stored Records

Although handwritten records may be penned in a distinctive handwriting style, computer-stored records consist of a long string of zeros and ones that do not necessarily identify their author. This is a particular problem with Internet communications, which offer their authors an unusual degree of anonymity. For example, Internet technologies permit users to send effectively anonymous e-mails, and Internet Relay Chat channels permit users to communicate without disclosing their real names. When prosecutors seek the admission of such computer-stored records against a defendant, the defendant may challenge the authenticity of the record by challenging the identity of its author.

Circumstantial evidence generally provides the key to establishing the authorship and authenticity of a computer record. For example, in *United States v. Simpson*, 152 F.3d 1241 (10th Cir. 1998), prosecutors sought to show that the defendant had conversed with an undercover FBI agent in an Internet chat room devoted to child pornography. The government offered a printout of an Internet chat conversation between the agent and an individual identified as "Stavron," and sought to show that "Stavron" was the defendant. The district court admitted the printout in evidence at trial. On appeal following his conviction, Simpson argued that "because the government could not identify that the statements attributed to [him] were in his handwriting, his writing style, or his voice," the printout had not been authenticated and should have been excluded. *Id.* at 1249.

The Tenth Circuit rejected this argument, noting the considerable circumstantial evidence that "Stavron" was the defendant. *See id.* at 1250. For example, "Stavron" had told the undercover agent that his real name was "B. Simpson," gave a home address that matched Simpson's, and appeared to be accessing the Internet from an account registered to Simpson. Further, the police found records in Simpson's home that listed the name, address, and phone number that the undercover agent had sent to "Stavron." Accordingly, the government had provided evidence sufficient to support a finding that the defendant was "Stavron," and the printout was properly authenticated. *See id.* at 1250. *See also United States v. Tank*, 200 F.3d 627, 630-31 (9th Cir. 2000) (concluding that district court properly admitted chat room log printouts in circumstances similar to those in *Simpson*). *But see United States v. Jackson*, 208 F.3d 638 (7th Cir. 2000) (concluding that Web postings purporting to be statements made by white supremacist groups were properly excluded on authentication grounds absent evidence that the postings were actually posted by the groups).

Hearsay

Federal courts have often assumed that all computer records contain hearsay. A more nuanced view suggests that in fact only a portion of computer records contain hearsay. When a computer record contains the assertions of a person, whether or not processed by a computer, the record can contain hearsay. In such cases, the government must fit the record within a hearsay exception such as the business records exception, Fed. R. Evid. 803(6). When a computer record contains only computer-generated data untouched by human hands, however, the record cannot contain hearsay. In such cases, the government must establish the authenticity of the record, but does not need to establish that a hearsay exception applies for the records to be admissible.

Inapplicability of the Hearsay Rules to Computer-Generated Records

The hearsay rules exist to prevent unreliable out-of-court statements by human declarants from improperly influencing the outcomes of trials. Because people can misinterpret or misrepresent their experiences, the hearsay rules express a strong preference for testing human assertions in court, where the declarant can be placed on the stand and subjected to cross-examination. *See Ohio v. Roberts*, 448 U.S. 56, 62-66 (1980). This rationale does not apply when an animal or a machine makes an assertion: beeping machines and barking dogs cannot be called to the witness stand for cross-examination at trial. The Federal Rules have adopted this logic. By definition, an assertion cannot contain hearsay if it was not made by a human being. Can we just use the word person? *See* Fed. R. Evid. 801(a) ("A 'statement' is (1) an oral or written assertion or (2) nonverbal conduct *of a person*, if it is intended by the person as an assertion.") (emphasis added); Fed. R. Evid. 801(b) ("A declarant is *a person* who makes a statement.") (emphasis added).

As several courts and commentators have noted, this limitation on the hearsay rules necessarily means that computer-generated records untouched by human hands cannot contain hearsay. One state supreme court articulated the distinction in an early case involving the use of automated telephone records:

> The printout of the results of the computer's internal operations is not hearsay evidence. It does not represent the output of statements placed into the computer by out of court declarants. Nor can we say that this printout itself is a "statement" constituting hearsay evidence. The underlying rationale of the hearsay rule is that such statements are made without an oath and their truth cannot be tested by cross-examination. Of concern is the possibility that a witness may consciously or unconsciously misrepresent what the declarant told him or that the declarant may consciously or unconsciously misrepresent a fact or occurrence. With a machine,

however, there is no possibility of a conscious misrepresentation, and the possibility of inaccurate or misleading data only materializes if the machine is not functioning properly.

— *State v. Armstead, 432 So.2d 837, 840 (La. 1983)*.
　　See also People v. Holowko, 486 N.E.2d 877, 878-79 (Ill. 1985)
　　(automated trap and trace records);
　　United States v. Duncan, 30 M.J. 1284, 1287-89 (N-M.C.M.R. 1990)
　　(computerized records of ATM transactions);
　　2 J. Strong, *McCormick on Evidence* §294, at 286 (4th ed.1992);
　　Richard O. Lempert & Stephen A. Saltzburg,
　　A Modern Approach to Evidence 370 (2d ed. 1983)
　　Cf. United States v. Fernandez-Roque, 703 F.2d 808, 812 n.2 (5th Cir. 1983)
　　(rejecting hearsay objection to admission of automated telephone records
　　because "the fact that these calls occurred is not a hearsay statement.").

Accordingly, a properly authenticated computer-generated record is admissible. *See* Lempert & Saltzburg, at 370.

The insight that computer-generated records cannot contain hearsay is important because courts that assume the existence of hearsay may wrongfully exclude computer-generated evidence if a hearsay exception does not apply. For example, in *United States v. Blackburn*, 992 F.2d 666 (7th Cir. 1993), a bank robber left his eyeglasses behind in an abandoned stolen car. The prosecution's evidence against the defendant included a computer printout from a machine that tests the curvature of eyeglass lenses. The printout revealed that the prescription of the eyeglasses found in the stolen car exactly matched the defendant's. At trial, the district court assumed that the computer printout was hearsay, but concluded that the printout was an admissible business record according to Fed. R. Evid. 803(6). On appeal following conviction, the Seventh Circuit also assumed that the printout contained hearsay, but agreed with the defendant that the printout could not be admitted as a business record:

> the [computer-generated] report in this case was not kept in the course of a regularly conducted business activity, but rather was specially prepared at the behest of the FBI and with the knowledge that any information it supplied would be used in an ongoing criminal investigation... . In finding this report inadmissible under Rule 803(6), we adhere to the well-established rule that documents made in anticipation of litigation are inadmissible under the business records exception.

— *Id. at 670. See also Fed. R. Evid. 803(6)*
　　(stating that business records must be
　　"made ... by, or transmitted by, a person")

Fortunately, the *Blackburn* court ultimately affirmed the conviction, concluding that the computer printout was sufficiently reliable that it could have been admitted under the residual hearsay exception, Rule 803(24). *See Id.* at 672. However, instead of flirting with the idea of excluding the printouts because Rule 803(6) did not apply, the court should have asked whether the computer printout from the lens-testing machine contained hearsay at all. This question would have revealed that the computer-generated printout could not be excluded on hearsay grounds because it contained no human "statements."

Applicability of the Hearsay Rules to Computer-Stored Records

Computer-stored records that contain human statements must satisfy an exception to the hearsay rule if they are offered for the truth of the matter asserted. Before a court will admit the records, the court must establish that the statements contained in the record were made in circumstances that tend to ensure their trustworthiness. *See, e.g., Jackson*, 208 F.3d at 637 (concluding that postings from the Web sites of white supremacist groups contained hearsay, and rejecting the argument that the postings were the business records of the ISPs that hosted the sites).

As discussed earlier in this section, courts generally permit computer-stored records to be admitted as business records according to Fed. R. Evid. 803(6). Different circuits have articulated slightly different standards for the admissibility of computer-stored business records. Some courts simply apply the direct language of Fed. R. Evid. 803(6). *See e.g.,United States v. Moore*, 923 F.2d 910, 914 (1st Cir. 1991); *United States v. Catabran*, 836 F.2d 453, 457 (9th Cir. 1988). Other circuits have articulated doctrinal tests specifically for computer records that largely (but not exactly) track the requirements of Rule 803(6). *See, e.g., United States v. Cestnik*, 36 F.3d 904, 909-10 (10th Cir. 1994) ("Computer business records are admissible if (1) they are kept pursuant to a routine procedure designed to assure their accuracy; (2) they are created for motives that tend to assure accuracy (e.g., not including those prepared for litigation); and (3) they are not themselves mere accumulations of hearsay.") (quoting *Capital Marine Supply v. M/V Roland Thomas II*, 719 F.2d 104, 106 (5th Cir. 1983)); *United States v. Briscoe*, 896 F.2d 1476, 1494 (7th Cir. 1990) (computer-stored records are admissible business records if they "are kept in the course of regularly conducted business activity, and [that it] was the regular practice of that business activity to make records, as shown by the testimony of the custodian or other qualified witness.") (quoting *United States v. Chappell*, 698 F.2d 308, 311 (7th Cir. 1983)). Notably, the printout itself may be produced in anticipation of litigation without running afoul of the business records exception. The requirement that the record be kept "in the course of a regularly conducted business activity" refers to the underlying data, not the actual printout of that data. *See United States v. Sanders*, 749 F.2d 195, 198 (5th Cir. 1984).

From a practical perspective, the procedure for admitting a computer-stored record pursuant to the business records exception is the same as admitting any other business record. Consider an e-mail harassment case. To help establish that the defendant was the sender of the harassing messages, the prosecution may seek the introduction of records from the sender's ISP showing that the defendant was the registered owner of the account from which the e-mails were sent. Ordinarily, this will require testimony from an employee of the ISP ("the custodian or other qualified witness") that the ISP regularly maintains customer account records for billing and other purposes, and that the records to be offered for admission are such records that were made at or near the time of the events they describe in the regular course of the ISP's business. Again, the key is establishing that the computer system from which the record was obtained is maintained in the ordinary course of business, and that it is a regular practice of the business to rely upon those records for their accuracy.

The business record exception is the most common hearsay exception applied to computer records. Of course, other hearsay exceptions may be applicable in appropriate cases. *See, e.g., Hughes v. United States*, 953 F.2d 531, 540 (9th Cir. 1992) (concluding that computerized IRS forms are admissible as public records under Fed. R. Evid. 803(8)).

Other Issues

The authentication requirement and the hearsay rule usually provide the most significant hurdles that prosecutors will encounter when seeking the admission of computer records. However, some agents and prosecutors have occasionally considered two additional issues: the application of the best evidence rule to computer records, and whether computer printouts are "summaries" that must comply with Fed. R. Evid. 1006.

The Best Evidence Rule

The best evidence rule states that to prove the content of a writing, recording, or photograph, the "original" writing, recording, or photograph is ordinarily required. *See* Fed. R. Evid. 1002. Agents and prosecutors occasionally express concern that a mere printout of a computer-stored electronic file may not be an "original" for the purpose of the best evidence rule. After all, the original file is merely a collection of 0's and 1's. In contrast, the printout is the result of manipulating the file through a complicated series of electronic and mechanical processes.

Fortunately, the Federal Rules of Evidence have expressly addressed this concern. The Federal Rules state that

> [i]f data are stored in a computer or similar device, any printout or other output readable by sight, shown to reflect the data accurately, is an "original."

> — Fed. R. Evid. 1001(3).

Thus, an accurate printout of computer data always satisfies the best evidence rule. *See Doe v. United States*, 805 F. Supp. 1513, 1517 (D. Hawaii. 1992). According to the Advisory Committee Notes that accompanied this rule when it was first proposed, this standard was adopted for reasons of practicality. While strictly speaking the original of a photograph might be thought to be only the negative, practicality and common usage require that any print from the negative be regarded as an original. Similarly, practicality and usage confer the status of original upon any computer printout. Advisory Committee Notes, Proposed Federal Rule of Evidence 1001(3) (1972).

Computer Printouts as "Summaries"

Federal Rule of Evidence 1006 permits parties to offer summaries of voluminous evidence in the form of "a chart, summary, or calculation" subject to certain restrictions. Agents and prosecutors occasionally ask whether a computer printout is necessarily a "summary" of evidence that must comply with Fed. R. Evid. 1006. In general, the answer is no. *See Sanders*, 749 F.2d at 199; *Catabran*, 836 F.2d at 456-57; *United States v. Russo*, 480 F.2d 1228, 1240-41 (6th Cir. 1973). Of course, if the computer printout is merely a summary of other admissible evidence, Rule 1006 will apply just as it does to other summaries of evidence.

Proposed Standards for the Exchange of Digital Evidence

Scientific Working Group on Digital Evidence (SWGDE)

The Scientific Working Group on Digital Evidence (SWGDE) was established in February 1998 through a collaborative effort of the Federal Crime Laboratory Directors. SWGDE, as the U.S.-based component of standardization efforts conducted by the International Organization on Computer Evidence (IOCE), was charged with the development of cross-disciplinary guidelines and standards for the recovery, preservation, and examination of digital evidence, including audio, imaging, and electronic devices.

The following document was drafted by SWGDE and presented at the International Hi-Tech Crime and Forensics Conference (IHCFC) held in London, United Kingdom, October 4–7, 1999. It proposes the establishment of standards for the exchange of digital evidence between sovereign nations and is intended to elicit constructive discussion regarding digital evidence. This document has been adopted as the draft standard for U.S. law enforcement agencies.

Purpose

The latter part of the twentieth century was marked by the electronic transistor and the machines and ideas made possible by it. As a result, the world changed from analog to digital. Although the computer reigns supreme in the digital domain, it is not the only digital device. An entire constellation of audio, video, communications, and photographic devices are becoming so closely associated with the computer as to have converged with it.

From a law enforcement perspective, more of the information that serves as currency in the judicial process is being stored, transmitted, or processed in digital form. The connectivity resulting from a single world economy, in which the companies providing goods and services are truly international, has enabled criminals to act transjurisdictionally with ease. Consequently, a perpetrator may be brought to justice in one jurisdiction while the digital evidence required to successfully prosecute the case may reside only in other jurisdictions.

This situation requires that all nations have the ability to collect and preserve digital evidence for their own needs as well as for the potential needs of other sovereigns. Each jurisdiction has its own system of government and administration of justice but, in order for one country to protect itself and its citizens, it must be able to make use of evidence collected by other nations.

Though it is not reasonable to expect all nations to know about and abide by the precise laws and rules of other countries, a means that will allow the exchange of evidence must be found. This document is a first attempt to define the technical aspects of these exchanges.

Organization

The format of this document was adopted in conformance with the format of the American Society of Crime Laboratory Directors/Laboratory Accreditation Board manual.

Definitions

- *Acquisition of Digital Evidence:* Begins when information and/or physical items are collected or stored for examination purposes. The term *evidence* implies that the collector of evidence is recognized by the courts. The process of collecting is also assumed to be a legal process and appropriate for rules of evidence in that locality. A data object or physical item only becomes evidence when so deemed by a law enforcement official or designee.
- *Data Objects:* Objects or information of potential probative value that are associated with physical items. Data objects may occur in different formats without altering the original information.
- *Digital Evidence:* Information of probative value stored or transmitted in digital form.
- *Physical Items*: Items on which data objects or information may be stored and/or through which data objects are transferred.
- *Original Digital Evidence:* Physical items and the data objects associated with such items at the time of acquisition or seizure.
- *Duplicate Digital Evidence:* An accurate digital reproduction of all data objects contained on an original physical item.
- *Copy*: An accurate reproduction of information contained on an original physical item, independent of the original physical item.

Standards

Principle 1

In order to ensure that digital evidence is collected, preserved, examined, or transferred in a manner safeguarding the accuracy and reliability of the evidence, law enforcement and forensic organizations must establish and maintain an effective quality system. Standard Operating Procedures (SOPs) are documented quality-control guidelines that must be supported by proper case records and use broadly accepted procedures, equipment, and materials.

- *Standards and Criteria 1.1* — All agencies that seize and/or examine digital evidence must maintain an appropriate SOP document. All elements of an agency's policies and procedures concerning digital evidence must be clearly set forth in this SOP document, which must be issued under the agency's management authority.
  - *Discussion:* The use of SOPs is fundamental to both law enforcement and forensic science. Guidelines that are consistent with scientific and legal principles are essential to the acceptance of results and conclusions by courts and other agencies. The development and implementation of these SOPs must be under an agency's management authority.
- *Standards and Criteria 1.2* — Agency management must review the SOPs on an annual basis to ensure their continued suitability and effectiveness.
  - *Discussion:* Rapid technological changes are the hallmark of digital evidence, with the types, formats, and methods for seizing and examining digital evidence changing quickly. In order to ensure that personnel, training, equipment, and procedures continue to be appropriate and effective, management must review and update SOP documents annually.
- *Standards and Criteria 1.3* — Procedures used must be generally accepted in the field or supported by data gathered and recorded in a scientific manner.
  - *Discussion:* Because a variety of scientific procedures may validly be applied to a given problem, standards and criteria for assessing procedures need to remain flexible. The validity of a procedure may be established by demonstrating the accuracy and reliability of specific techniques. In the digital evidence area, peer review of SOPs by other agencies may be useful.
- *Standards and Criteria 1.4* — The agency must maintain written copies of appropriate technical procedures.
  - *Discussion:* Procedures should set forth their purpose and appropriate application. Required elements such as hardware and software must be listed and the proper steps for successful use should be listed or discussed. Any limitations in the use of the procedure or the use or interpretation of the results should be established. Personnel who use these procedures must be familiar with them and have them available for reference.
- *Standards and Criteria 1.5* — The agency must use hardware and software that is appropriate and effective for the seizure or examination procedure.
  - *Discussion:* Although many acceptable procedures may be used to perform a task, considerable variation among cases requires that personnel have the flexibility to exercise judgment in selecting a method appropriate to the problem.

    Hardware used in the seizure and/or examination of digital evidence should be in good operating condition and be tested to ensure that it operates correctly. Software must be tested to ensure that it produces reliable results for use in seizure and/or examination purposes.
- *Standards and Criteria 1.6* — All activity relating to the seizure, storage, examination, or transfer of digital evidence must be recorded in writing and be available for review and testimony.

— *Discussion:* In general, documentation to support conclusions must be such that, in the absence of the originator, another competent person could evaluate what was done, interpret the data, and arrive at the same conclusions as the originator.

The requirement for evidence reliability necessitates a chain of custody for all items of evidence. Chain-of-custody documentation must be maintained for all digital evidence. Case notes and records of observations must be of a permanent nature. Handwritten notes and observations must be in ink, not pencil, although pencil (including color) may be appropriate for diagrams or making tracings. Any corrections to notes must be made by an initialed, single strikeout; nothing in the handwritten information should be obliterated or erased. Notes and records should be authenticated by handwritten signatures, initials, digital signatures, or other marking systems.

■ *Standards and Criteria 1.7* — Any action that has the potential to alter, damage, or destroy any aspect of original evidence must be performed by qualified persons in a forensically sound manner.

— *Discussion:* As outlined in the preceding standards and criteria, evidence has value only if it can be shown to be accurate, reliable, and controlled. A quality forensic program consists of properly trained personnel and appropriate equipment, software, and procedures to collectively ensure these attributes.

Comments

SWGDE's proposed standards for the exchange of digital evidence will be posted on the National Forensic Science Technology Center, Law Enforcement Online, and IOCE Web sites in the near future.

Comments and questions concerning the proposed standards may be forwarded to whitcomb@mail.ucf.edu or mpollitt.cart@fbi.gov

Recovering and Examining Computer Forensic Evidence

Michael G. Noblett, Mark M. Pollitt, and Lawrence A. Presley, in Forensic Science Communication, *Volume 2, Issue 4, October 2000*

Introduction

The world is becoming a smaller place in which to live and work. A technological revolution in communications and information exchange has taken place within business, industry, and our homes. America is substantially more invested in information processing and management than manufacturing goods, and this has affected our professional and personal lives. We bank and transfer money electronically, and we are much more likely to receive an e-mail than a letter. It is estimated that the worldwide Internet population is 349 million (CommerceNet Research Council 2000).

In this information technology age, the needs of law enforcement are changing as well. Some traditional crimes, especially those concerning finance and commerce, continue to be upgraded technologically. Paper trails have become electronic trails. Crimes associated with the theft and manipulations of data are detected daily. Crimes of violence also are not immune to the effects of the information age. A serious and costly terrorist act could come from the Internet instead of a truck bomb. The diary of a serial killer may be recorded on a floppy disk or hard disk drive rather than on paper in a notebook.

Just as the workforce has gradually converted from manufacturing goods to processing information, criminal activity has, to a large extent, also converted from a physical dimension, in which evidence and investigations are described in tangible terms, to a cyber dimension, in which evidence exists only electronically, and investigations are conducted online.

Computer Forensic Science

Computer forensic science was created to address the specific and articulated needs of law enforcement to make the most of this new form of electronic evidence. Computer forensic science is the science of acquiring, preserving, retrieving, and presenting data that has been processed electronically and stored on computer media. As a forensic discipline, nothing since DNA technology has had such a large potential effect on specific types of investigations and prosecutions as computer forensic science.

Computer forensic science is, at its core, different from most traditional forensic disciplines. The computer material that is examined and the techniques available to the examiner are products of a market-driven private sector. Furthermore, in contrast to traditional forensic analyses, there commonly is a requirement to perform computer examinations at virtually any physical location, not only in a controlled laboratory setting. Rather than producing interpretative conclusions, as in many forensic disciplines, computer forensic science produces direct information and data that may have significance in a case. This type of direct data collection has wide-ranging implications for both the relationship between the investigator and the forensic scientist and the work product of the forensic computer examination.

Background

Computer forensic science is largely a response to a demand for service from the law enforcement community. As early as 1984, the FBI Laboratory and other law enforcement agencies began developing programs to examine computer evidence. To properly address the growing demands of investigators and prosecutors in a structured and programmatic manner, the FBI established the Computer Analysis and Response Team (CART) and charged it with the responsibility for computer analysis. Although CART is unique in the FBI, its functions and general organization are duplicated in many other law enforcement agencies in the United States and other countries.

An early problem addressed by law enforcement was identifying resources within the organization that could be used to examine computer evidence. These resources were often scattered throughout the agency. Today, there appears to be a trend toward moving these examinations to a laboratory environment. In

1995, a survey conducted by the U.S. Secret Service indicated that 48 percent of the agencies had computer forensic laboratories and that 68 percent of the computer evidence seized was forwarded to the experts in those laboratories. As encouraging as these statistics are for a controlled programmatic response to computer forensic needs, the same survey reported that 70 percent of these same law enforcement agencies were doing the work without a written procedures manual (Noblett 1995).

Computer forensic examinations are conducted in forensic laboratories, data processing departments and, in some cases, the detective's squad room. The assignment of personnel to conduct these examinations is based often on available expertise, as well as departmental policy. Regardless of where the examinations are conducted, a valid and reliable forensic examination is required. This requirement recognizes no political, bureaucratic, technological, or jurisdictional boundaries.

There are ongoing efforts to develop examination standards and to provide structure to computer forensic examinations. As early as 1991, a group of six international law enforcement agencies met with several U.S. federal law enforcement agencies in Charleston, South Carolina, to discuss computer forensic science and the need for a standardized approach to examinations. In 1993, the FBI hosted an International Law Enforcement Conference on Computer Evidence that was attended by 70 representatives of various U.S. federal, state, and local law enforcement agencies and international law enforcement agencies. All agreed that standards for computer forensic science were lacking and needed. This conference again convened in Baltimore, Maryland, in 1995, Australia in 1996, and the Netherlands in 1997, and ultimately resulted in the formation of the International Organization on Computer Evidence. In addition, a Scientific Working Group on Digital Evidence (SWGDE) was formed to address these same issues among federal law enforcement agencies.

A New Relationship

Forensic science disciplines have affected countless criminal investigations dramatically and have provided compelling testimony in scores of trials. To enhance objectivity and to minimize the perception of bias, forensic science traditionally has remained at arms length from much of the actual investigation. It uses only those specific details from the investigation that are necessary for the examination. These details might include possible sources of contamination at the crime scene or fingerprints of individuals not related to the investigation who have touched the evidence. Forensic science relies on the ability of the scientists to produce a report based on the objective results of a scientific examination. The actual overall case may play a small part in the examination process. As a case in point, a DNA examination in a rape case can be conducted without knowledge of the victim's name, the subject, or the specific circumstances of the crime.

Conversely, computer forensic science, to be effective, must be driven by information uncovered during the investigation. With the average storage capacity in a personally owned microcomputer approaching 30 gigabytes (GB; Fischer 1997), and systems readily available that have 60-GB storage capacity or more, it is likely to be impossible from a practical standpoint to completely and exhaustively examine every file stored on a seized computer system. In addition, because computers serve such wide and varied uses within an organization or household, there may be legal prohibitions against searching every file. Attorney or physician computers may contain not only evidence of fraud but probably also client and patient information that is privileged. Data centrally stored on a computer server may contain an incriminating e-mail prepared by the subject as well as e-mail of innocent third parties who would have a reasonable expectation of privacy.

As difficult as it would be to scan a directory of every file on a computer system, it would be equally difficult for law enforcement personnel to read and assimilate the amount of information contained within the files. For example, 12 GB of printed text data would create a stack of paper 24 stories high. For primarily pragmatic reasons, computer forensic science is used most effectively when only the most probative information and details of the investigation are provided to the forensic examiner. From this information, the examiner can create a list of key words to cull specific, probative, and case-related information from very large groups of files. Even though the examiner may have the legal right to search every file, time limitations and other judicial constraints may not permit it. The examination in most cases should be limited to only well-identified probative information.

Forensic Results

Forensic science has historically produced results that have been judged to be both valid and reliable. For example, DNA analysis attempts to develop specific identifying information relative to an individual. To support their conclusions, forensic DNA scientists have gathered extensive statistical data on the DNA profiles from which they base their conclusions. Computer forensic science, by comparison, extracts or produces information. The purpose of the computer examination is to find information related to the case. To support the results of a computer forensic examination, procedures are needed to ensure that only the information exists on the computer storage media, unaltered by the examination process. Unlike forensic DNA analysis or other forensic disciplines, computer forensic science makes no interpretive statement as to the accuracy, reliability, or discriminating power of the actual data or information.

Beyond the forensic product and the case-related information needed to efficiently perform the work, there is another significant difference between most traditional forensic science and computer forensic science. Traditional forensic analysis can be controlled in the laboratory setting and can progress logically, incrementally, and in concert with widely accepted forensic practices. In comparison, computer forensic science is almost entirely technology and market driven, generally outside the laboratory setting, and the examinations present unique variations in almost every situation.

Common Goals

These dissimilarities aside, both the scientific conclusions of traditional forensic analyses and the information of computer forensic science are distinctive forensic examinations. They share all the legal and good laboratory practice requirements of traditional forensic sciences in general. They both will be presented in court in adversarial and sometimes very probing proceedings. Both must produce valid and reliable results from state-of-the-art procedures that are detailed, documented, and peer-reviewed and from protocols acceptable to the relevant scientific community (ASCLD/LAB 1994).

As laboratories begin to examine more computer-related evidence, they must establish policies regarding computer forensic examinations and, from these policies, develop protocols and procedures. The policies should reflect the broad, community-wide goal of providing valid and reproducible results, even though the submissions may come from diverse sources and present novel examination issues. As the laboratory moves from the policy statement to protocol development, each individual procedure must be well-documented and sufficiently robust to withstand challenges to both the results and methodology.

However, computer forensic science, unlike some of its traditional forensic counterparts, cannot rely on receiving similar evidence in every submission. For example, DNA from any source, once cleared of contaminants and reduced to its elemental form, is generic. From that point, the protocols for forensic DNA analysis may be applied similarly to all submissions. The criminal justice system has come to expect a valid and reliable result using those DNA protocols. For the following reasons, computer forensic science can rarely expect these same elements of standardized repetitive testing in many of its submissions:

- Operating systems, which define what a computer is and how it works, vary among manufacturers. For example, techniques developed for a personal computer using the Disk Operating System (DOS) environment may not correspond to operating systems such as UNIX, which are multi-user environments.
- Applications programs are unique.
- Storage methods may be unique to both the device and the media.

Typical computer examinations must recognize the fast-changing and diverse world in which the computer forensic science examiner works.

Examining Computer Evidence

Computer evidence represented by physical items such as chips, boards, central processing units, storage media, monitors, and printers can be described easily and correctly as a unique form of physical evidence. The logging, description, storage, and disposition of physical evidence are well understood. Forensic laboratories have detailed plans describing acceptable methods for handling physical evidence. To the extent that computer evidence has a physical component, it does not represent any particular challenge. However, the evidence, while stored in these physical items, is latent and exists only in a metaphysical electronic form. The result that is reported from the examination is the recovery of this latent information. Although forensic laboratories are very good at ensuring the integrity of the physical items in their control, computer forensics also requires methods to ensure the integrity of the information contained within those physical items. The challenge to computer forensic science is to develop methods and

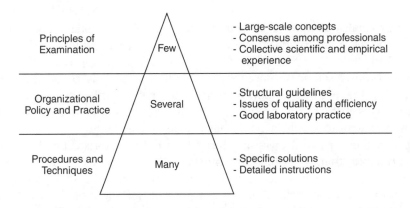

Principles of Examination	Few	- Large-scale concepts - Consensus among professionals - Collective scientific and empirical experience
Organizational Policy and Practice	Several	- Structural guidelines - Issues of quality and efficiency - Good laboratory practice
Procedures and Techniques	Many	- Specific solutions - Detailed instructions

Exhibit 1. Recovering and Examining Computer Forensic Evidence: A Three-Level Hierarchical Model for Developing Guidelines for Computer Forensic Evidence

techniques that provide valid and reliable results while protecting the real evidence — the information — from harm.

To complicate the matter further, computer evidence almost never exists in isolation. It is a product of the data stored, the application used to create and store it, and the computer system that directed these activities. To a lesser extent, it is also a product of the software tools used in the laboratory to extract it.

Computer forensic science issues must also be addressed in the context of an emerging and rapidly changing environment. However, even as the environment changes, both national and international law enforcement agencies recognize the need for common technical approaches and are calling for standards (Pollitt 1998). Because of this, a model (see Exhibit 1) must be constructed that works on a long-term basis even when short-term changes are the rule rather than the exception. The model that we describe is a three-level hierarchical model consisting of the following:

- An overarching concept of the principles of examination,
- Policies and practices, and
- Procedures and techniques.

Principles of examinations are large-scale concepts that almost always apply to the examination. They are the consensus approaches as to what is important among professionals and laboratories conducting these examinations. They represent the collective technical practice and experience of forensic computer examiners.

Organizational policy and practices are structural guidance that applies to forensic examinations. These are designed to ensure quality and efficiency in the workplace. In computer forensic science, these are the good laboratory practices by which examinations are planned, performed, monitored, recorded, and reported to ensure the quality and integrity of the work product.

Procedures and techniques are software and hardware solutions to specific forensic problems. The procedures and techniques are detailed instructions for specific software packages as well as step-by-step instructions that describe the entire examination procedure (Pollitt 1995).

As an overall example, a laboratory may require that examinations be conducted, if possible and practical, on copies of the original evidence. This requirement is a principle of examination. It represents a logical approach taken by the computer forensic science community as a whole, and it is based on the tenet of protecting the original evidence from accidental or unintentional damage or alteration. This principle is predicated on the fact that digital evidence can be duplicated exactly to create a copy that is true and accurate.

Creating the copy and ensuring that it is true and accurate involves a subset of the principle, that is, policy and practice. Each agency and examiner must make a decision as to how to implement this principle on a case-by-case basis. Factors in that decision include the size of the data set, the method used to create it, and the media on which it resides. In some cases it may be sufficient to merely compare the size and creation dates of files listed in the copy to the original. In others, it may require the application of more technically robust and mathematical rigorous techniques such as a cyclical redundancy check (CRC) or calculating a message digest (MD).

CRC and MD are computer algorithms that produce unique mathematical representations of the data. They are calculated for both the original and the copy and then compared for identity. The selection of tools must be based on the character of the evidence rather than simply laboratory policy. It is likely that examiners will need several options available to them to perform this one function.

An examiner responsible for duplicating evidence must first decide an appropriate level of verification to weigh time constraints against large file types. The mathematical precision and discriminating power of these algorithms are usually directly proportional to the amount of time necessary to calculate them. If there were [one] million files to be duplicated, each less than [one] kilobyte in size, time and computational constraints would likely be a major determining factor. This circumstance would probably result in a decision to use a faster, but less precise and discriminating, data integrity algorithm.

Having decided how best to ensure the copy process will be complete and accurate, the next step is the actual task. This is a subset of the policy and practice, that is, procedures and techniques. These most closely represent the standard cookbook approach to protocol development. They are complete and contain required detailed steps that may be used to copy the data, verify that the operation was complete, and ensure that a true and accurate copy has been produced.

Again, as Exhibit 1 illustrates, a principle may spawn more that one policy, and those policies can accept many different techniques. The path an examiner takes in each case is well-documented and technologically sound for that particular case. It may not, however, be the same path the examiner takes with the next case. Traditional forensic examinations, such as the DNA examination of blood recovered from a crime scene, lend themselves to a routine and standardized series of steps that can be repeated in case after case. There is generally no such thing as generic computer evidence procedures. The evidence is likely to be significantly different every time a submission is received by the laboratory and will likely require an examination plan tailored to that particular evidence. Although this situation may present a recurrent consideration of management checks and controls within the laboratory setting, it is a consideration that must be addressed and improved if this emerging forensic discipline is to remain an effective and reliable tool in the criminal justice system.

Conclusion

Valid and reliable methods to recover data from computers seized as evidence in criminal investigations are becoming fundamental for law enforcement agencies worldwide. These methods must be technologically robust to ensure that all probative information is recovered. They must also be legally defensible to ensure that nothing in the original evidence was altered and that no data was added to or deleted from the original. The forensic discipline of acquiring, preserving, retrieving, and presenting data that has been processed electronically and stored on computer media is computer forensic science.

This chapter examined issues surrounding the need to develop laboratory protocols for computer forensic science that meet critical technological and legal goals. Computer forensic scientists need to develop ongoing relationships with the criminal justice agencies they serve. The reasons for these relationships include the following:

- In their efforts to minimize the amount of data that must be recovered and to make their examinations more efficient and effective, computer forensic scientists must have specific knowledge of investigative details. This is a clear requirement that is generally more demanding than traditional forensic science requests, and it places more reliance on case information.
- Courts are requiring that more information rather than equipment be seized. This requires cooperative efforts between law enforcement officers and the computer forensic scientist to ensure that the technical resources necessary for the execution of the search warrant are sufficient to address both the scope and complexity of the search.
- Computers may logically contain both information identified in the warrant as well as information that may be constitutionally protected. The computer forensic scientist is probably the most qualified person to advise both the investigator and prosecutor as to how to identify technical solutions to these intricate situations.

Developing computer examination protocols for forensic computer analysis is unique for several reasons:

- Unlike some traditional forensic analyses that attempt to gather as much information as possible from an evidence sample, computer forensic analysis attempts to recover only probative information from a large volume of generally heterogeneous information.
- Computer forensic science must take into account the reality that computer forensic science is primarily market driven, and the science must adapt quickly to new products and innovations with valid and reliable examination and analysis techniques.
- The work product of computer forensic science examinations also differs from most traditional forensic work products. Traditional forensic science attempts to develop a series of accurate and reliable facts. For example, the DNA extracted from blood found at a crime scene can be matched to a specific person to establish the fact that the blood was shed by that person to the exclusion of all other individuals. Computer forensic science

generally makes no interpretive statement as to the accuracy or reliability of the information obtained and normally renders only the information recovered.

Computer forensic science protocols should be written in a hierarchical manner so that overarching principles remain constant, but examination techniques can adapt quickly to the computer system to be examined. This approach to computer forensic protocols may differ from those developed for many traditional forensic disciplines, but it is necessary to accommodate a unique forensic examination.

International Principles for Computer Evidence

International Organization on Computer Evidence (IOCE)

The International Organization on Computer Evidence (IOCE) was established in 1995 to provide international law enforcement agencies a forum for the exchange of information concerning computer crime investigation and other computer-related forensic issues. Comprised of accredited government agencies involved in computer forensic investigations, IOCE identifies and discusses issues of interest to its constituents, facilitates the international dissemination of information, and develops recommendations for consideration by its member agencies. In addition to formulating computer evidence standards, IOCE develops communications services between member agencies and holds conferences geared toward the establishment of working relationships.

In response to the G-8 Communique and Action plans of 1997, IOCE was tasked with the development of international standards for the exchange and recovery of electronic evidence. Working groups in Canada, Europe, the United Kingdom, and the United States have been formed to address this standardization of computer evidence.

During the International Hi-Tech Crime and Forensics Conference (IHCFC) of October 1999, the IOCE held meetings and a workshop which reviewed the United Kingdom Good Practice Guide and the SWGDE Draft Standards. The working group proposed the following principles, which were voted upon by the IOCE delegates present with unanimous approval.

IOCE International Principles

The international principles developed by IOCE for the standardized recovery of computer-based evidence are governed by the following attributes:

- Consistency with all legal systems;
- Allowance for the use of a common language;
- Durability;
- Ability to cross international boundaries;
- Ability to instill confidence in the integrity of evidence;

- Applicability to all forensic evidence; and
- Applicability at every level, including that of individual, agency, and country.

These principles were presented and approved at the International Hi-Tech Crime and Forensics Conference in October 1999. They are as follow:

- Upon seizing digital evidence, actions taken should not change that evidence.
- When it is necessary for a person to access original digital evidence, that person must be forensically competent.
- All activity relating to the seizure, access, storage, or transfer of digital evidence must be fully documented, preserved, and available for review.
- An individual is responsible for all actions taken with respect to digital evidence while the digital evidence is in their possession.
- Any agency that is responsible for seizing, accessing, storing, or transferring digital evidence is responsible for compliance with these principles.

Other items recommended by IOCE for further debate and/or facilitation included:

- *Forensic competency* and the need to generate agreement on international accreditation and the validation of tools, techniques, and training;
- Issues relating to practices and procedures for the examination of digital evidence; and
- The sharing of information relating to hi-tech crime and forensic computing, such as events, tools, and techniques.

References

1. American Society of Crime Laboratory Directors/Laboratory Accreditation Board (ASCLD/LAB). *ASCLD/LAB Manual.* American Society of Crime Laboratory Directors/ Laboratory Accreditation Board, Garner, NC, 1994, pp. 29–30.
2. CommerceNet Research Council. *2000 Industry Statistics.* Available at http:// www.commerce.net/research/stats/wwstats.html
3. Fischer, L. M. I.B.M. plans to announce leap in disk-drive capacity, *New York Times* (December 30, 1997), p. C-2.
4. Noblett, M. G. Report of the Federal Bureau of Investigation on development of forensic tools and examinations for data recovery from computer evidence. In: *Proceedings of the 11th INTERPOL Forensic Science Symposium,* Lyon, France. The Forensic Sciences Foundation Press, Boulder, CO, 1995.
5. Pollitt, M. The Federal Bureau of Investigation report on computer evidence and forensics. In: *Proceedings of the 12th INTERPOL Forensic Science Symposium,* Lyon, France. The Forensic Sciences Foundation Press, Boulder, CO, 1998.
6. Pollitt, M. *Computer Evidence Examinations at the FBI.* Unpublished presentation at the 2nd International Law Enforcement Conference on Computer Evidence, Baltimore, MD, April 10, 1995.

7. ASTM. *Form and Style for ASTM Standards*. American Society for Testing and Materials, Philadelphia, PA, 1996.

8. ASTM. *Standard Definitions*. American Society for Testing and Materials, Scranton, PA, 1994.

9. Osborn, A. S. *Questioned Documents*. Boyd, Albany, NY, 1929.

10. Hilton, O. Scientific Examination of Questioned Documents. Elsevier, New York, 1982.

11. Harrison, W. R. *Suspect Documents*. Sweet and Maxwell, London, 1958 and 1966.

12. Conway, J. V. P. *Evidential Documents*. Charles C Thomas, Springfield, IL, 1959.

13. Ellen, D. The Scientific Examination of Documents Methods and Techniques. Ellis Horwood, London, 1989.

14. American Society of Crime Laboratory Directors-Laboratory Accreditation Board Manual, January 1997.

15. ASTM. *Form and Style for ASTM Standards*. American Society for Testing and Materials, Philadelphia, PA, 1996.

16. ASTM. *Standard Definitions*. American Society for Testing and Materials, Scranton, PA, 1994.

17. Osborn, A. S. *Questioned Documents*. Boyd, Albany, NY, 1929.

18. Hilton, O. Scientific Examination of Questioned Documents. Elsevier, New York, 1982.

19. Harrison, W. R. *Suspect Documents*. Sweet and Maxwell, London, 1958 and 1966.

20. Conway, J. V. P. *Evidential Documents*. Charles C Thomas, Springfield, IL, 1959.

21. Ellen, D. The Scientific Examination of Documents Methods and Techniques. Ellis Horwood, London, 1989.

Chapter 9

Computer Crime Policy and Programs

The National Infrastructure Protection Center Advisory 01-003

On March 8, 2001, the National Infrastructure Protection Center (NIPC) issued the NIPC Advisory 01-003, an update to the NIPC Advisory 00-060, "E-Commerce Vulnerabilities," dated December 1, 2000.

This advisory is an update to the NIPC Advisory 00-060, "E-Commerce Vulnerabilities," dated December 1, 2000. Since the advisory was published, the FBI has continued to observe hacker activity targeting victims associated with e-commerce or e-finance/banking businesses. In many cases, the hacker activity had been ongoing for several months before the victim became aware of the intrusion. The NIPC emphasizes the recommendation that all computer network systems administrators check relevant systems and consider applying the updated patches as necessary, especially for systems related to e-commerce or e-banking/financial businesses. The patches are available on Microsoft's Web site.

The following vulnerabilities have been previously reported.

Unauthorized Access to IIS Servers through Open Database Connectivity (ODBC) Data Access with Remote Data Service (RDS)

Systems Affected: Windows NT running IIS with RDS enabled
Details: Microsoft Security Bulletin MS99-025, NIPC CyberNotes 99-22

- http://www.microsoft.com/technet/security/bulletin/ms99-025.asp
- http://www.nipc.gov/warnings/advisories/1999/99-027.htm
- http://www.nipc.gov/cybernotes/cybernotes.htm

Summary: Allows unauthorized users to execute shell commands on the IIS system as a privileged use; Allows unauthorized access to secured, non-published files on the IIS system; On a multi-homed Internet-connected IIS systems, using Microsoft Data Access Components (MDAC), allows unauthorized users to tunnel Structured Query Language (SQL) and other ODBC data requests through the public connection to a private back-end network.

SQL Query Abuse Vulnerability

Affected Software Versions: Microsoft SQL Server Version 7.0 and Microsoft Data Engine (MSDE) 1.0
Details: Microsoft Security Bulletin MS00-14, NIPC CyberNotes 20-05

- http://www.microsoft.com/technet/security/bulletin/ms00-014.asp
- http://www.nipc.gov/cybernotes/cybernotes.htm

Summary: The vulnerability could allow the remote author of a malicious SQL query to take unauthorized actions on a SQL Server or MSDE database.

Registry Permissions Vulnerability

Systems Affected: Windows NT 4.0 Workstation, Windows NT 4.0 Server
Details: Microsoft Security Bulletin MS00-008, NIPC CyberNotes 20-08 and 20-22

- http://www.microsoft.com/technet/security/bulletin/ms00-008.asp
- http://www.nipc.gov/cybernotes/cybernotes.htm

Summary: Users can modify certain registry keys such that:

- a malicious user could specify code to launch at system crash
- a malicious user could specify code to launch at next login
- an unprivileged user could disable security measures

Web Server File Request Parsing

While they have not been shown to be a vector for the current attacks, Microsoft has advised us that the vulnerabilities addressed by Microsoft bulletin MS00-086 are very serious, and we encourage Web site operators to consider applying the patch provided with this bulletin as well as the three that are under active exploitation.

- http://www.microsoft.com/technet/security/bulletin/ms00-014.asp
- http://www.nipc.gov/cybernotes/cybernotes.htm

Summary: The vulnerability could allow a malicious user to run system commands on a Web server. New Information: In addition to the above exploits, several filenames have been identified in connection with the intrusions, specific to Microsoft Windows NT systems. The presence of any of these files on your system should be reviewed carefully because they may indicate that your system has been compromised:

- ntalert.exe
- sysloged.exe
- tapi.exe
- 20.exe
- 21.exe
- 25.exe
- 80.exe
- 139.exe
- 1433.exe
- 1520.exe
- 26405.exe
- i.exe

In addition, system administrators may want to check for the unauthorized presence of any of the following executable files, which are often used as hacking tools:

- lomscan.exe
- mslom.exe
- lsaprivs.exe
- pwdump.exe
- serv.exe
- smmsniff.exe

Recipients of this Advisory are encouraged to report computer crime to the NIPC Watch at (202) 323-3204/3205/3206. Incidents may also be reported online at www.nipc.gov/incident/cirr.htm.

NIPC Advisory 01-003 Press Release (March 8, 2001)

Over the past several months, the National Infrastructure Protection Center (NIPC) has been coordinating investigations into a series of organized hacker activities specifically targeting U.S. computer systems associated with e-commerce or e-banking. Despite previous advisories, many computer owners have not patched their systems, allowing these kinds of attacks to continue, and prompting this updated release of information.

More than 40 victims located in 20 states have been identified and notified in ongoing investigations in 14 Federal Bureau of Investigation Field Offices and 7 United States Secret Service Field Offices. These investigations have been closely coordinated with foreign law enforcement authorities, and the private sector. Specially trained prosecutors in the Computer and Telecommunication Coordinator program in U.S. Attorneys' Offices in a variety of districts have participated in the investigation, with the assistance of attorneys in the Computer Crime and Intellectual Property Section at the Department of Justice.

The investigations have disclosed several organized hacker groups from Eastern Europe, specifically Russia and the Ukraine, that have penetrated U.S.

e-commerce computer systems by exploiting vulnerabilities in unpatched Microsoft Windows NT operating systems. These vulnerabilities were originally reported and addressed in Microsoft Security Bulletins MS98-004 (re-released in MS99-025), MS00-014, and MS00-008. As early as 1998, Microsoft discovered these vulnerabilities and developed and publicized patches to fix them. Computer users can download these patches from Microsoft for free.

Once the hackers gain access, they download proprietary information, customer databases, and credit card information. The hackers subsequently contact the victim company through facsimile, e-mail, or telephone. After notifying the company of the intrusion and theft of information, the hackers make a veiled extortion threat by offering Internet security services to patch the system against other hackers. They tell the victim that without their services, they cannot guarantee that other hackers will not access the network and post the credit card information and details about the compromise on the Internet. If the victim company is not cooperative in making payments or hiring the group for their security services, the hackers' correspondence with the victim company has become more threatening. Investigators also believe that in some instances the credit card information is being sold to organized crime groups. There has been evidence that the stolen information is at risk whether or not the victim cooperates with the demands of the intruders. To date, more than one million credit card numbers have been stolen.

The NIPC has issued an updated Advisory 01-003 at www.nipc.gov regarding these vulnerabilities being exploited. The update includes specific file names that may indicate whether a system has been compromised. If these files are located on your computer system, the NIPC Watch in Washington, D.C. should be contacted at (202) 323-3204/3205/3206. Incidents may also be reported online at www.nipc.gov/incident/cirr.htm. For detailed information on the vulnerabilities that are being exploited, please refer to the NIPC Advisory 00-60, and NIPC Advisory 01-003.

The National Information Infrastructure Protection Act of 1996

In October 1996, the National Information Infrastructure Protection Act of 1996 was enacted as part of Public Law 104-294. It amended the Computer Fraud and Abuse Act, which is codified at 18 U.S.C. § 1030. Below you will find links to the amended version of 18 U.S.C. § 1030, as well as a legislative analysis, prepared by attorneys from the Computer Crime and Intellectual Property Section. This legislative analysis was incorporated into the Senate Committee on the Judiciary's Report on the National Information Infrastructure Protection Act.

Legislative Analysis by the Computer Crime and Intellectual Property Section United States Department of Justice

Also see Computer Crime and Intellectual Property Section, U.S. Department of Justice, *Legislative Analysis of the 1996 National Information Infrastructure Protection Act*, 2 Electronic Info. Pol'y & L. Rep. 240, 240 (1997).

I. Introduction: The Need for Legislative Reform

Although there has never been accurate nationwide reporting of computer crime, it is clear from the reports which do exist and from anecdotal information that computer crime is on the rise. For example, the Computer Emergency and Response Team at Carnegie Mellon University reports that from 1991 through 1994, there was a 498 percent increase in the number of computer intrusions, and a 702 percent rise in the number of sites affected. *See* CERT Annual Report to ARPA. During 1994, for example, approximately 40,000 Internet computers were attacked in 2,460 incidents. *Id*. Similarly, the FBI's National Computer Crime Squad has opened over 200 hacker cases since the Squad was created in 1991.

That computer crime is on the rise is perhaps a natural result of introducing computers into American society. In an earlier era, the advent of the automobile opened the way for criminals to target the automobile itself (e.g., auto theft) or use it to facilitate traditional crimes (e.g., the bank robbery getaway vehicle). In addition, law enforcement had to learn to seize vehicles to search them for evidence of some offense unrelated to the vehicle itself (e.g., the box of documents in the trunk). In many of the same ways, computers, too, have proven important to criminal investigations. First, a computer may be the target of the offense. In these cases, the criminal's goal is to steal information from, or cause damage to, a computer, computer system, or computer network. Second, the computer may be a tool of the offense. This occurs when an individual uses a computer to facilitate some traditional offense such as fraud (e.g., a bank teller who once stole money from a cash drawer may now use a computer program to skim money directly from depositors' accounts). Last, computers are sometimes incidental to the offense, but significant to law enforcement because they contain evidence of a crime. Narcotics dealers, for example, may use a personal computer to store records pertaining to drug trafficking instead of relying on old-fashioned ledgers.

The different ways in which criminals can use computers have created a philosophical debate among law enforcement experts. Some argue that computer crime is nothing more than traditional crime committed with new, high-tech devices. Others contend that computer crime cannot be analogized to traditional crime and that combatting it requires both innovative law enforcement techniques and new laws designed to address abuses of emerging technologies. In 1984, Congress adopted the latter view and enacted discrete legislation to address crime in electronic environments. Although certain computer crimes appear simply to be old crimes committed in new ways (e.g., the bank teller who uses a computer program to steal money is still committing bank fraud), some computer offenses find their genesis in our new technologies and must be specifically addressed by statute. For example, the widespread damage caused by inserting a virus into a global computer network cannot be prosecuted adequately by relying upon common law criminal mischief statutes. Indeed, it is questionable whether Robert Morris, the individual responsible for launching the Morris worm and crippling 6,000 computers around the world, could have been prosecuted had Congress not had the foresight to enact the Computer Fraud and Abuse Act.

Whether classified as "old" or "new," computer crime creates unique problems for law enforcement and a concomitant threat to the public welfare. The most significant legislative problems stem from technology's shift from a corporeal to an intangible environment. This departure from a physical world (where items are stored in a tangible form that can be carried, such as information written on paper) to an intangible, electronic environment means that computer crimes (and the methods used to investigate them) are no longer subject to traditional rules and constraints. Consider, for example, the way the crimes of theft and criminal mischief have evolved. Before the advent of computer networks, the ability to steal information or damage property was to some extent determined by physical limitations. A burglar could break only so many windows and burglarize only so many homes in a week. During each intrusion, the burglar could carry away only so many items. This does not, of course, make this conduct trivial, but it points out that the amount of property a burglar could steal, or the amount of damage he could cause, had physical limits.

In the information age, of course, these limitations no longer apply. A criminal seeking information stored in a networked computer with dial-in access can acquire that information from virtually anywhere in the world. The quantity of information stolen or the amount of damage caused by malicious programming code may be limited only by the speed of the network and the criminal's computer equipment. Moreover, such conduct can easily occur across state and national borders.

This clear shift to a borderless, incorporeal environment and the increased risk that information will be stolen and transported in electronic form is difficult to address by relying upon older laws written to protect physical property. For example, the statute pertaining to interstate transportation of stolen property, 18 U.S.C. § 2314, speaks of "goods, wares and merchandise," and consequently has been held by at least one court not to apply to intangible property. *See United States v. Brown*, 925 F.2d 1301, 1308 (10th Cir. 1991). Similarly, the long-familiar extortion statute makes it illegal, in some cases, to threaten physical violence to property. 18 U.S.C. § 1951(a). Although a threat to fire bomb a building would clearly satisfy this test, a threat to delete files may not.

II. The Structure of Title 18 Reform

There are two ways, conceptually, to address the growing computer crime problem. The first would be to comb through the entire United States Code, identifying and amending every statute potentially affected by the implementation of new computer and telecommunications technologies. The second would be to focus substantive amendments on the Computer Fraud and Abuse Act to specifically address new abuses that spring from the misuse of new technologies.

The new legislation adopts the latter approach for a host of reasons:

1. The United States, in a single statute, continues to address the core issues driving computer and information security at both domestic and international levels; that is, protecting the confidentiality, integrity, and availability of data and systems. Indeed, these three themes provide the foundation for the Organization for Economic Cooperation and Development's (OECD) *Guidelines for the Security of Information Systems*. They also serve as the linchpin for emerging domestic works on information privacy. *See*, e.g., Draft Principles for Providing and Using Personal Information, 60 Fed. Reg.

4362 (January 20, 1995) [hereinafter "Draft Principles"]. By patterning the amended Computer Fraud and Abuse Act on the OECD guidelines, the U.S. is at the forefront of rethinking how information technology crimes must be addressed — simultaneously protecting the confidentiality, integrity, and availability of data and systems. And by choosing this path, we may encourage other countries to adopt a similar framework, thus creating a more uniform approach to addressing computer crime in the existing global information infrastructure.

2. In most cases, a single point of reference — The Computer Fraud and Abuse Act, 18 U.S.C. § 1030 — is provided for investigators, prosecutors, and legislators as they attempt to determine whether a particular abuse of new technology is covered under federal criminal law.

3. As new technologies are introduced and the criminal law requires reconsideration, fine-tuning § 1030 may well be adequate, and it will not be necessary to continually parse through the entire United States Code.

4. This statutory scheme will give us a better understanding of the scope of the computer crime problem by enabling more reliable statistics to be generated regarding computer abuse. Under current law, computer crimes can be charged under a host of criminal statutes, and this situation will continue if the U.S. chooses a patchwork approach and amends the various provisions of Title 18 to address new computer crimes. The existence of various computer crime provisions in different parts of Title 18 exacerbates an already obvious problem; i.e., computer crime experts have long admitted that there are no centralized computer crime statistics, not even within the law enforcement community. Indeed, a June 1996 study by the United States Sentencing Commission concluded that there were only 174 cases in which the statute of conviction included 18 U.S.C. § 1030, but conceded that

> ...pertinent questions remain unanswered. For example, how much criminal behavior that could have been successfully prosecuted under 18 U.S.C. § 1030 was prosecuted under other fraud statutes... ?

> — United States Sentencing Commission,
>   *Report to Congress:* Adequacy of Federal Sentencing Guideline Penalties for Computer Fraud and Vandalism Offenses, pp. 2, 6

By centralizing computer crimes under one statute, we may better measure existing harms, anticipate trends, and determine the need for further legislative reform. Additionally, amendments to the sentencing scheme of 18 U.S.C. § 1030 (and the Federal Sentencing Guidelines — 2F1.1 — upon which actual sentences are based), will be more effectively determined.

5. Last, 18 U.S.C. § 1030(f) specifically provides that certain government officials, if engaging in lawfully authorized investigative, protective, or intelligence activities, are not restricted by § 1030. By amending only 18 U.S.C. § 1030 to address new high-tech offenses, this exception clearly continues to apply to any newly defined criminal conduct.

III. Specific Amendments: Protecting the Confidentiality, Integrity, and Availability of Systems and Information

A. Section 1030(a)(1)

Title 18, Section 1030(a)(1) originally provided that anyone who knowingly accesses a computer without authorization or exceeds authorized access and obtains classified information "with the intent or reason to believe that such information so obtained *is to be used* to the injury of the United States, or to the advantage of any foreign nation" is subject to a fine or imprisonment for not more that ten years (for a first offense). 18 U.S.C. § 1030(a)(1) (emphasis added). This scienter element apparently was included when this subsection was originally drafted because it is contained in 18 U.S.C. § 794(a). Section 794(a), however, provides for life imprisonment, whereas § 1030(a)(1) is only a ten-year felony. Therefore, it is more appropriate that the language of § 1030(a)(1) should track the language of 18 U.S.C. § 793(e), which also provides a maximum penalty of ten years' imprisonment for obtaining from any source certain information connected with the national defense and thereafter communicating or attempting to communicate it in an unauthorized manner.

It should be noted that, although there is considerable overlap between § 793(e) and § 1030(a)(1) as amended, the two statutes do not reach exactly the same conduct. Section 1030(a)(1) would require proof that the individual knowingly used a computer without authority, or in excess of authority, for the purpose of obtaining classified information or restricted data, and subsequently performed some unauthorized communication or other improper act. In this sense then, it is the use of the computer which is being proscribed, not the unauthorized possession of, control over, or subsequent transmission of the information itself. Existing espionage laws would provide an adequate basis for the prosecution of individuals who attempt to peddle governmental secrets to foreign governments. However, a person who deliberately breaks in to a computer for the purpose of obtaining properly classified or restricted information, or attempts to do so, should be subject to criminal prosecution for this conduct.

B. Section 1030(a)(2)

Subsection (a)(2) is, in the truest sense, a provision designed to protect the confidentiality of computer data. As was noted in 1986 by the Senate Judiciary Committee,

> [t]he premise of 18 U.S.C. 1030(a)(2) will remain the protection, for privacy reasons, of computerized credit records and computerized information relating to customers' relationships with financial institutions... . Because the premise of this subsection is privacy protection, the Committee wishes to make clear that 'obtaining information' in this context includes mere observation of the data.
>
> — S. Rep. No. 99-432 at 6.

With the continued evolution of the National Information Infrastructure (NII), however, Congress has come to recognize that not only financial records and credit information warrant federal protection. As noted in the commentary to the Draft Principles, "with the NII, the assumption is that large amounts of sensitive information will be online, and can be accessed, perhaps without authority, by a large number of network users." 59 Fed. Reg. at 27207. Moreover, "the NII will only achieve its full potential if individual privacy is properly protected." *Id.* Therefore, the new subsection 1030(a)(2) is designed to insure that it is punishable to misuse computers to obtain government information and, where appropriate, information held by the private sector. Moreover, the provision has been restructured so that different paragraphs protect different types of information, thus allowing easy additions or modifications to offenses if events require.

Certainly not all computer misuse warrants federal criminal sanctions. The problem is that no litmus test can accurately segregate important from unimportant information, and any legislation may therefore be under- or over-inclusive. For example, a frequent test for determining the appropriateness of federal jurisdiction — a monetary amount — does not work well when protecting information. The theft from a computer of a judge's draft opinion in a sensitive case or the copying of medical records might not meet such a monetary threshold, but clearly such information should be protected. Therefore, the act of taking all of this kind of information is now criminalized. Even so, it is important to remember that the elements of the offense include not just taking the information, but abusing one's computer authorization to do so.

The need to protect information is highlighted by recent studies indicating that people are increasingly misusing computers to obtain information. In 1993, the General Accounting Office (GAO) presented testimony before the House Government Operations Committee, Subcommittee on Information, Justice, Agriculture, and Transportation, on the abuse of National Crime Information Center (NCIC) information. The testimony stated that, following an investigation, GAO determined that (1) NCIC information is valuable, (2) such information has been misused by "insiders" (individuals with authorized access), (3) this misuse included selling NCIC information to outsiders and determining whether friends and relatives had criminal records, and (4) incentives for misuse outweighed potential penalties. Statement of Laurie E. Ekstrand, July 28, 1993, p. 6 [hereinafter "Ekstrand Statement"]. The GAO found that some of this misuse jeopardized the safety of citizens and potentially jeopardized law enforcement personnel. *Id.* at 16. Moreover, because there were no federal or state laws specifically directed at NCIC misuse, most abusers of NCIC were not criminally prosecuted. *Id.* at 17. GAO concluded that Congress should enact legislation with strong criminal sanctions specifically directed at the misuse of NCIC. *Id.* at 20.

Of course, protecting only NCIC data (or, more broadly, criminal history information), would be underinclusive, because other types of sensitive data are clearly at risk. For example, during Operation Desert Storm, it was widely reported that hackers accessed sensitive but unclassified data regarding personnel performance reports, weapons development information, and logistics information regarding the movement of equipment and personnel. *Teen tapped computers of U.S. military*, Chicago Tribune, November 21, 1991 at 3. NASA computers have also been penetrated, *Computer Hacker Charged with Entering NASA System*, Washington Post, September 26, 1991 at A20, as have at least two federal courthouse computer systems. *See*, e.g., *U.S. Says Hackers Scanned Data*, The New York Times, November 15, 1992, at A40. Some Internal Revenue Service employees also improperly used IRS computers to examine tax return information. *I.R.S. Staff Is Cited in Snoopings*, The New York Times, July 19, 1994, at D1, D5.

Clearly, the government should be able to prosecute individuals who obtain government information by misusing computers. Importantly, 18 U.S.C. § 1030(a)(2), as amended, does not punish the mere acquisition of information (which might unduly impede the free flow of ideas), but prohibits intentionally accessing a computer without or in excess of authority *and* then obtaining such information. Moreover, to the extent that the information obtained is or should be available, it should be obtained through legal means (e.g., public sources or FOIA) and not through hacking.

Subsection 1030(a)(2)(C) is designed to protect against the interstate or foreign theft of information by computer. Such a provision is necessary in light of the Tenth Circuit's decision in *United States v. Brown*, 925 F.2d 1301, 1308 (10th Cir. 1991), where the court held that purely intangible intellectual property, such as a computer program, cannot constitute goods, wares, merchandise, securities, or moneys which have been stolen, converted, or taken within the meaning of § 2314. "Information" as used in this subsection is meant to be broadly construed and includes information stored in intangible form. Moreover, consistent with Congress's prior construction of § 1030(a)(2), "obtaining information" includes merely reading it; i.e., there is no requirement that the information be copied or transported. This is critically important because, in an electronic environment, information can be "stolen" without asportation, and the original usually remains intact.

Some computers may qualify under more than one subsection of § 1030(a)(2); for example, a particular government computer might be covered by both § 1030(a)(2)(B) and (a)(2)(C). This overlap serves to eliminate legal issues that might have arisen had Congress made the provisions mutually exclusive. Conceivably, in a given case, it may not be clear whether information taken from a government contractor's computer constitutes "information from any department or agency of the United States" under § 1030(a)(2)(B), but the offense might still be chargeable under § 1030(a)(2)(C) if the elements of that subsection are satisfied.

The seriousness of a breach in confidentiality depends, in considerable part, on either the value of the information or the defendant's motive in taking it. Thus, the statutory penalties are structured so that merely obtaining information of minimal value is only a misdemeanor, but certain aggravating factors make the crime a felony. More specifically, the crime becomes a felony if the offense was committed for purposes of commercial advantage or private financial gain, for the purpose of committing any criminal or tortious act in violation of the Constitution or laws of the United States or of any State, or if the value of the information obtained exceeds $5,000.

As for enhancements not based on the value of the property obtained, recent documented cases indicate that individuals misuse information for a variety of unacceptable purposes. The terms "for purposes of commercial advantage or private financial gain" and "for the purpose of committing any criminal or tortious act" are taken from the copyright statute (17 U.S.C. § 506(a)) and wiretap statute (18 U.S.C. § 2511(1)(d)), respectively.

As for the monetary threshold, any reasonable method can be used to establish the value of the information obtained. For example, the research, development, and manufacturing costs, or the value of the property "in the thieves' market," can be used to meet the $5,000 valuation. *See*, e.g., *United States v. Stegora*, 849 F.2d 291, 292 (8th Cir. 1988).

The relationship between the existing § 1030(a)(3) provision and the newly amended § 1030(a)(2) merits some discussion. Section 1030(a)(3) protects the computer from outsiders, even if the hacker obtains no information. Thus, an intruder who violates the integrity of a government machine to gain network access is nonetheless liable for trespass even when he has not jeopardized the confidentiality of data. Section 1030(a)(2), on the other hand, protects the confidentiality of data, even from intentional misuse by insiders. Additionally, although a first violation of § 1030(a)(3) is always a misdemeanor, a § 1030(a)(2) violation may constitute a felony if the information taken is valuable or sufficiently misused. *See* § 1030(c)(2)(B)(raising the offense to felony level based on the value or intended use of the improperly acquired data). Although a single act may violate both provisions, the provisions protect against different harms and, in any event, the actor's conduct would be aggregated for the purposes of sentencing.

C. Subsection 1030(a)(3)

Three substantive changes were made to § 1030(a)(3). First, the word "adversely" has been deleted because including this term suggests, inappropriately, that trespassing in a government computer may be benign.

Second, for clarity, the term "the use of the Government's operation of such computer" has been replaced with the term "that use by or for the Government of the United States." When a computer is used for the government, the government is not necessarily the operator, and the old term may have led to confusion. Consistent with this change, a similar change was made to the definition of "federal interest computer" (redesignated as "protected computer") in § 1030(e)(2)(A). Third, Congress inserted "non-public" to modify "computer of a department or agency of the United States." This change is intended to reflect the growing use of the Internet by government agencies and, in particular, the establishment of World Wide Web home pages and other public services. Arguably, a person charged under the old subsection (a)(3) might have asserted as a defense that he was not "without authorization to access *any* computer of a department or agency of the United States," because he was authorized to access some publicly available computer of that department or agency, such as a Web site. While this defense would almost have negated the law and thus defied a common-sense interpretation of the former law, Congress added the word "non-public" to make it perfectly clear that a person who has no authority to access any non-public computer of a department or agency may be convicted under (a)(3) even though permitted to access publicly available computers.

D. Subsection 1030(a)(4)

Subsection 1030(a)(4) has been amended to insure that felony level sanctions apply when unauthorized use of the computer (or use exceeding authorization) is significant. At the time the "computer use" exception was originally crafted, the Senate Judiciary Committee noted that:

[T]he mere use of a computer or computer service has a value all its own. Mere trespasses onto someone else's computer system can cost the system provider a "port" or access channel that he might otherwise be making available for a fee to an authorized user. At the same time, the Committee believes it is important to distinguish clearly between acts of fraud under (a)(4), punishable as felonies, and acts of simple trespass, punishable in the first instance as misdemeanors. That distinction would be wiped out were the Committee to treat every trespass as an attempt to defraud a service provider of computer time.

> — S. Rep. No. 99-432, 99th Cong., 2d Sess. 10 (1986).
> *See also* H.R. Rep. No. 99-612, 99th Cong., 2d Sess. 12 (1986).

Although Congress retains the concern about converting every trespass into a felony scheme to defraud, this new amendment clearly recognizes that a blanket exception for computer use may be too broad. Hackers, for example, have broken into Cray supercomputers for the purpose of running password cracking programs, sometimes amassing computer time worth far in excess of $5,000. In light of the large expense to the victim caused by some of these trespassing incidents, it is more appropriate to except from the felony provisions of subsection 1030(a)(4) only cases involving no more than $5,000 of computer use during any one-year period.

E. Subsection 1030(a)(5)

Subsection 1030(a)(5) was completely restructured in 1994, but the 1994 law may have had some unintended consequences. Most notably, certain government and financial institution computers may have been denied previously existing federal protection; some hacking activities may have been inappropriately decriminalized; and certain insider conduct may have been inappropriately criminalized.

In the 1994 amendments, the reach of this subsection was broadened by replacing the term "federal interest computer" with the term "computer used in interstate commerce or communications." The latter term is broader because the old definition of "federal interest computer" in 18 U.S.C. § 1030(e)(2)(B) covered a computer "which is one of two or more computers used in committing the offense, not all of which are located in the same State." This meant that a hacker who attacked other computers in the same state was not subject to federal jurisdiction, even when these actions may have severely affected interstate or foreign commerce. For example, individuals who attack telephone switches may disrupt interstate and foreign calls. The 1994 change remedied that defect.

However, the definition of federal interest computer actually covered more than simply interstate activity. More specifically, 18 U.S.C. § 1030(e)(2)(A) covered, generically, computers belonging to the United States Government or financial institutions, or those used by such entities on a non-exclusive basis if the conduct constituting the offense affected the Government's operation or the financial institution's operation of such computer. By changing § 1030(a)(5) from "federal interest computer" to "computer used in interstate commerce or communications," Congress may have inadvertently eliminated federal protection for those government and financial institution computers not used in interstate communications.

For example, the integrity and availability of classified information contained in an intrastate local area network may not have been protected under the 1994 version of 18 U.S.C. § 1030(a)(5), although its confidentiality continued to be protected under 18 U.S.C. § 1030(a)(1). To remedy this situation in the 1996 Act, 18 U.S.C. § 1030(a)(5) was redrafted to cover any "protected computer," a new term defined in § 1030(e)(2) and used throughout the new statute — in § 1030(a)(5), as well as in §§ 1030(a)(2), (a)(4), and the new (a)(7). The definition of "protected computer" includes government computers, financial institution computers, and any computer "which is used in interstate or foreign commerce or communications."

This broad definition addresses the original concerns regarding intrastate "phone phreakers" (i.e., hackers who penetrate telecommunications computers). It also specifically includes those computers used in "foreign" communications. With the continually expanding global information infrastructure, with numerous instances of international hacking, and with the growing possibility of increased global industrial espionage, it is important that the United States have jurisdiction over international computer crime cases. Arguably, the old definition of "federal interest computer" contained in 18 U.S.C. § 1030(e)(2) conferred such jurisdiction because the requirement that the computers used in committing the offense not all be located in the same state might be satisfied if one computer were located overseas. As a general rule, however, Congress's laws have been presumed to be domestic in scope only, absent a specific grant of extraterritorial jurisdiction. *E.E.O.C. v. Arabian American Oil Co.*, 499 U.S. 244 (1991). To ensure clarity, the statute was amended to reference international communications explicitly.

Another concern with the 1994 version of 18 U.S.C. § 1030(a)(5) involved the overall statutory scheme. Under the 1986 version of subsection 1030(a)(5), the actor causing the harm must have been *without* authority to access the victim computer. As such, the provision never applied to insiders, although insiders are often responsible for intentionally causing computer damage. Indeed, the Justice Department was forced to decline prosecution in some cases where individuals intentionally inserted malicious programming code into computers, because those individuals were authorized to access the attacked system. The 1994 law, in contrast to the 1986 version, appropriately applied to both insiders and those without authorized access who intentionally caused damage.

Unfortunately, however, by eliminating the trespassing requirement, *and at the same time* requiring the government to prove that the actor either intentionally or recklessly caused damage, the 1994 law no longer punished a person who broke into a federal interest computer and "thereby caused loss." *See* 18 U.S.C. § 1030(a)(5) [1986 version]. Thus, the enactment of the 1994 legislation decriminalized some hacking and inadvertently sent the message that breaking into computers was acceptable so long as the actor neither intended nor recklessly caused damage. However, in these 1996 amendments, criminal liability for such behavior has been restored. This was clearly necessary in light of the increased importance of computer networks in today's society and the nation's considerable interest in creating a trusted national information infrastructure that insures the confidentiality, integrity, and availability of information and systems.

This problem, now corrected, arose because the 1986 and 1994 versions of Section 1030(a)(5) defined improper conduct in completely different ways — the former by focusing only on the actor's authority to access the computer; the latter

Exhibit 1.   § 1030(a)(5) [1986 Version]
[Based on the defendant's authority to access the computer]

	Trespassers	Authorized Users
Intentional Damage	Felony	No crime
Reckless Damage	Felony	No crime
Negligent Damage	Felony	No crime

Exhibit 2.   18 U.S.C. § 1030(a)(5)[1994 Version]
[Based on the defendant's criminal intent to damage]

	Trespassers	Authorized Users
Intentional Damage	Felony	Felony
Reckless Damage	Misdemeanor	Misdemeanor
Negligent Damage	No crime	No crime

by considering solely the actor's intent. Of course, these two separate litmus tests each cover important aspects of criminal computer damage, but neither measure, taken alone, fully succeeds in describing the acts which should be criminal. For example, although those who intentionally damage a system should be punished regardless of whether they are authorized users, it is equally clear that anyone who knowingly invades a system without authority and causes significant loss to the victim should be punished as well, even when the damage caused is not intentional. In such cases, it is the intentional act of trespass that makes the conduct criminal. To provide otherwise is to openly invite hackers to break into computer systems, safe in the knowledge that no matter how much damage they cause, they commit no crime unless that damage was either intentional or reckless. Rather then send such a dangerous message (and deny victims any relief), it is better to insure that § 1030(a)(5) criminalizes all computer damage done by outsiders, as well as intentional damage by insiders, albeit at different levels of severity.

By using a matrix, [Exhibits 1 and 2 show] that neither the 1986 law nor the 1994 law was adequate, although they fail in different categories.

Conceptually, a comprehensive statutory scheme does not treat these two tests — mental state and authority to access — as mutually exclusive. Instead, it integrates them to cover all kinds of serious misconduct. Just as important, it recognizes that some behaviors are less serious, or should not be criminal offenses at all. For example, the 1994 law created a misdemeanor for reckless damage without distinguishing between trespassers and authorized users. Whether authorized users should ever be criminally liable for reckless damage is a debatable question. For example, it could be deemed reckless in today's computer environment to intentionally copy a file from a floppy diskette to a hard drive without first running a virus scan — although imposing criminal sanctions for such conduct is clearly inappropriate, absent other evidence of criminal intent. On the other hand, reckless trespassers warrant felony prosecutions, since they are unauthorized users who pose significant risks to computer systems. Thus, Congress has now

Exhibit 3.   18 U.S.C. § 1030(a)(5) [The New Law] [Based on the defendant's authority to access the computer and criminal intent to damage]

	Trespassers	Authorized Users
Intentional Damage	Felony	Felony
Reckless Damage	Felony	No crime
Negligent Damage	Misdemeanor	No crime

chosen an approach that integrates access and authority tests, as shown in Exhibit 3.

Essentially, this new statute provides that individuals who access protected computers without authority are responsible for the consequences of their actions, but those accessing with authority are criminally liable only if they intend to cause damage to the victim.

Although subsections § 1030(a)(5)(B) and (a)(5)(C) require that the actor cause damage as a result of his or her unauthorized access, damages are not limited to those caused by the process of gaining illegal entry. Rather, all damage, whether caused while gaining access or after entry, is relevant.

Another concern with the 1994 law was that it required both "damage" and "loss," without clearly articulating what constituted "damage." For example, intruders often alter existing log-on programs so that user passwords are copied to a file which the hackers can retrieve later. After retrieving the newly created password file, the intruder restores the altered log-on file to its original condition. Arguably, in such a situation, neither the computer nor its information has been damaged. Nonetheless, the intruder's conduct allowed him to accumulate valid user passwords to the system, required all system users to change their passwords, and required the system administrator to devote resources to re-securing the system. Thus, although there may be no permanent "damage," the victim does suffer "loss." If the loss to the victim meets the required monetary threshold, the conduct should be criminal, and the victim should be entitled to relief.

It would not have been possible to address all of these concerns by making only minor amendments to subsection 1030(a)(5). Thus, the statutory scheme was altered to both simplify its provisions and adopt the sanctions provided in Exhibit 3.

As discussed further below, the term "damage" remains, but is now defined in 18 U.S.C. § 1030(e)(8). Consistent with the view that § 1030(a)(5) protects the integrity and availability of data and systems, "damage" means any impairment of those attributes. The statutory language avoids listing specific acts that can cause such impairment to insure that its coverage is suitably broad. For example, in the 1986 version, the terms "alters, damages or destroys information," were included, inadvertently raising new issues (e.g., whether encrypting data satisfies this test since the underlying original information remains unchanged). Rather than providing a list of prohibited actions and risk being underinclusive, the statute focuses instead on the harms it seeks to prevent.

This harm-based definition of "damage" can now be found in subsections 1030(e)(8)(A) through (D). As in the past, the term "damage" will require meeting one of several significant thresholds. Two of these measures survive from earlier versions of § 1030: the first is significant financial losses — although raised in these amendments from $1000 to $5000 — [§ 1030(e)(8)(A)]; the second is potential impact on medical treatment [§ 1030(e)(8)(B)]. In addition, Congress has listed two new threshold harms in its definition of "damage": causing physical injury to any person [18 U.S.C. § 1030(e)(8)(c)] and threatening the public health or safety [18 U.S.C. § 1030(e)(8)(c)]. As the NII and other network infrastructures continue to grow, computers will increasingly be used for access to critical services such as emergency response systems and air traffic control, and will be critical to other systems that we cannot yet anticipate. Thus, any definition of "damage" must broadly encompass the types of harms against which people should be protected.

Having amended the structure of § 1030(a)(5), Congress needed to amend the civil penalty provision under § 1030(g). The subsection as amended provides that victims of computer abuse can maintain a civil action against the violator to obtain compensatory damages, injunctive relief, or other equitable relief, but damages are limited to economic damages for cases where the only damage suffered by the plaintiff is monetary loss as defined by § 1030(e)(8)(A).

F. Subsection 1030(a)(7)

New subsection (a)(7) is designed to respond to a growing problem: the interstate transmission of threats directed against computers and computer networks. Such threats, if accompanied by an intent to extort, may already be covered in some instances by the Hobbs Act, 18 U.S.C. § 1951, which applies to interference with commerce by extortion. They also may be covered in some instances by 18 U.S.C. § 875(d), which applies to interstate communication of a threat to injure the property of another. However, under both of these statutes, it is not absolutely clear that "property" includes the unimpaired operation of a computer or the unrestricted access to the data or programs stored in a computer and its peripheral equipment. Moreover, it is not clear that certain actions (such as encrypting someone's data and then demanding money for the key) constitute a threat to "injure the property of...another." *See* 18 U.S.C. § 875(d).

These concerns are not theoretical. In one recent case, for example, an individual threatened to crash a computer system unless he was granted access to the system and given an account. Another case involved an individual who penetrated a city government's computer system and encrypted the data on a hard drive, thus leading the victim to suspect an extortion demand was imminent. (This demand never came, however, and fortunately the victim was able to recover from the incident.) Although the number of such incidents is currently small, the explosion in network access has substantially increased the risk that such conduct will occur, and our nation's increased reliance on computers clearly suggests that such activities, if not deterred, will severely impair our ability to use the NII effectively. Moreover, since such extortion and threats will normally involve interstate and foreign communications, federal law enforcement needed a clear basis to address this new problem quickly.

It is worth noting that subsection (a)(7) covers any interstate or international transmission of threats against computers, computer networks, and their data and programs, whether the threat is received by mail, a telephone call, electronic mail, or through a computerized message service. The provision is worded broadly to cover threats to interfere in any way with the normal operation of the computer or system in question, such as denying access to authorized users, erasing or corrupting data or programs, or slowing down the operation of the computer or system. The extortion element is modeled after that in 18 U.S.C. §§ 875(b) and (d).

G. Sentencing Provisions: Subsection 1030(c)

The sentencing provisions of § 1030 have been altered to reflect the new statutory scheme and to address an old, technical error. As previously enacted, recidivists were only subject to enhanced penalties if they violated the same *subsection* twice. For example, if an individual violated the Act by committing fraud by computer [subsection (a)(4)] and later committed another computer crime offense by intentionally destroying medical records [subsection (a)(5)], he was not a recidivist because his conduct violated two separate subsections of § 1030. Congress has changed the statutory language to provide that anyone who is convicted twice of committing a computer offense will be subjected to enhanced penalties.

H. Jurisdiction: Subsection 1030(d)

Having created several new crimes in 18 U.S.C. § 1030, Congress needed to consider the jurisdictional grant in 18 U.S.C. § 1030(d). For some time, the Federal Bureau of Investigation and the United States Secret Service have shared concurrent jurisdiction over § 1030 based on a Memorandum of Understanding. This new Act, by creating certain new crimes, does not alter any existing agreements, nor limit or alter an agency's "traditional" jurisdiction. Thus, there is new language in 18 U.S.C. § 1030(d) to insure that the *status quo* is maintained. For example, the new 18 U.S.C. § 1030(a)(2)(C) addressed gaps in 18 U.S.C. § 2314 (interstate transportation of stolen property), and the new 18 U.S.C. § 1030(a)(7) addressed gaps in 18 U.S.C. § 1951 (the Hobbs Act) and 18 U.S.C. § 875 (interstate communications). All of these statutes are within the traditional jurisdiction of the FBI, therefore 18 U.S.C. § 1030(d) did not extend to the United States Secret Service concurrent jurisdiction over these types of offenses, even when committed by computer. Subsections over which the Secret Service maintains concurrent jurisdiction are § 1030(a)(2)(A) and (B), (a)(3), (a)(4), (a)(5), and (a)(6).

Distributed Denial of Service Attacks

In the week of February 7, 2000, hackers launched distributed denial of service (DDS) attacks on several prominent Web sites, including Yahoo!, E*Trade, Amazon.com, and eBay. In a DDS attack, dozens or even hundreds of computers all linked to the Internet are instructed by a rogue program to bombard the target site with nonsense data. This bombardment soon causes the target sites's servers to run out of memory, and thus cause it to be unresponsive to the queries of legitimate customers. On February 29, 2000, Deputy Attorney General Eric Holder and Director of the National Infrastructure Protection Center Michael A. Vatis testified before a House and Senate Joint Judiciary Subcommittee meeting to talk about the distributed denial of services attacks and about cybercrime in general.

Internet Denial of Service Attacks and the Federal Response

Eric Holder, Deputy Attorney General of the United States
Subcommittee on Crime of the House Committee on the Judiciary and the Subcommittee on Criminal Oversight of the Senate Committee on the Judiciary

Mr. Chairmen and other Members of the Subcommittees, I want to thank you for this opportunity to testify on the recent Internet "denial of service" attacks and the federal response to these incidents, with a particular focus on the challenges facing the Department of Justice in its fight against cybercrime. Both Subcommittees have been very helpful in providing the Department with the resources and tools we need to keep pace with the ever-changing demands of law enforcement and public safety, particularly the new challenge of cybercrime. At a time where new technologies abound and our society becomes increasingly reliant on computer networks and thus vulnerable to cybercrime, we look forward to working again with you to ensure that law enforcement, in cooperation with the private sector, can play an appropriate and critical role in protecting the well-being of Americans.

Comments on the Recent Attacks

I would be happy to address your questions on the recent attacks, to the extent I can do so without compromising our investigation. At this point, I would simply say that we are taking the attacks very seriously and that we will do everything in our power to identify those responsible and bring them to justice. In addition to the malicious disruption of legitimate commerce, so-called "denial of service" attacks involve the unlawful intrusion into an unknown number of computers, which are in turn used to launch attacks on the eventual target computer, in this case the computers of Yahoo, eBay, and others. Thus, the number of victims in these types of cases can be substantial, and the collective loss and cost to respond to these attacks can run into the tens of millions of dollars — or more.

Overview of Investigative Efforts and Coordination

Computer crime investigators in a number of FBI field offices and investigators from other agencies are investigating these attacks. They are coordinating information with the National Infrastructure Protection Center (NIPC) of the FBI. The agents are also working closely with our network of specially trained computer crime prosecutors who are available 24 hours a day/7 days a week to provide legal advice and obtain whatever court orders are necessary. Attorneys from the Criminal Division's Computer Crime and Intellectual Property Section (CCIPS) are coordinating with the Assistant United States Attorneys in the field. We are also obtaining information from victim companies and security experts, who, like many in the Internet community, condemn these recent attacks. We are also working closely with our counterparts in other nations. I am proud of the efforts being made in this case, including the assistance we are receiving from a number of federal agencies.

The Emergence of Cybercrime

It is worth remembering that just ten years ago, the Internet was largely unknown and unavailable to the average person. There was no e-commerce, no e-Bay, no amazon-dot-com, very little dot-anything. At that time, the Internet was a collection of military, academic, and research networks serving a small community of trusted users. Many of us were just learning about pagers and cell phones, VCRs, and videocams.

That world is history. The far-reaching, ever-expanding, and ever more rapid advances in computer and software technology over the last ten years have combined with the explosive growth of the Internet to change the world forever. For the most part, the Internet and other technologies are providing wonderful benefits to our society — from providing new, high-wage jobs to our economy, to expanding educational opportunities, to improving health care, and in countless other ways.

Unfortunately, these wonderful technologies also provide new opportunities for criminals. Online crime is rapidly increasing. We are seeing more "pure" computer crimes, that is, crimes where the computer is used as a weapon to attack other computers, as we saw in the distributed denial of service attacks I just spoke about, and in the spread of malicious code, like viruses. Our vulnerability to this type of crime is astonishingly high — it was only this past December that a defendant admitted, when he pled guilty in federal and state court to creating and releasing the Melissa virus, that he caused over 80 million dollars in damage. These crimes also include computer intrusions designed to obtain information of the most sensitive sort — such as credit cards, companies' trade secrets, or individual's' private information.

These crimes not only affect our financial well-being and our privacy; they also threaten our nation's critical infrastructure. Our banking system, the stock market, the electricity and water supply, telecommunications networks, and critical government services, such as emergency and national defense services, all rely on computer networks. For a real-world terrorist to blow up a dam, he would need tons of explosives, a delivery system, and a surreptitious means of evading armed security guards. For a cyberterrorist, the same devastating result could be achieved by hacking into the control network and commanding the computer to open the floodgates.

We are also seeing a migration of "traditional" crimes — including threats, child pornography, fraud, gambling, and extortion — from the physical to the online world. When these crimes are carried out online, perpetrators often find that the can reach more victims quickly and quite easily, turning what were once "local" scams into crimes that cross interstate and international borders. Computers and computer networks provide a cheap and powerful means of communications, and criminals take advantage of this just like everyone else. In addition, sophisticated criminals can readily use the easy anonymity that the Internet provides to hide their crimes.

Challenges of Cybercrime

The Internet and computers have brought tremendous benefits to our society, including greater freedom of expression and economic growth. But we must also recognize that as a result of our society's increasing reliance on technology, investigators and prosecutors at all levels — international, federal, state, and local — are encountering unique challenges. These challenges generally can be divided into three categories:

- *Technical challenges* that hinder law enforcement's ability to find and prosecute criminals operating online;
- *Legal challenges* resulting from laws and legal tools needed to investigate cybercrime lagging behind technological, structural, and social changes; and
- *Resource challenges* to ensure we have satisfied critical investigative and prosecutorial needs at all levels of government.

Before I discuss each of these challenges, let me say that we recognize that we in government will not be able to solve all of these problems. In fact, we believe the private sector should take the lead in protecting private computer networks, through more vigilant security efforts, information sharing, and, where appropriate, cooperation with government agencies. The private sector has the resources, the technical ability, and the trained personnel to ensure that, as technology continues to develop and change rapidly, the Internet is a safer place for all of us. Thus, the private sector can and should take the lead on improving security practices and the development of a more secure Internet infrastructure.

Our society will also need the assistance of the everyday user in making sure that safeguards are taken and practices are followed. The best infrastructure and most secure means of electronic commerce will be ineffective if the users of the technology, that is, all of us, don't follow the basic "rules of the road."

However, even assuming that users and companies do everything they can to provide a safe, secure, and vibrant Internet, there will be instances where the practices and safeguards fail. Criminals rob banks even though banks use numerous security measures. In such cases, law enforcement must be prepared and equipped to investigate and prosecute cybercriminals in order to stop their criminal activity, to punish them, and to deter others who might follow the same path. This is the reason that it is so important that we work together to address the challenges I am about to discuss.

Technical Challenges

When a hacker disrupts air traffic control at a local airport, when a child pornographer sends computer files, when a cyberstalker sends a threatening e-mail to a public school or a local church, or when credit card numbers are stolen from a company engaged in e-commerce, investigators must locate the source of the communication. Everything on the Internet is communications, from an e-mail to an electronic heist. Finding an electronic criminal means that law enforcement must determine who is responsible for sending an electronic threat or initiating an electronic robbery. To accomplish this, law enforcement must in nearly every case trace the "electronic trail" leading from the victim back to the perpetrator.

Tracking a criminal online is not necessarily an impossible task, as demonstrated last year when federal and state law enforcement agencies were able to track down the creator of the Melissa virus and the individual who created a false

Bloomburg News Service Web site in order to drive up the stock price of PairGain, a telecommunications company in California. In both cases, technology enabled us to find the individuals who were engaging in criminal activity.

Unfortunately, despite our successes in the Melissa and PairGain cases, we still face significant challenges as online criminals become more sophisticated, often wearing the equivalent of Internet electronic gloves to hide their fingerprints and their identity.

It doesn't take a master hacker to disappear on a network. Ironically, while the public is justifiably worried about protecting the legitimate electronic privacy of individuals who use networks, a criminal using tools and other information easily available over the Internet can operate in almost perfect anonymity. By weaving his or her communications through a series of anonymous remailers; by creating a few forged e-mail headers with powerful, point-and-click tools readily downloadable from many hacker Web sites; or by using a "free-trial" account or two, a hacker, online pornographer, or Web-based fraud artist can effectively hide the trail of his or her communications.

As we consider the challenge created by anonymity, we must also recognize that there are legitimate reasons to allow anonymity in communications networks. A whistleblower, a resistance fighter in Kosovo, a battered woman's support group — all of these individuals may understandably wish to use the Internet and other new technologies to communicate with others without revealing their identities.

In addition to problems related to the anonymous nature of the Internet, we are being challenged to investigate and prosecute criminals in an international arena. The Internet is a global medium that does not recognize physical and jurisdictional boundaries. A criminal no longer needs to be at the actual scene of the crime to prey on his or her victims. As a result, a computer server running a Web page designed to defraud U.S. senior citizens might be located in Europe or Asia. A child pornographer may distribute photographs or videos via e-mail, sending the e-mails through the communications networks of several countries before they reach their intended recipients. With more than 190 Internet-connected countries in the world, the coordination challenges facing law enforcement are tremendous. And any delay in an investigation is critical, as a criminal's trail might, in certain circumstances, end as soon as he or she disconnects from the Internet.

Likewise, evidence of a crime can be stored at a remote location, either for the purpose of concealing the crime from law enforcement and others, or simply because of the design of the network. In certain circumstances, the fact that the evidence is stored and held by a third party, such as an Internet service provider, might be helpful to law enforcement agencies who might be able to use lawful process to get that information. However, storing information remotely can also create a challenge to law enforcement, which cannot ignore the real-world limits of local, state, and national sovereignty and jurisdiction. Obtaining information from foreign countries, especially on an expedited basis, can be a daunting task, especially when a country may be in a different time zone, use a different language, have different legal rules, and may not have trained experts available. Consequently, even as the Internet and other new technologies have given us new abilities to find criminals remotely, our abilities can be hindered if we cannot obtain the necessary legal cooperation from our counterparts in other countries.

The vast majority of Internet companies are good corporate citizens and are interested in the safety of our citizens. In fact, several companies have been engaged in discussions with law enforcement regarding our concerns. Despite these efforts, we have learned that we cannot take for granted the nature of any Internet service provider's services, its record-keeping practices, and its ability or willingness to cooperate with us. We have encountered a handful of companies involved in criminal activity. In addition, even those companies that are not involved in criminal activities might not be able to assist us because of business reasons or privacy concerns that have resulted in them not keeping the records that are necessary to investigate a particular crime.

Moreover, users connect to the Internet from anywhere in the world over old-fashioned telephone lines, wireless phones, cable modems, and satellite systems. Each of these telecommunications systems has its own protocols for addressing and routing traffic, which means that tracking all the way back to the criminal at his or her computer will require agents to be fluent in each technical language. Gathering this evidence from so many kinds of providers is a very different proposition from the days when we simply obtained an order for a telephone company to trace a threatening call.

Legal Challenges

Deterring and punishing computer criminals requires a legal structure that will support detection and successful prosecution of offenders. Yet the laws defining computer offenses, and the legal tools needed to investigate criminals using the Internet, can lag behind technological and social changes, creating legal challenges to law enforcement agencies.

Some of the legal challenges we encounter can easily be corrected through legislative action. For example, the Computer Fraud and Abuse Act, 18 U.S.C. § 1030, arguably does not reach a computer hacker who causes a large amount of damage to a network of computers if no individual computer sustains over $5,000 worth of damage. The Department of Justice has encountered several instances in which intruders have gained unauthorized access to protected computers (whether publicly or privately owned) used in the provision of "critical infrastructure" systems and services — such as those that hospitals use to store sensitive information and to treat patients, and those that the military uses to defend the nation — but where proof of damage in excess of $5000 has not been readily available.

The laws under which we are able to identify the origin and destination of telephone calls and computer messages also need to be reviewed. For example, under current law we may have to obtain court orders in multiple jurisdictions to trace a single communication. Obtaining court orders in multiple jurisdictions does not advance any reasonable privacy safeguard, yet it can be a substantial impediment to a fast-paced investigation. As the Attorney General testified recently, it might be extremely helpful, for example, to provide nationwide effect for trap and trace orders.

Another concern focuses on the problem of online threats and serious harassment — that is, cyberstalking. Current federal law does not address those situations where a cyberstalker uses unwitting third parties to bombard a victim with messages, transmits personal data about a person — such as the route by which the victim's children walk to school — in order to place such person or his family in fear of injury, or sends an e-mail or other communications under someone else's name with the intent to abuse, harass, or threaten that person. We believe federal law may need to be amended to address this gap.

These aren't hypothetical changes that we are proposing to address. Just ask the California woman who was awakened six times in the middle of the night to find men knocking on her door offering to rape her. She discovered that a man whom she had told she was not romantically interested in had posted personal advertisements on a variety of Internet services pretending to be her. Each posting, which contained her home address and telephone number, claimed that she fantasized about being raped. We need to ensure that laws against harassment clearly prohibit such horrific actions, particularly since access to the Internet means immediate access to a wide audience.

Resource Challenges

In addition to technical and legal challenges, we face significant resource challenges. Simply stated, we need an adequate number of prosecutors and agents — at the federal, state and local level — trained with the necessary skills and properly equipped to effectively fight all types of cybercrime.

While Congress has been very supportive of the Department's cybercrime efforts, we need additional resources to ensure we are adequately equipped to continue our battle against cybercriminals. The President has requested $37 million in new money in FY 2001 to expand our staffing, training and technological capabilities to continue the fight against computer crime. Together, these enhancements will increase the Department's 2001 funding base for computer crime to $138 million, 28 percent more than in 2000.

Last, the Department of Justice would like to work with Congress to develop a comprehensive, five-year plan — with FY 2001 as our baseline — to prevent cybercrime and, when it does occur, to locate, identify, apprehend and bring to justice those responsible for these types of crimes. On February 16th, the Attorney General testified before Congress regarding a proposed a 10-point plan to identify the key areas we need to develop for our cybercrime capability. The key points of this plan she touched upon include:

- Developing a round-the-clock network of federal, state and local law enforcement officials with expertise in, and responsibility for, investigating and prosecuting cybercrime.
- Developing and sharing expertise — personnel and equipment — among federal, state and local law enforcement agencies.
- Dramatically increasing our computer forensic capabilities, which are so essential in computer crime investigations — both hacking cases and cases where computers are used to facilitate other crimes, including drug trafficking, terrorism, and child pornography.
- Reviewing whether we have adequate legal tools to locate, identify, and prosecute cybercriminals. In particular, we may need new and more robust procedural tools to allow state authorities to more easily gather evidence

located outside their jurisdictions. We also need to explore whether we have adequate tools at the federal level to effectively investigate cybercrime.

■ Because of the borderless nature of the Internet, we need to develop effective partnerships with other nations to encourage them to enact laws that adequately address cybercrime and to provide assistance in cybercrime investigations. A balanced international strategy for combating cybercrime should be at the top of our national security agenda.

■ We need to work in partnership with industry to address cybercrime and security. This should not be a top-down approach through excessive government regulation or mandates. Rather, we need a true partnership, where we can discuss challenges and develop effective solutions that do not pose a threat to individual privacy.

■ And we need to teach our young people about the responsible use of the Internet. The Department of Justice and the Information Technology Association of America have already taken steps to do so through the development of the Cybercitizen Partnership, but more needs to be done.

Efforts Against Cybercrime

Despite the technical, legal, and resource challenges, the Department has made strides in our fight against cybercrime. We have and will continue to develop extensive investigatory and prosecutorial programs to counter cybercrime. Let me take a few moments to details some of our efforts to date.

On the investigatory side, we have the FBI's National Infrastructure Protection Center (NIPC) and specialized squads located in 16 field offices.

On the prosecutorial side, we have trained attorneys, both in headquarters and in the field, who are experts in the legal, technological, and practical challenges involved in investigating and prosecuting cybercrime. The cornerstone of our prosecutor cybercrime program is the Computer Crime and Intellectual Property Section. CCIPS, which currently has 18 attorneys, was founded in 1991 as the Computer Crime Unit and was elevated to Section status in 1996. CCIPS works closely on computer crime cases with Assistant United States Attorneys known as "Computer and Telecommunications Coordinators" (CTCs) in U.S. Attorneys' Offices around the country. Each CTC is given special training and equipment, and serves as the district's expert in computer crime cases. As a result of these programs, the number of cases and prosecutions by the Department is growing at a tremendous rate. For example, in 1998, U.S. Attorneys' Offices filed 85 computer crime cases against 116 defendants. This represents a 29 percent increase in the number of cases filed and a 51 percent increase in the number of defendants, compared to the previous year. During that same period of time, a total of 62 cases against 72 defendants were terminated, with 78 percent of those defendants being convicted.

At the same time, our prosecutors are working with numerous other federal, state, and local investigators and prosecutors, providing assistance in any case involving computers and other high technology, such as computer searches and seizure. In sum, the Department and, in particular, its investigators and prosecutors take seriously our responsibility to protect the nation's computers and the Internet from computer crime.

In addition to the Department's efforts, other agencies including Customs, the Secret Service, the Securities and Exchange Commission, and the U.S. Postal's Inspectors General, have played a role in the investigation and prosecution of computer crimes.

Conclusion

On behalf of the Department, I want to thank Congress for all the support it has given to our efforts to combat cybercrimes. Advancements in technology indicate that our efforts are only just beginning. We look forward to working with Congress and the private sector to ensure that we have a robust and effective long-term plan for combating cybercrime, protecting our nation's infrastructure, and ensuring that the Internet reaches its full potential for expanding communications, facilitating commerce, and bringing countless other benefits to our society.

The Melissa Virus

The Melissa virus first appeared on the Internet in March of 1999. It spread rapidly throughout computer systems in the United States and Europe. It is estimated that the virus caused $80 million in damages to computers worldwide. In the United States alone, the virus made its way through 1.2 million computers in one-fifth of the country's largest businesses. David Smith pleaded guilty on December 9, 1999 to state and federal charges associated with his creation of the Melissa virus.

Three documents relating to the Melissa virus case are linked below:

- *Information in United States of America v. David Smith* — Court document filed by the U.S. Attorney's Office in Newark, New Jersey relating to charges against the creator of the Melissa computer virus. www.usdoj.gov/criminal/cybercrime/melinfo.htm
- *Plea Agreement* — David Smith agreed to plead guilty to creating and disseminating the Melissa virus and causing over $80 million in damages, in violation of federal computer crime laws. www.usdoj.gov/criminal/cybercrime/meliplea.htm
- *Creator of 'Melissa' Computer Virus Pleads Guilty in New Jersey to State and Federal Charges* — www.usdoj.gov/criminal/cybercrime/melissa.htm

Cybercrime Summit: A Law Enforcement/Information Technology Industry Dialogue

On April 5, 2000, the Department of Justice hosted a Cybercrime Summit at Stanford Law School, titled "Cybercrime Summit:A Law Enforcement/Information Technology Industry Dialogue on Prevention, Detection, Investigation and Cooperation," at which Attorney General Janet Reno and members of the Justice Department and other law enforcement agencies met with representatives of information technology and Internet companies. The main topic of the Summit was how to improve cooperation between law enforcement and industry in investigating computer network hacking. Linked below are the Attorney General's Opening Remarks from the Summit, as well as the Question & Answer session between industry representatives and the Attorney General.

- Opening Remarks of Attorney General Janet Reno at the Cybercrime Summit — www.usdoj.gov/criminal/cybercrime/agcybsum.htm
- Question and Answer Session with Attorney General Janet Reno at the Cybercrime Summit — www.usdoj.gov/criminal/cybercrime/4500agcyber crimes.htm

Chapter 10

International Aspects of Computer Crime

With the explosive growth of the Internet worldwide, computer crimes increasingly are prone to have international dimensions. Some of the challenges faced by law enforcement on the international front include: harmonization of countries' criminal laws; locating and identifying perpetrators across borders; and securing electronic evidence of their crimes so that they may be brought to justice. Complex jurisdictional issues arise at each step. The Department of Justice is working with foreign governments through many channels to address global threats related to computer crime.

Council of Europe Convention on Cybercrime

On April 27, 2000, the Council of Europe released its draft Convention on Cyber-Crime, which is the first multilateral instrument drafted to address the problems posed by the spread of criminal activity on computer networks. The United States has participated in the drafting of the Council of Europe Convention, which is still a work in progress, since the project began over two years ago. The drafting group is scheduled to complete its work by December 31, 2000, but it continually releases new drafts. The Convention will then be finalized by the Steering Committee on European Crime Problems and submitted to the Committee of Ministers for adoption before it is opened to members of the Council of Europe and observer nations, including the United States, for signature.

The text of the explanatory memorandum of the Convention, the draft Convention and the accompanying press release are available at conventions.coe.int/treaty/EN/cadreproject.htm

Draft Convention on Cyber-Crime

Version No. 27 Revised

This text prepared by Committee of Experts on Crime in Cyber-Space (PC-CY), was submitted to the European Committee on Crime Problems (CDPC) at its 50th plenary session (18–22 June 2001). The text will be submitted to the Committee of Ministers for adoption.

This document, provisionally entitled "Draft Convention on Cyber-Crime," is the first ever international treaty to address criminal law and procedural aspects of various types of criminal behavior directed against computer systems, networks or data and other types of similar misuse. A list of contact points in certain negotiating States is also provided herewith to allow interested parties to submit comments or questions on the draft treaty to national government experts.

It also contains the **draft Explanatory Memorandum** which has been made public to help readers of the draft Convention better understand the scope and meaning of its provisions, as intended by the drafters. Explanations provided in this document should therefore be read in conjunction with the draft treaty's provisions.

Supervisory Authorities and Transborder Data Flows

Additional Protocol to the Convention for the Protection of Individuals with regard to Automatic Processing of Personal Data (ETS No. 108)

[ETS No. 179]

[Strasbourg,8.XI.2001]

Preamble

The Parties to this additional Protocol to the Convention for the Protection of Individuals with regard to Automatic Processing of Personal Data, opened for signature in Strasbourg on 28 January 1981 (hereafter referred to as "the Convention"); convinced that supervisory authorities, exercising their functions in complete independence, are an element of the effective protection of individuals with regard to the processing of personal data;

Considering the importance of the flow of information between peoples; considering that, with the increase in exchanges of personal data across national borders, it is necessary to ensure the effective protection of human rights and fundamental freedoms, and in particular the right to privacy, in relation to such exchanges of personal data,

Have agreed as follows:

Article 1 — Supervisory authorities

1. Each Party shall provide for one or more authorities to be responsible for ensuring compliance with the measures in its domestic law giving effect

to the principles stated in Chapters II and III of the Convention and in this Protocol.

2. a. To this end, the said authorities shall have, in particular, powers of investigation and intervention, as well as the power to engage in legal proceedings or bring to the attention of the competent judicial authorities violations of provisions of domestic law giving effect to the principles mentioned in paragraph 1 of Article 1 of this Protocol.

    b. Each supervisory authority shall hear claims lodged by any person concerning the protection of his/her rights and fundamental freedoms with regard to the processing of personal data within its competence.

3. The supervisory authorities shall exercise their functions in complete independence.

4. Decisions of the supervisory authorities, which give rise to complaints, may be appealed against through the courts.

5. In accordance with the provisions of Chapter IV, and without prejudice to the provisions of Article 13 of the Convention, the supervisory authorities shall co-operate with one another to the extent necessary for the performance of their duties, in particular by exchanging all useful information.

Article 2 — Transborder flows of personal data to a recipient which is not subject to the jurisdiction of a Party to the Convention

1. Each Party shall provide for the transfer of personal data to a recipient that is subject to the jurisdiction of a State or organisation that is not Party to the Convention only if that State or organisation ensures an adequate level of protection for the intended data transfer.

2. By way of derogation from paragraph 1 of Article 2 of this Protocol, each Party may allow for the transfer of personal data:

    a. if domestic law provides for it because of:

        i.   specific interests of the data subject, or

        ii. legitimate prevailing interests, especially important public interests, or

    b. if safeguards, which can in particular result from contractual clauses, are provided by the controller responsible for the transfer and are found adequate by the competent authorities according to domestic law.

Article 3 — Final provisions

1. The provisions of Articles 1 and 2 of this Protocol shall be regarded by the Parties as additional articles to the Convention and all the provisions of the Convention shall apply accordingly.

2. This Protocol shall be open for signature by States Signatories to the Convention. After acceding to the Convention under the conditions provided by it, the European Communities may sign this Protocol. This Protocol is subject to ratification, acceptance or approval. A Signatory to this Protocol may not ratify, accept or approve it unless it has previously or simultaneously ratified, accepted or approved the Convention or has acceded to

it. Instruments of ratification, acceptance or approval of this Protocol shall be deposited with the Secretary General of the Council of Europe.

3. a. This Protocol shall enter into force on the first day of the month following the expiry of a period of three months after the date on which five of its Signatories have expressed their consent to be bound by the Protocol in accordance with the provisions of paragraph 2 of Article 3.

    b. In respect of any Signatory to this Protocol which subsequently expresses its consent to be bound by it, the Protocol shall enter into force on the first day of the month following the expiry of a period of three months after the date of deposit of the instrument of ratification, acceptance or approval.

4. a. After the entry into force of this Protocol, any State which has acceded to the Convention may also accede to the Protocol.

    b. Accession shall be effected by the deposit with the Secretary General of the Council of Europe of an instrument of accession, which shall take effect on the first day of the month following the expiry of a period of three months after the date of its deposit.

5. a. Any Party may at any time denounce this Protocol by means of a notification addressed to the Secretary General of the Council of Europe.

    b. Such denunciation shall become effective on the first day of the month following the expiry of a period of three months after the date of receipt of such notification by the Secretary General.

6. The Secretary General of the Council of Europe shall notify the member States of the Council of Europe, the European Communities and any other State which has acceded to this Protocol of:

    a. any signature;

    b. the deposit of any instrument of ratification, acceptance or approval;

    c. any date of entry into force of this Protocol in accordance with Article 3;

    d. any other act, notification or communication relating to this Protocol.

In witness whereof the undersigned, being duly authorised thereto, have signed this Protocol.

Done at [Strasbourg], this [8th day of November 2001], in English and in French, both texts being equally authentic, in a single copy which shall be deposited in the archives of the Council of Europe. The Secretary General of the Council of Europe shall transmit certified copies to each member State of the Council of Europe, the European Communities and any State invited to accede to the Convention.

The text will increase the protection of personal data and privacy by improving the original Convention of 1981 in two areas. First, it provides for the setting up of national supervisory authorities responsible for ensuring compliance with laws or regulations adopted in pursuance of the convention, concerning personal data protection and transborder data flows. The second improvement concerns transborder data flows to third countries. Data may only be transferred if the recipient State or international organisation is able to afford an adequate level of protection.

This Protocol will be open for signature in Strasbourg on 8 November 2001, on the occasion of the 109th Session of the Committee of Ministers of the Council of Europe.

The main aim of this Additional Protocol is to amend and supplement in certain areas, as between the Parties to the Protocol, the provisions of the Agreement, in particular with a view to increasing and improving the co-operation between Central Authorities, facilitating the communications between lawyers and applicants and improving the efficiency in the application of the Agreement by Central Authorities.

This Protocol will be open for signature in Strasbourg on 8 November 2001, on the occasion of the 109th Session of the Committee of Ministers of the Council of Europe.

Press Release on the Council of Europe Draft Convention on Cybercrime (April 27, 2000) is available at www.usdoj.gov/criminal/cybercrime/coepress.htm

Council of Europe Convention on Cybercrime Frequently Asked Questions

Background and Process

Q: What is the Council of Europe?

A: The Council of Europe ("CoE") (website: www.coe.int) consists of 41 member states, including all of the members of the European Union. It was established in 1949 primarily as a forum to uphold and strengthen human rights, and to promote democracy and the rule of law in Europe. Over the years, the CoE has been the negotiating forum for a number of conventions on criminal matters in which the United States has participated.

Q: What is the history of the Convention on Cyber Crime?

A: Since the late 1980s, the CoE has been working to address the growing international concern over the threats posed by hacking and other computer-related crimes. In 1989, it published a study and recommendations addressing the need for new substantive laws criminalizing certain conduct committed through computer networks. *See* Recommendation No. R. (89) 9. This was followed by a second study, published in 1995, which contained principles concerning the adequacy of criminal procedural laws in this area. *See* Recommendation No. R. (95) 13. (Both the 1989 and 1995 Recommendations are available at www.coe.int and www.cybercrime.gov.) Building on the principles developed in the 1989 and 1995 reports, in 1997 the CoE established a Committee of Experts on Crime in Cyberspace (PC-CY) to begin drafting a binding convention to facilitate international cooperation in the investigation and prosecution of computer crimes.

Q: What role has the United States played in drafting the Council of Europe Convention?

A: The United States was invited to participate as an "observer" in both the 1989 and 1995 Recommendations, as well as in the development of the Convention on Cyber Crime. Because of the vulnerability of the United States to cyber crime, the benefits to be gained from a well-crafted instrument focused on increasing international cooperation in this area, its desire to help shape such an important instrument, and the importance of the information technology sector, the United States accepted the CoE's invitation to participate in the Convention negotiations. The other non-CoE States participating in the negotiations are: Canada, Japan, and South Africa. By virtue of their having participated in the Convention's elaboration, the United States and these other non-CoE States will have the right to become parties to the Convention if they choose to do so.

The United States, represented by the Department of Justice and the Department of State, in close consultation with other U.S. government agencies, has actively participated in the negotiations in both the drafting and plenary sessions, working closely with both CoE and non-CoE member States. Because the provisions in the draft Convention are generally adopted by consensus both in the drafting and plenary groups, rather than by member state vote, the United States has had a real voice in the drafting process.

Q: What benefits would this Convention bring for the United States?

A: The United States is heavily dependent on computers that are networked, and it offers many targets across every sector of society. Left unchallenged, computer crime poses a serious threat to the health and safety of our citizens, and may stifle the Internet's power as a tool to communicate, engage in commerce, and expand people's educational opportunities around the globe. Thus, the United States has much to gain from a strong, well-crafted multilateral instrument that removes or minimizes the many procedural and jurisdictional obstacles that can delay or endanger international investigations and prosecutions of computer-related crimes.

As the February 2000 denial-of-service attacks on prominent commercial Internet sites and the recent dissemination of the "I Love You" virus have taught us, cyber crime is a serious international problem that requires an international solution. Recent surveys suggest that these types of computer crimes will continue to increase both in number and severity over the coming years, particularly since cyber criminals often have access to the newest technology, can reach vast numbers of victims, and can readily avoid detection. A survey conducted by the CERT (Computer Emergency Response Team) Coordination Center at Carnegie-Mellon University indicates a 183 percent increase in the number of computer attack incidents from 1998 to 1999. In addition, the Spring 2000 Computer Security Institute ("CSI")/FBI Computer Crime and Security Survey projected monetary losses exceeding $265,000,000 in 2000, up from $100,000,000 in 1997 (in all likelihood, these numbers are significantly underestimated because, while 74 percent of survey respondents acknowledged financial losses due to computer crimes, only 42 percent could quantify those losses). A more recent study by Computer Economics, an independent research institute, indicates that the dissemination of the "I Love You" virus, and subsequent copycat viruses, already resulted in $6.7 billion in damages to businesses worldwide this year. According to Computer Economics, virus attacks also resulted in more than $12.1 billion in damages to businesses during 1999.

In addition to the damage resulting from attacks on computer networks, criminals around the globe also are increasingly using computers to reach across borders to commit traditional crimes, including fraud, copyright infringement, distribution of child pornography, and other crimes. For example, in 1998, Vladimir Levin was convicted of hacking into a major international bank from Russia and transferring $12 million out of accounts located around the world. More recently, one study estimates that credit card fraud cost merchants $400 million in 1999. The Business Software Alliance ("BSA") also estimates that software piracy cost the U.S. some 109,000 jobs and $991 million in tax revenue in 1998; moreover, Computer Economics research shows that, by 2005, over $112 billion in software, music, video, and text will be pirated over the Internet. The Internet also has made it much easier for pedophiles to distribute child pornography and lure children. Prosecutions of child pornography and luring cases in the United States have increased by 10 percent every year since 1995; in 1999, the U.S. Department of Justice prosecuted over 400 such cases, many of which were international in scope.

Computer crimes that target our critical infrastructure, such as utilities, energy, transportation, and communications service companies, pose a particularly significant threat to the public. For example, in one case, a juvenile was prosecuted under federal law for disabling a telephone company computer that supported vital communications services to an airport; as a result of the computer intrusion, an FAA control tower was shut down for more than six hours. In addition, our military and political institutions are targeted by intruders daily. The United States government has expended tremendous resources over the last several years investigating such incidents and securing our sensitive networks.

The Convention breaks new ground by being the first multilateral agreement drafted specifically to address the problems posed by the international nature of computer crime. Although we believe the vast bulk of the obligations and powers contemplated by the draft Convention are already provided for under United States law, the Convention makes progress in this area by (1) requiring signatory countries to establish certain substantive offenses in the area of computer crime, (2) requiring parties to adopt domestic procedural laws to investigate computer crimes, and (3) providing a solid basis for international law enforcement cooperation in combating crime committed through computer systems. If the United States were to become a party to this Convention, it would directly benefit by having better methods of obtaining international assistance from other parties in computer-related crime cases, particularly because the other parties to the Convention would have similar minimum definitions of computer crimes and the domestic procedural tools needed to investigate those crimes.

Q: When will the Convention be completed and opened for signature?

A: The expected schedule as of this writing (late November 2000) is as follows: The terms of reference for the committee of experts to finish drafting the Convention expire December 31, 2000. A final plenary session is scheduled for December. It is also likely that additional experts' meetings will convene in early 2001 to, inter alia, review comments provided by the CoE Parliamentary Assembly, finalize the Convention's text, and complete drafting of the explanatory memorandum (the authoritative interpretation of the Convention's text). The Convention and the explanatory memorandum will then be forwarded to the Council of Europe's Committee on Crime Problems, and thereafter to its Committee of Ministers for consideration before it is opened for signature to Council members, other States participating in the negotiations, and any other States that have been invited to accede to the Convention. On the present schedule, the Convention could be opened for signature before the end of 2001.

Q: Has the United States already committed to sign this Convention once it is completed?

A: The United States will make a determination whether to sign the Convention only after the drafting work on the Convention has been completed and it is ready for signature. At that time, the Administration will assess whether it is in the interests of the United States to become a party to the Convention and whether any implementing legislation would be required.

Q: Will implementing legislation be required for the U.S. to join the Convention?

A: The Convention is still being drafted, and therefore is subject to change both in the final meetings in the committee of experts and during the subsequent process described above. However, we do not currently anticipate that implementing legislation would be required for the U.S. to become a Party.

First, the U.S. delegation has worked hard to balance attentiveness to the suggestions of other countries with respect for the strengths of current U.S. law. As a result, the central provisions of the draft Convention are consistent with the existing framework of U.S. law and procedure. Second, the terms of the draft Convention do permit us some flexibility if other provisions do not conform completely to our current law. This is because, in accordance with traditional CoE practice, Parties to the Convention will be permitted to take reservations on a limited number of specified articles, or parts thereof. For example, we would likely take a partial reservation to the Jurisdiction article (Article 23, Draft 24REV2) because the U.S. does not as a general matter assert jurisdiction over crimes committed by U.S. citizens abroad.

We are currently aware of three additional areas where U.S. law may not be as broad as the draft Convention. First, U.S. federal law (18 U.S.C. 1030) criminalizes intentional destruction only of specified types of data or where the amount of damage exceeds $5,000; our CoE colleagues have disfavored a monetary damage threshold for data interference (see Article 4). Second, while U.S. federal law reaches possession and trafficking in unauthorized access and interception devices, the Convention will likely also reach persons who, with the intent to commit one of the substantive offenses under the Convention, possess or traffic in other devices and programs (such as viruses) designed to damage systems or data (see Article 6). Third, under current U.S. law, a small set of copyright infringements covered in the draft Convention (see Article 10) are generally enforced through civil remedies.

Legislation proposed by the Administration earlier this year included an amendment to remove the monetary damage requirement in 18 U.S.C. 1030, and we understand that there may be interest in amending current law to reach illicit possession and trafficking in viruses and other destructive programs or devices. However, the U.S.'s ability to sign or ratify the Convention does not necessarily depend on securing such amendments, since we would likely be able to take, as an alternative, limited reservations in these three areas so that our obligations under the Convention would be consistent with U.S. law.

Q: What can be done at this point to comment on the Convention and recommend changes?

A: If you have concerns about the provisions of the draft Convention, both the CoE and the United States government want to hear about it. Part of the reason the United States encouraged the early release of the draft Convention and now supports prompt release of newer versions is to give the public the opportunity to comment on the provisions and allow us to seek changes where necessary to improve and clarify the terms of the Convention. Over the course of the last seven months, we have actively engaged in dialogue with industry groups, privacy groups, and other interested individuals, and we will consider all comments we receive as we continue to participate in the drafting of the Convention and the explanatory memorandum. Comments should be submitted to the Council of Europe directly through www.coe.int and to the U.S. Department of Justice using the contact information available at www.cybercrime.gov.

Structure of the Convention

Q: Because the Convention is drafted at a general level and leaves many of the details and safeguards up to national law, won't the differences in implementation actually undermine the goal of harmonization and lead to less certainty in this area?

A: The Convention would not itself create substantive criminal law offenses or detailed legal procedures. Parties agree to ensure that their domestic laws criminalize several categories of conduct and establish the procedural tools necessary to investigate such crimes under their own national laws. It is anticipated that Parties will discharge their international obligations consistent with their particular domestic legal systems. The Convention is thus typical of the way multilateral law enforcement conventions are drafted, including in the United Nations and the Council of Europe.

Q: How is the term "without right," which appears in all of the substantive offense provisions (Articles 2–12), intended to apply?

A: As the explanatory memorandum to the Convention will clarify, the term "without right" has a broad meaning and is intended to take into account well-established principles regarding criminal culpability, including application of legal defenses and justifications, contract law, and traditional legislative exemptions. The specific demarcation between conduct that is "with right" and that which is "without right" is, in general, left to national law. Thus, if conduct is "legitimate" under a particular signatory's national law, then it will not be "without right" under the same law.

For example, the Convention does not purport to exhaustively define the line between what sorts of "interception" are lawful and which are not under Article 3 ("Illegal Interception"). Therefore, nothing in this Convention would change the U.S. wiretap statute (18 U.S.C. 2511(2)(a)(I)), which specifically allows monitoring by a service provider of traffic on its own network undertaken to protect its rights and property. Exactly what sorts of interception are "with right" and which "without right" in a particular signatory country would continue to be determined under national law.

Substantive Offense and Domestic Procedural Provisions

Q: Article 6, Misuse of Devices: The Convention purports to outlaw illegal devices on the Internet. Doesn't this provision go too far by essentially banning network diagnostic tools or data deletion tools that have a legitimate use?

A: Nothing in the draft Convention suggests that states should criminalize the legitimate use of network security and diagnostic tools. On the contrary, Article 6 obligates parties to criminalize the trafficking and possession of "hacker" tools *only* where such conduct is (i) intentional, (ii) "without right," and (iii) *done with the intent to commit an offense* of the type described in Articles 2-5 of the Convention. Because of the criminal intent element, fears that such laws would criminalize legitimate computer security, research, or education practices are unfounded. Moreover, paragraph 2 of the Article 6 makes clear that legitimate scientific research and system security practices, for example, are not criminal under the Article. Finally, in practice, the existing U.S. laws that already criminalize possession and trafficking in "access" or "interception" tools (as opposed to "damage" tools) with similar criminal intent have not led to investigations of network security personnel.

Q: Article 9, Child Pornography: The Convention criminalizes images that "appear" to represent children engaged in sexual conduct. Is this constitutional? Does it effectively prohibit certain adult pornography?

A: Child pornography on the Internet is an extremely serious problem, and one on which all the negotiating States have agreed to adopt a strong position. The Convention is intended to cover virtual child pornography because it is nearly impossible to distinguish it from real child pornography, though in fact few instances of virtual child pornography have been found. Virtual child pornography, like real child pornography, can be and has been used to entice minors into sexual relationships and is often traded for real child pornography. We believe this provision of the Convention is consistent with United States law in this area.

Q: **I've read news reports that state that the Council of Europe Convention will require Internet service providers to collect and retain data, adopt mandatory business practices, and build certain technical capabilities into their infrastructures. Is this accurate?**

A: The Convention does not contain any mandatory retention provisions or requirements that service providers collect or maintain categories of data generally; nor does it require certain technical capabilities.

First, it is important to distinguish between data *retention requirements*, which would require providers to collect and keep all or a large portion of a provider's traffic as a routine matter, and *preservation requirements*, which enable law enforcement authorities, during the course of a criminal investigation, to instruct a service provider to set aside *specified* data that is *already in the service provider's possession*. There is no data retention in the Convention; there is, however, a data preservation provision. Preservation is not a new idea; it has been the law in the United States for nearly five years. 18 U.S.C. 2703(f) requires an electronic communications service provider to "take all necessary steps to preserve records and other evidence in its possession pending the issuance of a court order or other process" upon "the request of a governmental entity." This applies in practice only to reasonably small amounts of specified data identified as relevant to a particular case where the service provider already has control over that data. Similarly, as with traditional subpoena powers, issuance of an order to an individual or corporation to produce specified data during the course of an investigation carries with it an obligation not to delete or destroy information falling within the scope of that order when that information is in the person's possession or control.

Finally, the Convention does not require any particular architecture or capability; nothing in the Convention states that a service provider must be able to obtain evidence that it is not technically capable of collecting. However, while there are no mandatory technical requirements placed on service providers, there is no prohibition on States imposing such requirements if necessary under their legal systems.

Q: **Because there are no exemptions from liability for service providers, are service providers going to be held criminally liable for failing to monitor customer or user content, or for the criminal actions of their employees?**

A: Nothing in the Convention requires service providers to monitor content. Under the Convention, service providers do not face criminal liability if they have *only* an "intent to transmit data" without knowledge of what the data contains. Once a provider becomes specifically aware that its system is being used to transmit or store criminal content, instructions, etc., questions of liability may arise.

For example, Article 11 on aiding and abetting contemplates liability where the person who commits one of the substantive offenses in the Convention is aided by another person who shares the mental state required for the commission of the crime. However, individuals or legal persons (including service providers) that do not share the objective of committing the crime cannot incur liability through unknowing incidental assistance provided to a criminal actor. Indeed, the Convention explicitly requires that the actor intentionally aid or abet a crime under the convention.

In addition, Article 12, governing corporate liability, restates the traditional corporate liability principle that if a person with significant authority within a corporation intentionally undertakes or, through a lack of supervision, permits the undertaking of criminal activity for the corporation's benefit, the corporation may face criminal, civil or administrative liability. This Article is based on similar provisions in other multilateral law enforcement treaties and does not go beyond current U.S. law governing the vicarious liability of corporations. In fact, the Convention's liability requirements would apply to a more limited group of persons than under U.S. federal law.

Internet as the Scene of Crime

On May 29, 2000, Assistant Attorney General James K. Robinson spoke at the International Computer Crime Conference in Oslo, Norway, on "Internet as the Scene of Crime." His speech addressed the types of computer crime that exist, as well as the legal and technical challenges that face law enforcement and prosecutors in their efforts to combat this crime. The speech is available at www.usdoj.gov/criminal/cybercrime/roboslo.htm.

Challenges Presented to Law Enforcement by High-Tech and Computer Criminals

Attorney General Janet Reno's speech to Senior Experts representing the G-7 on January 21, 1997
On January 21, 1997, Attorney General Janet Reno spoke to Senior Experts representing the G-7 group of leading industrialized nations (now, with the inclusion of Russia, known as The Eight). The Attorney General's speech addressed the challenges presented to law enforcement by high-tech and computer criminals, and she suggested a number ways in which the United States and its allies can respond to this global threat. Her speech is available at www.usdoj.gov/criminal/cybercrime/agfranc.htm.

Problems of Criminal Procedural Law Connected with Information Technology

Council of Europe Recommendation 95(13)

In September 1995, the Council of Europe adopted eighteen (18) recommendations relating to problems of criminal procedural law connected with information technology. These recommendations are available at www.usdoj.gov/criminal/cybercrime/crycoe.htm.

Combating High-Tech and Computer-Related Crime

Meeting of the Justice and Interior Ministers of The Eight, on December 9 and 10, 1997, in Washington, D.C.

On December 9 and 10, 1997, Attorney General Reno convened a first-ever meeting on crime of her counterparts from The Eight (formerly known as the G-7 plus Russia) countries: England, France, Germany, Italy, Russia, Japan, and Canada. In all, sixteen Ministers and Deputy Ministers attended.

The subject of the meeting was transnational organized crime, and its focus was on combatting high-tech and computer-related crime. On December 10, the Ministers adopted a Communique which contained 10 Principles and 10 Action Items relating to high-tech crime. This document is the outgrowth of the work of the Subgroup of The Eight on High-tech Crime, which met five times in 1997, and is working to develop the tools that law enforcement needs to locate and identify computer criminals, and gather evidence of their crimes so that they may be brought to justice. The 10 Principles they adopted are given below:

Principles to Combat High-Tech Crime

1. There must be no safe havens for those who abuse information technologies.
2. Investigation and prosecution of international high-tech crimes must be coordinated among all concerned States, regardless of where harm has occurred.
3. Law enforcement personnel must be trained and equipped to address high-tech crimes.
4. Legal systems must protect the confidentiality, integrity, and availability of data and systems from unauthorized impairment and ensure that serious abuse is penalized.
5. Legal systems should permit the preservation of and quick access to electronic data, which are often critical to the successful investigation of crime.
6. Mutual assistance regimes must ensure the timely gathering and exchange of evidence in cases involving international high-tech crime.
7. Transborder electronic access bylaw enforcement to publicly available (open source) information does not require authorization from the State where the data resides.
8. Forensic standards for retrieving and authenticating electronic data for use in criminal investigations and prosecutions must be developed and employed.

9. To the extent practicable, information and telecommunications systems should be designed to help prevent and detect network abuse, and should also facilitate the tracing of criminals and the collection of evidence.

10. Work in this area should be coordinated with the work of other relevant international forums to ensure against duplication of efforts.

Action Plan to Combat High-Tech Crime

In support of the Principles, we are directing our officials to:

1. Use our established network of knowledgeable personnel to ensure a timely, effective response to transnational high-tech cases and designate a point-of-contact who is available on a twenty-four hour basis.

2. Take appropriate steps to ensure that a sufficient number of trained and equipped law enforcement personnel are allocated to the task of combating high-tech crime and assisting law enforcement agencies of other States.

3. Review our legal systems to ensure that they appropriately criminalize abuses of telecommunications and computer systems and promote the investigation of high-tech crimes.

4. Consider issues raised by high-tech crimes, where relevant, when negotiating mutual assistance agreements or arrangements.

5. Continue to examine and develop workable solutions regarding: the preservation of evidence prior to the execution of a request for mutual assistance; transborder searches; and computer searches of data where the location of that data is unknown.

6. Develop expedited procedures for obtaining traffic data from all communications carriers in the chain of a communication and to study ways to expedite the passing of this data internationally.

7. Work jointly with industry to ensure that new technologies facilitate our effort to combat high-tech crime by preserving and collecting critical evidence.

8. Ensure that we can, in urgent and appropriate cases, accept and respond to mutual assistance requests relating to high-tech crime by expedited but reliable means of communications, including voice, fax, or e-mail, with written confirmation to follow where required.

9. Encourage internationally recognized standards-making bodies in the fields of telecommunications and information technologies to continue providing the public and private sectors with standards for reliable and secure telecommunications and data processing technologies.

10. Develop and employ compatible forensic standards for retrieving and authenticating electronic data for use in criminal investigations and prosecutions.

Vienna International Child Pornography Conference

Deputy Attorney General Eric Holder's welcoming remarks, September 29, 1999

On September 29, 1999, Deputy Attorney General Eric Holder gave remarks on "Combating Child Pornography on the Internet" at Vienna, Austria International Child Pornography Conference. The conference sought to combat child pornography and exploitation on the Internet and was based on existing international obligations and commitments for the protection of children, including the Convention on the Rights of the Child. The conference built and acted upon commitments undertaken at the Stockholm World Congress against the Commercial Sexual Exploitation of Children (1996) and ongoing initiatives in many countries and regions.

Remarks of U.S. Deputy Attorney General Eric Holder on "Combating Pornography on the Internet" at the Vienna, Austria International Child Pornography Conference (September 29, 1999), are available at www.usdoj.gov/criminal/cybercrime/dagceos.htm

OECD Guidelines for Cryptography Policy

In early 1996 the Organization for Economic Cooperation and Development (OECD) initiated a project on cryptography policy by forming the Ad hoc Group of Experts on Cryptography Policy Guidelines. The Ad hoc Group was charged with drafting Guidelines for Cryptography Policy ("Guidelines") to identify the issues which should be taken into consideration in the formulation of cryptography policies at the national and international level. The Ad hoc Group had a one year mandate to accomplish this task and it completed its work in December 1996. Thereafter, the Guidelines were adopted as a Recommendation of the Council of the OECD on 27 March 1997.

Fighting Cybercrime: What are the Challenges Facing Europe?

Deputy Assistant Attorney General DiGregory's Remarks before the European Parliament on International Cooperation in Combating Cybercrime, September 19, 2000

On September 19, 2000 Deputy Assistant Attorney General Kevin DiGregory spoke before a conference in the European Parliament that was entitled "Fighting Cybercrime: What are the Challenges Facing Europe?" DiGregory discussed the Transatlantic perspective on combating cybercrime, including international cooperation.

Deputy Assistant Attorney General DiGregory's Remarks before the European Parliament (September 19, 2000) are available at www.usdoj.gov/criminal/cybercrime/EUremarks.htm.

Chapter 11

Privacy Issues in the High-Tech Context

The Department of Justice Privacy Council

On December 7, 1998, Attorney General Janet Reno established the Department of Justice Privacy Council. In her memorandum to heads of components of the Justice Department, the Attorney General cites new challenges that have arisen as a result of the proliferation of new technologies as the main reason for the establishment of the Council. The purpose of the Privacy Council is to address privacy concerns in a comprehensive and coordinated way.

Law Enforcement Concerns Related to Computerized Databases

The Computer Crime and Intellectual Property Section of the Department of Justice submitted comments in response to the request of the Federal Trade Commission ("FTC") for comments on its workshop on Consumer Information Privacy and its Database Study. The Department is deeply concerned about the safety and security of American citizens. The Department is vigilant to take appropriate measures to guard their privacy while using all the resources at its disposal, including information resources, to investigate and prosecute violations of the federal criminal law. The comments are listed in Exhibit 1.

Exhibit 1.   CCIPS Comments as Submitted to the FTC Workshop on Consumer Information Privacy and Database Study

---

Secretary, Federal Trade Commission

Room H-159

Sixth Street & Pennsylvania Ave., NW

Washington, D.C. 20580

Re: Database Study — Comment, P974806

Database Workshop — Request to Participate, P974806

To the Federal Trade Commission:

The Department of Justice ("Department") hereby submits these comments in response to the request of the Federal Trade Commission ("FTC") for comments on its workshop on Consumer Information Privacy and its Database Study. Pursuant to the FTC's request, the Department requests the opportunity to participate in the Database Workshop by submission of these comments.

The Department, of which Federal Bureau of Investigation is a part, is an executive branch agency charged with federal law enforcement responsibilities. The Department is deeply concerned about the safety and security of American citizens. The Department is vigilant to take appropriate measures to guard their privacy while using all the resources at its disposal, including information resources, to investigate and prosecute violations of the federal criminal law.

The FTC invited comment about the collection, compilation, sale, and use of computerized databases that provide sensitive consumer identifying information. Public Workshop on Consumer Information Privacy, 62 Fed. Reg. 10271, 10272-73 (1997) In particular, Question 1.24 asks about federal laws regulating such activity. Question 1.26 asks whether additional regulations or laws are necessary or appropriate.

No federal law regulates such activity on a general basis. The FTC is familiar with the scope and limitations of the Fair Credit Reporting Act, 15 U.S.C. § 1681 *et seq.,* which imposes restrictions on the furnishing of a "consumer report" by a "consumer reporting agency." FTC policy has been to treat market lists from a credit reporting database based on such "identifying information" as name, zip code, age, social security number or "substantially similar identifiers," as not rising to the level of a "consumer report." *See Trans Union Corp. v. FTC,* 81 F.3d 228, 232 (D.C. Cir. 1996) (discussing Letter from FTC to TRW, September 24, 1992).

Other federal laws are subject to their own limitations. The Privacy Act, for example, applies to government entities only. 5 U.S.C. § 552a. See 5 U.S.C. § 552(f) (definition of "agency"). The Social Security Act has an analogous provision prohibiting disclosure of Social Security account numbers and related records by "authorized persons," who are defined as including only government employees. 42 U.S.C. § 405(c)(2)(C)(vii). The Social Security Act also provides penalties for fraud related to procurement of Social Security number information. 42 U.S.C. § 1307(b).

Exhibit 1. CCIPS Comments as Submitted to the FTC Workshop on Consumer Information Privacy and Database Study (Continued)

On an ad hoc basis, Congress has occasionally protected privacy of records with regard to particular records or particular industries. These protections relate to financial records, 12 U.S.C. § 3401-34, drivers licenses, 18 U.S.C. § 2721, wire and electronic communications records, 18 U.S.C. § 2703, video rentals, 18 U.S.C. § 2710-2711, and telephone network customer information, 42 U.S.C. § 222.

These restrictions on use of sensitive records are important to protect American citizens. They serve not only to protect the dignity of Americans by keeping their personal information private, but also to deter identity fraud and other kinds of fraud. Deterring fraud is an important federal law enforcement interest. See, e.g., 18 U.S.C. § 1002 (possession of false papers to defraud the United States), 18 U.S.C. § 1028 (fraud and related activity in connection with identification documents), 18 U.S.C. § 1029 (fraud and related activity in connection with access devices). See also 18 U.S.C. § 1341 (mail fraud); 18 U.S.C. § 1343 (wire fraud); 18 U.S.C. § 1344 (bank fraud). This concern takes on added significance in the context of computers, where access often occurs without face-to-face interactions. See 18 U.S.C. § 1030.

Congress has repeatedly recognized that the needs for protecting privacy and deterring fraud must be balanced by the need for effective law enforcement. All of the industry-specific provisions mentioned above permit reasonable access by law enforcement. See, e.g., 12 U.S.C. § 3413(a)-(o) (financial records); 18 U.S.C. § 2703(c)(1)(C) (local and long distance telephone toll billing records); 18 U.S.C. § 2710(b)(2)(C) (video tape rental records).

In the absence of incentives to the contrary, collection, compilation, sale, and use of computerized databases that provide sensitive consumer identifying information will likely proliferate with the rise of electronic commerce and other cyberspace activity. This increase would be driven both on the supply side and on the demand side of the market. Because electronic commerce is conducted on computers, the supply of consumer identifying information stored on computers in an easily accessible format will increase as use of electronic commerce increases.

The demand for this information is likely to be potent because of its marketing value for those companies who collect it, both for evaluating preferences of particular customers and for estimating the appeal of particular products and services. This information will also be sought by other companies who would use it for similar purposes. In fact, as face-to-face interactions decrease, companies will increasingly rely on such information to "profile" market segments.

The proliferation of these computerized databases will simplify the perpetration of many kinds of fraud, including identity fraud. The Department is concerned about this potential.

Law enforcement is also faced with concerns about the decrease in direct interactions between individuals. The rise of electronic commerce will not only facilitate crimes such as money laundering, 18 U.S.C. § 1956, but it will also affect the availability of investigative leads and evidence. Computerized databases will become increasingly important in the investigation and prosecution of all kinds of crime. No longer will it be possible to interview bystanders about the whereabouts of an individual. Instead, crimes will have to be traced electronically.

Exhibit 1.   CCIPS Comments as Submitted to the FTC Workshop on Consumer Information Privacy and Database Study (Continued)

Society's continual recognition of the need for reasonable law enforcement access to otherwise protected records should be preserved in the area of computerized databases. A desire for anonymity in the world of electronic commerce should not be used as a cover to avoid accountability. Policy makers must be vigilant for unintended consequences of privacy laws that, if written without procedures for access by law enforcement, could severely hinder public safety efforts. Of course, the procedures for government access should be tailored to the type of information at issue and ensure that privacy is appropriately protected.

The Department appreciates the opportunity to share these views with the FTC.

Respectfully submitted,

Scott Charney
Chief, Computer Crime and Intellectual Property Section

Enforcing the Criminal Wiretap Statute

The Computer Crime and Intellectual Property Section helps to protect the privacy of Americans by enforcing the criminal wiretap statute, 18 U.S.C. § 2511. One well-publicized interception involved a conference call in which the Speaker of the House Newt Gingrich participated. The couple that intercepted the call pleaded guilty on April 25, 1997, as is described in the press release at www.usdoj.gov/criminal/cybercrime/177crm.htm.

On September 8, 1998, a Sheriff in North Carolina pled guilty to wiretapping and recording a high school teacher's telephone calls, which the Sheriff intended to use to force the teacher out of his job. The information is available at www.usdoj.gov/criminal/cybercrime/sheriff.htm.

Referring Potential Privacy Violations to the Department of Justice for Investigation and Prosecution

Recently, Deputy Attorney General Eric Holder wrote a memo to the Inspector General community encouraging them to refer potential violations of federal privacy statutes to the Department of Justice for investigation and prosecution. The letter provides an overview of federal privacy laws, including the Privacy Act, and explains the sentencing guidelines associated with particular violations. The letter further directs that all suspected 1030(a)(2) offenses should be referred to the Computer Crime and Intellectual Property Section. The information is available at www.usdoj.gov/criminal/cybercrime/igprivacy.htm.

Testimony on Digital Privacy

On September 6, 2000, Deputy Assistant Attorney General Kevin V. DiGregory testified before Senate Committee on the Judiciary about the FBI computer program "Carnivore." He addressed the imperative of protecting individual privacy on the Internet from unwarranted governmental intrusion, and the critical role the Department plays to ensure that the Internet is a safe and secure place for our citizens. [See http://www.cybercrime.gov/kvd_0906b.htm.]

On September 6, 2000, Deputy Assistant Attorney General Kevin V. DiGregory testified before the Subcommittee on the Constitution of the House Committee on the Judiciary on the subject of the two new bills proposed by members of the Subcommittee: H.R. 5018, "The Electronic Communications Privacy Act of 2000," and H.R. 4987, "The Digital Privacy Act of 2000." His testimony detailed the ways in which technological advances challenge law enforcement ability to fulfill its duty to protect public safety and discussed the serious concerns raised by the introduced bills. [See http://www.cybercrime.gov/kvd_060900.htm.]

Kevin V. DiGregory, Deputy Assistant Attorney General, testified before the Subcommittee on the Constitution of the House Committee on the Judiciary on July 24, 2000. This statement addressed the law enforcement tool "Carnivore" and its impact on Internet privacy and the Fourth Amendment. [See http://www.cyber-crime.gov/carnivore.htm.]

On April 6, 2000, Deputy Assistant Attorney General Kevin V. DiGregory testified before the Subcommittee on the Constitution of the House Committee on the Judiciary on the subject of the Fourth Amendment and the Internet. His testimony detailed the ways in which the Fourth Amendment protects the privacy of Internet users. Also covered were the new technical challenges that face law enforcement and possible solutions for overcoming these challenges. [See http://www.cybercrime.gov/inter4th.htm.]

On March 27, 2000, John T. Bentivoglio, Special Counsel for Health Care Fraud and Chief Privacy Officer at the U.S. Department of Justice, gave remarks on the prosecution of health care fraud and the protection of health care privacy on the Internet. His speech focused on the federal government's fraud, consumer protection, and privacy protection efforts as they relate to the Internet healthcare industry. [The information is available at www.usdoj.gov/criminal/cybercrime/healthsp.htm.]

On May 27, 1999, the Subcommittee on Courts and Intellectual Property of the Judiciary Committee, United States House of Representatives, convened a hearing on medical records privacy. John T. Bentivoglio, the Justice Department's Chief Privacy Officer, testified before the committee on the subject of digital privacy in general. The testimony outlines the Department's privacy initiatives, including the work of the Privacy Council and comments on industry-led privacy safeguarding measures. The testimony also addresses problems that result from failures to protect privacy, from Internet fraud to identity theft. [The information is available at www.usdoj.gov/criminal/cybercrime/digpriv.htm.]

Chapter 12

Critical Infrastructure Protection

Our national defense, public safety, economic prosperity, and quality of life have long depended on the efficient delivery of essential services — energy, banking and finance, transportation, vital human services, and telecommunications. The rapid growth and integration of the telecommunications infrastructure has made all of these sectors interdependent, and in the process, created unprecedented risks. CCIPS has long been involved in investigations of cyber-attacks; the entire federal sector is now organizing to address these new threats.

The Department of Justice and the FBI rose to the challenge by creating the National Infrastructure Protection Center (NIPC) in early 1998. On May 22, 1998, the President issued Presidential Decision Directive 63 (PDD-63), which called for the creation of a national plan to protect the services on which we depend daily.

Attorney General Janet Reno's Speech on Critical Infrastructure Protection

On February 27, 1998, Attorney General Janet Reno addressed the Conference on Critical Infrastructure Protection, held at Lawrence Livermore Laboratories, in Livermore, California, to announce the formation of the National Infrastructure Protection Center (NIPC) at FBI Headquarters in Washington, D.C. The Center is a joint government and private sector partnership, including representatives from the relevant agencies of federal, state, and local governments, and the private sector, to address the daunting challenge of protecting the critical infrastructures on which our nation depends. The NIPC is designated as the national focal point for threat assessment, warning, investigation, and response to attacks on the critical infrastructures. The concept for the NIPC grew out of the Report of the President's Commission on Critical Infrastructure Protection [see "Protecting the Nation's

Critical Infrastructures: Presidential Decision Directive 63" below] and from the government's experiences in dealing with illegal intrusions into government and private sector computer systems over the last five years.

Protecting the Nation's Critical Infrastructures: Presidential Decision Directive 63

On May 22, 1998, President Clinton announced two new directives designed to strengthen the Nation's defenses against terrorism and other unconventional threats: Presidential Decision Directives (PDD) 62 and 63. PDD-63 focuses specifically on protecting the Nation's critical infrastructures from both physical and "cyber" attack. These attacks may come from foreign governments, foreign and domestic terrorist organizations, and foreign and domestic criminal organizations. The NIPC is a part of the broader framework of government efforts established by PDD-63.

This Presidential Directive builds on the recommendations of the President's Commission on Critical Infrastructure Protection. In October 1997 the Commission issued its report, calling for a national effort to assure the security of the United States' increasingly vulnerable and interconnected infrastructures, such as telecommunications, banking and finance, energy, transportation, and essential government services.

Presidential Decision Directive 63 is the culmination of an intense, interagency effort to evaluate those recommendations and produce a workable and innovative framework for critical infrastructure protection. The President's policy:

- Sets a goal of a reliable, interconnected, and secure information system infrastructure by the year 2003, and significantly increased security for government systems by the year 2000, by:
  — Immediately establishing a national center to warn of and respond to attacks
  — Building the capability to protect critical infrastructures from intentional acts by 2003
  — Addresses the cyber and physical infrastructure vulnerabilities of the Federal Government by requiring each department and agency to work to reduce its exposure to new threats
- Requires the Federal Government to serve as a model to the rest of the country for how infrastructure protection is to be attained;
- Seeks the voluntary participation of private industry to meet common goals for protecting our critical systems through public–private partnerships;
- Protects privacy rights and seeks to utilize market forces. It is meant to strengthen and protect the nation's economic power, not to stifle it.
- Seeks full participation and input from the Congress.

PDD-63 sets up a new structure to deal with this important challenge:

- A *National Coordinator* whose scope will include not only critical infrastructure but also foreign terrorism and threats of domestic mass destruction (including biological weapons) because attacks on the U.S. may not come labeled in neat jurisdictional boxes;

- The *National Infrastructure Protection Center* (NIPC) at the FBI which will fuse representatives from FBI, DOD, USSS, Energy, Transportation, the Intelligence Community, and the private sector in an unprecedented attempt at information sharing among agencies in collaboration with the private sector. The NIPC will also provide the principal means of facilitating and coordinating the Federal Government's response to an incident, mitigating attacks, investigating threats and monitoring reconstitution efforts;
- An *Information Sharing and Analysis Center* (ISAC) is encouraged to be set up by the private sector, in cooperation with the federal government;
- A *National Infrastructure Assurance Council* drawn from private sector leaders and state/local officials to provide guidance to the policy formulation of a National Plan;
- The *Critical Infrastructure Assurance Office* will provide support to the National Coordinator's work with government agencies and the private sector in developing a national plan. The office will also help coordinate a national education and awareness program, and legislative and public affairs.

The Clinton Administration's Policy on Critical Infrastructure Protection: Presidential Decision Directive 63

This White Paper explains key elements of the Clinton Administration's policy on critical infrastructure protection. It is intended for dissemination to all interested parties in both the private and public sectors. It will also be used in U.S. Government professional education institutions, such as the National Defense University and the National Foreign Affairs Training Center, for course work and exercises on interagency practices and procedures. Wide dissemination of this unclassified White Paper is encouraged by all agencies of the U.S. Government.

A Growing Potential Vulnerability

The United States possesses both the world's strongest military and its largest national economy. Those two aspects of our power are mutually reinforcing and dependent. They are also increasingly reliant upon certain critical infrastructures and upon cyber-based information systems.

Critical infrastructures are those physical and cyber-based systems essential to the minimum operations of the economy and government. They include, but are not limited to, telecommunications, energy, banking and finance, transportation, water systems and emergency services, both governmental and private. Many of the nation's critical infrastructures have historically been physically and logically separate systems that had little interdependence. As a result of advances in information technology and the necessity of improved efficiency, however, these infrastructures have become increasingly automated and interlinked. These same advances have created new vulnerabilities to equipment failures, human error, weather and other natural causes, and physical and cyber attacks. Addressing these vulnerabilities will necessarily require flexible, evolutionary approaches that span both the public and private sectors, and protect both domestic and international security.

Because of our military strength, future enemies, whether nations, groups or individuals, may seek to harm us in non-traditional ways including attacks within the United States. Our economy is increasingly reliant upon interdependent and cyber-supported infrastructures and non-traditional attacks on our infrastructure and information systems may be capable of significantly harming both our military power and our economy.

President's Intent

It has long been the policy of the United States to assure the continuity and viability of critical infrastructures. President Clinton intends that the United States will take all necessary measures to swiftly eliminate any significant vulnerability to both physical and cyber attacks on our critical infrastructures, including especially our cyber systems.

A National Goal

No later than the year 2000, the United States shall have achieved an initial operating capability and no later than five years from the day the President signed Presidential Decision Directive 63 the United States shall have achieved and shall maintain the ability to protect our nation's critical infrastructures from intentional acts that would significantly diminish the abilities of:

- The Federal Government to perform essential national security missions and to ensure the general public health and safety;
- State and local governments to maintain order and to deliver minimum essential public services;
- The private sector to ensure the orderly functioning of the economy and the delivery of essential telecommunications, energy, financial and transportation services.

Any interruptions or manipulations of these critical functions must be brief, infrequent, manageable, geographically isolated and minimally detrimental to the welfare of the United States.

A Public–Private Partnership to Reduce Vulnerability

Since the targets of attacks on our critical infrastructure would likely include both facilities in the economy and those in the government, the elimination of our potential vulnerability requires a closely coordinated effort of both the public and the private sector. To succeed, this partnership must be genuine, mutual and cooperative. In seeking to meet our national goal to eliminate the vulnerabilities of our critical infrastructure, therefore, the U.S. government should, to the extent feasible, seek to avoid outcomes that increase government regulation or expand unfunded government mandates to.the private sector.

For each of the major sectors of our economy that are vulnerable to infrastructure attack, the Federal Government will appoint from a designated Lead Agency a senior officer of that agency as the Sector Liaison Official to work with the private sector. Sector Liaison Officials, after discussions and coordination with private sector entities of their infrastructure sector, will identify a private sector counterpart (Sector Coordinator) to represent their sector.

Together these two individuals and the departments and corporations they represent shall contribute to a sectoral National Infrastructure Assurance Plan by:

- Assessing the vulnerabilities of the sector to cyber or physical attacks;
- Recommending a plan to eliminate significant vulnerabilities;
- Proposing a system for identifying and preventing attempted major attacks;
- Developing a plan for alerting, containing and rebuffing an attack in progress and then, in coordination with FEMA as appropriate, rapidly reconstituting minimum essential capabilities in the aftermath of an attack.

During the preparation of the sectoral plans, the National Coordinator (see ["Structure and Organization"]), in conjunction with the Lead Agency Sector Liaison Officials and a representative from the National Economic Council, shall ensure their overall coordination and the integration of the various sectoral plans, with a particular focus on interdependencies.

Guidelines

In addressing this potential vulnerability and the means of eliminating it, President Clinton wants those involved to be mindful of the following general principles and concerns.

- We shall consult with, and seek input from, the Congress on approaches and programs to meet the objectives set forth in this directive.
- The protection of our critical infrastructures is necessarily a shared responsibility and partnership between owners, operators and the government. Furthermore, the Federal Government shall encourage international cooperation to help manage this increasingly global problem.
- Frequent assessments shall be made of our critical infrastructures' existing reliability, vulnerability and threat environment because, as technology and the nature of the threats to our critical infrastructures will continue to change rapidly, so must our protective measures and responses be robustly adaptive.
- The incentives that the market provides are the first choice for addressing the problem of critical infrastructure protection; regulation will be used only in the face of a material failure of the market to protect the health, safety or well-being of the American people. In such cases, agencies shall identify and assess available alternatives to direct regulation, including providing economic incentives to encourage the desired behavior, or providing information upon which choices can be made by the private sector. These incentives, along with other actions, shall be designed to help harness the latest technologies, bring about global solutions to international problems, and enable private sector owners and operators to achieve and maintain the maximum feasible security.

- The full authorities, capabilities and resources of the government, including law enforcement, regulation, foreign intelligence and defense preparedness shall be available, as appropriate, to ensure that critical infrastructure protection is achieved and maintained.
- Care must be taken to respect privacy rights. Consumers and operators must have confidence that information will be handled accurately, confidentially and reliably. The Federal Government shall, through its research, development and procurement, encourage the introduction of increasingly capable methods of infrastructure protection.
- The Federal Government shall serve as a model to the private sector on how infrastructure assurance is best achieved and shall, to the extent feasible, distribute the results of its endeavors.
- We must focus on preventative measures as well as threat and crisis management. To that end, private sector owners and operators should be encouraged to provide maximum feasible security for the infrastructures they control and to provide the government necessary information to assist them in that task. In order to engage the private sector fully, it is preferred that participation by owners and operators in a national infrastructure protection system be voluntary.
- Close cooperation and coordination with state and local governments and first responders is essential for a robust and flexible infrastructure protection program. All critical infrastructure protection plans and actions shall take into consideration the needs, activities and responsibilities of state and local governments and first responders.

Structure and Organization

The Federal Government will be organized for the purposes of this endeavor around four components (elaborated in Exhibit 1).

1. *Lead Agencies for Sector Liaison:* For each infrastructure sector that could be a target for significant cyber or physical attacks, there will be a single U.S. Government department which will serve as the lead agency for liaison. Each Lead Agency will designate one individual of Assistant Secretary rank or higher to be the Sector Liaison Official for that area and to cooperate with the private sector representatives (Sector Coordinators) in addressing problems related to critical infrastructure protection and, in particular, in recommending components of the National Infrastructure Assurance Plan. Together, the Lead Agency and the private sector counterparts will develop and implement a Vulnerability Awareness and Education Program for their sector.

2. *Lead Agencies for Special Functions:* There are, in addition, certain functions related to critical infrastructure protection that must be chiefly performed by the Federal Government (national defense, foreign affairs, intelligence, law enforcement). For each of those special functions, there shall be a Lead Agency which will be responsible for coordinating all of the activities of the United States Government in that area. Each lead agency will appoint a senior officer of Assistant Secretary rank or higher to serve as the Functional Coordinator for that function for the Federal Government.

Exhibit 1.   Structure and Organization

Lead Agencies:

Clear accountability within the U.S. Government must be designated for specific sectors and functions. The following assignments of responsibility will apply:

Lead Agencies for Sector Liaison:

Commerce	Information and communications
Treasury	Banking and finance
EPA	Water supply
Transportation	Aviation
	Highways (including trucking and intelligent transportation systems)
	Mass transit
	Pipelines
	Rail
	Waterborne commerce
Justice/FBI	Emergency law enforcement services
FEMA	Emergency fire service
	Continuity of government services
HHS	Public health services, including prevention, surveillance, laboratory services and personal health services
Energy	Electric power
	Oil and gas production and storage

Lead Agencies for Special Functions:

Justice/FBI	Law enforcement and internal security
CIA	Foreign intelligence
State	Foreign affairs
Defense	National defense

In addition, OSTP shall be responsible for coordinating research and development agendas and programs for the government through the National Science and Technology Council. Furthermore, while Commerce is the lead agency for information and communication, the Department of Defense will retain its Executive Agent responsibilities for the National Communications System and support of the President's National Security Telecommunications Advisory Committee.

National Coordinator:

The National Coordinator for Security, Infrastructure Protection and Counter-Terrorism shall be responsible for coordinating the implementation of this directive. The National Coordinator will report to the President through the Assistant to the President for National Security Affairs. The National Coordinator will also participate as a full member of Deputies or Principals Committee meetings when they meet to consider infrastructure issues. Although the National Coordinator will not direct Departments and Agencies, he or she will ensure interagency coordination for policy development and implementation, and will review crisis activities concerning infrastructure events with significant foreign involvement. The National Coordinator will provide advice, in the context of the established annual budget

---

Exhibit 1.   Structure and Organization (Continued)

---

process, regarding agency budgets for critical infrastructure protection. The National Coordinator will chair the Critical Infrastructure Coordination Group (CICG), reporting to the Deputies Committee (or, at the call of its chair, the Principals Committee). The Sector Liaison Officials and Special Function Coordinators shall attend the CICG's meetings. Departments and agencies shall each appoint to the CICG a senior official (Assistant Secretary level or higher) who will regularly attend its meetings. The National Security Advisor shall appoint a Senior Director for Infrastructure Protection on the NSC staff.

A National Plan Coordination (NPC) staff will be contributed on a non-reimbursable basis by the departments and agencies, consistent with law. The NPC staff will integrate the various sector plans into a National Infrastructure Assurance Plan and coordinate analyses of the U.S. Government's own dependencies on critical infrastructures. The NPC staff will also help coordinate a national education and awareness program, and legislative and public affairs.

The Defense Department shall continue to serve as Executive Agent for the Commission Transition Office, which will form the basis of the NPC, during the remainder of FY98. Beginning in FY99, the NPC shall be an office of the Commerce Department. The Office of Personnel Management shall provide the necessary assistance in facilitating the NPC's operations. The NPC will terminate at the end of FY01, unless extended by Presidential directive.

Warning and Information Centers

As part of a national warning and information sharing system, the President immediately authorizes the FBI to expand its current organization to a full scale National Infrastructure Protection Center (NIPC). This organization shall serve as a national critical infrastructure threat assessment, warning, vulnerability, and law enforcement investigation and response entity. During the initial period of six to twelve months, the President also directs the National Coordinator and the Sector Liaison Officials, working together with the Sector Coordinators, the Special Function Coordinators and representatives from the National Economic Council, as appropriate, to consult with owners and operators of the critical infrastructures to encourage the creation of a private sector sharing and analysis center, as described below.

National Infrastructure Protection Center (NIPC)

The NIPC will include FBI, USSS, and other investigators experienced in computer crimes and infrastructure protection, as well as representatives detailed from the Department of Defense, the Intelligence Community and Lead Agencies. It will be linked electronically to the rest of the Federal Government, including other warning and operations centers, as well as any private sector sharing and analysis centers. Its mission will include providing timely warnings of intentional threats, comprehensive analyses and law enforcement investigation and response. All executive departments and agencies shall cooperate with the NIPC and provide

---

Exhibit 1. Structure and Organization (Continued)

---

such assistance, information and advice that the NIPC may request, to the extent permitted by law.

All executive departments shall also share with the NIPC information about threats and warning of attacks and about actual attacks on critical government and private sector infrastructures, to the extent permitted by law. The NIPC will include elements responsible for warning, analysis, computer investigation, coordinating emergency response, training, outreach, and development and application of technical tools. In addition, it will establish its own relations directly with others in the private sector and with any information sharing and analysis entity that the private sector may create, such as the Information Sharing and Analysis Center described below.

The NIPC, in conjunction with the information originating agency, will sanitize law enforcement and intelligence information for inclusion into analyses and reports that it will provide, in appropriate form, to relevant federal, state and local agencies; the relevant owners and operators of critical infrastructures; and to any private sector information sharing and analysis entity. Before disseminating national security or other information that originated from the intelligence community, the NIPC will coordinate fully with the intelligence community through existing procedures. Whether as sanitized or unsanitized reports, the NIPC will issue attack warnings or alerts to increases in threat condition to any private sector information sharing and analysis entity and to the owners and operators. These warnings may also include guidance regarding additional protection measures to be taken by owners and operators. Except in extreme emergencies, the NIPC shall coordinate with the National Coordinator before issuing public warnings of imminent attacks by international terrorists, foreign states or other malevolent foreign powers.

The NIPC will provide a national focal point for gathering information on threats to the infrastructures. Additionally, the NIPC will provide the principal means of facilitating and coordinating the Federal Government's response to an incident, mitigating attacks, investigating threats and monitoring reconstitution efforts. Depending on the nature and level of a foreign threat/attack, protocols established between special function agencies (DOJ/DOD/CIA), and the ultimate decision of the President, the NIPC may be placed in a direct support role to either DOD or the Intelligence Community.

Information Sharing and Analysis Center (ISAC):

The National Coordinator, working with Sector Coordinators, Sector Liaison Officials and the National Economic Council, shall consult with owners and operators of the critical infrastructures to strongly encourage the creation of a private sector information sharing and analysis center. The actual design and functions of the center and its relation to the NIPC will be determined by the private sector, in consultation with and with assistance from the Federal Government. Within 180 days of this directive, the National Coordinator, with the assistance of the CICG including the National Economic Council, shall identify possible methods of providing federal assistance to facilitate the startup of an ISAC.

Exhibit 1.   Structure and Organization (Continued)

Such a center could serve as the mechanism for gathering, analyzing, appropriately sanitizing and disseminating private sector information to both industry and the NIPC. The center could also gather, analyze and disseminate information from the NIPC for further distribution to the private sector. While crucial to a successful government-industry partnership, this mechanism for sharing important information about vulnerabilities, threats, intrusions and anomalies is not to interfere with direct information exchanges between companies and the government. As ultimately designed by private sector representatives, the ISAC may emulate particular aspects of such institutions as the Centers for Disease Control and Prevention that have proved highly effective, particularly its extensive interchanges with the private and non-federal sectors. Under such a model, the ISAC would possess a large degree of technical focus and expertise and non-regulatory and non-law enforcement missions. It would establish baseline statistics and patterns on the various infrastructures, become a clearinghouse for information within and among the various sectors, and provide a library for historical data to be used by the private sector and, as deemed appropriate by the ISAC, by the government. Critical to the success of such an institution would be its timeliness, accessibility, coordination, flexibility, utility and acceptability.

3. *Interagency Coordination:* The Sector Liaison Officials and Functional Coordinators of the Lead Agencies, as well as representatives from other relevant departments and agencies, including the National Economic Council, will meet to coordinate the implementation of this directive under the auspices of a Critical Infrastructure Coordination Group (CICG), chaired by the National Coordinator for Security, Infrastructure Protection and Counter-Terrorism. The National Coordinator will be appointed by and report to the President through the Assistant to the President for National Security Affairs, who shall assure appropriate coordination with the Assistant to the President for Economic Affairs. Agency representatives to the CICG should be at a senior policy level (Assistant Secretary or higher). Where appropriate, the CICG will be assisted by extant policy structures, such as the Security Policy Board, Security Policy Forum and the National Security and Telecommunications and Information System Security Committee.

4. *National Infrastructure Assurance Council:* On the recommendation of the Lead Agencies, the National Economic Council and the National Coordinator, the President will appoint a panel of major infrastructure providers and state and local government officials to serve as the National Infrastructure Assurance Council. The President will appoint the Chairman. The National Coordinator will serve as the Council's Executive Director. The National Infrastructure Assurance Council will meet periodically to enhance the partnership of the public and private sectors in protecting our critical infrastructures and will provide reports to the President as appropriate. Senior Federal Government officials will participate in the meetings of the National Infrastructure Assurance Council as appropriate.

Protecting Federal Government Critical Infrastructures

Every department and agency of the Federal Government shall be responsible for protecting its own critical infrastructure, especially its cyber-based systems. Every department and agency Chief Information Officer (CIO) shall be responsible for information assurance. Every department and agency shall appoint a Chief Infrastructure Assurance Officer (CIAO) who shall be responsible for the protection of all of the other aspects of that department's critical infrastructure. The CIO may be double-hatted as the CIAO at the discretion of the individual department. These officials shall establish procedures for obtaining expedient and valid authorizations to allow vulnerability assessments to be performed on government computer and physical systems. The Department of Justice shall establish legal guidelines for providing for such authorizations.

No later than 180 days from issuance of this directive, every department and agency shall develop a plan for protecting its own critical infrastructure, including but not limited to its cyber-based systems. The National Coordinator shall be responsible for coordinating analyses required by the departments and agencies of inter-governmental dependencies and the mitigation of those dependencies. The Critical Infrastructure Coordination Group (CICG) shall sponsor an expert review process for those plans. No later than two years from today, those plans shall have been implemented and shall be updated every two years. In meeting this schedule, the Federal Government shall present a model to the private sector on how best to protect critical infrastructure.

Tasks

Within 180 days, the Principals Committee should submit to the President a schedule for completion of a National Infrastructure Assurance Plan with milestones for accomplishing the following subordinate and related tasks.

1. *Vulnerability Analyses:* For each sector of the economy and each sector of the government that might be a target of infrastructure attack intended to significantly damage the United States, there shall be an initial vulnerability assessment, followed by periodic updates. As appropriate, these assessments shall also include the determination of the minimum essential infrastructure in each sector.
2. *Remedial Plan:* Based upon the vulnerability assessment, there shall be a recommended remedial plan. The plan shall identify time lines for implementation, responsibilities and funding.
3. *Warning:* A national center to warn of significant infrastructure attacks will be established immediately (see Exhibit 1). As soon thereafter as possible, we will put in place an enhanced system for detecting and analyzing such attacks, with maximum possible participation of the private sector.
4. *Response:* A system for responding to a significant infrastructure attack while it is underway, with the goal of isolating and minimizing damage.
5. *Reconstitution:* For varying levels of successful infrastructure attacks, we shall have a system to reconstitute minimum required capabilities rapidly.

6. *Education and Awareness:* There shall be Vulnerability Awareness and Education Programs within both the government and the private sector to sensitize people regarding the importance of security and to train them in security standards, particularly regarding cyber systems.

7. *Research and Development:* Federally-sponsored research and development in support of infrastructure protection shall be coordinated, be subject to multi-year planning, take into account private sector research, and be adequately funded to minimize our vulnerabilities on a rapid but achievable timetable.

8. *Intelligence:* The Intelligence Community shall develop and implement a plan for enhancing collection and analysis of the foreign threat to our national infrastructure, to include but not be limited to the foreign cyber/information warfare threat.

9. *International Cooperation:* There shall be a plan to expand cooperation on critical infrastructure protection with like-minded and friendly nations, international organizations and multinational corporations.

10. *Legislative and Budgetary Requirements:* There shall be an evaluation of the executive branch's legislative authorities and budgetary priorities regarding critical infrastructure, and ameliorative recommendations shall be made to the President as necessary. The evaluations and recommendations, if any, shall be coordinated with the Director of OMB.

The CICG shall also review and schedule the taskings listed in Exhibit 2.

Implementation

In addition to the 180-day report, the National Coordinator, working with the National Economic Council, shall provide an annual report on the implementation of this directive to the President and the heads of departments and agencies, through the Assistant to the President for National Security Affairs. The report should include an updated threat assessment, a status report on achieving the milestones identified for the National Plan and additional policy, legislative and budgetary recommendations. The evaluations and recommendations, if any, shall be coordinated with the Director of OMB. In addition, following the establishment of an initial operating capability in the year 2000, the National Coordinator shall conduct a zero-based review.

Foreign Ownership Interests in the American Communications Infrastructure

On September 7, 2000, Kevin V. DiGregory, Deputy Assistant Attorney General, Department of Justice, testified before the House Subcommittee on Telecommunications, Trade, and Consumer Protection, Committee on Commerce, about foreign ownership interests and foreign government ownership interests in the American communications infrastructure. His statement discusses the various policy and law enforcement implications that arise from this issue. This statement can be viewed at www.doj.gov/criminal/cybercrime/kvd_telecom.htm

---

Exhibit 2.   Additional Taskings

Studies

The National Coordinator shall commission studies on the following subjects:

- Liability issues arising from participation by private sector companies in the information sharing process.
- Existing legal impediments to information sharing, with an eye to proposals to remove these impediments, including through the drafting of model codes in cooperation with the American Legal Institute.
- The necessity of document and information classification and the impact of such classification on useful dissemination, as well as the methods and information systems by which threat and vulnerability information can be shared securely while avoiding disclosure or unacceptable risk of disclosure to those who will misuse it.
- The improved protection, including secure dissemination and information handling systems, of industry trade secrets and other confidential business data, law enforcement information and evidentiary material, classified national security information, unclassified material disclosing vulnerabilities of privately owned infrastructures and apparently innocuous information that, in the aggregate, it is unwise to disclose.
- The implications of sharing information with foreign entities where such sharing is deemed necessary to the security of United States infrastructures.
- The potential benefit to security standards of mandating, subsidizing, or otherwise assisting in the provision of insurance for selected critical infrastructure providers and requiring insurance tie-ins for foreign critical infrastructure providers hoping to do business with the United States.

Public Outreach

In order to foster a climate of enhanced public sensitivity to the problem of infrastructure protection, the following actions shall be taken:

- The White House, under the oversight of the National Coordinator, together with the relevant Cabinet agencies shall consider a series of conferences: (1) that will bring together national leaders in the public and private sectors to propose programs to increase the commitment to information security; (2) that convoke academic leaders from engineering, computer science, business and law schools to review the status of education in information security and will identify changes in the curricula and resources necessary to meet the national demand for professionals in this field; (3) on the issues around computer ethics as these relate to the K through 12 and general university populations.
- The National Academy of Sciences and the National Academy of Engineering shall consider a round table bringing together federal, state and local officials with industry and academic leaders to develop national strategies for enhancing infrastructure security.
- The intelligence community and law enforcement shall expand existing programs for briefing infrastructure owners and operators and senior government officials.

Exhibit 2. Additional Taskings (Continued)

- The National Coordinator shall (1) establish a program for infrastructure assurance simulations involving senior public and private officials, the reports of which might be distributed as part of an awareness campaign; and (2) in coordination with the private sector, launch a continuing national awareness campaign, emphasizing improving infrastructure security.

Internal Federal Government Actions

In order for the Federal Government to improve its infrastructure security, these immediate steps shall be taken:

- The Department of Commerce, the General Services Administration, and the Department of Defense shall assist federal agencies in the implementation of best practices for information assurance within their individual agencies.
- The National Coordinator shall coordinate a review of existing federal, state and local bodies charged with information assurance tasks, and provide recommendations on how these institutions can cooperate most effectively.
- All federal agencies shall make clear designations regarding who may authorize access to their computer systems.
- The Intelligence Community shall elevate and formalize the priority for enhanced collection and analysis of information on the foreign cyber/ information warfare threat to our critical infrastructure.
- The Federal Bureau of Investigation, the Secret Service and other appropriate agencies shall: (1) vigorously recruit undergraduate and graduate students with the relevant computer-related technical skills for full-time employment as well as for part-time work with regional computer crime squads; and (2) facilitate the hiring and retention of qualified personnel for technical analysis and investigation involving cyber attacks.
- The Department of Transportation, in consultation with the Department of Defense, shall undertake a thorough evaluation of the vulnerability of the national transportation infrastructure that relies on the Global Positioning System. This evaluation shall include sponsoring an independent, integrated assessment of risks to civilian users of GPS-based systems, with a view to basing decisions on the ultimate architecture of the modernized NAS on these evaluations.
- The Federal Aviation Administration shall develop and implement a comprehensive National Airspace System Security Program to protect the modernized NAS from information-based and other disruptions and attacks.
- GSA shall identify large procurements (such as the new Federal Telecommunications System, FTS 2000) related to infrastructure assurance, study whether the procurement process reflects the importance of infrastructure protection and propose, if necessary, revisions to the overall procurement process to do so.
- OMB shall direct federal agencies to include assigned infrastructure assurance functions within their Government Performance and Results Act strategic planning and performance measurement framework.

Exhibit 2. Additional Taskings (Continued)

- The NSA, in accordance with its National Manager responsibilities in NSD-42, shall provide assessments encompassing examinations of U.S. Government systems to interception and exploitation; disseminate threat and vulnerability information; establish standards; conduct research and development; and conduct issue security product evaluations.

Assisting the Private Sector

In order to assist the private sector in achieving and maintaining infrastructure security:

- The National Coordinator and the National Infrastructure Assurance Council shall propose and develop ways to encourage private industry to perform periodic risk assessments of critical processes, including information and telecommunications systems.
- The Department of Commerce and the Department of Defense shall work together, in coordination with the private sector, to offer their expertise to private owners and operators of critical infrastructure to develop security-related best practice standards.
- The Department of Justice and Department of the Treasury shall sponsor a comprehensive study compiling demographics of computer crime, comparing state approaches to computer crime and developing ways of deterring and responding to computer crime by juveniles.

On September 7, 2000, Larry R. Parkinson, General Counsel for the Federal Bureau of Investigation, testified before the House Subcommittee on Telecommunications, Trade, and Consumer Protection, Committee on Commerce, about foreign government ownership of American telecommunications companies. His statement discusses the various policy and law enforcement implications that arise from this issue. This statement can be viewed at www.usdoj.gov/criminal/cybercrime/lrp_telecom.htm

Carnivore and the Fourth Amendment

Statement of Kevin V. DiGregory, Deputy Assistant Attorney General, United States Department of Justice, July 24, 2000
Subcommittee on the Constitution of the House Committee on the Judiciary
Mr. Chairman and Members of the Subcommittee, thank you for allowing me this opportunity to testify about the law enforcement tool "Carnivore" and the Fourth Amendment. On April 6, 2000, I had the privilege of testifying before you during a hearing on Internet privacy and the Fourth Amendment; I am pleased to continue to participate in the discussion today about "Carnivore" and its role in protecting individual privacy on the Internet from unwarranted governmental intrusion, and about the critical role the Department plays to ensure that the Internet is a safe and secure place.

Privacy and Public Safety

It is beyond dispute that the Fourth Amendment protects the rights of Americans while they work and play on the Internet just as it does in the physical world. The goal is a long-honored and noble one: to preserve our privacy while protecting the safety of our citizens. Our founding fathers recognized that in order for our democratic society to remain safe and our liberty intact, law enforcement must have the ability to investigate, apprehend and prosecute people for criminal conduct. At the same time, however, our founding fathers held in disdain the government's disregard and abuse of privacy in England. The founders of this nation adopted the Fourth Amendment to address the tension that can at times arise between privacy and public safety. Under the Fourth Amendment, the government must demonstrate probable cause before obtaining a warrant for a search, arrest, or other significant intrusion on privacy.

Congress and the courts have also recognized that lesser intrusions on privacy should be permitted under a less exacting threshold. The Electronic Communications Privacy Act ("ECPA") establishes a three-tier system by which the government can obtain stored information from electronic communication service providers. In general, the government needs a search warrant to obtain the content of unretrieved communications (like e-mail), a court order to obtain transactional records, and a subpoena to obtain information identifying the subscriber. See 18 U.S.C. §§ 2701-11.

In addition, in order to obtain source and destination information in real time, the government must obtain a "trap and trace" or "pen register" court order authorizing the recording of such information. See 18 U.S.C. 3121, *et seq.*

Because of the privacy values it protects, the wiretap statute, 18 U.S.C. §§ 2510-22, commonly known as Title III, places a higher burden on the real-time interception of oral, wire and electronic communications than the Fourth Amendment requires. In the absence of a statutory exception, the government needs a court order to wiretap communications. To obtain such an order, the government must show that normal investigative techniques for obtaining the information have or are likely to fail or are too dangerous, and that any interception will be conducted so as to ensure that the intrusion is minimized.

The safeguards for privacy represented by the Fourth Amendment and statutory restrictions on government access to information do not prevent effective law enforcement. Instead, they provide boundaries for law enforcement, clarifying what is acceptable evidence gathering and what is not. At the same time, those who care deeply about protecting individual privacy must also acknowledge that law enforcement has a critical role to play in preserving privacy. When law enforcement investigates, successfully apprehends and prosecutes a criminal who has stolen a citizen's personal information from a computer system, for example, law enforcement is undeniably working to protect privacy and deter further privacy violations. The same is true when law enforcement apprehends a hacker who compromised the financial records of a bank customer.

As we move into the 21st century, we must ensure that the needs of privacy and public safety remain in balance and are appropriately reflected in the new and emerging technologies that are changing the face of communications. Although the primary mission of the Department of Justice is law enforcement, Attorney General Reno and the entire Department understand and share the legitimate concerns of all Americans with regard to personal privacy. The Department has been and will remain committed to protecting the privacy rights of individuals. We look forward to working with Congress and other concerned individuals to address these important matters in the months ahead.

Law Enforcement Tools in Cyberspace

Although the Fourth Amendment is over two centuries old, the Internet as we know it is still in its infancy. The huge advances in the past ten years have changed forever the landscape of society, not just in America, but worldwide. The Internet has resulted in new and exciting ways for people to communicate, transfer information, engage in commerce, and expand their educational opportunities. These are but a few of the wonderful benefits of this rapidly changing technology. As has been the case with every major technological advance in our history, however, we are seeing individuals and groups use this technology to commit criminal acts. As Deputy Attorney General Eric Holder told the Crime Subcommittee of this Committee in February, our vulnerability to computer crime is astonishingly high and threatens not only our financial well-being and our privacy, but also this nation's critical infrastructure.

Many of the crimes that we confront everyday in the physical world are beginning to appear in the online world. Crimes like threats, extortion, fraud, identity theft, and child pornography are migrating to the Internet. The Fourth Amendment and laws addressing privacy and public safety serve as a framework for law enforcement to respond to this new forum for criminal activity. If law enforcement fails properly to respect individual privacy in its investigative techniques, the public's confidence in government will be eroded, evidence will be suppressed, and criminals will elude successful prosecution. If law enforcement is too timid in responding to cybercrime, however, we will, in effect, render cyberspace a safe haven for criminals and terrorists to communicate and carry out crime, without fear of authorized government surveillance. If we fail to make the Internet safe, people's confidence in using the Internet and e-commerce will decline, endangering the very benefits brought by the Information Age. Proper balance is the key.

To satisfy our obligations to the public to enforce the laws and preserve the safety, we use the same sorts of investigative techniques and methods online as we do in the physical world, with the same careful attention to the strict constitutional, statutory, internal and court-ordered boundaries. Carnivore is simply an investigative tool that is used online only under narrowly defined circumstances, and only when authorized by law, to meet our responsibilities to the public.

To illustrate, law enforcement often needs to find out from whom a drug dealer, for example, is buying his illegal products, or to whom the drug dealer is selling. To investigate this, it is helpful to determine who is communicating with the drug dealer. In the "olden days" of perhaps 10 years ago, the drug dealer would have communicated with his supplier and customers exclusively through use of telephones and pagers. Law enforcement would obtain an order from a court authorizing the installation of a "trap and trace" and a "pen register" device on the drug dealer's phone or pager, and either the telephone company or law enforcement would have installed these devices to comply with the court's order.

Thereafter, the source and destination of his phone calls would have been recorded. This is information that courts have held is not protected by any reasonable expectation of privacy. Given the personal nature of this information, however, the law requires government to obtain an order under these circumstances. In this way, privacy is protected and law enforcement is able to investigate to protect the public.

Now, that same drug dealer may be just as likely to send an e-mail as call his confederates. When law enforcement uses a "trap and trace" or "pen register" in the online context, however, we have found that, at times, the Internet service provider has been unable or even unwilling to supply this information. Law enforcement cannot abdicate its responsibility to protect public safety simply because technology has changed. Rather, the public rightfully expects that law enforcement will continue to be effective as criminal activity migrates to the Internet. We cannot do this without tools like Carnivore.

When a criminal uses e-mail to send a kidnapping demand, to buy and sell illegal drugs or to distribute child pornography, law enforcement needs to know to whom he is sending messages and from whom he receives them. To get this information, we obtain a court order, which we serve on the appropriate service provider. Because of the nature of Internet communications, the addressing information (which does not include the content of the message) is often mixed in with a lot of other non-content data that we have no desire to gather. If the service provider can comply with the order and provide us with only the addressing information required by court order, it will do so and we will not employ Carnivore. If, however, the service provider is unwilling or unable to comply with the order, we simply cannot give a criminal a free pass. It is for that narrow set of circumstances that the FBI designed "Carnivore."

Carnivore is, in essence, a special filtering tool that can gather the information authorized by court order, and only that information. It permits law enforcement, for example, to gather only the e-mail addresses of those persons with whom the drug dealer is communicating, without allowing any human being, either from law enforcement or the service provider, to view private information outside of the scope of the court's order. In other words, Carnivore is a minimization tool that permits law enforcement strictly to comply with court orders, strongly to protect privacy, and effectively to enforce the law to protect the public interest. In addition, Carnivore creates an audit trail that demonstrates exactly what it is capturing.

As with any other investigative tools, there are many mechanisms we have in place to prevent against possible misuse of Carnivore, and to remedy misuse that has occurred. The Fourth Amendment, of course, restricts what law enforcement can do with Carnivore, as do the statutory requirements of Title III and the Electronic Communications Privacy Act, and the courts.

For federal Title III applications, the Department of Justice imposes its own guidelines on top of the privacy protections provided by the Constitution, statutes and the courts. For example, before Carnivore may be used to intercept wire or electronic communications, the requesting investigative agency must obtain approval for the Title III application from the Department of Justice. Specifically, the Office of Enforcement Operations (OEO) in the Criminal Division of the Department reviews each proposed Title III application to ensure that the interception satisfies the Fourth Amendment requirements, and is in compliance with applicable statutes and regulations. Even if the proposal clears the OEO, approval must be given by a Deputy Assistant Attorney General. Although this requirement of high-level review is required by Title III only with regard to proposed intercepts of wire and oral communications, the Department voluntarily imposes the same level of review for proposed interceptions of electronic communications (except digital-display pagers). Typically, investigative agencies such as the Federal Bureau of Investigation have similar internal requirements, separate and apart from Constitutional, statutory or Department of Justice requirements.

If the investigative agency and the Department of Justice approve a federal Title III request, it still must, of course, be approved by the proper court. The court will evaluate the application under the Fourth Amendment and using the familiar standards of Title III. By statute, for example, the application to the court must show, through sworn affidavit, why the intercept is necessary as opposed to other less-intrusive investigative techniques. The application must also provide additional detail, including whether there have been previous interceptions of communications of the target, the identity of the target (if known), the nature and location of the communications facilities, and a description of the type of communications sought and the offenses to which the communications relate. By statute and internal Department regulation, the interception may last no longer than 30 days without an extension by the court.

Courts also often impose their own requirements. For example, many federal courts require that the investigators provide periodic reports setting forth information such as the number of communications intercepted, steps taken to minimize irrelevant traffic, and whether the interceptions have been fruitful. The court may, of course terminate the interception at any time.

The remedies for violating Title III or ECPA by improperly intercepting electronic communications can include criminal sanctions, civil suit, and for law enforcement agents, adverse employment action. For violations of the Fourth Amendment, of course, the remedy of suppression is also available.

Carnivore itself also contains self-regulating features. For example, because of its sophisticated passive filtering features, it automates the process of minimization without intrusive monitoring by investigators, and simply disregards packets of information that do not satisfy the criteria in the court's authorization. Indeed, one of the most powerful privacy-protecting features of Carnivore is its ability to ignore information that is outside the scope of the court-ordered authority. For later verification, it also logs the filter settings. In addition, as a practical matter, Carnivore is not deployed except with close cooperation with the appropriate system provider. In any event, the FBI does not use Carnivore in every instance in which the court orders a Title III electronic communication intercept. Indeed, I understand that the Bureau uses Carnivore only in those instances when the service provider is unable to comply with the court order using its own equipment, or when the provider asks the FBI to use Bureau equipment.

As I testified in April, we face three major categories of challenges in trying to keep the Internet a safe and secure place for our citizens. These are:

1. Technical challenges that hamper law enforcement's ability to locate and prosecute criminals that operate online;
2. Certain substantive and procedural laws that have not kept pace with the changing technology, creating significant legal challenges to effective investigation and prosecution of crime in cyberspace; and

3. Resource needs that must be addressed to ensure that law enforcement
    can keep pace with changing technology and has the ability to hire and
    train people to fight cybercrime.

Carnivore is an investigative tool that assists us in meeting the first challenge.
As we have witnessed, tracking a criminal online is not always an impossible task
using our investigative tools. For example, last year federal and state law enforcement combined to successfully apprehend the creator of the Melissa virus and
the individual who created a fraudulent Bloomberg News Service Web site in
order to artificially drive up the stock price of PairGain, a telecommunications
company based in California. Although we are proud of these important successes,
we still face significant challenges as online criminals become more and more
sophisticated.

In nearly every online case, tracking the online criminal requires law enforcement to attempt to trace the "electronic trail" from the victim back to the
perpetrator. In effect, this "electronic trail" is the fingerprint of the twenty-first
century — only much harder to find and not as permanent as its more traditional
predecessor. In the physical world, a criminal and his victim are generally in the
same location. But cybercriminals do not have to physically visit the crime scene.
Instead they cloak their illegal activity by weaving communications through a
series of anonymous remailers, by creating forged e-mail headers with powerful
point and click tools readily downloadable from hacker Web sites, by using a
"free-trial" account or two, or by "wiping clean" the logging records that would
be evidence of their activity.

In some cases, the criminal may not even be in the same country as the
victim. The global nature of the Internet, while one of the greatest assets of the
Internet to law-abiding citizens, allows criminals to conduct their illegal activity
from across the globe. In these cases, the need to respond quickly and track the
criminal is increasingly complicated and often frustrated by the fact that the activity
takes place throughout different countries. With more than 190 countries connected to the Internet, it is easy to understand the coordination challenges that
face law enforcement. Furthermore, in these cases, time is of the essence and the
victim may not even realize they have been victimized until the criminal has long
since signed-off. Clearly, the technical challenges for law enforcement are real
and profound.

This fact was made clear in the findings and conclusions reached in the
recently released report of the President's Working Group on Unlawful Conduct
on the Internet, entitled, "The Electronic Frontier: The Challenge of Unlawful
Conduct Involving the Use of the Internet." This extensive report highlights in
detail the significant challenges facing law enforcement in cyberspace. As the
report states, the needs and challenges confronting law enforcement, "are neither
trivial nor theoretical." The Report outlines a three-pronged approach for responding to unlawful activity on the Internet:

1. Conduct on the Internet should be treated in the same manner as similar
    conduct offline, in a technology neutral manner.
2. We must recognize that the needs and challenges of law enforcement posed
    by the Internet are substantial, including our need for resources, up-to date
    investigative tools and enhanced multi-jurisdictional cooperation.

3. Finally, we need to foster continued support for private sector leadership in developing tools and methods to help Internet users to prevent and minimize the risks of unlawful conduct online.

I would encourage anyone with an interest in this important topic to review carefully the report of the Working Group. The report can be found on the Internet by visiting the Web site of the Department of Justice's Computer Crime and Intellectual Property Section, located at www.cybercrime.gov. In addition to the report, www.cybercrime.gov also contains other useful information on a wide array of Internet related issues, including the topic of today's hearing — privacy.

Despite the type of difficulties outlined in the Unlawful Conduct Report and discussed today, the Justice Department and law enforcement across this nation are committed to continuing to work together and with their counterparts in other countries to develop and implement investigative strategies to successfully track, apprehend, and prosecute individuals who conduct criminal activity on the Internet. In so doing, the same privacy standards that apply in the physical world remain effective online.

Mr. Chairman, the Department of Justice has taken a proactive leadership role in making cyberspace safer for all Americans. The cornerstone of our cybercrime prosecutor program is the Criminal Division's Computer Crime and Intellectual Property Section, known as CCIPS. CCIPS was founded in 1991 as the Computer Crime Unit, and became a Section in 1996. CCIPS has grown from five attorneys in 1996 to nineteen today, and we need more to keep pace with the demand for their expertise. The attorneys in CCIPS work closely on computer crime cases with Assistant United States Attorneys known as "Computer and Telecommunications Coordinators," or CTC's, in U.S. Attorney's Offices around the nation. Each CTC receives special training and equipment and serves as the district's expert on computer crime cases. CCIPS and the CTC's work together in prosecuting cases, spearheading training for local, state and federal law enforcement, working with international counterparts to address difficult international challenges, and providing legal and technical instruction to assist in the protection of this nation's critical infrastructures. We are very proud of the work these people do and we will continue to work diligently to help stop criminals from victimizing people online.

I also note that public education is an important component of the Attorney General's strategy on combating computer crime. As she often notes, the same children who recognize that it is wrong to steal a neighbor's mail or shoplift do not seem to understand that it is equally wrong to steal a neighbor's e-mail or copy a proprietary software or music file without paying for it. To remedy this problem, the Department of Justice, together with the Information Technology Association of America (ITAA), has embarked upon a national campaign to educate and raise awareness of computer responsibility and to provide resources to empower concerned citizens. The "Cybercitizen Awareness Program" seeks to engage children, young adults, and others on the basics of critical information protection and security and on the limits of acceptable online behavior. The objectives of the program are to give children an understanding of cyberspace benefits and responsibilities, an awareness of consequences resulting from the misuse of the medium and an understanding of the personal dangers that exist on the Internet and techniques to avoid being harmed.

Finally, Mr. Chairman, the Subcommittee may be aware that the Administration will soon be transmitting to Congress a legislative proposal addressing various issues relating to cyber-security. I know that the focus of today's hearing is the Carnivore program, and this is not the time to undertake any detailed discussion of the Administration's proposal. I would, however, like to mention two points that relate directly to today's discussion. First, the Administration supports raising the statutory standards for intercepting the content of electronic communications so they are the same as those for intercepting telephone calls: high-level approval, use only in cases involving certain predicate offenses that are specified by statute, and statutory suppression of evidence derived from improper intercepts. Second, the Administration supports requiring federal judges to confirm that the appropriate statutory predicates have been satisfied before issuing a pen register or trap-and-trace order. Those changes would apply to the use of Carnivore — and would, in important respects, simply confirm by statute the policies and procedures already followed by the Department of Justice. Beyond those specific points, I will simply note here that the Administration supports a balanced updating of laws to enhance protection of both privacy and public safety, and that the forthcoming proposal will contain important provisions whose enactment would be most helpful in the ongoing fight against cyber-crime.

Conclusion

Mr. Chairman, I want to thank you again for this opportunity to testify today about our efforts to fight crime on the Internet while preserving the rights conferred by the Fourth Amendment and statute. Ultimately, the decision as to the appropriate parameters of law enforcement activity lies squarely within the Constitution and the elected representatives of the people, the Congress. The need to protect the privacy of the American people, not just from the government but also from criminals, is a paramount consideration, not just in the context of the Internet, but in general. The Department of Justice stands ready to work with this Subcommittee and others to achieve the proper balance between the important need for protecting privacy and the need to respond to the growing threat of crime in cyberspace.

Mr. Chairman, that concludes my prepared statement. I would be pleased to attempt to answer any questions that you may have at this time.

Chapter 13

Electronic Commerce: Legal Issues

The Electronic Commerce Working Group (ECWG), Department of Justice

The Electronic Commerce Working Group (ECWG) of the Department of Justice consists of lawyers from throughout the Department who are in regular contact to discuss legal issues related to electronic commerce. The ECWG provides a convenient vehicle for Justice Department attorneys to disseminate information quickly regarding electronic commerce developments.

The ECWG has studied complex and novel legal issues, and helps to coordinate Justice Department positions on emerging legal issues. For example, the ECWG has a sub-group that meets regularly to study legal issues related to electronic filing and electronic transactions; representatives of this sub-group have met with representatives of other federal agencies to discuss these issues in the context of a particular agency's processes.

For more information about the Department of Justice's Electronic Commerce Working Group, please call the Department of Justice's Computer Crime and Intellectual Property Section at 202-514-1026.

Guide for Federal Agencies on Implementing Electronic Processes

This guide addresses legal issues that agencies are likely to face in converting to electronic processes and provides suggestions on how to address these issues. The rise of electronic commerce offers departments and agencies exciting opportunities to convert or redesign existing processes. At the same time, creating a more accessible and efficient government requires us to maintain public confidence in the security and reliability of the Government's electronic transactions, processes, and systems. Thus, in designing electronic systems, departments and agencies should ensure that essential data are available when need[ed] and that the data and the underlying processes are legally sufficient, reliable and in compliance with all applicable legal requirements.

Attorney General Reno's Cover Memorandum to the Guide (November 22, 2000)

Office of the Attorney General
Washington, D.C. 20530
November 22, 2000
Memorandum for the Heads of Departments and Agencies
From: The Attorney General
Subject: Guidance on Legal Considerations Related to the Government Paperwork Elimination Act

Under the Government Paperwork Elimination Act (GPEA), Pub. L. No. 105-277. §§1701-1710 (1998) (codified as 44 U.S.C.A. §3504 n. (West Supp. 1999)), executive agencies are required, by October 21, 2003, to provide "for the option of the electronic maintenance, submission, or disclosure of information, when practicable as a substitute for paper" and "for the use and acceptance of electronic signatures, when practicable." (GPEA §1704.) To assist agencies implementing GPRA, the Office of Management and Budget (OMB) has developed Procedures and Guidance on Implementing the Government Paperwork Elimination Act (OMB Guidance). 65 Fed. Reg. 25,511 (May 2, 2000). Under the OMB Guidance, the Department of Justice is charged with developing, in consultation with federal agencies and OMB, practical guidance on legal considerations related to agency use of electronic filing and record keeping. 65 Fed. Reg. at 25,513.

I am enclosing a copy of the Department's guidance, entitled "Legal Considerations in Designing and Implementing Electronic Processes: A Guide for Federal Agencies" (the Guide). The Guide, which was prepared in consultation with OMB and other federal agencies, addresses legal issues that agencies are likely to face in converting to electronic processes and provides suggestions on how to address these issues.

The rise of electronic commerce offers departments and agencies exciting opportunities to convert or redesign existing processes. GPEA is an important tool in assisting departments and agencies in improving customer service and government efficiency through the use of information technology. At the same time, creating a more accessible and efficient government requires us to maintain public confidence in the security and reliability of the Government's electronic transactions, processes, and systems. Thus, in designing electronic sytems, departments and agencies should ensure that essential data are available when needed and that the data and the underlying processes are legally sufficient, reliable, and in compliance with all applicable legal requirements.

This Guide was prepared to assist your department or agency in protecting its legal rights and minimizing the leqal risks as you develop and implement electronic-based processes and transactions. The Guide also includes the names of attorneys at the Department of Justice who may be contacted if your department or agency has additional questions.

I hope you find the Guide useful, and I look forward to our continued work together in using information technology to make our Government processes and transactions more efficient, secure, reliable, and responsive to the needs of the American people.

Guide to the Federal Agencies on Implementing Electronic Processes
November 2000
Reference Appendix 43

Consumer Protection in the Global Electronic Marketplace

The Justice Department submitted comments to the Federal Trade Commission on the subject of "Consumer Protection in the Global Electronic Marketplace." The Justice Department submitted these comments on March 29, 1999. The full text of the Justice Department comments is available at www.usdoj.gov/criminal/cybercrime/ftcconsu.htm

The Government Paperwork Elimination Act

The Justice Department submitted comments to the Office of Management and Budget on the Proposed Procedures and Guidance on Implementing the Government Paperwork Elimination Act. The OMB's proposal was published at 64 Fed. Reg. 10.896 (March 5, 1999). The Justice Department filed these comments on June 25, 1999. The full text of the Justice Department comments, including the cover letter from Associate Attorney General Raymond Fisher is available via the link below:

> http://www.cybercrime.gov/gpea.htm

Internet Gambling

1. Federal Legislation Related to Internet Gambling

Kevin V. DiGregory, Deputy Assistant Attorney General, testified before the House of Representatives Committee on Banking and Financial Services on June 20, 2000, on Gambling on the Internet. As with earlier testimony, this statement addressed the Department of Justice's concerns with proposed Internet gambling legislation and the problems inherent in creating a solution that is not technology-neutral. [http://www.cybercrime.gov/kvd0600.html]

Questions and Answers

- How can the Department prosecute Internet gambling under existing law?
- How would new legislation prohibiting Internet gaming affect Indian tribes?

- Give us more details about the cases in the Southern District of New York?
- How would pending legislation affect fantasy sports leagues conducted on the Internet?
- What have other countries done with regard to Internet gaming?

2. Prosecution of Internet Gambling

On February 28, 2000, Jay Cohen was convicted in Manhattan federal court of operating a sports betting business that illegally accepted bets and wagers on sporting events from Americans over the Internet and telephones. Cohen is the first defendant to stand trial in a series of Internet offshore sports gambling cases that were the first prosecutions brought under the federal Wire Wager Act. Sentencing is scheduled for May 23, 2000.

Jay Cohen Convicted of Operating an Off-Shore Sports Betting Business that Accepted Bets from Americans Over the Internet (February 28, 2000). The statement can be found at www.usdoj.gov/criminal/cybercrime/cohen.htm.

In New York, twenty-one owners, managers and employees of Internet sports betting companies have been charged in Manhattan federal court with conspiracy to transmit bets and wagers on sporting events via the Internet and telephones. Information about the filing of these charges is available below.

Owners, Managers and Employees of Internet Sports Betting Companies Charged with Violating Federal Law The statement can be found at www.usdoj.gov/criminal/cybercrime/nypr.htm.

Sale of Prescription Drugs Over the Internet

On October 25, 2000, a New Jersey man pleaded guilty to one count of fraud. The man, Stanley Lapides, admitted to selling via the Internet home HIV test kits. However, Lapides neglected to tell his customers that these kits had not yet been approved for use by the FDA. The statement can be found at www.usdoj.gov/criminal/cybercrime/hivtest.htm.

On May 25, 2000, Deputy Associate Attorney General Ethan M. Posner testified before the Subcommittee on Oversight and Investigations of the House Committee on Commerce on the subject of Online Pharmaceutical Drug Sales. His testimony detailed the role of the Department of Justice in Internet drug sales, including current specific efforts by the Department and information on the Internet Prescription Drug Sales Act of 2000. The statement can be found at www.usdoj.gov/criminal/cybercrime/posner.htm.

On December 9, 1999, a federal grand jury charged Kent Aoki Lee with selling Viagra over the Internet without a prescription. Lee was also charged with wire fraud and trademark violations growing out of his operation of a separate pirated Internet Web site. The statement can be found at www.usdoj.gov/criminal/cybercrime/kaokilee.htm.

Ivan K. Fong, Deputy Associate Attorney General, Department of Justice, testified before the Subcommittee on Oversight and Investigations, Committee of Commerce of the United States House of Representatives regarding Sale of Prescription Drugs over the Internet on July 30, 1999. The statement can be found at www.usdoj.gov/criminal/cybercrime/fong9907.htm.

Guidance on Implementing the Electronic Signatures in Global And National Commerce Act (E-SIGN)

The Electronic Signatures in Global and National Commerce Act (E-SIGN) was enacted on June 30, 2000. E-SIGN applies broadly to Federal and state statutes and regulations governing private sector (including business-to-business and business-to-consumer) activities. The Act generally requires that agencies permit private parties to conduct business and retain records electronically, using electronic signatures. Agencies may also establish appropriate performance standards for the accuracy, integrity, and accessibility of electronic records. Agency activities and requirements that do not relate to business, commercial, or consumer transactions are not within the scope of this legislation; they are instead addressed by the Government Paperwork Elimination Act. ESIGN begins to take effect on October 1 of this year, with later dates for recordkeeping and certain other activities regulated by the Federal Government. The OMB has issued a guidance memorandum on implementing this Act. Any questions related to specific legal issues regarding this guidance may be referred to the Justice Department at ESIGN@usdoj.gov; specific questions about the legislative history of E-SIGN may be referred to the Commerce Department at ESIGN@doc.gov.

Part I: General Overview of the E-SIGN Act

Public Law No. 106-229 (As it Relates to Federal Agencies)
On June 30, 2000, the President signed into law the Electronic Signatures in Global and National Commerce Act ("E-SIGN"). This version explains E-SIGN as it relates to federal agencies, to assist them in becoming familiar with these new requirements.

A. Basic Areas Covered by E-SIGN

E-SIGN promotes the use of electronic contract formation, signatures, and record-keeping in private commerce by establishing legal equivalence between:

- Contracts written on paper and contracts in electronic form;
- Pen-and-ink signatures and electronic signatures; and
- Other legally-required written documents (termed "records") and the same information in electronic form.

E-SIGN applies broadly to commercial, consumer, and business transactions affecting interstate or foreign commerce, and to transactions regulated by both Federal and state government. If there is no writing required by another law, E-SIGN does not apply. In general, subject to the limits discussed in B. below, E-SIGN applies to the following areas:

1. *Regulation of Private Parties' Contract Formation* — If all parties to a contract choose to use electronic signatures and records, E-SIGN generally grants legal recognition to those methods. E-SIGN provides that no contract, signature, or record shall be denied legal effect solely because it is in

electronic form. Nor may a contract relating to a transaction be denied legal effect solely because an electronic signature or record was used in its formation (Section 101(a)). Beginning October1, 2000, E-SIGN will supersede all statutes or agency rules containing paper-based requirements that might otherwise deny effect to electronic signatures and records in consumer, commercial or business transactions between two or more private parties, providing that all the contracting parties agree to the use of electronic methods. E-SIGN preserves agencies' existing authority, however, to set standards for the integrity, accuracy, and accessibility of electronic records and the authentication of electronic signatures. Such standards must be consistent with E-SIGN and substantially justified. They must also satisfy other statutory criteria (as described in detail in Part III).

2. *Legally Required Notices and Disclosures in Private Transactions* — Many Federal, State, and local laws or rules require that parties receive notices and disclosures in connection with private transactions (for example real estate purchases and settlements). To the extent these laws or rules require paper notices, E-SIGN largely supersedes them. Effective October 1, 2000, the notices may be in electronic form, provided that all involved parties agree. E-SIGN establishes special requirements for the use of electronic notices and disclosures in consumer transactions. A consumer must specifically "opt-in" to receiving electronic notification according to requirements spelled out in detail in the statute (Section 101(c)). Please note that E-SIGN does not give legal effect to the use of electronic notices of home mortgage foreclosures, evictions, repossessions, termination of utility services, cancellation of health or life insurance, and product recalls (Section 103(b)(2)). Also, E-SIGN does not affect the proximity requirements of any other law with respect to any warning, notice, disclosure, or other record required to be posted or displayed.

3. *Record Retention Requirements* — If a Federal law or regulation requires that a document (or particular information) be retained by an individual or company, E-SIGN adds an electronic option. Effective March 1 (if no new regulation is in process), or June 1, 2001 (if a regulation is being revised), retention may be electronic so long as the electronic record accurately reflects the information set forth in the record, and remains accessible in a form that can be accurately reproduced for later reference (Section 101(d)). As noted below, agencies also may promulgate performance standards to ensure the accuracy, integrity and accessibility of electronic records (Section 104(b)(3)).

4. *Filings* — E-SIGN generally preserves an agency's existing authority to specify standards and formats for records filed with the agency (Section 104(a)). Federal agencies have separate obligations, however, under the Government Paperwork Elimination Act ("GPEA")(Title XVII of Pub. L. No. 105-277) to accept most electronic records submitted by the public (See Section 104(c)(2)).[1] Under GPEA, agencies must generally provide for the optional use and acceptance of electronic documents, signatures, and recordkeeping, when practicable, by October 2003. GPEA seeks to increase the ability of citizens to interact with the Federal government electronically.

5. *Federal Agency Contracts* — E-SIGN does not force contracting parties
    (whether the government or the private sector) to use or accept electronic
    signatures and records. If agencies and the parties with whom they contract
    choose to use electronic methods, E-SIGN gives legal effect to those
    methods. Moreover, E-SIGN expressly permits agencies to require the use
    of specific technologies (such as specific authentication methods) in con-
    nection with Federal procurement contracts (Section 104(b)(4)). It is impor-
    tant to distinguish these points from other, non-procurement electronic
    transactions provided for under GPEA, where Federal agencies *are* com-
    pelled (when practicable) to accept electronic forms with electronic sig-
    natures by October 2003.

B. Governmental Activities

Congress specifically rejected the inclusion of the term A "governmental transactions" in the definition of transactions subject to E-SIGN, although that term did
appear in earlier versions of the bill. See Section 106(13) (defining covered
transactions). E-SIGN does not prescribe requirements pertaining to activities that
are governmental (as opposed to business, consumer, or commercial) in nature,
including activities conducted by private parties principally for governmental
purposes. One example of an activity that is governmental is census reporting
and related requirements. When government agencies choose to engage in commercial transactions, E-SIGN does apply, permitting (but not required) the use of
electronic methods. See above ("Federal Agency Contracts").

   Note that if a transaction is not within the scope of E-SIGN because it is
governmental, rather than commercial, consumer, or business in nature, agencies
must still pursue options for electronic collection, maintenance, and disclosure of
information, as well as electronic signatures, under GPEA. The latter statute
generally requires agencies to recognize the validity of electronic submissions in
their programs by October 2003 (when practicable), in accordance with guidance
issued by the Office of Management and Budget.

C. Preservation of Agency Authority

If an agency is responsible for issuing rules under a statute (pursuant to rulemaking
authority granted by that statute or some other statute), E-SIGN preserves that
agency's authority to issue a rule, order or other guidance of general applicability
interpreting the impact of E-SIGN on that statute (Section 104(b)). These rules
must be:

- Consistent with Section 101 of E-SIGN and not add to its requirements;
- Supported by a substantial justification;
- Substantially equivalent to similar requirements imposed with respect to
  non-electronic contracts, notices, and retained records;
- Reasonable in the costs they impose; and
- Technology neutral (Section 104(b)(2)).

To the extent authorized by statute, an agency may:

- Issue rules requiring the use of an authentication technology providing a particular level of security (but generally not the use of one specific technology, unless certain requirements are met) for contract formation or for signing of notices or disclosures;
- Issue interpretive rules or other guidance regarding the application of the consumer consent provisions to the particular notices or disclosures within the agency's jurisdiction;
- Issue interpretive rules or other guidance regarding the agency's record retention rules, including the specification of performance standards required to assure accuracy, record integrity, and accessibility of the records that are required to be retained (Section 104(b)(3)).

An agency may not require the use of a specific technology unless necessary to meet an important government objective (for example, ensuring that personal information is kept private). It also may not require that a record be retained in paper form unless it is essential to attaining a compelling governmental interest relating to law enforcement or national security.

Part II: Suggested Steps for the Implementation of E-SIGN

Beginning on October 1, 2000, E-SIGN will supersede many provisions in Federal and State statutes and agency regulations requiring the use of paper records and ink signatures in commercial, consumer, and business transactions.

The statutes and regulations affected by E-SIGN include those that impose requirements for contract formation, record retention, and notices and disclosures by private parties (that relate to business, consumer, or commercial, rather than governmental, activities). E-SIGN also provides special rules and effective dates for government and government-guaranteed loans.

Agencies should immediately begin to identify which of their regulations or other requirements may be subject to E-SIGN. They should decide whether they need to revise any of their regulations or requirements in light of the legal status accorded to electronic records and signatures under E-SIGN. They should work with their customers and regulated communities in this process to help ensure that they understand the scope of E-SIGN. They should issue a general notice or group of notices for comment as to what guidance or regulations should be amended.

We recommend that agencies follow these steps:

1. *Identify Affected Agency Regulations, Policies, and Procedures.* E-SIGN could potentially affect any statute or agency regulation, policy, or procedure that requires private parties to conduct transactions using paper records and ink signatures. As a first step, you should review your statutes, regulations, policies, and procedures to determine whether they come within the scope of E-SIGN. You should specifically examine those relating to transactions between private parties (for example, contract formation, notices, disclosures), record retention, filings, government guaranteed loans

and mortgage insurance, as well as those governing situations in which the government is a market participant. Part III of this Guidance contains a detailed discussion of the scope of E-SIGN and how it may apply to these specific areas.

2. Determine Whether it is Necessary to Issue Guidance or Regulations Concerning the Use of Electronic Records or Signatures in Particular Transactions. Consistent with the intent of E-SIGN, you generally should not restrict whether and how private parties use electronic records and signatures in their dealings. You may need to provide guidance or standards for the use of electronic records or signatures in some contexts in order to implement statutory requirements that you administer. Part III discusses the types of situations in which there may be substantial justification for you to issue guidance or set standards on the use of electronic records and signatures.

3. Determine the Extent to Which You Have Authority to Issue Guidance or Regulations Concerning the Use of Electronic Records or Signatures in Particular Transactions. E-SIGN generally allows you to interpret how its requirements apply to your statutes and regulations. You have varying levels of discretion to issue guidance or regulations for different types of transactions. You have more discretion to establish standards in connection with record retention requirements than in connection with the formation of contracts between private parties. Part III discusses the scope of discretion with respect to the use of electronic records and signatures in various types of transactions affected by E-SIGN.

4. *Adopt Guidance or Regulations for the Use of Electronic Records and Signatures, Where Necessary.* If you determine that it is necessary to issue new or amended regulations, policies, or procedures to establish standards for electronic records or signatures, you should ensure that you do so in compliance with the requirements of E-SIGN as well as other applicable laws, such as GPEA. If your regulation contains information collections under the Paperwork Reduction Act ("PRA"), and thus is subject to GPEA, you should address options for automating these collections as part of your planning for GPEA implementation.[2]

You should initiate any needed changes to your regulations that affect contract formation, notices, or disclosures between private parties involving business, consumer, or commercial transactions — or draft new regulations if necessary — by October 1, 2000, the general effective date for E-SIGN, or as soon as possible thereafter. In light of the close proximity of E-SIGN's effective date, you may wish to consider whether interim final or direct final regulations are appropriate. You should not wait to complete your GPEA plans that are due October 31, 2000 to pursue such regulatory actions.

A. *Special Rules for Specific Types of Regulations*

1. *Record Retention Requirements* — Once E-SIGN becomes effective, private parties may keep electronic records instead of paper records of covered transactions provided the electronic records meet certain accuracy and

accessibility requirements in the E-SIGN statute. Agencies should review their record retention regulations to determine whether changes are needed for mission performance or for future audit or law enforcement purposes. An agency may need to update requirements for paper records or adopt performance standards for accuracy, integrity, and accessibility of electronic records in order to maintain the effectiveness of record retention requirements. Part III discusses an agency's authority to issue performance standards for the use of electronic records.

Record retention requirements imposed by Federal laws and by State laws administered by a State agency will be subject to E-SIGN beginning on March 1, 2001. (Record retention requirements imposed by State laws that are not administered by a State agency are subject to E-SIGN beginning October 1, 2000.) If on March 1, 2001, an agency has announced, proposed or initiated (but not completed) a rulemaking to prescribe performance standards for electronic records used to meet a record retention requirement, the effective date of E-SIGN as to that requirement will be June 1, 2001. Accordingly, agencies should commence any rulemaking as soon as possible but no later than March 1, 2001, in order to complete the rulemaking by June 1, 2001. Agencies may wish to combine proposed changes relating to record retention in a single proposed rule for administrative ease.

The PRA covers many regulatory record retention requirements for business, consumer, or commercial transactions. When these regulations are information collections under the PRA, and thus subject to GPEA (see discussion under Step Four above), agencies should address options for automating these collections as part of their GPEA planning. Given the considerably earlier effective dates for E-SIGN than for GPEA, changes in record retention regulations should be given high priority in the GPEA plans that are due by October 31, 2000.

2. *Filing Requirements* — Under E-SIGN, agencies generally can specify standards and formats for records. They must adapt standards for the filing of electronic filings for most of their processes, consistent with the standards and timetables in GPEA. Agencies should review their regulations that relate to filings to determine whether changes are needed. They should decide any on such changes by October 31, 2000, the deadline for GPEA plans. Agencies should refer to OMB Memorandum M-00-10, "Implementation of the GPEA," for general guidance in this area, and to OMB's procedural guidance on developing GPEA plans, issued July 25, 2000, for specific instructions.

3. *Federal Loan Guarantees and Mortgage Insurance* — Agencies should also examine their regulations governing transactions related to federal loan guarantees, mortgage insurance, and commitments for these obligations. Some agency regulations set rules for communication between lenders (for example, financial institutions) and borrowers (for example, homeowners or students) in such transactions. Due to the importance of preserving loan documentation, an agency should carefully examine the extent to which it needs to specify standards for the accuracy, integrity, and accessibility of electronic loan documentation methods.

E-SIGN applies to transactions involving mortgage insurance, loan guarantees, loan guarantee commitments, and other programs listed in the Federal Credit Supplement, Budget of the United States (FY 2001). E-SIGN applies to such transactions and to any loan or mortgage which is made, insured, or guaranteed by the United States under this supplement on or after June 30, 2001 (one year after E-SIGN became law). If agency regulations related to these loan transactions contain information collections under the PRA, they are subject to GPEA, and agencies should address options for automating these collections as part of their GPEA planning.

Part III: A Description of E-SIGN's Requirements

The following discussion seeks to explain E-SIGN's specific requirements. Agencies may also benefit from the discussion of E-SIGN's legislative history in Exhibit 1.[3]

A. *Regulating Transactions Between Private Parties (Contract Formation, Notices, and Disclosures)*

1. **When Does E-Sign Apply?**
    a. **Contract formation.** Regulations that directly regulate the form or content of legal agreements in commercial, consumer or business transactions between private parties are generally within the scope of E-SIGN. They must allow the parties to use electronic contracts.

    Illustration 1: Person A is selling substance S to person B in a commercial transaction. Agency ABC currently requires that all private contracts for the sale of substance S be recorded on blue paper. E-SIGN applies to this requirement, so assuming A and B agree to use an electronic record to evidence their contract, they do not need to use paper of any type.

    Illustration 2: Person A is selling substance S to person B in a commercial transaction. Agency ABC has adopted a regulation requiring that all electronic contracts for the sale of substance S be electronically signed with a particular signature method. E-SIGN applies, and the regulation must meet the standards set forth in Section 104 governing the use of agency interpretive authority (see Section III(A)(3) below).

    b. **Notice and disclosure requirements.** E-SIGN generally applies to all requirements that private parties undertake such activities as signing documents or exchanging disclosures during the course of commercial, consumer or business transactions.

    Illustration 1: Person A is selling substance S to person B in a commercial transaction. Agency ABC requires that when substance S is sold, a separate disclosure form must be provided. E-SIGN applies to the disclosure form, so (assuming the parties agree) the disclosure may be in electronic form.

Exhibit 1.   Legislative History of E-SIGN

At the time E-SIGN was passed, a number of Senators and Representatives made floor statements about E-SIGN, Especially comprehensive statements were delivered by Senators Hollings, Wyden, and Sarbanes, who made a joint statement, and by Congressman Dingell, who made two statements. The joint Senate statement and the first statement of Congressman Dingell were very similar. 146 Cong. Rec. S5229 (June 16, 2000); 146 Cong. Rec. H4357 (June 14, 2000); 146 Cong. Rec. E1071 (June 21, 2000). Senator Abraham and Congressman Bliley also made extensive statements, which were likewise similar to one another. 146 Cong. Rec. S5283 (June 16, 2000); 146 Cong. Rec. H4352 (June 14, 2000). In signing E-SIGN, the President stated that he did so

> with the understanding, reflected in the Congressional Record statements of Senators Hollings, Wyden, and Sarbanes, and Congressman Dingell, that this Act gives State and Federal governments the authority they need to establish record retention requirements, prescribe standards and formats for filings, and issue other regulations and orders to implement the legislation necessary to prevent waste, investigate and enforce the law, operate programs effectively, and protect consumers and the public interest. As they explained, this legislation principally addresses commercial and consumer activities, not governmental activities that have already been addressed by the Government Paperwork Elimination Act. To the extent that these two laws overlap, I instruct Federal agencies to construe them in a manner consistent with protecting the public interest and effectively carrying out agency missions.

The floor statements of the legislation's sponsors contain a number of statements that may be helpful to agencies seeking to construe E-SIGN. Of particular help may be the statements specifically cited by the President in his signing statement. These statements include, for example, Congressman Dingell's statement about the scope of E-SIGN:

> [t]he Conferees specifically rejected including 'Governmental' transactions. Members should understand that this bill will not in any way affect most Governmental transactions, such as law enforcement actions, court actions, issuance of Government grants, applications for or disbursement of Government benefits, or other activities that the Government conducts that private actors would not conduct. Even though some aspects of such Governmental transactions (for example, the Government's issuance of a check reflecting a Government benefit) are commercial in nature, they are not covered by this bill because they are part of a uniquely governmental operation. Likewise, activities conducted by private parties principally for governmental purposes are not covered by this bill. Thus, for example, the act of collecting signatures to place a nomination on a ballot would not be covered, even though it might have some nexus with commerce (such as the signature collectors' contract of employment).

There may be narrow circumstances in which requirements imposed on private-party transactions are not
within the scope of E-SIGN, for example, where they do
not "relate to" the transaction. We expect such situations
to arise infrequently.[4] In addition, private-party transactions that are principally undertaken for a governmental
purpose do not fall under the scope of E-SIGN.

c. **Additional requirements for consumer transactions.** Section 101(c)
requires that for transactions that involve a consumer,[5] electronic records
may be substituted for paper versions only if the consumer affirmatively
consents to receive the documents in electronic form and several other
requirements are met. These include, among other things, that the
consumer receive a clear and conspicuous statement of: (1) the consumer's right to receive paper records; (2) the consequences of later
withdrawing consent to receive electronic records; and (3) the hardware
and software requirements for access to and retention of electronic
records. This provision is especially significant, since many laws require
that individuals receive information in paper form in connection with
private transactions, including extensions of credit by financial institutions and the sale of real estate.

The consumer must provide the affirmative consent electronically
in a manner that reasonably demonstrates that the consumer is able to
access the electronic records that are the subject of the consent.
Section 101(c) seeks to ensure that existing consumer protections based
on paper disclosures to consumers are not undermined by the use of
electronic disclosures in cases where consumers do not have the
capability to receive such disclosures or may not be fully aware of the
consequences of agreeing to receive such disclosures electronically.

Agencies should review the extensive consumer disclosure provisions
contained in Section 101(c) of E-SIGN, which are not reviewed in full here.

2. Should Agencies Issue Guidance or Regulations on How Parties May Contract or Provide Notices Electronically?

When agencies assess their regulations affecting private-party transactions,
they should first consider two things:

- what the regulated persons might do on their own (that is, forms they
  might choose to use in their transactions), and
- whether there are any substantial policy reasons to issue guidance or
  regulations with respect to the parties' choice of method

a. **What would regulated parties do in the absence of rule revision?**
In general, starting on October 1, 2000, those who formerly had to use
paper-and-ink contracts, notices, and disclosures need no longer do so.
At least in the short run, however, most contracting parties will continue
to use paper B perhaps out of habit, or due to unfamiliarity with new
methods, or for other purposes. Other parties will begin immediately
to use electronic formats for their contracts. Agencies should ensure
that they are aware of what approach regulated parties are taking to
electronic transactions.

Illustration 1: Person A is contracting with person B to sell product M in a commercial transaction. Agency ABC requires that contracts for the sale of product M be in writing. (They need not, however, be filed or retained.) Agency ABC elects not to issue a new regulation in response to E-SIGN. Starting on October 1, 2000, A and B may use any electronic form they agree on for their contracts. E-SIGN ensures that Agency ABC's regulation will not deny the contracts legal effect solely because they are in electronic form.

b. Is there a substantial policy reason to issue guidance or regulations concerning the parties' choice of contracting or disclosure method? As a rule, parties should be left to choose the electronic contracting method they will use. There may be some circumstances, however, in which substantial policy reasons require that agencies issue guidance or regulations concerning this issue. For example, the agency may want to ensure that consumers or businesses have accessible copies of electronic contracts or disclosures relating to certain types of transactions. An agency may wish to solicit comments from regulated entities, consumers, and the public at large as to whether issuance of guidance or regulations is appropriate to address substantial policy concerns. These comments could help the agency identify issues that should be addressed in any guidance or regulation.

Illustration 1: Product M is often counterfeited. Agency ABC has issued a regulation requiring that all contracts for the sale of Product M be in writing and contain certain terms, for the protection of consumers who later discover that they have purchased a counterfeit product. Agency ABC is concerned that, if product M is sold electronically in a way that leaves many consumers with poor records of the transaction, those who buy counterfeits may be unable to obtain relief. Agency ABC may conclude that it is appropriate to issue regulations interpreting the provisions of E-SIGN to address this risk.

3. What is an Agency's Interpretive Authority?

If E-SIGN applies (section (1) above) and it is necessary to interpret E-SIGN (section (2) above), agencies should consider issuing rules or guidance to do so, as discussed in part I.C., above. Section 104(b)(1) of E-SIGN provides that only agencies with statutory authority to issue rules may do so. Agencies with authority to issue guidance and orders as well as rules may elect to issue guidance or orders. An agency's rules should interpret one of the provisions in Section 101. A regulation or guidance could specify standards for signatures or records used in meeting a particular statutory requirement. Agencies whose regulations implement consumer disclosure requirements may consider the need to interpret various terms used in Section 101(c) as they apply to the disclosure requirements the agency administers. For example, an agency may consider the need to interpret the "clear and conspicuous" requirement (Section 101(c)(1)(B)) or how a consumer "reasonably demonstrates" the ability to access electronic records (Section 101(c)(1)(C)(2)).

Of course, agencies need not promulgate rules unless there are substantial reasons for doing so. When agencies choose to do so, E-SIGN contains a number of specific restrictions on agency rulemaking authority. While E-SIGN may help grant legal recognition to electronic signatures and records, agencies still have the authority to impose some rules to ensure the reliability, availability and integrity of contracts and records or when necessary for other agency purposes.

a. **Rules must be consistent with and not add to Section 101. (Section 104(b)(2)(A), (B)).** These provisions require that regulations, orders, or guidance be "consistent with" Section 101 and "not add to" the requirements of that Section. Agency interpretations of these provisions are subject to the usual test for judicial review of an agency's interpretation of a statute that it is charged with administering. The agency may not deviate from the clear language of a statute but may construe a statute where Congress' intent is not clear.[6]

b. **Rules must be substantially justified. (Section 104(b)(2)(C)(i)).** This provision requires that the agency find that there is a "substantial justification" for the regulation, order, or guidance. Agencies should not promulgate regulations unless substantial policy reasons justify that they do so. If such policy reasons exist, regulation may be appropriate.[7]

c. **Rules must be substantially equivalent to those for paper records. (Section 104(b)(2)(C)(ii)(I)).** This provision requires that "the methods selected to carry out" the agency's purpose must be "substantially equivalent to the requirements imposed on records that are not electronic records." In some circumstances, it may be appropriate to assess "substantial equivalence" by considering general features of a process (such as security, proof of identity, and the like), since electronic and paper systems often operate by means that are not directly analogous. Systems may be substantially equivalent at this higher level of generality even though their details are quite dissimilar.

d. **Rules may not impose unreasonable costs. (Section 104(b)(2)(C) (ii)(II)).** This provision requires that "the methods selected to carry out" the agency's purpose must "not impose unreasonable costs on the acceptance and use of electronic records." One factor in the reasonableness determination may be a comparison of the cost and benefits of the proposed regulation. This comparison will presumably resemble other analysis of regulatory costs and benefits.

e. **Rules must be technology-neutral. (Section 104(b)(2)(C)(iii)).** This provision requires that "the methods selected to carry out" the agency's purpose must not "require, or accord greater legal status or effect to, the implementation or application of a specific technology or technical specification for performing the functions of creating, storing, generating, receiving, communicating, or authenticating electronic records or electronic signatures." Although this provision bars agencies from prescribing specific technologies, it does not bar an agency from adopting a performance standard for a particular technology. Such standards could address such issues as security, record integrity, record or identity authentication, or interoperability of systems. In some instances, agencies may be able to require the use of a specific technology or technical specification. See Section 104(b)(3)(A), discussed in Section III(B)(3), below.

f. **Rules may not require the use of paper. (Section 104(c)(1)).** This provision states that agencies may not use their interpretive authority to "impose or reimpose any requirement that a record be in a tangible printed or paper form." But see the exception in Section 104(b)(3)(B), discussed in Section III(B)(3), below.

B. Record Retention Requirements

E-SIGN does not define "record retention" requirements. In its usual sense, however, the term refers to requirements that a private party retain certain records so they will be available for audit or law enforcement purposes.

Section 101 of E-SIGN contains specific provisions permitting the use of electronic records to comply with record retention requirements if the record "accurately reflects the information set forth in the contract or record," (Section 101(d)(1)(A)), and "remains accessible to all persons who are entitled to access by statute, regulation, or rule of law, for the period required by such statute, regulation, or rule of law, in a form that is capable of being accurately reproduced for later reference, whether by transmission, printing, or otherwise," (Section 101(d)(1)(B)).

1. When Does E-SIGN Apply?

Record retention requirements for records generated in a commercial, consumer, or business transaction are subject to E-SIGN.

Illustration 1: Person A is selling substance S to person B in a commercial transaction. Agency ABC requires that, when substance S is sold, a copy of the contract of sale be retained for future audit or law enforcement purposes. E-SIGN applies to this requirement, so the contract may be retained in electronic form.

Records generated solely to comply with regulations (see illustration 2), rather than records generated as part of a preexisting commercial transaction, are generally not subject to E-SIGN. Record retention requirements of the former type are subject to GPEA, however, and should be reviewed and addressed under the processes set forth in that Act.

Illustration 2: Agency ABC requires that certain categories of businesses periodically commission audits of their consumption of substance S. The audits are self-contained documents, created to government specifications, and do not contain records of the underlying transactions. Agency ABC requires that the businesses retain a copy of the audit, but does not require that the audits be reported. E-SIGN does not apply. The requirement is not "related to" a commercial transaction. The contract between the audited and auditing entity is a commercial transaction, but one that occurs only to comply with this governmental requirement.

2. **Should the Agency Allow the Parties to Choose any Method for Retaining Records Electronically?**
   As with regulation of private-party transactions, agencies should consider two things regarding their record retention requirements. First, they should consider what the regulated persons might do on their own (that is, what forms might they choose for retention absent regulation). Second, agencies should consider whether there are any substantial policy reasons to regulate the parties' choice of method.

   a. **What would regulated parties do in the absence of a rule revision?**
      In general, starting on March 1, 2001, regulated parties need no longer retain records in paper form (so long as they keep them in an acceptable electronic form). Many parties may continue to keep their records on paper, others may prefer that electronic forms of record retention. This is especially true for transactions that were originally undertaken in electronic, rather than written form.

      Illustration 1: Agency ABC regulates the sale of a commodity that raises significant regulatory concerns. Agency ABC requires suppliers of the commodity to keep written records of all sales, so that, if necessary, it can track and trace major purchasers and uses of the commodity. Starting on March 1, 2001, Corporation C and others begin to sell the commodity over the Internet. C's computers keep an electronic copy of certain key information on each purchase. Now that this information is stored electronically, C and other distributors who use similar systems no longer keep paper records of the transactions. Agency ABC should review its record keeping regulations to insure that they are consistent with the practices permitted by E-SIGN.

   b. Is there a substantial policy reason to issue guidance or regulations with respect to the parties' choice of record retention methods? Parties should be left to select an electronic storage form of their own choosing where appropriate. There may be some circumstances, however, in which substantial policy reasons require that agencies regulate the parties' choice. For example, the agency may want to ensure that the record has not been tampered with, that it is safe from inadvertent loss or destruction, that the agency can read and access it, or that it contains all the necessary information. We believe that many agencies will wish to issue guidance or regulations addressing these issues.

      Illustration 1: The information about the regulated commodity transactions stored on C's system is kept in a database that is updated every minute. Any of C's employees have access to the database and can change any of the data in it. Agency ABC may wish to update its regulations to require that the commodity sale records be maintained in a secure format if C's current database management substantially impedes audits or enforcement.

      Illustration 2: Agency ABC is also concerned about its ability to identify purchasers of the commodity through the sales records. Agency ABC has concluded that regulated entities do not always preserve this information adequately in their electronic systems. The agency may also wish to issue an updated regulation requiring that records be maintained in a format that accurately and reliably reflects the identity of the purchaser.

Illustration 3: In some cases, Agency ABC has a need to refer to the commodity sales records for several years after a sale occurs. Realizing that computer systems and database software used in the industry change frequently as technology advances, Agency ABC may want to issue an updated regulation requiring that records be maintained over time in a format that is reasonably accessible to government investigators.

3. What is an Agency's Interpretive Authority?

If E-SIGN applies (Section 1 above) and it is necessary to interpret E-SIGN (Section 2 above), agencies may wish to issue rules or guidance to do so. E-SIGN provides, in Section 104(b)(1), that only agencies with preexisting statutory authority to issue rules may do so. Agencies with authority to issue guidance and orders as well as rules may elect to issue guidance or orders. These rules or guidance would interpret the provisions of Section 101(d). For example, agencies having the requisite rulemaking authority might interpret the following aspects of Section 101(d)'s provisions with regard to their programs:

- What types of records will be deemed to "accurately reflect the information" (Section 101(d)(1)(A)) in a contract or record? Must the record be of a type that is read-only or otherwise is non-alterable?

- What particular information "in the contract or record" (Section 101(d)(1)(A)) must be reflected?

- What does it mean to "remain accessible" (Section 101(d)(1)(B))? Does that mean that the hardware and software necessary to read the record must be kept available too? If so, where must those materials be kept? To whom must they be available? Who pays for that?

- Who are the persons "entitled to access" (Section 101(d)(1)(B))?

- What is the applicable period of time (Section 101(d)(1)(B)) for which the records must be accessible?

- Regarding checks, what comprises the "information on the front and the back of the check" (Section 101(d)(4))? Is this requirement satisfied by merely typing into a database the handwritten name(s) that appears on the signature line and the endorsement, or does it require scanning the signature and maintaining the image of it in the database?

The general limitations on agency rulemaking authority discussed in part A.3. (See p. 12) also apply here in the case of agency interpretations related to record retention requirements. E-SIGN also contains specific provisions in Section 101 addressing record retention, and provisions providing agencies with additional authority to regulate record retention, including authority to adopt performance standards, and to require the use of specific technologies or of paper in certain circumstances.

a. **Requiring specific technologies. (Section 104(b)(3)(A)).** As explained above, E-SIGN generally permits agencies to adopt performance standards in regulations interpreting Section 101. With respect to record retention requirements, E-SIGN provides agencies with additional authority, stating that agencies may "specify performance standards to assure accuracy, record integrity, and accessibility of records that are required to be retained." Such standards would be interpretations of the general provisions of Section 101(d).

E-SIGN permits agencies to adopt standards that are "specified in a manner that imposes a requirement in violation of paragraph (2)(C)(iii)," — that is, that require the use of a specific technology or technical specification — if the agency finds that the requirement serves an *important* government objective and is *substantially* related to the achievement of that objective.

Agencies may not "require use of a particular type of software or hardware in order to comply with Section 101(d)." This provision is probably best read to mean that agencies may not require use of the hardware or software of a specific manufacturer, not that they may not set performance standards for hardware and software. The statute permits agencies to require the use of a particular technology or technical specification if the required findings are made.

Illustration 1: Agency ABC wishes to ensure that records retained by private parties are kept in a format that cannot be tampered with and that it can easily read with its equipment. The agency requires that records be retained on a write-once, read-many device meeting an established industry standard S. The only manufacturer that currently makes equipment meeting that industry standard is Manufacturer M. The regulation is permissible, assuming the other provisions of E-SIGN and any other applicable laws are met.

Illustration 2: The same situation as in Illustration 1, but Agency ABC specifically requires the use of equipment made by the Manufacturer M. The regulation is not permissible.

b. **Requiring use of paper. (Section 104(b)(3)(B)).** This provision permits agencies to require retention of a record in a tangible printed or paper form if there is a "compelling governmental interest relating to law enforcement or national security for imposing such requirement" and "imposing such requirement is essential to attaining such interest."

C. Filing Requirements

E-SIGN preserves agencies' authority to specify standards and formats for records filed with the agency (Section 104(a)). Therefore, as a rule, filing requirements will be governed by GPEA, not by E-SIGN. GPEA generally provides for agencies to allow for the use and acceptance of electronic signatures and records when practicable. GPEA sets timetables for this.

Agencies should review their regulations regarding filings to determine what changes, if any, are needed in those regulations. Agencies should make any changes needed in this area by October 2003, the deadline under GPEA. To the extent that regulated filings are also information collections under the PRA, agencies should address options for automating these transactions as part of their GPEA planning.

D. Government Guaranteed Loans and Mortgage Insurance

These programs generally involve at least two contracts: A contract between the borrower and a private lender, and a separate guarantee or insurance contract between the private lender and the government. The government generally is not a party to the first contract (the loan or mortgage transaction), but is a party to the second contract (the guarantee or insurance).

Although E-SIGN would not require the government to use or accept electronic signatures in its guarantee or insurance contract (Section 101(b)(2)), the government may do so because of GPEA's requirements. An agency can specify the format (for example, paper, with ink signatures, or a particular technology or software) for records filed with that agency (Section 104(a)). An agency could also require that crucial documents in the transaction (for example, copy of note and mortgage) be filed with the agency or its contractor in whatever form the agency chooses.

Aside from the filing requirements discussed above, the agency might have less control over how the loan or mortgage contract would be documented between the parties. To the extent that the agency has rulemaking authority with regard to the transaction, however, it could interpret Section 101 accordingly. The agency also could interpret the record retention provisions of Section 101(d) (subject to applicable restrictions in Section 104(b)). For example:

- The agency could interpret the terms (such as "accessibility") used in Section 101(d).
- Under Section 104(b)(3)(A) the agency could specify "performance standards to ensure accuracy, record integrity, and accessibility of records."
- The agency could specify the specific technology that must be used to keep the records, if the agency determines that such a requirement (i) serves an important governmental objective, and (ii) is substantially related to the achievement of that objective.

Agencies need to act on loan provisions in time to meet the effective dates outlined in Part F below.

E. Government as Market Participant

1. When Does E-SIGN Apply?

Whether a particular action or interaction by a government agency is covered by Section 101(a) can be a complicated question. As explained in Part I, section B above, distinctively governmental activities are not within the scope of E-SIGN. For example, particular activities undertaken by an agency involving the government's obligations regarding Medicare are not covered by Section 101(a), even though those activities may be analogous to activities engaged in by a private party (e.g., provision of health insurance).

When the government engages in "business, consumer or commercial affairs," its actions could be deemed "transactions" within the meaning of Section 101(a). In that event, the question of whether Section 101(a) mandates the government's use or acceptance of electronic signatures and records might depend on whether the transaction is a contract to which the government is a party.

a. **Contract to which agency is a party.** Section 101(b)(2), in effect, states that Title I of E-SIGN does not require agencies to "use or accept" electronic signatures or records for contracts to which they are parties.[8]

An agency and a private party with whom it is contracting may choose by mutual agreement whatever particular methodologies they wish to use. For example, they could specify in the contract that certain notices or records must be on paper, with an ink signature, or that the contract, notices or related records must be in a particular electronic format or must use a particular type of software. Section 101 states "[n]otwithstanding any statute, regulation, or other rule of law ... ." Thus, the operative portions of Section 101 trump statutes, regulations and rules of law, but this should be read narrowly to leave open the option for parties to agree to limitations on the use of electronic methods. The restrictions of Section 104 should not apply to consensual agreements between the government and another party to a government contract. The restrictions in Section 104 apply only to what the government may require by regulations, not to what the government and those with whom it contracts may agree upon.

Illustration 1: An agency seeks to lease office equipment. E-SIGN would not require the agency to use or accept electronic signatures and records for the lease itself, because the agency would be a party to the contract, but the agency is likely to implement an electronic method under GPEA.

Illustration 2: Assume the agency and the lessor enter into the lease (on paper, with ink signatures), and the lessor seeks to serve a notice (such as a notice of a breach or foreclosure) electronically. The lease expressly states that notices must be given in writing, signed with an ink signature. In this case, the electronic notice was not sufficient. Even under E-SIGN, parties to a contract (including the government, when it is a party) are free to specify contract terms such as the form of notices.[9]

b. **Agency is not a party to a contract.** If an activity involves a "transaction" (generally, the conduct of business, consumer or commercial affairs) that is not a contract, or if it involves a contract to which the agency is not a party, Section 101(a) might require recognition of electronic signatures and records (Section 101(b)(2)). This could arise, for example, in the context of government loan guarantees and mortgage insurance, to the extent that they are considered business, consumer or commercial activities (See Section D).

To the extent the agency has rulemaking authority in connection with the transaction, it may have the ability to interpret Section 101 in ways that will allow it some control over the format of the transaction. It also might be able to require that records be filed with the agency in specified formats.

2. Should an Agency Agree to Use Electronic Records and Signatures for Contracts to Which It is a Party?

When the government is a party to a contract, it has the ability to determine, subject to GPEA, whether to use and accept electronic methods, even if the other parties to the contract wish to do so. Agencies should use their discretion, taking into account the applicable requirements of GPEA as applied to the contract, and considering any policy implications. Even when the government is not a party to a contract, in many instances it may have a significant financial stake (such as the mortgage insurance and loan guarantee contracts described above). It must assess whether it needs to take steps to ensure that it is protected from financial loss that might occur if the private parties do not use means that will allow the government to protect its rights in the transaction.

3. What is an Agency's Interpretive Authority?

To the extent that agencies determine that they need to have some control over, for example, contracts between private parties that expose the government to liability or loss (for example, government guaranteed loans by a private lender to a borrower), agencies may use their rule-making authority, as discussed above. Further, to the extent that agencies need to require that certain documents in the underlying transaction (for example, the underlying loan contract) need to be submitted to the agency (directly or to a loan servicer (a contractor) who maintains the records for the agency) Section 104(a) preserves the agency's ability to require this.

4. How Does E-SIGN Apply to Transactions in which the Government is a Party?

Section 101(c) establishes a special rule for the use of electronic records in consumer transactions (see Section A(1)(c) above). If a statute, regulation, or other rule of law requires that information be provided to a consumer in writing, an electronic record of the information may be used to fulfill this requirement only if the consumer affirmatively consents to the use of the electronic record and several other requirements spelled out in Section 101(c) are satisfied. Under the Act, a consumer is an individual who obtains products or services primarily for personal, family, or household purposes (Section 106(1)).

The requirements of Section 101(c) likely will apply to a federal agency in very limited circumstances. First, these requirements will apply only where the agency is engaging in a transaction as a market participant (as opposed to strictly governmental transactions related to taxation or public benefits administration) and the agency is providing products or services directly to a consumer. Second, there must be a statute, regulation, or other law requiring the consumer to receive certain information relating to the transaction in writing. Third, the agency must seek to require the consumer to receive that information electronically. Fourth, the information must not be part of a contract to which the agency is a party.

F.   Effective Dates

See Exhibit 2 for effective dates of the provisions.

The Electronic Frontier: the Challenge of Unlawful Conduct Involving the Use of the Internet

In August 1999, President Clinton established an interagency Working Group on Unlawful Conduct on the Internet. Executive Order 13,133 directed the Working Group, under the leadership of the Attorney General, to prepare a report with recommendations on:

- The extent to which existing federal laws provide a sufficient basis for effective investigation and prosecution of unlawful conduct that involves the use of the Internet;
- The extent to which new technology tools, capabilities, or legal authorities may be required for effective investigation and prosecution of unlawful conduct that involves the use of the Internet; and
- The potential for new or existing tools and capabilities to educate and empower parents, teachers, and others to prevent or to minimize the risks from unlawful conduct that involves the use of the Internet.

Press Release

Attorney General Janet Reno today issued a report that presents an analysis of legal and policy issues created by unlawful conduct on the Internet. The report, entitled The Electronic Frontier: The Challenge of Unlawful Conduct Involving the Use of the Internet, is a product of the President's Working Group on Unlawful Conduct on the Internet. The report finds that the Internet presents new and significant investigatory challenges for law enforcement at all levels.

"The Internet has afforded our society unparalleled opportunities, many of which we are just discovering, but it is also providing new opportunities for criminals to engage in crime," said Attorney General Janet Reno. "Through the continued efforts of law enforcement and private industry we will ensure that the Internet reaches its full potential for expanding communications, facilitating commerce, and bringing countless other benefits to our society."

The report recommends a three-part approach to address unlawful conduct on the Internet and concludes that:

Exhibit 2. Effective Dates

Provision	Effective Date
General effective date for the provisions of Title I (Electronic Records and Signatures in Commerce) except for the provisions discussed below.	October 1, 2000
Any record retention requirement imposed by: (i) a Federal statute, regulation, or other rule of law, or (ii) a State statute, regulation, or other rule of law administered or promulgated by a State regulatory agency.	March 1, 2001
If on March 1, 2001, a Federal regulatory agency or State regulatory agency has announced, proposed, or initiated, but not completed, a rulemaking proceeding to prescribe a regulation under Section 104(b)(3), with respect to a record retention requirement, Title I (Electronic Records and Signatures in Commerce) shall be effective on June 1, 2001, with respect to such requirement.	June 1, 2001
With regard to any transaction involving a loan guarantee or loan guarantee commitment (as those terms are defined in Section 502 of the Federal Credit Reform Act of 1990), or involving a program listed in the Federal Credit Supplement, Budget of the United States, FY 2001, Title I (Electronic Records and Signatures in Commerce) applies only to such transactions entered into, and to any loan or mortgage made, insured, or guaranteed by the United States Government thereunder. Note that this includes most transactions involving loan guarantees and mortgage insurance programs of federal agencies.	June 30, 2001 (On or after one year after the date of enactment of the bill)
Any records that are provided or made available to a consumer pursuant to an application for a loan, or a loan made, pursuant to title IV of the Higher Education Act of 1965	Section 101(c) shall not apply until the earlier of C(a) such time as the Secretary of Education publishes revised promissory notes under Section 432(m) of the Higher Education Act of 1965; or (b) June 30, 2001.
General effective date for the provisions of Title II (transferable records)	September 29, 2000 (90 days after date of enactment of the bill).

- Regulation of unlawful conduct involving the use of the Internet should be analyzed through a framework that ensures that online conduct is treated in a manner consistent with the way offline conduct is treated, in a technology-neutral manner, and in a manner that recognizes and protects privacy and civil liberties.

- Cybercrime presents unique and significant challenges to law enforcement which requires resources for training, new investigative tools, legal authorities and capabilities.
- Continued support of private sector leadership is needed to promote and teach "cyberethics" to empower Internet users to prevent and minimize the risks of unlawful activity.

The Working Group analyzed existing federal law for its applicability in cybercrime cases. It determined that current law is appropriate in most cases of fraud, child pornography, sale of prescription drugs and controlled substances, firearms, gambling, alcohol, securities fraud and intellectual property over the Internet. It also indicated a need for modification of certain procedural and evidentiary laws in order for law enforcement to confront the challenges created by the Internet.

According to the report, the challenge facing law enforcement is the difficulty in finding criminals in the Internet's multi-jurisdictional, global environment. The inability to track down sophisticated criminals who hide their identities online, the need for better coordination among law enforcement agencies, and the need for trained and well-equipped personnel at all levels of law enforcement is critical to fighting cybercrime.

The report also states that when addressing these challenges, the government should carefully consider all societal interests. A balance must be struck when investigating and prosecuting criminals which takes into account free speech, protecting children, reasonable expectations of privacy, broad access to public information, and legitimate commerce.

The interagency Working Group was established in August 1999 by a Presidential Executive Order, under the leadership of the Attorney General, to address the issue of unlawful conduct involving the use of the Internet. The working group was directed to perform their evaluation within the context of current Administration policy which included promoting self-regulation in the industry, supporting technology-neutral laws and recognizing that the Internet is an important resource for commerce, communication and education.

The Working Group benefitted from the views of a variety of sources. Those providing input included various entities of the federal government, state and local groups, industry groups, and non-profit advocacy and civil liberties groups.

Fact Sheet (August 6, 1999)

- The Vice President announced today a new effort by the Administration to address unlawful conduct involving the use of the Internet. Specifically, the Executive Order will create a Working Group, chaired by the Attorney General, that will address legal and policy issues relating to unlawful conduct on the Internet.
- While the Internet provides dramatic and exciting benefits to enhance our lives, it also allows those who want to violate or evade the law an opportunity to reach exponentially greater numbers of people. The Working Group provides a mechanism to take a comprehensive look at our policies and assess the scope and applicability of current law to unlawful

activity on the Internet, the extent to which new technological tools or resources can help in the fight against crime, and the potential to use other means to lower the risks from unlawful acts on the Internet.

■ In the spirit of the Administration's Framework for Global Electronic Commerce, the Working Group will undertake its review in the context of Administration policy that emphasizes industry self-regulation where possible, technology-neutral laws and regulations, and an appreciation of the Internet as an important medium both domestically and internationally for commerce and free speech.

— The Attorney General will serve as Chair for the Working Group, which will include:
— The Director of the Office of Management and Budget,
— The Secretary of the Treasury,
— The Secretary of Commerce,
— The Secretary of Education,
— The Director of the Federal Bureau of Investigation,
— The Director of the Bureau of Alcohol, Tobacco, and Firearms,
— The Administrator of the Drug Enforcement Administration,
— The Chairman of the Federal Trade Commission
— The Administrator of the Food and Drug Administration, and
— Other federal officials deemed appropriate by the Chair of the Working Group.

The Chair and Vice Chair of the Vice President's Electronic Commerce Working Group will serve as liaisons to the Group.

■ As it carries out its mandate, the Working Group will seek input from industry, consumer, and other private sector groups, along with state and local law enforcement officials.

■ The Executive Order provides that the Working Group will provide a report and recommendations to the President and Vice President within 120 days on:

— The applicability of existing federal laws to unlawful conduct involving the use of the Internet (e.g., sale of guns, explosives, controlled substances, and prescription drugs);
— The need for new technological and legal tools to investigate and prosecute such conduct; and
— The potential for new or existing tools to educate and empower parents, teachers, and others to prevent or to minimize the risks from unlawful conduct on the Internet.

Questions and Answers (August 6, 1999)

Q: Why is the Executive Order necessary? Is there a specific problem with the Internet that you are trying to address?

A: The Executive Order is a recognition that, apart from the Internet's dramatic and exciting benefits, it also allows those who want to violate or evade the law an opportunity to reach exponentially greater numbers of people. We want to make the Internet safe for commerce and safe for all Americans. One way to do that is to take a step back from the discrete issues — Internet sale of drugs, guns, explosives — and take a more comprehensive look at our policies to see what we need to do to address the challenges posed by this new technology. The Working Group provides a mechanism to understand the scope and applicability of current law, the extent to which new techno-logical tools or resources can help in the fight against crime, and the potential to use other means to lower the risks from unlawful acts on the Internet.

Q: What is industry's role in this process?

A: The Working Group will seek input from industry, consumer, and other private sector groups as it carries out its work. In addition, the Working Group will undertake its review in the context of current Administration policy, which includes support for industry self-regulation where possible, technology-neu-tral laws and regulations, and an appreciation for the Internet as an important medium both domestically and internationally for commerce and free speech[.]

Q: You say that this review will be done in the context of current Admin-istration policy, which favors self-regulation. Isn't the approach described in the Executive Order inconsistent with self-regulation?

A: No. The Administration continues to believe strongly in the need for self-regulation of this growing engine of our economy, but unlawful conduct does not become lawful simply because it happens to involve the use of the Internet. If you break the law by sending child pornography through the mails or planning a terrorist attack, your conduct does not suddenly become insulated from legal scrutiny simply because you used e-mail to commit the crime. Our criminal laws, by hypothesis, exist because we as a society do not believe self-regulation works to prevent conduct that is so harmful or morally unacceptable that we decide to make it a crime.

Q: Isn't this just the first step toward having Big Brother monitor all content on the Internet? How does this effort relate to the FIDNET (Federal Intrusion Detection Network) proposal?

A: The Administration has no plans to monitor all content on the Internet. The Working Group's review is intended as a forum to develop a comprehensive and coordinated policy approach to address unlawful conduct that involves the use of the Internet. Furthermore, as for FIDNET, this is merely a proposal to protect the security of Federal networks that contain sensitive information or perform critical functions to prevent unauthorized break-ins.

Q: What kind of international issues will the Working Group address?

A: We are finding that much of the conduct that may be of concern — such as the sale of prescription drugs without a valid prescription — may originate from Web site operators or other who happen to be abroad. The borderless aspect of the Internet raises difficult jurisdictional issues and investigatory challenges. We are working on a number of fronts to secure increased cooperation with our foreign counterparts on these issues, but we want to address the international aspects in a coordinated fashion, and it will therefore be important for the Working Group to consider these issues in the context of the report and recommendations.

Q: Will the Administration's review also cover Internet gambling? Other Internet crimes?

A: One of the initial tasks for the Attorney General and the Working Group will be to define the scope of the report. While the Executive Order does not limit the review to specific topics or crimes, the intent of the Executive Order is to primarily target and seek solutions to criminal activity on the Internet.

Q: What is the outcome likely to be?

A: The Working Group will produce a report and recommendations to the President and Vice President within 120 days, assessing: (1) the extent to which existing laws and technologies can be applied to unlawful conduct on the Internet; (2) the extent to which new technological tools may be required for effective investigation and prosecution of unlawful conduct on the Internet; and (3) the potential for new or existing tools to educate and empower parents, teachers, and others to prevent or to minimize the risks from unlawful conduct involving the use of the Internet.

On August 5, 1999, President Clinton issued Executive Order 13133, which established a Working Group to analyze the existence of unlawful conduct on the Internet and to prepare and report recommendations based on its findings within 120 days. The specific topics that the group will be addressing include the extent to which existing Federal laws provide a sufficient basis for effective investigation and prosecution of unlawful conduct that involves the Internet; the extent to which new tools, capabilities, or authorities may be required for effective investigation and prosecution of Internet crime; and the potential for educating and empowering parents, teachers and others to prevent or minimize risks from such unlawful conduct.

Internet Health Care Fraud

One Privacy Officer at the U.S. Department of Justice gave remarks on the prosecution of health care fraud and the protection of health care privacy on the Internet. His speech focused on the Federal government's fraud, consumer protection, and privacy protection efforts as they relate to the Internet healthcare industry.

Remarks of John T. Bentivoglio, Special Counsel for Health Care Fraud and Chief Privacy Officer, U.S. Department of Justice, at the Symposium on Healthcare Internet and E-Commerce: Legal, Regulatory and Ethical Issues. The statement can be found at www.usdoj.gov/criminal/cybercrime/healthsp.htm.

Jurisdiction in Law Suits

On June 29, 2000 D. Jean Veta, Deputy Associate Attorney General, testified before the House Subcommittee on the Courts and Intellectual Property, Committee on the Judiciary, about on how the Internet is changing the way in which federal and state courts and regulatory agencies conceive of their jurisdiction in civil lawsuits involving private litigants.

D. Jean Veta, Deputy Associate Attorney General, United States Department of Justice

Subcommittee on the Courts and Intellectual Property, Committee on the Judiciary, United States House of Representatives

10:00 AM

JUNE 29, 2000

Good morning, Mr. Chairman and Members of the Subcommittee. On behalf of the Department of Justice, I appreciate this opportunity to appear before this Subcommittee and to share with you our thoughts on how the Internet is changing the way in which federal and state courts and regulatory agencies conceive of their jurisdiction in civil lawsuits involving private litigants.

"Jurisdiction" is a broad concept and can be used to refer to four separate concepts. First and most commonly, jurisdiction refers to whether a court has the power to adjudicate claims against a litigant — in legal parlance, whether the court has "personal jurisdiction" over the litigant. Second, jurisdiction may loosely refer to whether a court proceeding is being held in the proper location, or venue. A court that possesses personal jurisdiction over a defendant, but which is not the proper venue for the action, might be said not to have "jurisdiction" over the lawsuit. Third, jurisdiction has sometimes been used to refer to the decision of a court to apply one state's law over another's, when the law of two or more states are relevant to a dispute. This is often referred to as "choice of law." Last, jurisdiction can refer to the statutory grant of authority a state or federal regulatory agency possesses. For example, when a court holds that an agency does not have "jurisdiction" to regulate a certain activity, it is expressing its view that the legislature did not invest that agency with substantive authority over that activity.[10]

Although all four concepts are longstanding and well-developed, their application to the Internet raises new and difficult questions. As a starting point in addressing these issues, we believe the principle articulated in the Report of the President's Working Group on Unlawful Conduct on the Internet, which was chaired by the Attorney General, applies with equal force in the civil context — online conduct should be treated the same as offline conduct, to the extent feasible. Additionally, we do not believe that it is necessary or appropriate to develop an entirely new body of federal statutory law to address cyber-jurisdiction issues. Rather, and for the reasons explained more fully below, we believe that the courts are adequately developing jurisdictional jurisprudence under applicable state and federal law, and should continue to take the lead on these issues.

We have narrowed the focus of this testimony in two ways we believe that the Subcommittee will find helpful. First, we will concentrate on how these jurisdictional issues affect litigation and regulation in the civil context. Second, we will focus on how these issues play out within the boundaries of the United States, leaving most of the international jurisdictional issues for the State Department to discuss in its testimony. We will therefore give the most attention to how jurisdictional issues among the states and within the United States are being addressed. Not surprisingly, most of these issues involve application of state long-arm statutes and other state laws, and are not appropriate subjects of federal regulation. We nevertheless agree with the Subcommittee that these issues warrant careful thought and discussion by policymakers and other interested parties.

On behalf of the Department, I commend this Subcommittee for its foresight in holding this hearing to assess the current state of the law regarding jurisdiction and the Internet. We believe that we can best contribute to this dialogue by identifying the issues we think will likely present the greatest challenges in the coming years in this difficult area.

Background

As the Supreme Court noted in its first major decision to grapple with Internet issues, the Internet is "an international network of interconnected computers."[11] Cyberspace renders geographical boundaries between states and nations less meaningful. Information placed on the Internet is instantly available to anyone else who accesses the data, no matter where they are on the globe. Indeed, while current Internet architecture allows Web site operators to restrict access to their sites through the use of passwords or credit card numbers, such screening mechanisms do not usually operate to screen people based on where they live and can be subverted by persons "posing" as someone else using their credit card or password.

As the Commerce Department has stated, the Internet is now a driving force in our economy, generating more than $5.3 billion in retail sales in the first quarter of 2000 alone.[12] The federal government and the states have largely opted not to regulate this fledgling new medium at this time, and businesses and individuals have taken advantage of this faster, less-capital-intensive means of transacting business. Other individuals have availed themselves of the Internet's ability to "broadcast" around the world to sell their products or speak their minds.

Some of these activities, as one might expect, have resulted in lawsuits. Businesses have sued one another for breach of contract, based on contracts entered into over the Internet or involving Internet-based services. Other companies have sued for infringement of their trademarks or under statutes prohibiting "cybersquatting" (the practice of reserving a "Web address," such as www.mtv.com, in order to force MTV to purchase that name for its own use) or "spamming" (the practice of sending unsolicited commercial electronic mail, or e-mail). Individuals maligned in Internet publications have sued for defamation.

Because jurisdiction historically has been tied to physical location — whereby the key to jurisdictional questions was determining where, geographically, an activity took place — the advent of cyberspace and the Internet has predictably required policymakers, litigants, and academics to step back and re-evaluate how jurisdiction is to apply in this new medium. We will now address these jurisdictional issues.

Personal Jurisdiction

One of the most vexing issues raised in litigation involving the Internet is this: When a person engages in wrongful behavior in cyberspace, where can he or she be sued?

The answer to this question generally depends, first and foremost, on state law. State long-arm statutes govern the reach of a state's courts. Most states, however, define their long-arm statutes to reach as far as the federal Due Process Clause will constitutionally permit.

The definition of permissible personal jurisdiction under the Due Process Clause has changed over time. Until the 1940s, a court's jurisdiction depended upon a defendant's physical presence (or the presence of her property) within the geographical boundaries of a state. In other words, a person residing in State B could only be sued in a court in State A if she were served with process while traveling in State A or if she owned property in State A and the lawsuit dealt with the property.[13]

Since 1945, the Court has interpreted the Due Process Clause more flexibly.[14] Under current law, a state may exercise jurisdiction over an out-of-state resident if the court finds that "there exist minimum contacts between the defendant and the forum state" and the state's exercise of personal jurisdiction over the defendant would not offend "traditional notions of fair play and substantial justice."[15]

A person is said to have "minimum contacts" with a state if she purposefully directs her activities toward that state.[16] The existence of minimum contacts confers "specific" personal jurisdiction over her and empowers a state to hale her into that state's court with respect to a lawsuit "aris[ing] out of or relat[ing] to those" contacts.[17] If she has "continuous and systematic" interaction with the state, the state has "general" personal jurisdiction over her and may exert its jurisdiction over her with respect to any valid cause of action.[18]

Whether the exertion of personal jurisdiction is reasonable — that is, whether it adheres to "traditional notions of fair play and substantial justice" — depends upon five factors: (i) the burden of the out-of-state lawsuit on the defendant; (ii) the forum state's interest in resolving the dispute; (iii) the plaintiff's interest in receiving convenient and effective relief; (iv) the interstate judicial system's interest in obtaining the most efficient resolution of controversies; and (v) the shared interest of the several states in furthering fundamental substantive social policies.[19]

The Court adopted this more flexible standard in recognition of the "fundamental transformation of ... [the] national economy over the years" and "the increasing nationalization of commerce."[20] Under these circumstances, requiring a company that conducted business in several states to be sued in those states was not unreasonable; most companies able to engage in interstate activities were financially well-off enough to be able to defend themselves in legal actions in those distant jurisdictions. The Internet arguably works another "fundamental transformation of ... [the] national economy" if the financial indicators are to be given any weight. Moreover, this transformation may affect one of the principle assumptions of the "minimum contacts" rule. The barriers to entering the Internet market — and offering goods on an interstate and international basis — are low, which arguably makes it less reasonable to expect Internet start-up companies to defend themselves in lawsuits throughout the United States.

The federal and state courts grappling with how personal jurisdiction applies on the Internet have not questioned the "minimum contacts" framework.[21] Instead, they have devoted time to analogizing Internet phenomena (Web pages, e-mail, the use of Internet equipment, and interactive online activity) to "real-world" phenomena (national print or broadcast advertisements, telemarketing, and physical distribution of goods).

Surveying these opinions reveals four primary approaches to determining whether a state court may exert personal jurisdiction over a person based on her Internet activities consistent with the constraints of the Due Process Clause. *First*, and most easy to analogize to the "real" world, a court may ask whether the defendant specifically availed herself of Internet machinery located in a particular state. Just recently, for example, the 10th Circuit Court of Appeals held that Oklahoma had personal jurisdiction over Bell Atlantic because Bell Atlantic knowingly used an Oklahoma Internet service provider's server equipment located in Oklahoma.[22] This rationale may also apply when a person enters into a contract to use such services or equipment in a known jurisdiction.[23]

Second, and most useful for persons who post Web pages, a court may look to the level of interactivity between the person's Web site and the users he is reaching in a particular state. The leading case on the "interactivity" standard is *Zippo Manuf. Co. v. Zippo Dot Com, Inc.*[24] There, the District Court defined a three-point, "sliding-scale" spectrum of interactivity. At one end of the spectrum is the defendant who "clearly does business over the Internet."[25] Over him, personal jurisdiction is appropriately exercised. At the other end is the defendant who has "simply posted information on an Internet Web site which is accessible to users in foreign jurisdictions."[26] This sort of "passive" activity, under the *Zippo* test, is insufficient to warrant the exercise of personal jurisdiction.[27] The "middle ground" of the spectrum — which, admittedly, accounts for most of the spectrum — is left to "interactive Web sites where a user can exchange information with the host computer" and where "the exercise of jurisdiction is determined by examining the level of interactivity and commercial nature of the exchange of information that occurs on the Web site."[28] In this last context, jurisdiction may hinge on whether the party simply exchanged information from the Web site or entered into a full-fledged contract for goods or services on that site.

Third, a court may look to the volume of business that an Internet company conducts with the residents of the forum state.[29] Under such a test, companies doing substantial business with residents of a state would be subject to jurisdiction, while companies engaged in a few small transactions could not be hauled into that state's court. This test may, to some extent, take into account the relatively small size of many Internet start-up companies; on the other hand, such an approach may also disadvantage consumers.

Fourth, a court may examine the "effects" that a particular person's behavior has in a specific state. In a trademark case alleging that a party's use of "nissan.com" and "nissan.net" infringed on Nissan Motor Company's trademark, the District Court held that the defendant's collection of advertising revenue from a state where the effects of its deception were felt was sufficient to confer specific jurisdiction.[30] Similarly, the New Jersey Supreme Court recently held that a person sued for defamation could be sued in New Jersey because the effects in New Jersey of his use of an electronic bulletin board physically located elsewhere was sufficient to confer jurisdiction over him in the New Jersey courts.[31]

These approaches, while seemingly different, actually dovetail nicely and will often yield the same outcome when applied to the same facts. If, for example, a Web site operator "targets" residents of a certain state — or, more broadly, residents living in the United States — the courts of that state (or the United States, in the latter example) will likely be able to assert personal jurisdiction over the site operator under any of the tests: such an operator is likely to have used machinery or entered into contracts in that state, is likely to have a highly interactive site designed to reach customers of the targeted jurisdiction, is likely to generate a substantial volume of business, and is likely to have some effect in the target jurisdiction. This is not surprising, as this sort of purposeful direction at a jurisdiction is part of the very definition of what amounts to "minimum contacts" under the Court's post-1940s due process jurisprudence.[32]

As this brief survey of leading cases indicates, the courts are busy grafting the uniqueness of the Internet onto the already-existing framework set out by the Supreme Court's due process jurisprudence. At this point in time, they seem to be handling the task well, which counsels strongly in favoring of allowing this precedent to develop without legislative intervention.

We observe that persons transacting business on the Internet are not entirely powerless to influence whether another state's courts will have personal jurisdiction over them. In many cases, the parties enter into contracts. One of the terms the parties may negotiate is a "forum selection clause" that dictates where jurisdiction is appropriate. Such clauses may present unique problems where Internet transactions are concerned; nonetheless, in appropriate circumstances they may encourage the parties to reach a "meeting of the minds" in advance and simply resolve disputes in the agreed-upon forum.

Internet users may also be able to take some unilateral actions to indicate that they do not wish to "purposefully direct" their business to a certain forum. For example, a company could place a banner on its Web site that stated that it intended to do business solely with New York residents (and back that up by listing a 1-800 number that only worked from within New York, or requiring purchasers to enter New York mailing addresses). As the Internet architecture evolves, Web site operators may also be able to "screen out" users who do not claim to be from only those states with which they want to do business. While these actions are no guarantee against the exertion of authority, they would be relevant to a court's inquiry into intent.

Venue

The next "jurisdictional" topic is venue — that is, assuming that the state or federal court has personal and subject matter jurisdiction over the lawsuit, where should the suit be litigated?

Like personal jurisdiction, venue has traditionally been pegged to geographic location. The federal venue rule for diversity cases, for example, provides that venue is proper in one of three possible judicial districts: a judicial district where any defendant resides if they all reside in the same state; one where a substantial part of the events or omissions giving rise to the claim occurred; or, if venue is not otherwise available, in a judicial district where any of the defendants is subject to personal jurisdiction at the time the action is commenced.[33]

Because Internet communications and the attendant online activities "occur" somewhere, but not necessarily in an easily identified judicial district, courts must address how these rules are to be applied when an Internet transaction is implicated in a lawsuit. Of course, the parties can designate by agreement where the suit is to be litigated. If the parties have not provided for venue by agreement, the three traditional venue possibilities prescribed by federal statute will still provide the full range of appropriate venues in most cases. Courts sitting in districts in which either of the parties reside or in which significant parts of the disputed transactions occurred each have a sufficient connection to the lawsuit to hear and decide it. One can also imagine disputes in the online world in which, for example, courts in the district where one of the party's Internet service provider maintains its equipment (and possibly evidence relating to the suit) may be a proper site for the lawsuit. These situations may occur so infrequently that no special rules are necessary, and resolution of them can be left to the courts on a case-by-case basis as they arise.

Choice of Law

A third question that courts adjudicating Internet disputes involving residents from different state are forced to address is this: Which state's substantive law applies?

When the parties have entered into a contract, the answer is usually straight-forward — look to the contract to see whether the parties have agreed upon which state's law is to govern any disagreements involving the contract. As a general rule, as long as the contractual provision is reasonable, courts will honor it.[34] Thus, as with personal jurisdiction and venue, parties entering into business transactions can avoid some of the uncertainty in the law by including such clauses in their negotiated documents.[35]

When a person commits a tort or does not enter into a contract with an enforceable forum selection clause, the "default" choice of law controls. It is important to keep in mind that the state court deciding the choice of law issue applies its own state's "choice of law" rule to render its decision.[36] The states are currently split in using one of three "choice of law" rules.

Some states apply the rule from Restatement (First) of Conflict of Laws, which hinges its selection of law on the state where the right to be asserted vested. This often translates into a requirement that a state court apply the law of the state where the "last act" necessary to complete the tort occurred.[37] Other states follow the Restatement (Second), which looks to the law of the state with the "most significant relationship" to the action, and lists several factors to be considered in making this assessment.[38] A last group of states follows an "interest" test and will apply the substantive law of the state having the greatest policy interest in its law to the case.[39]

Choice of law issues are largely subject to debate in the "real world," and the complications attendant to the doctrine are multiplied when the doctrine is applied to cyberspace. If, for example, a person posts defamatory language on a Web site, a court following the First Restatement choice of law rule might apply the law of the states where the defamatory statements are read, if reading the defamatory material is deemed to be the "last act" of the tort. There is no evidence, however, that the choice of law principles currently applied by the courts are inadequate to apply to lawsuits involving the Internet. Thus, although choice of law issues are often difficult — in both the physical world and the cyberspace cases — we again believe that the state and federal courts are best suited to addressing these issues at this time.

Substantive Authority to Regulate

Unlike personal jurisdiction, venue, and choice of law, which are defined largely by constitutional constraints and decisional law, jurisdiction as it refers to the substantive authority of a state or federal agency is largely a creature of legislative design.

The substantive authority of federal agencies to regulate companies and individuals domestically — that is, within the boundaries of the United States — is plenary once the terms of the authorizing statute are satisfied. Likewise, the authority of a federal court to review such action is typically set forth by statute. For example, the Administrative Procedure Act generally provides for the court's review of final agency action.

Federal authority to regulate extraterritorially is less certain. The Restatement (Third) of Foreign Relations provides a set of default rules that tie authority to regulate to one of several sovereign interests. More specifically, § 402 the Restatement provides that a nation has jurisdiction to prescribe law with respect to: (i) conduct that takes place within its geographic borders; (ii) the status of persons within its geographic borders; (iii) conduct outside its territory that has or is intended to have a substantive effect within its geographic borders; (iv) the activities, interest, status, or relations of its citizens regardless of where they are in the world; and (v) certain conduct outside its territory by any other person that is directly against the security of the state or against a limited class of other state interests.[40]

Nations are also in the process of further clarifying and developing this area of law through treaty negotiation. For example, as the State Department discusses in its written testimony, a Hague convention on Jurisdiction and the Recognition and Enforcement of Foreign Civil Judgments is currently under negotiation.

States, within the United States, are currently grappling with similar issues — namely, when it is permissible to 'regulate the activity of companies that do business with its residents over the Internet, but are physically located outside its boundaries. The reach of permissible state regulation, like the reach of nations, is constrained. In the case of individual states, the constraint is imposed by the state's authorizing statutes and the prohibitions of the so- called "dormant Commerce Clause," which in essence prohibits a state from discriminating against out-of-state businesses.

Conclusion

Through this brief overview of the four major "jurisdictional" issues involving the Internet today, we hope we have aided this Subcommittee in its thinking about the challenges that lie ahead and which are most appropriate for federal oversight and involvement.

Thank you for the opportunity to testify today. I will be pleased to respond to your questions.

Electronic Case Filing at the Federal Courts

On February 9, 2001, the Department of Justice submitted comments to the Administrative Office of the U.S. Courts in response to the federal judiciary's request for comments regarding the privacy and security implications of public access to electronic case files. The issue of privacy and public access to electronic case files is very important to the Department of Justice.

Abel J. Mattos
Chief, Court Administration Policy Staff
Court Administration Building, Suite 4-560
Administrative Office of the United States Courts
One Columbus Circle, N.E.
Washington, D.C. 20544

Dear Mr. Mattos:

I am pleased to enclose the comments of the Department of Justice in response to the federal judiciary's request for comments regarding the privacy and security implications of public access to electronic case files. The issue of privacy and public access to electronic case files is very important to the Department of Justice, as we know it is to the judiciary. We welcome the opportunity to continue the productive dialogue regarding these issues on an ongoing basis.

I would like to take this opportunity again to thank the Judicial Conference for allowing the Department an extension of time to produce these comments. As you know this has been, and remains, a period of transition for the Department. However, these comments represent the joint efforts of a working group of attorneys from a variety of components of the Department of Justice, including the Executive Office for United States Attorneys, the United States Trustee Program, the Office of Information and Privacy, the Fraud and Computer Crimes and Intellectual Property Sections of the Criminal Division, the Commercial Litigation, Federal Programs, and Torts Branches of the Civil Division, the Tax Division, the Federal Bureau of Investigation, the Environment and Natural Resources Division, the Justice Management Division, and the Office of Policy Development. With the appointment of the new Attorney General, the Department will be returning to full force at the leadership levels. We look forward to providing further thoughts and input, whether in the form of continued communication between our staffs or more formal testimony.

If you have any questions regarding this document, please do not hesitate to call Jonathan Meyer, Deputy Assistant Attorney General in the Office of Policy Development (202-307-3024), or Jeanette Plante, Special Assistant United States Attorney (202-616-6459). Thank you again for the opportunity to comment.

Sincerely,

/S/

Kevin R. Jones
Deputy Assistant Attorney General

Notes

1. Agencies should refer to OMB Memorandum M-00-10, *Implementation of the GPEA*, for general guidance in this area, and to OMB's procedural guidance on developing GPEA plans, issued July 25, 2000, for specific instructions on actions to be taken.
2. The PRA defines an information collection as:

   > the obtaining, causing to be obtained, soliciting, or requiring the disclosure to an agency, third parties or the public of information by or for an agency by means of identical questions posed to, or identical reporting, record keeping or disclosure requirements imposed on, ten or more person, whether such collection of information is mandatory, voluntary, or required to obtain or retain a benefit.
   >
   > — 5 C.F.R. 1320.3 (2000)

3. The examples and discussion that follow are intended as guidance and do not address every possible situation. In some instances other circumstances may render a particular discussion or illustration inapplicable.
4. There are also certain categories of requirements that are not subject to E-SIGN at all. See, for example, Section 101 (f) (referring to public notices).
5. Section 106(1) defines consumer as an individual who obtains, through a transaction, products or services which are used primarily for personal, family, or household purposes, and also means the legal representative of such individual.
6. Agencies should be aware of Congress's decision to reiterate this standard and be cautious in exercising their interpretive authority. Congressman Dingell and Senators Hollings, Wyden and Sarbanes explained in Senate and House floor statements that, because "each agency will be proceeding under its preexisting rulemaking authority, ... regulations or guidance interpreting Section 101 will be entitled to the same deference that the agency's interpretations would usually receive." 146 Cong. Rec. E1071 (June 21, 2000).
7. The Legislation's sponsors said in their floor statements that they intended that federal agencies have authority to interpret E-SIGN in order to protect industry and consumers, address abusive electronic practices, prevent waste, fraud and abuse, and enforce the law. 146 Cong. Rec. H4346, H4358-59 (June 14, 2000); 146 Cong. Rec. E1071 (June 21, 2000).
8. Section 101(b)(2) states that Title I "does not...require any person to agree to use or accept electronic records or electronic signatures, other that a governmental agency with respect to a record other that a contract to which it is a party." Thus, Title I of E-SIGN does not require governmental agencies to use or accept electronic records or signatures with regard to contracts to which they are parties.
9. Some might argue that, while Section 101(b)(2) states that the government will not be forced to use or accept electronic records and signatures for contracts, that might not apply to records other that the contract itself. They might assert that the government must accept electronic notices under a contract. We would disagree with that position. Section 101(b)(2) applies broadly to the entire transaction involving a government contract, including all records relating to the contract. *See id.* at H4357.
10. Jurisdiction can also refer to subject matter jurisdiction, which is prescribed to the federal courts by statute.
11. *ACLU v. Reno*, 521 U.S. 844, 849 (1997).
12. See http://www.census.gov/mrts/www/current.html (visited June 24, 2000). Business to business commerce may be even greater than this. According to a summary prepared by The Industry Standard, forecasts for 2003 of the dollar value of transactions between U.S. businesses that are conducted electronically range from $634 billion to $2.8 trillion. *See* Stacy Lawrence, Behind the Numbers: The Mystery of B2B Forecasts Revealed, The Industry Standard, Feb. 21, 2000, http://www.the-standard.com (visited June 28, 2000).

13. See, e.g., *Pennoyer v. Neff*, 95 U.S. 714 (1877).
14. *International Shoe Co. v . Washington*, 326 U.S. 310 (1945).
15. See *World Wide Volkswagen Corp. v. Woodson*, 444 U.S. 286, 491 (1980) (quotations omitted); *Burger King Corp. v. Rudzewicz*, 471 U.S. 462, 476 (1982).
16. *Burger King*, 471 U.S. at 472.
17. *Id.*
18. See *Helicopteros Nacionales de Colombia v. Hall*, 466 U.S. 408 (1984).
19. *Burger King*, 471 U.S. at 477.
20. *McGee v. International Life Ins. Co.*, 355 U.S. 220, 222-23 (1957).
21. We recognize that the courts could not depart from the standard, which is binding Supreme Court precedent. We simply mean to observe that the courts have also not questioned whether the premises of this precedent apply equally in cyberspace.
22. *Intercon, Inc. v. Bell Atlantic Internet Solutions, Inc.*, 205 F.3d 1244 (10th Cir. 2000). Although this case was heard in federal court on diversity jurisdiction grounds, the District Court applied Oklahoma's long-arm statute.
23. *See CompuServe, Inc. v. Patterson*, 89 F.3d 1257 (6th Cir. 1996) (finding personal jurisdiction over an Ohio defendant where defendant entered into a contract to distribute software through plaintiff's Ohio Internet server and defendant repeatedly sent his software files to the Ohio server via e-mail).
24. 952 F. Supp. 1119 (W.D. Pa. 1997).
25. *Id.* at 1124.
26. *Ibid.*
27. In some respects, this is a rejection of the "stream of commerce" theory, which provides that a defendant should be subject to personal jurisdiction in any state where his product, floating down the "stream of commerce," might foreseeably end up. *See Asahi Metal Indus. Co. v. Superior Court of California*, 480 U.S. 102 (1987).
28. *Zippo*, 952 F. Supp. At 1124.
29. See, e.g., Note, Richard A. Rochlin, "Cyberspace, International Shoe, and the Changing Context for Personal Jurisdiction," 32 Conn. L. Rev. 653, 671-72 (2000).
30. See *Nissan Motor Co., Ltd. v. Nissan Computer Corp.*, 89 F. Supp. 2d 1154 (C.D. Cal. 2000).
31. See *Blakey v. Continental Airlines, Inc.*, 164 N.J. 38 (N.J. 2000).
32. See *supra* note 6 and accompanying text.
33. See 28 U.S.C. § 1391(a). A defendant also has the right to ask the court to move venue to a different, appropriately authorized venue, "[f]or the convenience of parties and witnesses [and] in the interest of justice." *See* 28 U.S.C. § 1404(a).
34. See Gary B. Born, International Civil Litigation in the United States Courts: Commentary and Materials 655 (1996).
35. On the other hand, courts may question whether the parties have come to a meeting of the minds with regard to choice of law when a consumer has simply clicked "I agree" to a Web site operator's extensive boilerplate as a condition to proceeding further into the Web site.
36. See Restatement (Second) of Conflict of Laws § 6(1) ("A court, subject to constitutional restrictions, will follow a statutory directive of its own state on choice of law.").
37. See Restatement (First) of Conflict of Laws § 377 (1934).
38. See Restatement (Second) of Conflict of Laws § 145 (1971). Factors to be considered in assessing which jurisdiction has the "most significant relationship" include: (i) the place where the injury occurred; (ii) the place where the conduct causing the injury occurred; (iii) the domicile, residence, nationality, place of incorporation and place of business of the parties; and (iv) the place where the relationship, if any, between the parties is centered. *Id.* at § 145(2).
39. See generally Kermit Roosevelt III, "The Myth of Choice of Law: Rethinking Conflicts," 97 Mich. L. Rev. 2448, 2461-65 (1999).
40. See Restatement (Third) of Foreign Relations § 402 (1986).

Chapter 14

Legal Considerations in Designing and Implementing Electronic Processes: A Guide for Federal Agencies

Executive Summary

Under the Government Paperwork Elimination Act (GPEA), Pub. L. No. 105-277, §§1701-1710 (1998) (codified as 44 U.S.C.A. § 3504 n. (West Supp. 1999)), Federal Executive agencies are required, by October 21, 2003, to provide for (1) "the option of the electronic maintenance, submission, or disclosure of information, when practicable, as a substitute for paper," and (2) "the use and acceptance of electronic signatures, when practicable." The Office of Management and Budget (OMB) has developed guidance to assist agencies in implementing GPEA's requirements. "Procedures and Guidance; Implementation of the Government Paperwork Elimination Act," 65 FR 25508, May 2, 2000 ("OMB Guidance"). As part of the OMB Guidance, the Department of Justice is charged with developing, in consultation with federal agencies and OMB, practical guidance on legal considerations related to agency use of electronic filing and recordkeeping. The purpose of this Guide is to identify legal issues that agencies are likely to face in converting to electronic processes and to provide some suggestions on how to address them. Agencies should also consider the significance of the "Electronic Records and Signatures in Global and National Commerce Act" (E-SIGN) (Pub.L. 106-229, § 1, June 30, 2000, 114 Stat. 464, codified at 15 U.S.C. §§ 7001–7006), although a detailed discussion of that statute's impact on the federal agencies is beyond the scope of this Guide.

The rise of electronic commerce offers agencies exciting opportunities to convert — or redesign — paper-based processes to electronic ones. While some agencies have experience using electronic processes, others are just beginning to examine the opportunity of electronic processing, or are just beginning to consider electronic processing for more sensitive transactions. In moving to electronic processes, agencies face many important decisions. Among those decisions is one crucial question of interest to the Department of Justice: When an agency converts each type of transaction to an electronic-based process, how should the agency design that process so as to protect its legal rights and minimize legal risks that may compromise the agency's mission? In accordance with the OMB Guidance on GPEA, agency considerations of cost, risk, and benefit, as well as any measures taken to minimize risks, should be commensurate with the level of sensitivity of the transaction. Low-risk information processes may need only minimal safeguards, while high-risk processes may need more. In the context of legal and litigation risks, "low-risk information processes" are those that have a small chance of generating significant liability, financial impact, or litigation that would have a significant effect on the agency.[1]

The many potential benefits of re-designing (or designing) agency processes to use electronic-based processes are apparent: increased efficiency, accessibility, and reliability. Advances in technology, public expectations, Congress's mandate in the GPEA, and Administration policy all require that agencies of the United States move expeditiously to adopt electronic processes. Some agencies are already seeing benefits from increasing their use of and reliance on electronic recording and transaction systems. These benefits may not be fully realized unless the agency designs its processes with care. This Guide explains the legal issues an agency is likely to face in designing electronic-based processes (Part I), examines four overarching legal issues that should be considered with respect to converting any given type of system or operation (Part II), and discusses general and specific steps agencies should consider in converting to electronic processes (Part III). The reader who already recognizes the legal issues presented by electronic processes and those involved in replacing paper processes with electronic ones may wish to turn first to Part III, which does not depend on the analysis of Parts I and II for an understanding of its suggestions.

In deciding whether and how to convert any given process from paper to an electronic one, agencies should consider at least the following four issues, which are examined in Part II:

- *Availability.* Will the important information regarding a transaction be collected, retained, and accessible whenever needed despite changes to computer hardware or software? How long should the information be kept given legal record-keeping needs? The important transaction information to be collected and accessible typically includes the *content or substance* of the transaction (for example, the text of a contract); the processing of the transaction (such as when and from where a communication was sent and when and where it was received); the *identities* of the parties and the specific individuals involved in the transaction; and the *intent* of the parties (such as whether they intended to enter into a binding contract).

- *Legal Sufficiency.* Certain types of transactions must be in "writing" and "signed" in order to be legally enforceable. The law is still developing with respect to whether such requirements will be satisfied by all electronic processes in all circumstances. By using electronic processes that address the issues raised in this Guide, agencies can increase the likelihood that their electronic transactions will meet such legal standards. Federal laws, such as GPEA, address the legal validity and enforceability of electronic records and signatures. GPEA states that: "electronic records submitted or maintained in accordance with procedures developed under this title, or electronic signatures or other forms of electronic authentication used in accordance with such procedures, shall not be denied legal effect, validity, or enforceability because such records are in electronic form." E-SIGN similarly provides that records relating to commercial, financial, or consumer transactions shall not be denied legal effect solely because they are in electronic form or signed by electronic signature. Although Federal activities are usually governed by federal rather than state law, it is also noteworthy that various state laws, such as versions of the Uniform Electronic Transactions Act (UETA) that are currently being introduced in the states, similarly address the legal validity of electronic records and signatures, including in the formation of a contract. UETA states: "a record or signature may not be denied legal effect or enforceability solely because it is in electronic form.... [A] contract may not be denied legal effect or enforceability solely because an electronic record was used in its formation."

- *Reliability.* Will electronic records be sufficiently reliable and persuasive to satisfy courts and others who must determine the facts underlying agency actions? Will the electronic records be maintained in such a way so as to satisfy admissibility requirements? Will sufficient context be preserved so that the electronic records are usable?

- *Compliance with Other Laws.* Will the agency's use of electronic methods to obtain, send, disclose, and store information comply with applicable laws such as those governing privacy, confidentiality, recordkeeping, and accessibility to persons with disabilities? Myriad federal laws govern the use and disclosure of information gathered by the federal government. Agencies generally have developed systems for addressing such laws with regard to paper-based information. Electronic processes also will have to be designed to allow an agency to comply with such laws.

Part III of the Guide provides both general and specific steps an agency may take to reduce the potential legal risks of moving to electronic transactions. The general steps include:

1. Conduct an analysis of the nature of a transaction or process to determine the level of protection needed and the level of risk that can be tolerated;
2. Consider potential costs, quantifiable and unquantifiable, direct and indirect, in performing a cost/benefit analysis;
3. Use available sources of expertise, such as legal, programmatic, and technical experts, inside and outside your agency, including the OMB Guidance;
4. Consider developing a comprehensive plan when converting a traditional process to an electronic one, especially if converting means re-engineering the existing process;
5. Consider the kinds of information relevant to the process and ensure that necessary information is gathered;

6.   Consider using a "terms and conditions" agreement;

7.   Incorporate an appropriate retention and access policy for the records produced by electronic processes, including long-term retention where necessary;

8.   Be aware of legal concerns that implicate effectiveness of or impose restrictions on electronic data or records;

9.   Just as should be done with paper processes, document the various steps in your electronic process so that you can demonstrate the reliability of your process to courts and others who must determine the facts underlying an agency action;

10. Analyze the full range of technological options and follow commercial trends where appropriate;

11. If an agency considers using an outside entity to manage information, the agency should consider the various liability and privacy issues that may arise as a result of this system; and

12. Retain paper-based information in important or sensitive contexts where necessary.

The specific suggestions in Part III detail the types of information that should be gathered, retained, and made available on demand. They also make recommendations that address particular agency activities, including contracting, regulatory programs and other programs that require reporting of information, and benefit programs.

Exhibit 1 provides key legal issues for agencies to consider in adopting an electronic process. The exhibit is intended to serve as a resource for agencies; it is not a required checklist and it is not an exhaustive listing of the possible issues such processes may raise. Exhibit 2 provides the names and contact information for the attorneys who may be contacted should readers have specific questions or comments about this Guide.

Introduction

Under the Government Paperwork Elimination Act (GPEA), Pub. L. No. 105-277, §§1701-1710 (1998) (codified as 44 U.S.C.A. § 3504 n. (West Supp. 1999)), Federal Executive agencies[2] are required, by October 21, 2003, to provide for (1) "the option of electronic maintenance, submission, or disclosure of information, when practicable, as a substitute for paper," and (2) "the use and acceptance of electronic signatures, when practicable." The Office of Management and Budget (OMB) has developed guidance to assist agencies in implementing GPEA's requirements. "Procedures and Guidance; Implementation of the Government Paperwork Elimination Act," 65 FR 25508, May 2, 2000 ("OMB Guidance"). As part of the OMB Guidance, the Department of Justice is charged with developing, in consultation with federal agencies and OMB, practical guidance on legal considerations related to agency use of electronic filing and recordkeeping. The purpose of this Guide is to identify legal issues that agencies are likely to face in converting to electronic processes and to provide some suggestions on how to address them. Agencies should also consider the significance of the "Electronic Records and Signatures in Global and National Commerce Act" (E-SIGN) (Pub.L. 106-229, § 1, June 30, 2000, 114 Stat. 464, codified at 15 U.S.C. §§ 7001 — 7006), although a detailed discussion of that statute's impact on the federal agencies is beyond the scope of this Guide.

Exhibit 1.   Key Legal Issues to Consider in Adopting an Electronic Process

---

This exhibit is provided as a resource for agencies to identify the legal issues to consider in adopting an electronic process. There are two general ways of identifying the legal issues associated with adopting electronic processes. One convenient approach is to consider the features of an existing paper-based process, and decide how the electronic process must be designed in order to provide the same functions. In the alternative, one can turn to first principles and seek to identify legal issues without reference to any existing process. These two approaches may be complementary; concerns that might be immediately apparent when one approach is used may not be under the other approach. Accordingly, this exhibit incorporates elements of both approaches.

This exhibit focuses on legal issues associated with adopting an electronic process. (This analysis has many features of a requirements analysis, which agencies might already be conducting as part of their business process.) Although electronic processes can have many significant advantages over paper processes, those benefits will not be addressed in detail as they are outside the scope of this Guide. This exhibit also does not comprehensively address issues associated with archiving of records; for a more detailed review of that topic, please consult the guidance prepared by the National Archives and Records Administration. Although this exhibit is intended as a resource to federal agencies, some agencies may conclude that other approaches are more appropriate in addressing legal issues related to the development, use, and maintenance of those agencies' electronic processes.

A. *Comparison of Paper and Electronic Processes*

1. What is the type or purpose of the process — is it a benefits application, a contract, a bid proposal, a legally required report, or some other type of process?
2. What does each party to the communication need in order to achieve that purpose? This may include dates, identities, intent, signatures, the sources of particular information, and the informational content of the transaction itself. Who uses the information in your agency, and for what purpose? Are there types of information that are needed only for certain narrow purposes or only infrequently, but are very important for those purposes?
3. How will the electronic process collect this information?
4. What is it about the existing process that satisfies this need? A signature may serve a range of purposes, including proving identity and intent, and deterring abuse. Likewise, mailing of paper documents to a known address both helps to complete a transaction and helps to confirm the identity of the other party to the transaction. How will the electronic process be designed to meet these needs?
5. How do you ensure that information, once obtained, continues to be available when and where you need it? How is information organized, stored, and retrieved? When is information likely to be needed again, and for what purposes? How can appropriate availability of information be assured in an electronic process?

Exhibit 1.   Key Legal Issues to Consider in Adopting an Electronic Process (Continued)

---

6. What security procedures do you have, and why? Who has access to information and who does not, and why? How can equivalent or better security be obtained in an electronic process?

7. What elements of your program and process have historically been susceptible to fraud or other abuse, and why? How do you deter these activities? How will you ensure similar or greater deterrence in the electronic process? Will evidence of abuse be as available and persuasive in the new system as in the old one? Are there any features of the electronic process that are likely to facilitate fraud, abuse or disputes that did not occur before, or conversely, that are likely to discourage such acts which have occurred in the past?

8. What do you do in your existing system to comply with applicable laws and regulations, including any signature requirements, the Freedom of Information Act, the Privacy Act, the Rehabilitation Act, discovery procedures, and confidentiality laws? How will you ensure that you will continue to comply with those laws and regulations in your electronic system?

9. Have you adopted a plan to address the issues raised by moving to an electronic system, and planned to consult relevant offices and agencies (including general counsels, inspectors general, and relevant components of the Justice Department)?

B. Legal Issues Raised by Electronic Processes

1. Have applicable legal and practical requirements been considered?
   - Is any information used in the process required by law or regulation to be in a particular form, paper or otherwise?
   - Is the transaction required by law or regulation to be "signed?" If so, how do you plan to satisfy that requirement?
   - Will your process comply with the Government Paperwork Elimination Act?
   - What steps in the plan are taken to ensure confidentiality if confidentiality is required?
   - Will the process comply with:
     — The Privacy Act?
     — The Rehabilitation Act?
     — The Freedom of Information Act?
     — The Federal Records Act?
     — Other requirements applicable to the agency's programs?

2. How necessary is the information?
   - Is there a legal requirement to maintain the information?
   - Is the information of importance to national security, public health or safety, public welfare, the protection of the environment, or other important public purposes?
   - How many people would be affected by the unavailability of this information?

Exhibit 1.   Key Legal Issues to Consider in Adopting an Electronic Process (Continued)

- What is the importance of the information to the agency's programs?
- Could the information be used to collect money from the United States? Used by the United States in collecting money? How much money is at issue in each individual transaction? In the process as a whole?
- Does the information otherwise reflect rights or obligations of the United States or of other parties?
- Might the information be needed for use in criminal proceedings? In other legal proceedings?
- Is the information needed for proper agency management or for maintenance of agency financial records?
- Is the agency confident that the information will not be needed in the future for any important purpose?
- Is the information needed for any other reason?

If the foregoing analysis reveals that the information will not be necessary in the future and is not required to be retained under applicable law, there is likely to be little need to consider the risks associated with collection, use, and retention of the information discussed below. If, however, the information is likely to be of legal significance, the agency may wish to consider the following items in addressing potential risks. If the information is a "record," applicable law may nevertheless require it to be preserved in some form. Refer to guidance prepared by the National Archives and Records Administration for more detail on this topic.

3. What are the risks that private parties will seek to commit fraud or otherwise misuse the process?
    - How much money or other benefits are at issue in each individual transaction? Can transactions be aggregated?
    - Is the transaction conducted with people with whom the agency has had a long-term relationship?
    - Is the program one with a history of fraud?
    - Are there any other reasons to anticipate fraud in this process?

4. What are the risks that information will be damaged or lost?
    - Will the information be stored in a way that is accessible in a timely fashion if it is needed?
    - Will the information be retrievable in a way that is easy to understand?
    - What steps will be taken to control, log, and audit modifications to stored information?
    - How long will the agency need to keep its records?
    - Is it appropriate to involve outside contractors in information management tasks?
    - If so, does the contract and oversight process protect the interests of the agency and the public?
    - What plans are in place for migration of information when system technology is upgraded?
    - What parts of the process are unusual, distinctive, or unique to the agency? Do these steps give rise to unusual risks of harm to stored information?
    - Are there other risks?

Exhibit 1.   Key Legal Issues to Consider in Adopting an Electronic Process (Continued)

5. Will the information collected be complete?
    - Does an identity need to be associated with a transaction? How will identity be proved?
    - Does intent need to be associated with a transaction? Can the agency prove that the person who transmitted the information understood its significance and appreciated that his or her transmittal was legally binding on him or her?
    - Does a signature need to be associated with a transaction? If so, what is the function of the signature — identification, intent, evidentiary use, or some other function? What is an appropriate electronic equivalent? Is a digital signature required, or will some lesser form of electronic signature suffice?
    - What information about the processing of the document (such as when a document was sent or from where it was received) must be retained?
    - Are documents ever modified upon receipt? If so, how is information (including context, identity and intent information) regarding the modifications collected, retained, and made available? How is this information segregated from information associated with the original submission?
    - Is there some other necessary legal element required to conclude the transaction (delivery of a deed, for example)?
    - What contextual information is necessary (e.g., the questions to which a set of stored answers correspond)? How will it be collected and maintained?
    - Is there any information that is used only infrequently, or only for one narrow purpose, but that is nevertheless critical to the success of the system?
    - What other information needs to be collected by virtue of the distinctive features of the transaction?
6. Will the information be otherwise usable and credible for all necessary purposes, including possible legal proceedings?
    - Can the agency show that the information it received accurately reflects the information that was intended to be transmitted?
    - Can the agency show that the information it possesses accurately reflects the information originally submitted to it? Is the original information available as well as any subsequent edits?
    - Is a "terms and conditions" agreement appropriate? Is the information retained sufficient to be persuasive to a judge, jury, or other third party? Does it provide simple, straightforward and corroborated evidence of what occurred?
    - Has the agency addressed any other potential obstacles to the use of the information in a legal proceeding?
7. Have all relevant offices and agencies been consulted? Potentially interested offices and entities may include:
    - Agency program offices
    - Agency information technology specialists
    - General Counsel's office

Exhibit 1.   Key Legal Issues to Consider in Adopting an Electronic Process (Continued)

- Inspector General's office (audit and investigative personnel)
- Records management personnel
- FOIA, Privacy Act, and civil rights officers
- Agency enforcement personnel
- Other agency personnel
- Office of Management and Budget
- The Department of Justice
- National Archives and Records Administration
- Other government offices or agencies (federal, state, local and tribal) that are involved in the process, use the resulting information, or otherwise have a stake in process design
- Private and non-governmental organizations, including as appropriate contractors, the regulated community, and representatives of the general public

8. Have you developed a plan to address the foregoing issues?
   - Does the plan assign responsibility for particular tasks or problems to specific offices or individuals?
   - Does the plan provide for any auditing of the process, including auditing of any outside contractor who manages information on behalf of the agency?
   - Does the plan provide for periodic reassessment?
   - Have you consulted with interested parties on the development of this plan?
   - Have you shared the final plan with interested parties?

Exhibit 2.   Contact Information, Department of Justice

Electronic Commerce Working Group Co-Chairs

David Goldstone (Co-chair)
  Computer Crime and Intellectual Property Section, Criminal Division
  (202) 514-1026
  (202) 514-6113 fax
  E-Mail: David.Goldstone@usdoj.gov

Chris Kohn (Co-chair)
  Director, Corporate/Financial Litigation Section, Commercial Litigation
    Branch, Civil Division
  202-514-7450
  202-514-9163 fax
  E-Mail: Chris.Kohn@usdoj.gov

Electronic Processes Subgroup

Tony Whitledge (Chair)
  Criminal Appeals and Tax Enforcement Policy Section, Tax Division
  (202) 514-2832
  (202) 305-8687 fax
  E-Mail: Tony.Whitledge@usdoj.gov

Exhibit 2.   Contact Information, Department of Justice (Continued)

David Goldstone
   Computer Crime & Intellectual Property Section, Criminal Division
   (202) 514-1026
   (202) 514-6113 fax
   E-Mail: David.Goldstone@usdoj.gov
Joan Hartman
   Fraud Section, Commercial Litigation Branch, Civil Division
   (202) 307-6697
   (202) 616-3085/9029 fax
   E-Mail: Joan.Hartman@usdoj.gov
Brian Kennedy
   Federal Programs Branch, Civil Division
   (202) 514-3357
   (202) 616-8470 fax
   E-Mail: Brian.Kennedy@usdoj.gov
Sylvia Liu
   Policy, Legislation, and Special Litigation Section, Environment and Nat. Res.
      Division
   (202) 305-0639
   (202) 616-8543 fax
   E-Mail: Sylvia.Liu@usdoj.gov
Ken S. Nakata
   Disability Rights Section, Civil Rights Division
   (202) 307-2232
   (202) 307-1198 fax
   Ken.Nakata@usdoj.gov
Marc Gordon
   Land Acquisition Section, Environment and Natural Resources Division
   (202) 305-0291
   (202) 305-8273 fax
   E-Mail: Marc.Gordon@usdoj.gov
David Gottesman
   Corporate/Financial Litigation Section, Commercial Litigation Branch, Civil
      Division
   (202) 307-0183
   (202) 514-9163 fax
   E-Mail: David.Gottesman@usdoj.gov
Jennie Plante
   Executive Office for United States Attorneys
   (202) 616-6444
   (202) 616-6647 fax
   E-Mail: Jeanette.Plante@usdoj.gov
Richard Phillips
   Federal Programs Branch, Civil Division
   (202) 514-4778
   E-Mail: Richard.Phillips@usdoj.gov

Exhibit 2.   Contact Information, Department of Justice (Continued)

Justin Smith
> Policy, Legislation, and Special Litigation Section, Environment and Natural
> Resources Division
> (202) 514-9369
> (202) 514 4231 fax
> E-Mail: Justin.Smith@usdoj.gov

The rise of electronic commerce offers agencies exciting opportunities to convert — or redesign — paper-based processes to electronic ones. While some agencies have experience using electronic processes, others are just beginning to examine the opportunity of electronic processing, or are just beginning to consider electronic processing for more sensitive transactions. In moving to electronic processes, agencies face many important decisions. Among those decisions is one crucial question of interest to the Department of Justice: when an agency converts each type of transaction to an electronic-based process, how should the agency design that process so as to protect its legal rights and minimize legal risks that may compromise the agency's mission?

In accordance with the OMB Guidance on GPEA, agency considerations of cost, risk, and benefit, as well as any measures taken to minimize risks, should be commensurate with the level of sensitivity of the transaction. Low-risk information processes may need only minimal safeguards, while high-risk processes may need more. In the context of legal and litigation risks, "low-risk information processes" are those that have a small chance of generating significant liability, financial impact or litigation that would have a significant effect on the agency.[3]

The many potential benefits of re-designing (or designing) agency processes to use electronic-based processes are readily apparent: increased efficiency, accessibility, and reliability. Some agencies are already seeing benefits from increasing their use of and reliance on electronic recording and transaction systems. Yet, these benefits may not be fully realized unless the agency designs its processes with care. The collection and management of electronic records is becoming increasingly important for federal agencies.

Agencies must electronically receive, transmit, and store information in ways that will be acceptable to their program participants and others, while not violating legal restrictions, jeopardizing the government's legal rights, or unduly exposing the government to liabilities, criminal acts or other waste, fraud or abuse. The shift away from paper-based records raises serious record collection, management and retention issues, some of which are familiar to the world of paper records and some of which are unique to electronic record retention and retrieval. On the other hand, electronic records can offer benefits, like easier search and retrieval, that may reduce some of the problems of paper-based records management. Thus, the objective of any conversion to electronic processes is to maximize the benefits that such systems can offer, while simultaneously minimizing any risks, including legal risks.

The term "electronic processes" includes any use of computers or other electronic devices to conduct transactions or business, to store data or records, or to transmit communications or information (whether text, voice or visual images). Electronic processes encompass not only the hardware and software applications, but also the personnel, procedures, and policies that make the system work properly.

This Guide raises issues that agencies should consider in deciding when each of their processes and functions should be partially or entirely converted to an electronic process and how such electronic processes should be designed in order to reduce legal risks that may be identified. The first two parts of this Guide discuss the importance of the legal issues to the conversion process and explore the issues that electronic processes present to the agencies. The last part provides a list of suggested steps that agencies may incorporate into their decision-making process to address the issues raised in Parts I and II. The reader who already recognizes the legal issues presented by electronic processes and those involved in replacing paper processes with electronic ones may wish to turn first to Part III, which does not depend on the analysis of Parts I and II for [an] understanding of its suggestions.[4]

This Guide is intended only to provide information and analysis to the Department's client agencies. It is intended only to assist those agencies in identifying general issues in process design and is not intended to provide binding rules or standards for the use of electronic processes. The Department anticipates that agencies will exercise their own discretion in determining how to address the issues discussed in this Guide. Nothing herein is intended for use in resolving particular cases or to confer any right on any person or group. *See, e.g., United States v. Caceres*, 440 U.S. 741 (1979). The function of providing opinions and legal advice to executive agencies is conferred by regulation on the Office of Legal Counsel. 28 C.F.R. §0.25 (1999). To the extent that an agency seeks the legal opinion of the Department of Justice regarding these matters, we recommend that the agency contact the Office of Legal Counsel.

I. Why Agencies Should Consider Legal Risks

Government agencies are enmeshed in law: they are creatures of law; they act pursuant to legal authority; they are bound to carry out legal duties in a way legally accountable to the public; and they are subject to special restrictions imposed by law. For example, government procurement processes are regulated by law. Over time, agencies have developed processes to respond to obligations and practices imposed by these responsibilities. Therefore, agencies should be aware of the legal implications of converting or re-engineering existing processes and the legal changes that can occur in the move from traditional to electronic processes.[5]

Advances in technology, public expectations, Congress's mandate in GPEA, and Administration policy all require that agencies of the United States [G]overnment move expeditiously to adopt electronic processes. As this Guide explains, it is important to consider carefully the legal requirements and risks associated with the process involved. In many cases, the legal aspects of the process may be apparent and adopting an electronic process may be comparatively simple. In others, designing an electronic process that adequately protects an agency's ability to carry out its programs and legal obligations, and that deters fraud and misconduct by private parties, may be more difficult. In such cases, adopting electronic processes may require a substantial and long-term commitment of agency staff and resources, including close involvement at an agency's highest levels.

Finally, we note that our comparisons in this Guide of electronic processes to paper systems should not in any way be taken as an endorsement of the continued use of those paper processes. Rather, because everyone is familiar with paper systems, we refer to those systems to assist agencies in issue-spotting as they develop their electronic processes.[6]

A. Legal Issues Involved in Conversion to Electronic Processes

Agencies keep records for several reasons: to carry out their public responsibility to conduct agency business with due care in a fiscally responsible manner, to meet statutory recordkeeping requirements, and to provide the information necessary to protect the government's interest when disputes arise over agency operations. Paper-based systems of records have evolved over time to satisfy those needs. Many of those systems are being replaced by electronic processes that are being deployed over short time periods. Often, problems arise because the re-engineered process does not fully capture the needs of the agency. As a result, the adoption of electronic systems, or the conversion of paper-based records systems to electronic ones, can present significant legal issues that need to be identified and addressed as part of the decision-making process. New legal issues may arise from the use of the new storage media and the new electronic mechanisms that allow agencies to conduct business and deal with the public in a manner that was not possible in the paper world. On the other hand, other legal issues may be reduced with an effective electronic process. For example, the use of a digital signature on a document can cryptographically bind the signature to the entire document, whereas a written signature on the last page of a such a document may leave questions as to which of the preceding pages are part of the signed document.

Electronic processes can be designed in such a way that the electronic transactions and their terms can be recorded in a legally adequate manner. For example, an agency can design its electronic processes so that program participants can readily ascertain when they become eligible for benefits and the agency can establish that program participants agreed to certain limitations on the agency's obligations. Even if it is determined that some legal obligations cannot be established electronically, perhaps most of the program's business can be conducted and recorded electronically if just a few crucial paper instruments are used and saved.

B. Identifying Legal Issues

At this point, no one can provide definitive guidelines as to what program safeguards will ultimately be necessary to protect an agency's interests and create binding and enforceable obligations on the agency and those with whom it does business. What we can say, however, is that agencies should attempt to understand which risks have increased and which have decreased through the adoption of electronic processes. If agencies incorporate within their processes mechanisms to account for those risks, they will be far less likely to be surprised by unfavorable rulings than an agency that simply converts paper systems to electronic ones without undertaking such an analysis. The act of addressing these risks will give agency decision-makers a better understanding of the differences between paper and electronic processes and put them in a better position to design and implement electronic systems that will preserve the strengths of paper processes while avoiding the weaknesses inherent to paper and the flaws that have been incorporated into the paper systems over the years.

A key question agencies face in converting to or adopting electronic processes is whether the system under consideration meets the applicable legal requirements and provides adequate evidence of its transactions and actions. In certain situations, an agency may determine that an electronic process is "good enough" to meet its legal needs without regard to whether it is comparable to or as good as its prior process. At the other extreme, some agencies may decide that electronic conversion will require a complete re-engineering of their business processes in order to address the legal risks and issues that a particular system presents or that are not being addressed as effectively in their existing system.

Because most of our common experience and legal precedent comes from the paper-based world, many agencies will use their existing paper-based systems as a reference point in their analysis. So long as agencies recognize that most paper processes have risks associated with them, they may wish to consider whether the new systems will work at least as well as the traditional ones, and consider the significance of the risks posed by their conversion. The discussion that follows compares some aspects of paper systems to electronic processes as a method to identify legal issues that need to be considered in designing electronic processes. No disparagement of electronic processes, nor praise for paper ones, is meant by this analytical device.

Well-designed paper systems have advantages: paper records are more or less permanent; alterations usually can be detected; important contextual information may be added as the paper is processed; access to documents often can be controlled easily; many documents can be preserved for long periods of time and remain readable without special equipment; and there are well-settled rules that have developed over time to address issues such as the validity, authenticity, and reliability of paper documents. But paper also has limitations: storage of paper documents consumes vast amounts of space; single documents may easily be lost or become irretrievable; access is limited to those having physical possession of the document or a copy; extracting information from multiple paper sources is difficult and time-consuming; search capabilities are limited; some paper deteriorates and can become unreadable within a few years; and paper is bulky and difficult to transport in large volumes. By contrast, effective electronic processes can overcome some of paper's weaknesses: electronic records, when properly organized or archived, are easier to store, search, and retrieve than paper and allow for much broader access than paper documents.

An example describing both an agency's traditional process and its electronic process serves to illustrate this point. Suppose that an agency program involves transactions with an individual, and that the agency receives data about the transaction not only from the individual participant (e.g., an application form, financial statements), but also from other sources (e.g., agency personnel's reports on the transaction). In the traditional paper-based system, the agency probably would have kept a file with the specific paper documents submitted by each source (e.g., the paper application form and financial statements from the participant, and internal reports from agency staff). If a dispute ever arose that required a determination of who submitted what information, the paper documents in the file probably would reflect the needed information. (If the system were flawed, however, misfiled paper documents might not be retrievable at all.) A well-designed electronic process should ordinarily be able to provide the same information as the paper system: who submitted the information; what information was submitted; when the information was submitted; and whether all the relevant information was retrieved.

Agencies traditionally file paper communications by subject or by a name of a person or entity. The challenge in such a system is to ensure that all communications are properly filed in the appropriate place. When such a system works properly, agency employees (and the lawyers who represent the agency) have a permanent record (typically arranged chronologically) of all the significant documents pertaining to the matter. When it does not, documents may be irretrievably lost through misfiling. Electronic documents, on the other hand, may be maintained in a way that uses identifiers to associate the documents with a particular matter or "file," which often allows for easier access. However, for certain types of electronic records systems, processes and procedures must be developed to address such issues as creating accurate and correct associations in the electronic files, ensuring that each document is maintained in an unaltered state, and identifying the source, date, and content of additional information added.[7]

C. Assessing the Significance of the Risk

An agency that routinely found itself able to enforce its programmatic requirements when they were embodied in written documents could face significant problems if it converts to an electronic process that does not capture information legally sufficient to enforce its interests. The full scope of agency operations can be affected by the government's ability to litigate successfully any disputes involving agency programs and operations. The outcome of litigation can dictate whether an agency can:

- Collect money owed it on various loans, grants or other debts;
- Enforce security interests it received to secure various financial transactions and thereby protect a lending or granting program;
- Enforce important regulatory requirements;
- Continue to interpret its program, statute or regulations in accordance with current practices;
- Enforce contracts with third parties that are necessary for the successful running of its programs or mission; or
- Avoid unintended liabilities.

To be able to protect the government's interests in litigation, the Department of Justice needs available, reliable, and persuasive agency records: records that are complete, uniform, easily understood, easily accessible and have been kept under a system that ensures a chain of custody of submissions and information gathered from all sources. Those requirements will not disappear merely because the medium of transactions changes from paper to electronic.

Even relatively infrequent litigation can have a very substantial impact on an agency. A government victory in a single case may provide binding precedent that approves an agency practice or establishes the validity of agency regulations. Conversely, a loss in a single case might establish adverse precedent that rejects an agency practice or even invalidates an agency regulation. The agency may be able to seek a different result in future cases, but an initial loss may generate precedent that will affect the outcome of those cases, and may open the door to litigation by other parties who might not even have been aware that an argument was available. Even disputes and litigation over monetary claims against an agency may establish controlling interpretations of statutes and regulations. On the other hand, agencies should note that for transactions that an agency determines have low risk of being involved in litigation and that involve low financial risk, many of the considerations described in this Guide may not apply.

Moreover, while criminal prosecutions and civil fraud cases involve a relatively small number of transactions within any given agency, such actions are critical to the integrity of agency programs because they serve to deter others from engaging in similar conduct. When an agency does not have a credible deterrent to fraud through vigorous detection and prosecution policies, fraud typically increases dramatically. Without effective and successful litigation on the agency's behalf, fraud in agency programs may increase and legal challenges to agency actions could have a greater chance of success. Essential to such litigation is the consistent accuracy and reliability of an agency's recordkeeping system, whether paper or electronic.

Finally, agencies must be able to satisfy a variety of people besides judges and juries. Agencies are accountable to the public, customers, auditors, and Congress, and may have varying legal obligations to each. Electronic processes sufficient to protect an agency's position in court should also be able to address any legal responsibilities to these other audiences just as well-designed paper processes.

II. Legal Issues to Consider in "Going Paperless"

As an agency identifies processes for conversion from paper to electronic, the agency should ask how it should design those processes so as to protect its legal rights and minimize legal risks that may compromise the agency's mission.

In answering these questions, agencies should consider the following four issues:

1. Will the electronically gathered and stored information be collected, retained, and accessible whenever needed?
2. Will the electronic collection, transmission, or storage of "documents" or information comply with applicable legal requirements, including, for example, laws requiring that certain records be maintained in a particular form or format?
3. Will electronic records be sufficiently reliable to be useful to Congress, agency decision-makers, private disputants, judges, juries, and others who must determine the facts underlying agency actions?

4. Will the agency's use of electronic methods to obtain, send, disclose and store information comply with applicable laws, such as those governing recordkeeping, privacy, confidentiality, and accessibility?

Our discussion of each of these issues is an attempt to assist the agencies in spotting relevant issues; this discussion is not intended to provide authoritative answers or to endorse any particular technology.

A. Availability of Information

To ensure the availability of information in an electronic process, agencies should ensure: (1) that an electronic process collects all relevant information; (2) that the information is retained properly; and (3) that the information is readily accessible. The potentially lengthy period of time between the collection of information and its use in many situations, including litigation, highlights the importance of these issues.

Most agencies now file and retain significant paper documents themselves. Some agencies converting to electronic processes have considered requiring the party that submits electronic information to retain the original form and source documents relating to the filing, perhaps in paper and perhaps electronically. Other agencies, recognizing the technical complexity of electronic records management, may hire contractors to maintain the information and provide more than ministerial support. If agencies rely on the people or entities submitting information to retain legally significant documents, they might find some of those documents unavailable if a dispute over the transaction arises. Similarly, if an agency uses an outside information manager, it should contractually ensure that its information is properly retained and that the agency has access to its own information. In either case, the agency should take appropriate steps to ensure that information in third-party hands is available when needed.

1. Will the Electronic Process Gather Necessary Information?

Agencies should carefully examine the processes that they will be converting to electronic processes, and determine what information must be collected from each transaction. In adopting electronic processes, agencies should ascertain whether the following four specific types of information should be captured and retained: (1) content of the transaction, including all records that comprise the substance of the transaction or filing; (2) records that contain information about how the transaction was processed, including dates received and changes or modifications that were made in records; (3) a means to authenticate the identity of all people who participated in the transaction both inside and outside the agency, and the scope of each person's participation; and (4) for appropriate transactions, a means for establishing the intent of the participants to enter into the transaction or agreement. *See also, e.g., Public Citizen v. Carlin,* 184 F.3d 900, 910 (D.C. Cir. 1999) (discussing preservation of content, structure, and context of federal records).

Information gathering issues can be demonstrated through the following example:

An agency operates a direct loan program. Formerly, the agency received loan applications on paper, but now receives them electronically through its Web site. Four applicants (Abel, Baker, Company and Donald) submit loan applications that contain materially false and misleading information. When challenged by the agency, Abel, Baker, Company and Donald offer the following excuses:

- Abel claims that he sent his application along with an explanatory electronic note that concerned key information on his application.
- Baker claims that he submitted truthful information, and that someone must have altered it after he sent it.
- Company, a large corporation, claims that no employee was authorized to apply for a loan, so a rogue employee (identity unknown) must have sent the application without the company's knowledge. The agency's electronic process does not show who or even what office at Company submitted the application.
- Donald claims he was only working on a draft application with only preliminary information that he never meant to send, and that he must have pushed the "enter" button by accident, thus unwittingly transmitting his "draft" as though it were a real application.

Does the agency's electronic process provide adequate safeguards, just as paper processes must, to refute the arguments raised by Abel, Baker, Company and Donald?

Content

When agencies collect information in paper form, additional information beyond that requested by the four corners of the form is frequently supplied. The document received by an agency might include additional attachments not necessarily required, and the agency might supplement the record with interlineations or notes. The physical composition of the document can attest to its completeness — for example, pages that were stapled together by the sender suggest that this was the document that was intended to be submitted to the agency. The agency's electronic process should include safeguards so that an agency can establish all of the information that was submitted by the sender as a single electronic document.

In the above example, the agency's electronic process should be designed in such a way that the agency can demonstrate that Abel's submission included only the application form and no attached electronic note or other information. In a paper system, the agency would point out that it has standardized its filing procedures in a way that ensures that all attachments are saved with the documents. (Of course, this presumes that the agency has such standards.) Abel would be faced with convincing the agency or a court that he did, in fact, include an attachment to his filing. In the electronic as in the physical world, the agency must also be able to show that its processes have been designed to capture entire communications and that its files contain everything that it received from Abel.

Processing

Agencies should also ensure that their electronic processing captures all relevant information, such as when and where the document was sent and received and whether the document was subsequently altered, and, if so, the source, date, and content of the alteration. Electronic systems can be designed to capture such information, including alterations or changes to a document. In the above example, if the agency's electronic process reliably kept track of all alterations to the applications after receipt, it could prove that Baker's application was not altered.

Identities

Often it is crucial to be able to prove who (i.e., a specific individual) submitted a communication or agreed to a transaction with an agency. Paper documents generally accomplish this fairly well, most commonly by containing a handwritten signature that can be matched with a specific person, a letterhead or return address on the document or envelope, and so on. Some transactions are so important that agencies require a personal appearance before some designated official in order to establish identity, e.g., having a notary endorse or certify the signature.

Agencies should consider whether, in appropriate circumstances, a proposed electronic process will gather information sufficient to identify the person who submitted a communication or agreed to a transaction. For important transactions, particularly those that require proof of an individual's identity, or that he or she is creating a legally binding obligation, an agency may wish to require those individuals to employ some form of electronic signature. In the above example, the use of a digital signature could provide the agency a reliable means of identifying the name, position, and location of the specific individual who submitted the document, and thus, it would be difficult for Company to deny that one of its employees filed the application. See the discussion below in Section II.B.2 regarding the legal significance of signatures.

Intent of the Parties

Enforcement of an agency's rights often depends upon being able to prove what was intended by a communication. Did the parties intend a transmission of information to be a draft of a possible contract or a final, legally binding contract? Did an individual who transmitted information to the agency intend it to be a formal report which, if false, could result in his criminal prosecution? Paper-based transactions and communications typically answer such questions in a number of ways, for example, by whether a document "looks" like a contract or just an informal letter, whether it contains a handwritten signature, or whether it contains a warning that it is submitted under "penalty of perjury." Similar methods can be used in the electronic world.

The agency could probably defeat Donald's argument in the above example by showing, for example, that (1) its electronic process would not allow an application to be transmitted unless Donald had clicked "yes" after being shown a message explaining that by doing so, he was submitting a final application upon which the agency would rely; (2) it had provided a telephone number or e-mail address for Donald to notify the agency that an application had been submitted in error; or (3) the agency had actually notified Donald that it had received his application.[8]

2. Will the Information Be Retained?

Audits, Congressional inquiries, litigation and other dispute resolution often take place years after the agency's acts and transactions occurred and the "files" are considered closed. But such information remains essential to the agency's abilities to protect its program and to the ability of the Department of Justice to investigate and litigate the agency's cases. Information no longer necessary for day-to-day operations also may be useful to the agency itself (for example, when agencies update procedures and revise regulations). Additionally, different types of information require different levels of retention. Thus, agencies should determine which information should be retained and for what period of time, as well as which information may be discarded soon after receipt.

Electronic systems should be designed and maintained to guard against data corruption, whether through accidental deletion, equipment failures, storage media deterioration over time, stray electromagnetic forces, or myriad other hardware and software problems. Such systems should also be designed to limit access to authorized users — for example, by requiring controlled password identification for access to certain information. Finally, an electronic system should be designed to ensure proper file retention and tracing of alterations and updates (as to source, date, and content, and all other internal controls that are required to produce a secure and reliable record maintenance and retention system).[9]

Electronic data are frequently transferred or converted from one storage medium or software system to another. In this process (sometimes referred to as "data migration"), important information, such as formatting and the structure and content of electronic forms, may be lost, or even the record itself destroyed unless appropriate steps are taken. Similarly, unless such changes are thoroughly documented, it can be difficult to demonstrate that the critical information was not changed in the process. In transition between systems, agencies sometimes maintain multiple, over-lapping systems, particularly in the transition from paper to electronic based systems. Because information from all systems may be required to be maintained under the Federal Records Act,[10] and may be needed for various purposes, agencies should address retention issues for all systems, even overlapping ones.

3. Will the Information Continue to be Accessible?

Unlike paper files which, when properly organized and maintained in the ordinary course of business, are readily available and usable without any special equipment, electronic information is not always accessible without special equipment and software. Agencies should consider several factors related to the accessibility of electronic records. First, computer technology is rapidly changing and software and formatting standards may quickly become obsolete. Computer-stored data may become useless unless the agency can provide the continued capability with the older technologies or can accurately translate the document as more modern systems are implemented. Second, if in the future, an agency no longer has staff who are familiar and competent to work with the electronic processes necessary to read older data, such data could be functionally unavailable.[11] Electronic files might be stored while encrypted by software or protected by passwords no longer available or remembered years later, unless steps are taken to preserve the software or passwords. As noted above, these concerns are no less serious if the information is held by an outside party.

B. Legal Sufficiency of Electronic Records

Various state and federal laws require that certain types of transactions or events be reflected by written or signed documents. Case law and other legal authorities offer some guidance as to what types of transactions are covered and what types of records satisfy such requirements. GPEA addresses this situation by providing that electronic records and signatures shall not be denied legal effect because they are in electronic form. The recently enacted E-SIGN legislation contains similar provisions as to certain transactions, but a discussion of its provisions is beyond the scope of this Guide.

1. The Importance of Writings

In many circumstances, the law requires that the terms of an agreement or other legal obligation be in "writing."[12] The essence of the "writing" requirement is to establish a record that is not subject to imperfect memory or to competing claims as to what parties to an agreement intended. The formal requirement that legal documents be reduced to "writing" has been justified on many bases, including: providing the type of ceremony needed to make the parties appreciate the fact that they are undertaking enforceable legal obligations; creating evidence that the legal instrument exists and was entered into; simplifying litigation by narrowing the scope of relevant evidence; and providing evidence more permanent than a witness's recollection.

A statutory "writing" requirement does not necessarily imply that this writing must be on paper. Indeed, E-SIGN and GPEA may limit the courts' authority to restrict the term "writing" to paper documents. But the functional purposes underlying a "writing" requirement are important, and courts might require that these purposes be satisfied (whether through interpreting the term "writing" or in some other fashion) whether a document is on paper or is in electronic form. Electronic documents that satisfy the purposes of the "writing" requirement should be acceptable to the courts so long as they have the same (or better) indicia of reliability as their paper counterparts. Thus, electronic documents that provide a documentary recording of a transaction in a manner that establishes and memorializes the terms should constitute a "writing." To the extent that an electronic document is more like a traditional "writing" than an oral agreement, it should be treated by the law similarly to a paper document.[13] The challenge in creating electronic documents is to ensure that disparate communications (such as exchanges of e-mail) are reduced to a single document in a manner that provides evidence that the parties understand that the document memorializes the underlying terms and conditions. Electronic documents that satisfy those purposes are more likely to be given legal effect.

Federal and state laws traditionally have required that many types of documents, particularly contracts,[14] be in writing and signed by the parties to be bound. State laws known as the "Statute of Frauds" also require many contracts be written.[15] *See* Restatement (Second) of Contracts § 110 (1979).[16] Many states have introduced amendments that relate to electronic contracts, and these amendments are likely to have an impact on the "writing" and "signature" requirements contained in state statutory codes.

A federal statute, 31 U.S.C. §1501(a)(1)(A) (1994), provides that United States government obligations may be enforced "only when supported by documentary evidence of ... a binding agreement between an agency and another person (including an agency) that is ... in writing, in a way and form, and for a purpose authorized by law." As of the date of this Guide, no federal court has construed this writing requirement in the context of electronic commerce nor has a court squarely addressed the question of whether a purely electronic record, created as part of an automated system, would alone meet the Statute of Frauds.[17] However, case law and other legal authorities offer limited guidance as to whether federal and state statutes of frauds or other statutory requirements of writings will be satisfied by electronic substitutes. The Comptroller General has concluded, for example, that contracts formed using some electronic technologies may constitute valid obligations of the government for purposes of 31 U.S.C. §1501, so long as the technology used provides the same degree of assurance and certainty as traditional "paper and ink" methods of contract formation.[18]

As to state statutes, many state statutes of frauds do not define "writing." However, courts have accepted electronic communications that result in a paper document at the end of the communications process, such as a telegram, as a "writing." *See, e.g., Hillstrom v. Gosnay*, 614 P.2d 466 (Mont. 1980).[19] To the extent that the electronic process clearly records the terms of agreements and is adequate to show that the parties intended to make those agreements — that is, they serve the purposes that the law has required and relied on paper to serve — it is more likely that they will be accepted by the courts.[20]

Many court systems will themselves soon be allowing electronic filing of formal pleadings and briefs. As courts become more familiar with electronic records through electronic filings, they presumably will become more likely to recognize the validity of records and agreements recorded solely in electronic form in sensibly implemented electronic recording systems. Courts, however, might be reluctant to interpret legal requirements liberally merely because of technological advances, and the risk that courts may lag in doing so cannot be discounted altogether.

2. The Importance of Signatures

Signatures have been given a unique place in the law partly because they reflect physical characteristics of individuals that were applied to the particular document at issue. Generally, the presence of a signature on a document is sufficient to identify the person who signed the document (although courts might require that someone identify the signature as belonging to the signor), to indicate that the person read and was familiar with the contents of the document (or at least had the opportunity to read it before she signed it), and to demonstrate that the person agreed and intended to be bound by the contents of the documents she signed.[21]

These may be only assumptions, but agencies, businesses and the courts routinely rely on them.[22] Such "presumptions" provide a set of rules for associating an individual with a document and establishing his or her intent to accept or acknowledge its contents. Many of those rules are supported by centuries of case law and, in some cases, statutes that enforce them. Of course, signatures can be forged, may be illegible, or may have been placed on a document in a manner that does not satisfy the rules. In those situations, the party challenging the signature generally has the burden to rebut or overcome the presumption.

Unlike traditional signatures, electronic alternatives do not yet necessarily enjoy the long history of use and common expectations that surround traditional signatures. However, other steps have been taken — and undoubtedly more will be taken in the future — to support the validity of electronic signatures. For example, an increasing number of statutes and regulations impose the same presumptions of identity, intent, or familiarity with content that are typically associated with paper signatures. The proper design of legal instruments can reduce the need for such presumptions. Until such presumptions become widely accepted for electronic signatures, agencies should ensure that the electronic signature technologies they adopt identify the signers of the document and clearly express their intent and familiarity with the document.

For example, statutes that require certain agency officials to authorize or approve an agency action might not be satisfied with something less than a signature on a document. Thus, simply affixing a "/s/[Named Official]" on an electronic document authorizing a particular agency action may not satisfy any requirement that agency actions be authorized in a signed writing by the appropriate official, any more than it would on a paper document. The official's signature on a paper authorization demonstrates that the official saw and signed the authorization; the law presumes that the official was aware of the contents and the effect of signing the document. To the extent that an agency adopts electronic processes for such approvals, it must ensure that the technology utilized provides a legally acceptable method for indicating approval of the action.

3. Electronic Alternatives to Traditional Signatures

Electronic signatures generally fall into three broad methods of identifying an individual: something the individual knows, something the individual possesses, and something about the individual. Examples of techniques that use these methods include user identification codes and passwords (i.e., numbers or codes known to the individuals such as a "PIN," a passcode, or a private key used to make a digital signature[23]), tokens, smart cards or other physical objects that the user possesses that may be inserted into a reading device, and devices that measure physical, or "biometric,"[24] characteristics of the individual.[25] The National Institute of Standards and Technology has recognized that use of a combination of authentication techniques can "substantially increase" the security of an authentication system. For example, public key digital signature technology is designed to work only when the private key which is used to make a signature is used in conjunction with the proper PIN, password, or biometric identifier.[26]

Properly implemented, various types of electronic signatures, like traditional signatures, can offer increasing degrees of reliability, although no system — either electronic or traditional — can completely prevent fraud or misuse. Depending on the nature of the transactions, smart cards and sophisticated digital signatures that use public key cryptography can frequently offer a reasonable degree of reliability. The risk with these technologies is that any number that can be typed or any card or token that can be inserted can also be disclosed to others or stolen. Parties seeking to avoid a transaction might claim that their identifying number, card or token was given to others who then acted as imposters.[27] Of even greater reliability is a properly implemented biometric-based digital signature. When coupled with public key cryptography, biometric-based digital signatures become an even more powerful tool that holds much promise. However, the widespread use of biometrics would be expensive to implement, its commercial application is still relatively limited, and not every transaction requires this very high degree of security.[28]

Moreover, electronic signature methods vary in their ability to ensure that an electronic document to which they are bound has not been altered after signing. Some methods provide no assurance at all, but systems using "public key, private key" digital signatures generally are designed to reveal such alterations. Thus, the better approach is to vary the level of security, depending on the significance of the underlying documents. For those records where the need for reliability is even higher, agencies should consider using a combination of security methods.[29]

Indeed, a well-designed electronic system can make the indication of agreement more trustworthy than paper documents that are ambiguous as to intent. The creative design of the agreement formation stage of an electronic process offers agencies the possibility to develop an indication of intent that is even more meaningful than one arising from traditional paper processes. For example, when a multi-page paper document is signed only on the last page, the question is sometimes raised whether all of the pages were included in the document the signer signed. An electronic signature bound to the entire document eliminates any question as to the contents of the document signed by the signer. With high value transactions, exceeding, rather than merely meeting, the reliability standards of paper signatures, should be an agency's goal.

4. *Federal and state statutes will affect agencies' use of electronic processes*

a. The Government Paperwork Elimination Act

On October 21, 1998, Congress enacted the Government Paperwork Elimination Act, Pub. L. No. 105-277, §§1701-1710 (1998) (codified as 44 U.S.C.A. §3504 n. (West Supp. 1999)).[30] Among other things, the GPEA provides for the development of procedures for agencies by October 21, 2003, to use and accept electronic signatures,[31] and for agencies to provide "for the option of the electronic maintenance, submission, or disclosure of information, when practicable as a substitute for paper" and "for the use and acceptance of electronic signatures, when practicable." GPEA §1704. Moreover, "to the extent feasible and appropriate," agencies that expect receipt by electronic means of 50,000 or more submittals are to have "multiple methods of electronic signatures" available. GPEA §1703(b)(1)(E).

GPEA may leave issues unresolved. For example, GPEA may not necessarily make electronic records valid and enforceable under all circumstances (any more than paper signatures are valid under all circumstances). GPEA Section 1707 provides that certain electronic records or signatures "shall not be denied legal effect, validity, or enforceability because such records are in electronic form." (Section 101 of E-SIGN contains similar language about the validity of electronically recorded commercial transactions.) While that wording bars courts from invalidating electronic records and signatures merely because they are in electronic form, it does not require courts to accept electronic records and signatures that are deficient in other respects merely because they are in electronic form. For example, if there are reasons to doubt that it was actually the electronic signature holder who affixed the signature in question, a court might not accept the electronic signature, just as it might decline to accept a paper signature that could not be verified. Also, GPEA may apply only to certain types of electronic signatures and to records that meet certain requirements, such as the records submitted, used, or maintained in accord with the OMB Guidance required by GPEA.[32]

b. State Statutes

Some states have enacted statutes designed to make certain electronic submissions as enforceable as signed paper documents.[33] Because those statutes might only give effect to electronic submissions that meet specified requirements, each statute must be examined for other provisions affecting the proof of the transaction, such as who (the sender or receiver) has the burden of proving whether the sender named in the transmission really sent it and whether its contents were altered.[34] Some states have enacted broader statutes, including variants on the Uniform Electronic Transactions Act (1999), which was promulgated by the National Conference of Commissioners on Uniform State Laws. It is unclear to what extent the GPEA (discussed above in Section II.B.4.a) might preempt certain of such state laws or parts of them, or the extent to which such state laws are applicable to transactions to which the government is a party or acquires an interest (e.g., government-insured loans).

C. Reliability of Electronic Information

To be useful, agency information must be reliable and meaningful. While litigators are primarily concerned about the persuasiveness of information in a courtroom, the usability of agency information affects many aspects of agency work. Agency employees must be able to rely on the information to function effectively within the agency as well as to discuss the results of agency work with those outside the agency.

1. The Legal Significance of Context Surrounding the Collection or Creation of Electronic Information

Any information collection system should provide a means to define, limit and show the context of the information supplied to the extent it is necessary for a particular transaction. For example, a "form" to be filled out may require specified information to be supplied on particular lines or in boxes, and such forms usually are accompanied by explanatory instructions. Completed paper forms include a means of identifying not only the answers, but also the questions and instructions. The meaning of the answers is evident from the document itself.

Electronic processes that use "forms" generally display a template of the form to the person filling it out. The person enters the information requested by the form. If the system is designed to retain and reproduce only the *answers*, and not the questions or instructions, disputes may arise over the meaning of the information supplied. Knowing an answer without knowing the corresponding question is of little value. Electronic submission systems generally should be designed to provide a copy of the form (including all questions and instructions) in response to which information was supplied to the agency, or bind the form to the answers provided. If an agency's forms change over time, and the information on the form is important either to the underlying transaction or to an agency process or program, then the electronic process should be designed to keep track of the exact form used by each submitter of information.

2. The Perceived Reliability of Electronic Data

Even though many people routinely rely on electronic information, such as electronic mail, some people are skeptical about the reliability of electronic data that are created by unfamiliar government processes. Electronic information may not be perceived as reliable if the underlying processes that create or maintain the data themselves are not viewed as reliable. For example, many people believe that information in electronic storage is vulnerable to tampering, either by internal (i.e., within the agency) or external sources.[35] The internal vulnerability concerns can be addressed by demonstrating that there are sufficient electronic procedures in place to prevent accidental or unauthorized alteration of information and to provide an audit trail to trace all changes. The concerns about external vulnerability may be met by showing that the computer system has measures in place to prevent and detect intrusions from outside and to store important information securely, off the network, where outsiders cannot obtain access to it.

3. Persuasiveness of Electronic Processes and Information Derived from Them

Because electronic processes in many respects are more complex than paper methods, explaining them or their reliability may be more difficult. Whatever systems or methods are ultimately chosen by the agency, the agency will need to provide reliable information regarding its systems (verified by periodic audits) to a variety of audiences including judges and juries, agency employees, and members of the general public with whom the agency has dealings. The agency should be able to communicate this information in a straightforward and sensible manner and should recognize that people are likely to have varying degrees of knowledge about such processes.

4. Admissibility of Information Derived from Electronic Processes

As with evidence in any form, electronic records must meet the legal requirements for "admissibility" before the government can use them in court. Generally, the party seeking to introduce records must show that the evidence is "authentic" (that is, provides proof that it is what it purports to be), and that it is the "best evidence" (that is, that it is the original or an acceptable duplicate). In addition, in order to be able to use electronic or any other agency records as evidence, the government in most cases must establish that the records were generated and maintained by a "trustworthy" process. If an electronic process does not reliably show who transmitted a piece of information to the agency, when it was transmitted, and that it has not been altered either intentionally or inadvertently, then, depending on the circumstances, the electronic record might not even be admissible, which means that the record could not even be considered by the judge or jury in deciding the merits of the government's claims or defenses.[36]

It is consequently of paramount importance that agencies using electronic processes ensure that their processes store and reproduce records in a manner that will result in records that will be admissible in court. In general, an agency's electronic processes must be able to produce reliably the information that we discuss in Section III.C., below, and any other relevant information. To determine what other information might be relevant for this purpose, agencies should consult the Department of Justice or agency attorneys who litigate the particular agency's cases.

D. Legal Requirements Affecting Electronic Processes

The government has long-established systems for handling paper records in ways that generally meet legal requirements regarding the use, storage, and disclosure of information. As agencies convert to electronic processes, they must ensure that those processes also facilitate and comply with such legal requirements. If disregarded, these restrictions could be a source of legal liability.

Legal requirements can affect the use of electronic processes in many contexts, some requiring that the government be able to produce or disclose information, others prohibiting the government from releasing specified information. Such requirements include:

- The Freedom of Information Act (FOIA), 5 U.S.C. §552 (Supp. IV 1998), requires release of certain information in agency records to members of the public upon request. This statute has been applied to computer records. *See, e.g., Cleary, Gottlieb, Steen & Hamilton v. Department of Health & Human Servs.*, 844 F. Supp. 770 (D.D.C. 1993). The FOIA statute was recently amended to clarify the status of electronic records under public access law. See Pub. L. No. 104-231, 110 Stat. 3048, §§ 1-12 (1996) (codified as amended in scattered sections of 5 U.S.C. § 552). *See also* David MacDonald, Note, *The Electronic Freedom of Information Act Amendments: A Minor Upgrade to Public Access Law*, 23 Rutgers Computer & Tech. L.J. 357 (1997).
- Discovery in litigation. The federal government could be subject to discovery in any litigated case (even if it is not a party).[37] Such discovery can reach electronic records as well as paper records. Depending on the circumstances, the agency might be required to gather all electronic records pertaining to a specified person, topic, transaction or event.

- The Federal Records Act (FRA) requires federal agencies to ensure adequate and proper documentation of their policies, decisions, procedures, and essential transactions, by maintaining "records" as defined under the FRA. See 44 U.S.C. §§3101 and 3301 (1994). The National Archives and Records Administration has promulgated standards for the creation, use, preservation, and disposition of electronic records, which also specifically address the minimum requirements for electronic recordkeeping systems that maintain the official file copy of text documents on electronic media, including e-mail systems. 36 C.F.R. §§1234.22, 1234.24(b) (1999). The government's compliance with its FRA obligations as they affect the preservation of e-mail and word processing documents has been the subject of extensive litigation in the D.C. Circuit. *See Public Citizen v. Carlin*, 184 F.3d 900 (D.C. Cir. 1999); *Armstrong v. Executive Office of the President*, 1 F.3d 1274 (D.C. Cir. 1993).[38]

- The Privacy Act, 5 U.S.C. § 552a (Supp. IV 1998), imposes certain restrictions on agency use of personal data. In enacting the Privacy Act, Congress was concerned predominantly with the increasing use of computers and sophisticated information systems and the potential abuse of such technology. *Thomas v. United States Dept of Energy*, 719 F.2d 342 (10th Cir. 1983). The Privacy Act also (1) requires agencies to provide notice about how information in a system of records is stored, accessed and used; (2) requires agencies to provide a means for subjects to challenge, correct or rebut information relating to those records; and (3) provides specific standards for computer matching of electronic records containing personal information.

- The Rehabilitation Act of 1973, 29 U.S.C. 701 *et seq.,* prohibits federal agencies from discriminating against otherwise qualified persons with disabilities. Sections 501 and 504 of the Act prohibit disability-based discrimination against qualified individuals (employees and members of the public) participating in federal programs. New Section 508 of the Act, 29 U.S.C.A. 794d (West Supp. 1999), as amended in 1998, requires that all electronic and information technology systems and products used by any federal agency be accessible to persons with disabilities, including both employees and members of the public. Agencies will have to adhere to specific standards for accessibility of electronic products and systems. Section 508 also authorizes individuals to file administrative complaints or to sue agencies that have procured inaccessible electronic systems in violation of the law.[39]

- Other laws restricting agency disclosure of information, such as the Trade Secrets Act, 18 U.S.C. § 1905 (Supp. II 1996), prohibit federal officials from disclosing trade secrets or certain other types of confidential information about persons or businesses, unless authorized by law.

- Other laws and regulations require systems of records to be capable of verifying that information in an agency's possession is used solely for authorized purposes and restrict access to information for certain defined purposes and by only those agency officials who are involved in those authorized purposes. These statutes and regulations will require electronic processes to guard against unauthorized use of such information and track access to that information. (For example, 26 U.S.C. § 6103 (Supp. III 1997) limits access to a taxpayer's tax return information to only those Internal

Revenue Service employees who are directly involved in a matter involving that taxpayer; 8 U.S.C. § 1255a(c)(2)(B)(4), (5) (1994), prohibits Immigration and Naturalization Service employees from using applications for legalization for any immigration-related purpose other than the legalization program.)

Other statutes or regulations unique to a given agency might impose further requirements or restrictions on the availability or disclosure of agency information. For example, an agency decision to allow electronic submissions by the public raises many potential issues that should be considered, such as the notice requirements of the Privacy Act, the requirements of the Rehabilitation Act, and the requirements that the FOIA may impose on access to information regarding submissions, including providing the electronic forms or templates used to capture the submission.

III. Reducing The Legal Risks in "Going Paperless"

The concerns highlighted in Part II, some of which have not yet been clearly decided by the courts, should not unduly deter agencies from taking advantage of electronic processes for many of their functions. Agencies should first analyze whether total conversion would be appropriate for each existing process, and examine what new processes may be needed. For those processes that are to be converted, agencies should take steps to reduce the legal risks in "going paperless."

This part of the Guide provides suggested steps that agencies may incorporate into their decision-making process to address the issues raised above. The first section of this part provides an analytic process of general considerations, and the second provides specific suggestions, including the types of information that should be gathered, retained, and made available on demand. The second section also makes recommendations that address particular agency activities, including contracting, regulatory programs, and other programs that require reporting of information, and benefit programs. These suggested steps will be helpful to agencies as they attempt to reduce legal risk when converting their processes. In accordance with the OMB Guidance on GPEA, agency considerations of cost, risk, and benefit, as well as any measures taken to minimize risks, should be commensurate with the level of sensitivity of the transaction. Low-risk information processes may need only minimal safeguards, while high-risk processes may need more. In the context of legal and litigation risks, "low-risk information processes" are those that have a small chance of generating significant liability, financial impact or litigation that would have a significant effect on the agency.[40]

In addition, Exhibit 1 provides key legal issues for agencies to consider in adopting an electronic process. The exhibit is intended as a helpful resource for agencies; it is not intended to be a required checklist or an exhaustive listing of the possible issues such processes may raise.

A. Should Every Agency Function Be Completely "Paperless"?

Before attempting to make every agency process paperless, agencies should analyze whether total conversion would be appropriate for each process. Even if parts of an agency function are converted to an electronic process, agencies should consider whether some paper documents still should be used. The GPEA requires that, by October 21, 2003, agencies provide for "the option of the electronic maintenance, submission, or disclosure of information, when practicable as a substitute for paper," and for "the use and acceptance of electronic signatures, when practicable." GPEA §1704. If an agency concludes that such use for a particular type of transaction or process is not practicable, the agency is not required by the GPEA to so use electronic processes.

We note, however, that conversion to electronic processes need not be an "all or nothing proposition." An agency may conclude that it is appropriate to convert most of its processes, while continuing to use paper (at least for the time being) for one particular part of its process. This reflects the common-sense recognition that, for some important transactions, retaining a paper document might be the best, most certain, and easiest to prove medium for establishing a legally significant transaction or event.

B. General Guidelines

In considering whether each agency function or type of transaction should be converted to an electronic process, and, if so, how that process should be designed, agencies can take the following steps to address the concerns discussed above.

1. Conduct an Analysis of the Nature of a Transaction or Process to Determine the Level of Protection Needed and the Level of Risk that Can Be Tolerated

Different agency functions and types of data pose different levels of legal risk. The greater the risk, the more carefully the agency should consider whether that particular function or type of data should be converted to an electronic process, and if so, how the electronic process will be designed. Riskier functions and processes dealing with more important data may require more stringent safeguards when converted to electronic processes. The following types of functions are likely to pose greater legal risks:

- Transactions that have legal significance. This includes transferring funds, forming a contract or other obligation, or fulfilling a legal responsibility, such as submitting a required filing.
- Transactions open to the public. Other things being equal, transactions with the general public generally pose more of a litigation risk than transactions among agency employees or other federal agencies.
- Transactions with newcomers. Some processes occur in the context of a long-term relationship, such as a contractual or an ongoing regulatory relationship. Other transactions, such as a one-time submission of information, take place in the absence of a relationship between the submitter and the government agency, and might be riskier.
- Processes historically susceptible to fraud or litigation. These include claims for funds or reporting debts and liabilities to the government. (On the

other hand, some kinds of fraud are difficult to find in a paper process, simply because human beings cannot wade through all the submissions to catch inconsistencies or patterns that warrant further investigation the way a well-instructed computer can.)

In addition, the following types of agency information or data generally need the greatest protection:

- Instruments reflecting rights and obligations. These include contracts, task orders, and other instruments by which the government or those dealing with the government undertake an obligation.
- Information traditionally used in agency litigation. For example, documents in administrative records of agency decisions or agency rulemaking, and information from agency files about individuals who are involved in disputes are often of critical importance in litigation. These and other types of information that are more likely to be needed in litigation need greater protection than, for example, generalized information on the agency's Web site. Agencies might wish to confer on this point with this Department's litigating divisions that represent them in court.
- Legally protected or sensitive data. This includes data protected by the Privacy Act or the Trade Secrets Act, or information that is otherwise sensitive, such as national security or law enforcement information, attorney-client or other privileged information, and personnel or medical records.

The above-mentioned principles should also be used to determine the type of authentication procedure needed for the transaction. Higher risk transactions should use more reliable forms of authentication, while lower risk transactions may use less rigorous methods. Such an appraisal may allow for greater security for very important transactions, while reducing the burden on agencies in connection with transactions that may not need the assurances of more rigorous forms of authentication.

2. Consider Potential Costs and Benefits, Quantifiable and Unquantifiable, Direct and Indirect, in Performing a Cost/Benefit Analysis

Costs and benefits for government processes are not measured in strictly monetary terms. Consider whether conversion to an electronic process might change the effectiveness of the system, the amount of fraud, the amount of litigation, and the success rate in litigated cases — all of which could impose costs or benefits on the agency. Consider the costs of complying with the legal requirements described in Section II.D, above, the cost of retaining and ensuring accessibility of data, the cost of personnel to manage the system, and other indirect costs. Consider, too, the benefits such a conversion could create, such as an increased ability to analyze data, greater ease in retrieving information, and more efficient storage of information. These various benefits and costs should also be compared to those in an agency's existing system.

3. Use Available Sources of Expertise Inside and Outside Your Agency, Including the OMB Procedures

Many of the issues discussed in this Guide are unquestionably complex and draw on many kinds of knowledge, including both technical and legal experience. On legal and risk analysis issues, expertise in an agency can reside both in the General Counsel's office and in the Inspector General's office. Outside of an agency, such expertise exists in the Department of Justice. An agency might wish to consult with the particular Department of Justice components that typically litigate its cases.

As discussed above, the GPEA requires the OMB to issue procedures for use and acceptance of electronic signatures. See above at footnote 27. This guidance may be helpful to agencies. Moreover, opposing litigants might argue that the GPEA confers benefits only on systems adopted and used in accord with the OMB Guidance. Therefore, to avoid such challenges, agencies should conform their procedures to the OMB Guidance and affirmatively note their usage of the OMB Guidance on the record.

4. Consider Developing a Comprehensive Plan when Converting a Traditional Process to an Electronic One, Especially if Converting Means Re-engineering the Existing Process

Agencies should design electronic processes to ensure that the processes are at least as reliable, and serve the same purposes, as the paper-based systems they replace. Agencies also should consider any existing deficiencies in their paper processes and remedy those when converting to electronic processes; they should be especially careful to identify and correct any deficiencies that will be magnified by the transition to the new system. Use of electronic processing provides unprecedented opportunities for adopting processes that would be impractical, unknown, and unimaginable in a paper-based system.

Agencies should consider developing a comprehensive plan that identifies issues and fixes responsibility for addressing those issues, including the legal concerns outlined here. In developing such a plan, an agency should encourage participation by all those affected by the conversion inside the agency, including program managers, lawyers, technical staff, persons familiar with each of the statutes that impose particular requirements (e.g., the Privacy Act, FOIA, and the Rehabilitation Act), and those interested parties from outside the agency, such as OMB and other client or sister agencies. By following such an approach, an agency is more likely to assure that all needs are being addressed during system development and over the long run, at least to the extent expressed in the plan.

For example, agencies may risk legal liabilities if their electronic processes are not designed to comply with the Rehabilitation Act, 29 U.S.C. §794d (West Supp. 1999), that generally requires all processes to be accessible to persons with disabilities. The Rehabilitation Act and other applicable statutes may be overlooked in the planning process unless those within the agency responsible for complying with or administering such statutes are consulted and involved in the planning process. If these issues are not addressed in the system design, agencies may risk legal liability and incur large costs in redesigning non-compliant components.

5. Consider the Kinds of Information Relevant to the Process; Ensure that Necessary Information Is Gathered

Electronic processes should be designed to gather all relevant information pertaining to each transaction, including the four types of information discussed above: content, processing, identities, and intent of the parties. *See* above at Section II.A.1; *see also, e.g., Public Citizen v. Carlin*, 184 F.3d 900, 910 (D.C. Cir. 1999) (discussing preservation of content, structure, and context of federal records). In deciding what information should be gathered by an electronic process, it is useful to consider what information the agency gathers in its paper transactions or recordkeeping. To the extent such information is or might be useful or important, the electronic process must be designed to capture the same or comparable information. For example, when converting a process by which a contractor submits invoices from subcontractors supporting progress payment requests to document costs, agencies should consider ways to capture equivalent information about the authenticity of the invoices. Conversion to an electronic system also presents a useful opportunity to do a zero-assumption review of what different or additional information, not previously gathered by paper, can and ought to be gathered by a new electronic system (and, perhaps, what information can be omitted). In some respects, a good design of an electronic system should not merely strive to replicate the paper system it replaces, but should aim at fulfilling the necessary information functions even better.[41]

6. Consider Using a "Terms and Conditions" Agreement

Agency managers could consider formalizing an agreement, sometimes referred to as a "terms and conditions agreement," among the parties to the electronic process, to ensure that all conditions of submission and receipt of data electronically are mutually known and understood. This process can assist in avoiding repudiation, rebutting a claim of ignorance, and even, where appropriate, shifting allocation of risk. Agencies should consult with their general counsel for guidance on the most appropriate terms for such agreements.

7. Incorporate a Long-Term Retention and Access Policy for Electronic Processes

Aside from any requirements mandated by statutes or regulations governing government recordkeeping (see Section II.D, above), agencies should maintain the data that will be needed to protect their rights in litigation and otherwise. Litigation about an agency's program can take place many years after the program has come to an end, and the information to support that litigation should remain available and unaltered. The amount of time for which records must be kept varies by agency and type of data. Agencies should consult with their general counsel, the Department of Justice, or the National Archives and Records Administration for advice on these matters.

Keeping data available in electronic form means not only having the data stored on an electronic medium that is available and can be accessed through appropriate software, but it also includes having available staff or contractors who are familiar with operating the computer programs that can read data of a particular format. Auditing legacy systems can also be helpful. Further, the agency should retain the means to recover data that might have been encrypted or password-protected with long-forgotten or canceled passwords. Where agencies have multiple overlapping systems that are used during transition periods, agencies should generally retain necessary information from all of the systems.

8. Be Aware of Legal Concerns that Implicate Effectiveness of or Impose Restrictions on Electronic Data or Records

Before permitting the electronic submission of information, agencies should review the wording of all applicable statutes and any implementing regulations to verify that electronic reporting or submission would be permitted without a legislative or rule change. The criteria agencies require for electronic transactions involving the public, such as electronic reporting, should be published to the regulated community, either by way of formal rule-making, legislative amendment, or some other appropriate means.

In addition, many uses of data are subject to restrictions under general regimes of federal law. Some agencies are subject to legal regimes that are specific to their particular work. Therefore, it may be necessary to create a mechanism for protecting disclosure of the contents of electronically transmitted information. *See* above Section II.D.

9. Develop Processes that Can Form the Basis of Persuasive Evidence

To be usable, electronic information must be persuasive. Electronic processes that can be shown to gather, retain, and reproduce data reliably and without alteration are likely to be more persuasive. Electronic processes should be designed to enhance these characteristics.

Generally, there are at least four factors that agencies should consider in developing persuasive electronic processes, which may offset each other but should be considered separately:

- *Simplicity and directness of the evidence.* Simple and more direct evidence is generally far more effective than complex or complicated evidence.
  - *Example*: A videotape of an individual conducting a transaction would be more persuasive to many juries than a detailed examination of computer logs from the agency's system. Similarly, because fingerprints generally are familiar to most people as reliable identifiers, digitized fingerprints incorporated into an electronic signature might be more persuasive to many people than other electronic signature techniques.
- *Corroboration of the evidence.* Rebuttable evidence can be made substantially stronger if it is corroborated by other evidence.
  - *Example*: If the evidence shows that a fraud was committed at a particular time reliably authenticated, and that a smart card used to commit that fraud had previously been issued to an individual, and that the individual had the same smart card after the fraud was committed, it suggests that the individual had the card when the fraud took

place. If the use of the smart card required the use of a password that had also been issued to the individual and the individual had not reported the loss of either, the evidence against that individual would be even stronger.

■ *Quality of the technology at issue*. Different technological solutions can provide different levels of quality for persuasiveness to the jury.

■ *Quality of the management and implementation of the electronic process*. Even the best technology can be inadequately implemented, managed, audited, or certified, leading to a loss of credibility.

— *Example*: An agency receives an important communication from an outside party, sent in encrypted form, with an electronic signature. The agency "opens" the message, prints it in plain text on paper, and places it in the file, without keeping proof of how the message was received, or retains a copy of the data without the electronic signature attached. If the sender later denies sending the communication, the agency may be unable to prove who sent it or that it was not altered after receipt.

10. Analyze the Full Range of Technological Options and Follow Commercial Trends Where Appropriate

Not all available technologies are necessarily suitable for an agency's needs, nor should it be assumed that all methods used by the private sector are necessarily appropriate for government use. For example, private institutions generally can select their customers, reducing the risk of fraud and abuse by choosing to do business only with those who appear trustworthy and by taking affirmative steps to control fraud. But many government programs are open to all comers, thus exposing government systems to greater risk. Agencies also might face greater obstacles than private businesses in implementing complex technology programs or quickly changing them as circumstances dictate. Government agencies should generally use proven technology. The government operates under legal restrictions, such as the Privacy Act, that may not bind the private sector.

11. Consider the Unique Legal Risks Presented by Outsourcing an Agency's Data Management and Storage Functions

Many agencies are considering using outside parties to help manage information stored in electronic form. Some agencies are requiring private parties with whom they deal to retain originals and source documents instead of filing them with the agency. Other agencies are contracting out information management and storage functions to varying degrees. The future will present creative uses of third parties to serve many other roles, such as, for example, providing so-called "electronic notary" services to validate data and time-stamp electronic information. These creative strategies can address some agency information management needs, such as ensuring the accessibility or the reliability of information.

However, these uses of outside parties to perform data storage functions traditionally performed by agency personnel can also create a variety of additional legal risks that should be carefully considered before turning over an agency's files to a private party. In addition to other terms, contractual arrangements to provide data maintenance or storage services should, at a minimum, contain provisions providing the agency complete access to its records, specifying that the records will be kept in accord with standards that ensure the long-term availability, integrity, and reliability of the records; that the records will be legally adequate to defend the agency's rights in court or administrative dispute resolution procedures; and that the contractor's personnel will be available when necessary to authenticate records or testify as to the recordkeeping procedures.

Steps to consider include: choosing outside parties with care, clearly outlining responsibilities before initiating the relationship, placing reliance on an outside party only gradually, closely monitoring the outside party, regularly revisiting the nature and success of the relationship, taking advantage of appropriate industry standards, and developing backup plans. Agencies should especially consider the regular use and re-use of auditing or certification procedures to examine whether the outside party is following appropriate practices. Other steps may be helpful as well in reducing particular risks associated with the use of outside parties.[42]

Moreover, the use of outside parties generally will not relieve an agency of its responsibilities, such as those described in Section II.D. Any contractual arrangement should contain terms that require that the contractor meet the standards imposed by, for example, the Privacy Act, the Rehabilitation Act, and the Federal Records Act. In fact, the use of these outside parties may increase the possibility that those kinds of duties will not be met, unless the outside parties are managed with special care.

Agencies should recognize the potential problems that can arise when private parties who submit information to the federal government are required to retain originals or source documents relating to transactions with an agency. Many such documents may not be available to the agency in the future. Agencies should consider the potential impact on their programs and enforcement activities if they are unable to obtain such information.

12. Retain Extrinsic Information in Important or Sensitive Contexts

Even if an agency decides to implement an electronic process, prudence might still counsel for retaining paper instruments for important or sensitive transactions, or at least for the core part of transactions. For example, an agency might conduct substantial phases of a process, such as negotiation, electronically, and then formalize an agreement with a signed writing. Agencies might also consider requiring written certifications or signatures for some of their claim forms, if it would provide a helpful basis for a fraud claim years later.

C. Specific Guidelines

The following are specific guidelines for designing electronic processes to accommodate the concerns addressed in this Guide regarding the protection of agency rights, particularly in litigation. These guidelines are in addition to any record-keeping requirements imposed by statute or regulation. Sections 1 and 2 list some of the basic information and the kinds of factual information that electronic processes should be able to reliably produce, both in general and with regard to particular types of agency functions. Section 3 suggests procedures for retention and availability of information. But these are only generally applicable suggestions, not all-inclusive lists. Agencies should not assume that, if they merely do what these lists suggest, their job is complete. Moreover, in some instances, the items we suggest might not be necessary. Each agency must assess its own transactions and programs to determine what characteristics should be built into its electronic processes.

Throughout the sections that follow, we refer to processes that are adequate to "prove" certain characteristics of the transactions described. By the term "proof" we are not referring to absolute certainty beyond all doubt. We instead are referring to evidence that will be admissible in court and sufficient to demonstrate the point under applicable law. Agency personnel with questions over what information satisfies those standards should consult with their agency's general counsel or attorneys within the Department of Justice who litigate the agency's cases.

1. General Information to Gather, Retain, and Have Available

Electronic processes should be designed so that at least the following information can be proved with regard to sensitive or significant communications and transactions by, with, or within an agency:

- Date and time that the communication or transaction was sent or initiated.
- Identity and location of each particular person who transmitted such items. This includes an identifier traceable to a particular individual (e.g., digital or digitized signatures, or other identifiers, depending on which is appropriate), and a means of identifying the source of the transmission (e.g., mail server identification, e-mail account name, time-stamped Internet Protocol ("IP") address). Identity of an individual can be established to varying degrees of certainty by the individual's transmission or use of any of the following:
  — Something the individual knows (e.g., a password or secret number, personal information);
  — Something the individual possesses (e.g., a token or magnetic card);
  — Something the individual is (i.e., a physical or biometric attribute); or
  — Combinations of the above. As we noted previously (at Section II.B.3), using a combination of techniques can substantially increase the security of an authentication system (e.g., requiring the use of a password and a token, or a unique user identification and a password).

    Agencies should assess which of the above methods are suitable for each type of transaction or function, and should implement such methods in a careful way (for example, making sure that the electronic process does not readily permit someone's electronic signature to be pirated and misapplied in other transactions).

    The ideal electronic signature system deployed by an agency would produce electronic signatures that are (1) unique to the signer, (2) under the signer's sole control, (3) capable of being verified by a third party, and (4) linked to data in such a manner that changes to the data invalidate the signature. The degree to which these attributes are necessary depends on the risks of the particular transaction.

Each of those attributes may be used to serve different purposes in different procedures. A password or secret number may serve a different function when creating an electronic signature, than when creating a digital signature. Additionally, a biometric attribute may be used to authenticate a transaction, or it may be used as a passcode to generate a digital signature. Therefore, agencies should be aware that these attributes can be used in isolation or combination with each other, depending on the process used.

For each process, an agency should define the roles to be played by the electronic signature and adopt the electronic signature technology or technologies that best serve those purposes. If its primary function is to prove identity, other techniques or information may provide better proof in an electronic environment than a weak electronic signature. On the other hand, an electronic means that may be unconvincing at proving identity may be adequate for other functions, such as proving receipt or proving intent.

- That the communication or transmission actually was received, by whom it was received, and the date and time it was received.
- What the sender or originator of the communication or transmission intended by it, and the date and time he or she signed it. For example, certain electronic processes should be able to prove that a person who submits a report certifies to the agency that his report is true, accurate and correct at the time submitted. If the submitter of a document is shown a banner on his computer screen on which he must click "yes," the electronic process must be able to prove that the banner (including its precise text) was in fact displayed and that he clicked "yes."
- The complete contents of the communication or transaction, including any attachments or exhibits.
- This can include the terms unique to a given transaction and "boilerplate" terms that, on paper, might have been printed on the back of a form or in a set of instructions;
  — If the communication contains answers or responses to questions on a form, include a means of proving the precise questions, instructions, or contents of the version of the form actually used; and
  — For communication with attachments, there must be a means for preserving the attachments and permanently "binding" them to the electronic communications.
  — Some means of proving that the information in the transmission was not altered. This includes proving that no one (e.g., neither the submitter nor the agency) altered the information after the submitter sent it, perhaps by proving that the electronic system allows no one the ability to alter such documents. Or the electronic process might be designed to provide an "audit trail" showing all alterations, the date and time they were made, identifying who made them, and so on.
  — As appropriate, some means of showing all relevant communications and documents on a given subject or point.
  — Some means of distinguishing final documents from drafts.

2. Information Regarding Particular Types of Transactions

In addition to the preceding guidelines, electronic processes generally should be designed to provide additional or more specific information with regard to particular types of interactions.

a. Contracts and Related Transactions

Agencies that enter into contracts (which may have follow-on invoices or progress payment requests) or otherwise seek to enforce rights in connection with liens, mortgages, insurance, or guarantees, generally should design their electronic processes so as to be able to establish at least the following:

- Date and time of the contract or other instrument, any amendments to it, and any claims for payment (including invoices or progress payment requests) submitted under it;
- Date and time that each party submitted its offer, acceptance, or claim for payment, the date and time it was received (including proof that it was in fact received), and proof of the identity and location of each particular person who transmitted such items. This includes an identifier traceable to a particular individual (see Section III.C.1, above), and a means of identifying the source of the transmission (e.g., mail server identification, e-mail account names);
- Every term, provision and certification that applies to the transaction. Such terms include standard or "boilerplate" terms, as well as the terms unique to the particular transaction. Because agencies might change the standard terms used in later contracts, the system must be able to show what terms were in effect in each particular transaction. If the contract involves filling out a form or responding to a prior communication, then include the questions on the form or the content of the prior communication;
- That the text of all terms (specific terms and any boilerplate terms) was actually made available to each party;
- That all required parties agreed to the contract or transaction. This includes at least three components:
  — The identity of the specific individuals (see Section III.C.1, above) who entered into the contract or transaction on behalf of each party, and any appropriate identifying information about them (such as their titles, divisions, and so on);
  — Proof that the transaction was an agreement (i.e., text stating that the party or parties "agree"); and
  — Proof that each party intended to be legally bound (again, through use of, for example, an electronic signature traceable to a particular individual with authority to contract on behalf of the party, combined with proof that the "signature" was applied to that specific contract, and the date and time on which that occurred).
  — Where applicable, proof that the individual has certified to the truth and accuracy of the information submitted on any claims or required certifications and has submitted the information under penalty of perjury;

— All amendments, if any, to the transaction, including each of the above items for each amendment, along with proof that no other changes, amendments, or alterations have been made by the submitter, the government, or anyone else.

b. Regulatory Programs (and Any Programs That Require Reporting of Information)

Agencies that accept in electronic form information that is required to be collected under statutory or regulatory programs (or in connection with contracting), and that rely on such information in the conduct of agency business, generally should design their electronic processes so as to be able to establish at least the following:

- Date and time of transmission (either date and time of transmission or date and time of receipt or both, depending on program or agency requirements) and proof that the communication was actually received by the agency;
- The identity and location of each particular person who transmitted the report or data. This includes an identifier traceable to a particular individual (see Section III.C.1, above), and a means of identifying the source of the transmission (e.g., mail server identification, e-mail account names);
- Proof that the submitting individual was authorized to report for the company or other entity (e.g., his position or title);
- Complete contents of the communication, including any attachments or exhibits. Complete contents include both data and information submitted by the individual or company and the agency forms, questions or certifications to which the information responded;
- All amendments, if any, to the report, including each of the above items for each amendment, along with proof that no other changes, amendments, or alterations have been made by the submitter, the government, or anyone else;
- Where applicable, proof that the individual has certified to the truth and accuracy of the information submitted and has submitted the information under penalty of perjury. This might include, for example, proof that a banner was displayed to the submitter, informing him that by clicking "yes" he acknowledges those matters.

c. Benefit Programs

Agencies that accept electronically submitted applications or communications involving the receipt of government benefits of any kind (e.g., loans, grants, or entitlements), generally should design their electronic processes so as to be able to establish at least the following:

- Date and time of receipt of the application or communication (either date and time of transmission or date and time of receipt or both, depending on program or agency requirements) and proof that the application or communication was actually received by the agency;

- Proof of the identity and location of each particular person who transmitted such items. This includes an identifier traceable to a particular individual (see Section III.C.1, above), and a means of identifying the source of the transmission (e.g., mail server identification, e-mail account names);
- Complete contents of the application or communication, including any attachments or exhibits. Complete contents including all data and information submitted by the individual corresponding to requests for information or certifications on an application form, as well as the substance of the requests or certifications themselves;
- Where applicable, proof that the individual has certified to the truth and accuracy of the information submitted on the application and has submitted the information under penalty of perjury;
- Where applicable, some means to prove that the confidentiality of the applicant's submission or communication has not been compromised;
- All amendments, if any, to the application, including each of the above items for each amendment, along with proof that no other changes, amendments, or alterations have been made by the submitter, the government, or anyone else.

3. Retention and Availability

Once an agency determines which electronically gathered information must or should be gathered, retained and available in light of the issues discussed in this Guide, the agency should establish policies to fulfill those goals. Of course, various statutes and regulations impose requirements for the retention and availability of official records in electronic recordkeeping systems.[43] But in addition to those requirements, agencies generally should ensure that their electronic records that are important in light of the issues discussed in this Guide are:

- Retrievable in a form that can be viewed or printed in a "user-friendly" form;[44]
- Indexed in a manner sufficient to be able to retrieve needed data (for example, by subject, by name of program participant, by date and time, etc., in a manner that allows compilation of all relevant documents into a usable "file");
- Retained and retrievable in an electronic recordkeeping system for the length of time required by law, agency policy, or records retention schedules;
- Fully retrievable, printable, and adequately indexed even if the agency later modifies its electronic system (hardware or software), or later changes the contractor who manages the electronic process for the agency;
- Accessible, even if the electronic document originally was encrypted or restricted by a password;
- Capable of being promptly located, retrieved, printed, and interpreted by staff or otherwise immediately available personnel. (Where appropriate, promptly locating a record may include locating a notation that the record itself has been disposed of in accordance with an approved records schedule.)

Agencies may need to take specific measures to ensure the long-term accessibility of data in light of changes over time in technology, personnel turnover, or changes in contractors.

Conclusion

As agencies move forward in adopting electronic processes and making judicious use of technology, they face many decisions. This Guide has been provided to help agencies in considering the legal aspects of such decisions and to help them design their processes in a way that will reduce their legal risk and thus fully realize the benefits of electronic processing. For further information, consultation, or to provide feedback on this Guide, please contact any of the Department of Justice lawyers listed in Exhibit 2 of this Guide.

In accordance with the OMB Guidance on GPEA, agency considerations of cost, risk, and benefit, as well as any measures taken to minimize risks, should be commensurate with the level of sensitivity of the transaction. Low-risk information processes may need only minimal safeguards, while high-risk processes may need more. In the context of legal and litigation risks, "low-risk information processes" are those that have a small chance of generating significant liability, financial impact or litigation that would have a significant effect on the agency.[45] Agencies may wish to use the following twelve suggestions as a starting point in their analysis of legal risks:

1. Conduct an analysis of the nature of a transaction or process to determine the level of protection needed and the level of risk that can be tolerated.
2. Consider potential costs, quantifiable and unquantifiable, direct and indirect, in performing a cost/benefit analysis.
3. Use available sources of expertise inside and outside your agency, including the OMB GPEA Guidance and other OMB guidance.
4. Consider developing a comprehensive plan when converting a traditional process to an electronic one, especially if converting means re-engineering existing process.
5. Consider the kinds of information relevant to the process; ensure that necessary information is gathered.
6. Consider using a "terms and conditions" agreement.
7. Incorporate a long-term retention and access policy for electronic processes where necessary.
8. Be aware of legal concerns that implicate effectiveness of or impose restrictions on electronic data or records.
9. Develop processes that can form the basis of persuasive evidence.
10. Analyze the full range of technological options and follow commercial trends where appropriate.
11. Consider using outside parties to manage information as well as developing methods to manage the particular risks of doing so; and
12. Retain sufficient extrinsic records in important or sensitive contexts.

In addition, Exhibit 1 provides issues for agencies to consider in adopting an electronic process.

Notes

1. For example, even small transactions that take place in great volume could expose the agency to a large overall risk, even though each particular transaction does not.
2. GPEA, Section 1710(2), refers to 5 U.S.C. 105, which provides: "For the purpose of this title, 'Executive agency' means an Executive department, a Government corporation, and an independent establishment."
3. For example, even small transactions that take place in great volume could expose the agency to a large overall risk, even though each particular transaction does not.
4. Further information on the topics discussed in this Guide may be obtained by contacting the lawyers whose names appear in Exhibit 2.
5. The term "electronic process" is intended to encompass all systems in which records may be created or stored in electronic form as part of the agency's overall electronic process. These systems may or may not fall within the strict definition of an "electronic recordkeeping system," as defined by the National Archives and Records Administration. See 36 C.F.R. §§ 1234.2, 1234.22 (1999). Adherence to laws governing federal records is one of the legal considerations involved when agencies convert to electronic systems.
6. By the same token, we do not mean to imply that all existing paper systems are well designed (or indeed even capable of being designed) to eliminate such risks, or that well-designed paper systems are always properly implemented. That this Guide does not elaborate at length on problems with some paper transaction systems is due, in short, to its focus on electronic systems rather than any belief that paper systems are always adequate to satisfy agency needs or legal requirements.
7. As electronic mail ("e-mail") becomes a more common means of official communication and deliberation concerning agency actions, an agency's e-mail records will become a more significant repository of significant information reflecting agency deliberations, actions and decisions. Where an agency elects to preserve e-mail records electronically, the agency should design its electronic processes properly from the outset, to ensure that its e-mail system has appropriate mechanisms for capturing and storing those e-mail messages that ought to be a part of the official record.
8. Equally important is the need for any system — paper or electronic — to identify and authenticate the government employees who acted on or approved the claim or transaction, and to record all pertinent information about their actions.
9. Paper systems, of course, have their own retention and access control problems. Paper can be destroyed by age or by fire, or the warehouse in which it is kept can be made inaccessible. Moreover, paper records are expensive to store and can be difficult to locate. Employees must remember to secure sensitive records under lock and key to prevent unauthorized access. Federal agencies are generally familiar with these concerns. Electronic record systems properly implemented may provide many advantages over their paper counterparts.
10. 44 U.S.C. §§ 2101-2118, 2901-2910, 3101-3107, and 3301-3324
11. *See* Jeff Rothenberg, *Ensuring the Longevity of Digital Documents*, Scientific American, January 1995, at 42-47.
12. The term "writing" is defined by statute as any "reproduction of visual symbols." § 1 U.S.C. § 1 (1994).
13. Technology can blur the line between oral and written communications. For example, speech recognition technology automatically (without a human intermediary) converts oral statements (e.g., by phone) into text. Whether such a transmission is oral or written is a perplexing issue, and might depend on the particular situation and statute involved.

14. "Contracts" are simply legally binding agreements between two or more parties. Government contracts can involve activities as diverse as government procurement, making and guaranteeing loans to students or farmers, and making payments to providers under Medicare and other government contracted-for benefit programs.

15. Although the federal government's transactions generally are governed by federal law, in some instances, state laws supply the applicable rule.

16. The Uniform Commercial Code (UCC) also incorporates a Statute of Frauds in several of its articles. Whether and to what extent a state Statute of Frauds or the UCC applies to federal government contracts can be a complex question that depends upon the circumstances. *See United States v. Kimbell Foods, Inc.*, 440 U.S. 715, 728-29 (1979); *United States v. Kelley*, 890 F.2d 220 (10th Cir. 1989) (applying UCC § 9-504 to contract with SBA guaranty contract). The UCC requires a "writing" — defined as any "intentional reduction to tangible form," UCC § 1-201(46) — that is "signed." *See* UCC §§ 2-201, 8-319, 9-203(1)(a). A "signature" includes "any symbol executed or adopted by a party with present intention to authenticate a writing." UCC § 1-201(39).

17. *See generally* R.J. Robertson, Jr., *Electronic Commerce on the Internet and the Statute of Frauds*, 49 S.C. L. Rev. 787, 808 (1998) ("[T]here is a substantial likelihood that courts may balk at finding that electronic messages satisfy the Statute of Frauds").

18. National Institute of Standards and Technology B Use of Electronic Data Interchange Technology to Create Valid Obligations, 71 Comp. Gen. 109 (1991). Although opinions of the Comptroller General are not binding upon the executive branch, see *Bowsher v. Synar*, 478 U.S. 714, 727-32 (1986), or on the federal courts, they may offer helpful or persuasive authority. That opinion would not preclude a party in an action from asserting that an electronically formed contract was unenforceable. Thus, there exists a risk that courts would decline to enforce electronic federal contracts that have not been reduced to a traditional writing. That risk may be significantly reduced by procedures that ensure that electronically recorded transactions fulfill the purposes for which the law requires a "writing."

19. Tape recordings of oral agreements have failed to meet the requirements of the Statute of Frauds. *Sonders v. Roosevelt*, 476 N.Y.S.2d 331, 331-32 (App. Div. 1984) (not a writing), *aff'd mem.*, 476 N.E.2d 996 (N.Y. 1985); *Swink & Co. v. Carroll McEntee & McGinley*, 584 S.W. 2d 393, 399 (Ark. 1979) (not "signed"). See also *Parma Tile Mosaic & Marble Co. v. Estate of Short*, 663 N.E.2d 633, 635 (N.Y. 1996) (holding that sender's name at the top of a faxed page was not a "signature" for purposes of the Statute of Frauds where the sender's fax machine was programmed to imprint the name automatically).

20. By contrast, courts sometimes refuse to find oral communications binding, and it will be important for agencies to ensure that their electronic processes are not regarded as so haphazard or informal that they are considered the equivalent of an oral communication. For example, courts have construed 31 U.S.C. § 1501 (or its predecessor provision, 31 U.S.C. § 200(a)(1) (1976)) to hold oral contracts unenforceable because they are not "in writing." So, too, could we expect the courts to reject electronic documents that are more conversation-like than formal. In *In re Kaspar*, 125 F.3d 1358, 1359 (10th Cir. 1997), the court refused to hold that one party's oral statement was a written one, even though the other party entered the information into an electronic document. Similarly, oral contracts alleged to have been entered into by the federal government have been denied enforcement on state law Statute of Frauds grounds. *See, e.g., American Int'l Enters., Inc. v. FDIC*, 3 F.3d 1263, 1269 (9th Cir. 1993) (applying California Statute of Frauds; citing other federal courts applying Statutes of Frauds from Minnesota, Nevada, and Tennessee).

21. Experience teaches that signatures are important to connect the individual to the act, and in some cases we have failed to prove our case where we have not had the defendant's signature. For example, in *United States v. Larm*, 824 F.2d 780 (9th Cir. 1987), an allergist was acquitted of Medicare fraud concerning claim forms he did not personally sign. In *United States v. Brown*, 763 F.2d 984 (8th Cir.), *cert. denied*, 474 U.S. 905 (1985), the conviction of a pharmacist was reversed on some counts because the government could not link him, through a signature or initials, to claims submitted to the government for brand-name drugs when generic drugs were dispensed.

22. Thus, for example, courts normally prohibit individuals from avoiding their obligations by contending that they did not read what they signed, or that the contents were not explained, or that they did not understand them. *In re Cajun Elec. Power Co.*, 791 F.2d 353, 359 (5th Cir. 1986); *see Jones v. New York Life & Annuity Corp.*, 985 F.2d 503, 508 (10th Cir. 1993); *Hill v. A.O. Smith Corp.*, 801 F.2d 217, 221 (6th Cir. 1986); *O'Neel v. National Ass'n of Sec. Dealers, Inc.*, 667 F.2d 804, 806 (9th Cir. 1982).

23. A "digital signature" is generated by using an algorithm that ensures the identity of the signatory and the integrity of the data can be verified. Signature generation makes use of a value (commonly referred to as the "private key") to generate a digital signature. Signature verification makes use of another value (commonly referred to as the "public key") which corresponds to, but is not the same as, the private key. Each user possesses a private and public key pair, and the private key is not deducible from the public key. Public keys are permitted to be known widely, and assumed to be known to the public in general. Private keys should not be shared. Anyone can verify the "digital signature" of a user by employing that user's public key. However, signature generation can only be performed by the possessor of the user's private key. *See* National Inst. of Standards & Tech., *Federal Information Processing Standards Publication 186- 1, Digital Signature Standard*, at 1 (1998).

24. By "biometric," we mean attributes arising from a person's physical characteristics or actions that are unique to that person. These include codes derived from electronic analysis of fingerprints and retinal scans, among others.

25. Exclusive reliance upon one biometric identification without providing any alternatives, however, may run afoul of the Rehabilitation Act, 29 U.S.C. § 794d (West Supp. 1999), which may require agencies to provide alternative means of identification for those who do not possess the requisite physical characteristics (e.g., persons with prosthetic hands cannot provide fingerprints).

26. National Inst. of Standards & Tech., Federal Information Processing Standards Publication 190, Guideline for the Use of Advanced Authentication Technology Alternatives, at 39-40 (1994).

27. On the other hand, paper signatures are susceptible to forgery. Forgeries of traditional signatures can often be detected by handwriting analysis and forensic examination. Proving that someone else used an electronic signature can be more difficult because the electronic signature has no attributes that associate it with the individual unless a biometric method is used. However, it may be difficult for an individual to explain how and why someone else was able to obtain access to an electronic signature that had been assigned to her with instructions to safeguard it and keep it private.

28. As with other technologies, signatures in a biometric signature system that was not properly implemented might be subject to challenge. If the method of recording and preserving the signature is flawed, the signatures may not be considered reliable and may not be legally adequate to establish binding obligations.

29. For a more detailed discussion of various types of electronic signatures, and the advantages and disadvantages of each, see the OMB GPEA Guidance, "Implementation of the Government Paperwork Elimination Act," May 2, 2000, Part II, Section 7, 65 FR at 25518.

30. Other federal bills have been introduced in Congress that may affect agencies' use of electronic processes. Agencies should monitor the enactment of any such bill into law.

31. GPEA§ 1703(a) requires the Director of the Office of Management and Budget (OMB), in consultation with others, to develop procedures for the use and acceptance of electronic signatures by Executive agencies.

32. The GPEA Section 1707 safe harbor applies only to those records submitted, used, or maintained in accord with the OMB procedures required by the GPEA. That raises the question whether Section 1707 applies if an agency did not follow the OMB-mandated procedures in implementing its electronic signatures. Also, the GPEA defines "electronic signature" as: "a method of signing an electronic message that (A) identifies and authenticates a particular person as the source of the electronic message; and (B) indicates such person's approval of the information contained in the electronic message." GPEA § 1710(1). A court might decline to give effect to electronic signatures that do not technically meet this definition (e.g., those that do not identify a specific person or that do not indicate that person's approval).

33. For example, Illinois has enacted the Electronic Commerce Security Act, 5 Ill. Comp. Stat. 175/10-120(b) (West 1999), effective July 1, 1999, which provides that, subject to certain exceptions, "[w]here a rule of law requires information to be 'written' or 'in writing' ... an electronic record satisfies that rule of law." *Id*. at 5-115(a). The statute does not apply to specified documents such as wills, trusts, negotiable instruments, and instruments of title.

34. The Illinois statute (see preceding note), for example, provides that, if the parties use certain types of security procedures, then it "shall be rebuttably presumed that the electronic record has not been altered." *Id*. at 10-120(a).

35. Many may have the perception that electronic data are easily fabricated or forged. People recognize that digital data can be copied perfectly, and then edited without difficulty. (Thanks to popular computer photo-processing programs, there is even a growing awareness that digital photographs can be created or modified with much greater ease than traditional photographs.) Agency security procedures that prevent such modification should be robust and well documented.

36. For example, Rule 803(6) of the Federal Rules of Evidence (FRE) generally allows records of regularly conducted activity (commonly called "business records") to be admitted into evidence. The government frequently relies upon that rule to introduce agency records into evidence. But the rule also provides that such record will not be admissible if "the source of information or the method or circumstances of preparation indicate lack of trustworthiness." Similar provisions are contained in, for example, FRE 803(8) (pertaining to admissibility of public records and reports) and 804(b)(3) (statements against interest).

37. See Jay E. Grenig, Electronic Discovery: Making Your Opponent's Computer a Vital Part of Your Legal Team, 21 Am. J. Trial Advoc. 293 (1997).

38. *See also Electronic Records Work Group* <http://www.nara.gov/records/grs/20/index.html> (viewed Oct. 30, 2000) (collecting currently applicable guidance provided by the National Archives and Records Administration governing federal agency submission of records schedules covering the retention of electronic versions of e-mail and word processing documents).

39. For further information about agency obligations and liabilities under Section 508, visit the Department of Justice's Section 508 home page. Section *508 Home Page* (viewed Jan. 20, 2000) <http://www.usdoj.gov/crt/508/508home.html>. The General Services Administration also maintains an inter-agency Web site that contains current information about Section 5008 at <http://www.section508.gov>.

40. For example, even small transactions that take place in great volume could expose the agency to a large overall risk, even though each particular transaction does not.

41. At the same time, an agency might wish to consider establishing a system to cull from its files genuinely extraneous and redundant information in order to prevent unnecessary bloat in agency files. Unneeded duplicates of documents and e-mail messages that the agency is not obligated to retain under its record management systems can be difficult to manage and make retrieval of relevant documents more difficult. A sensible record retention and destruction policy should provide for routine purging of unnecessary information in an orderly and regular manner. A sensible policy can also ensure that information which may be useful for ongoing contract administration or possible dispute resolution is not inadvertently deleted.

42. In one recent case where at least 43,000 electronic messages were "lost," there was a misunderstanding between the agency, which believed that backups were being made both on a daily basis and a periodic system-wide basis, and the agency's contractor, which had been doing neither. A contributing factor to the loss of the messages may have been that the audit log features had been turned off to improve system performance.

43. *See, e.g.,* 36 C.F.R. § 1234.2 (1999) (National Archives and Records Administration definition of "electronic recordkeeping system"); *see also* 36 C.F.R. § 1234.22; 1234.24(b) (1999) (providing functional requirements for electronic recordkeeping systems, including e- mail).

44. To the extent that an electronic transmission includes data that cannot practicably be printed in paper form (e.g., an audio file attached to an e-mail), the agency should have some means of storing and being able to retrieve the image or sound of such items.

45. For example, even small transactions that take place in great volume could expose the agency to a large overall risk, even though each particular transaction does not.

Chapter 15

Encryption

The nation's policy on encryption must carefully balance important competing interests. The Department of Justice has a vital stake in the country's encryption policy because encryption may be used not only to protect lawful data against unauthorized intruders, [but] it may also be used to conceal illegitimate materials from law enforcement. While we support the spread of strong encryption, we believe that the widespread dissemination of unbreakable encryption without any accommodation for law enforcement access is a serious threat to public safety and to the integrity of America's commercial infrastructure. Our goal is to encourage the use of strong encryption to protect privacy and commerce, but in a way that preserves (without extending) law enforcement's ability to protect public safety and national security. Accordingly, the Administration has promoted the manufacture and use of key recovery products, aided the development of a global key management infrastructure ("KMI"), and liberalized United States restrictions on the export of robust cryptographic products. We anticipate that market forces will make key recovery products a *de facto* industry standard and thus preserve the balance of privacy and public safety that our Constitution embodies.

Department of Justice FAQ on Encryption Policy (April 24, 1998)

The Department of Justice is often asked for its concerns about encryption, or for the Administration viewpoint on encryption policy. The Department appreciates the opportunity to respond to such questions on this complex subject. A set of frequently asked questions (and answers) are below:

General Policy Issues

Q: What is the Administration's Policy on Encryption?

A: The Administration's policy is to promote the development and use of strong encryption which enhances the privacy of communications and stored data while preserving law enforcement's ability to gain access to evidence as part of a legally authorized search or surveillance. We are willing to look at any options that advance these goals, as well as protecting national security, securing electronic commerce and preserving U.S. competitiveness. The Administration has identified one method to achieve the necessary balance — the use of encryption products that incorporate recovery systems. With such products, law enforcement agents can, pursuant to lawful process, obtain recovered "plaintext." The Administration is open to other approaches.

Q: Aren't you really trying to force the market where it won't go?

A: Not at all. Indeed, we know that hardware and software companies have begun to develop data recovery products in response to the needs of businesses and individuals. For example, dozens of companies are now members of the "Key Recovery Alliance," including some of the largest computer companies in the United States. That such products are economically viable is not surprising. For example, companies may need access to encrypted data when employees are ill or otherwise unavailable, and individuals may forget their keys.

However, while industry must take the lead in developing cryptographic products and services, it is also true that market forces alone will not adequately protect public safety and national security. For example, market forces alone are not permitted to determine whether an airline should be allowed to fly — the government grounds unsafe airlines to protect public safety. Market forces alone do not determine whether meat is safe to sell in supermarkets and restaurants. Likewise, when the government pursues a cryptographic policy, it must take into account the need to protect public safety and national security.

Q: Some bills currently before Congress, such as H.R. 695, would make the criminal use of encryption a crime. Isn't this sufficient?

A: Making the use of encryption a crime if in furtherance of the commission of another crime makes an important statement, because encryption can pose a significant obstacle to the investigation and prosecution of criminal offenses.

That said, the mere fact that the criminal use of encryption would itself be a crime would be unlikely, standing alone, to prevent most criminals from using encryption. Moreover, since the encrypted data cannot be decrypted without recovery systems — and the plaintext cannot be ascertained — it would be difficult, if not impossible, to prove in most cases that the encryption was used in the furtherance of a crime. Finally, such a prohibition would fail to address the true public safety threat: that terrorists, child pornographers, drug dealers, and any other criminals could render useless court-authorized searches and wiretaps.

Q: Does the government want to hold everyone's private keys?

A: No, the government does not want to hold the keys of private citizens or commercial enterprises.

Actually, the Administration encourages the design, manufacture, and use of encryption products and services that allow for recovery of the plaintext of encrypted data, including the development of plaintext recovery systems, which permit through a variety of technical approaches timely access to plaintext either by the owners of data or by law enforcement authorities acting under lawful authority. Only the widespread use of such systems will both provide greater protection for data and protect public safety.

The Administration is not advocating any single product, technology, or even technical approach, and is certainly not insisting upon "escrow" of keys with the government. Key recovery, for example, where the encryption key is held by a trusted third party, is merely one possible approach, and is by no means the only one that would meet law enforcement's goals. Rather, we are flexible — provided that the resulting solutions and arrangements preserve the Nation's critical abilities to protect the public safety and defend our national security.

Law Enforcement Issues

Q: Why does law enforcement oppose the use of encryption? Don't you realize that it will make your job easier by stopping crime?

A: We do not oppose the use of encryption — just the opposite, because strong encryption can be an extraordinary tool to prevent crime. We believe that the use of strong cryptography is critical to the development of the "Global Information Infrastructure," or the GII. We agree that communications and data must be protected — both in transit and in storage — if the GII is to be used for personal communications, financial transactions, medical care, the development of new intellectual property, and other applications.

The widespread use of unrecoverable encryption by criminals, however, poses a serious risk to public safety. Encryption may be used by terrorist groups, drug cartels, foreign intelligence agents, and other criminals to secure their data and communications, thus nullifying the effectiveness of search warrants and wiretap orders. The Department's goal — and the Administration's policy — is to promote the development and use of strong encryption that enhances the privacy of communications and stored data while also preserving law enforcement's current ability to gain access to evidence as part of a legally authorized search or surveillance.

At bottom, it is important to recognize that society has an important choice to make. On the one hand, it can promote the use of unrecoverable encryption, and give a powerful tool to the most dangerous elements of our global society. On the other hand, it can promote the use of recoverable encryption and other techniques, achieve all of the benefits, and help protect society from these criminals. Faced with this choice, there is only one responsible solution.

Q: We don't ban cars, do we? Then why are you trying to ban encryption?

A: The Administration generally, and law enforcement particularly, are not trying to ban encryption. Law enforcement supports the responsible spread of strong encryption. Use of strong encryption will help deter crime and promote a safe national information infrastructure.

The more fundamental point raised by the analogy to the rise of the automobile is that society "managed" the automobile, not by letting it develop completely unfettered and without regard to public safety concerns, but first by recognizing that cars could cause substantial damage to the public safety, and then by regulating the design, manufacture, and use of cars to protect the public safety. Cars must be inspected for safety on a regular basis. Cars are subject to minimum gasoline mileage requirements and maximum pollutant emission requirements. Cars built today must include seat belts and air bags. Indeed, the laws of every jurisdiction in the United States closely regulate every aspect of driving cars on the public streets and highways, from driver's licenses to regulation of speed to direction and flow of traffic. Congress and the state legislatures recognized the public safety and health threats posed by the technology of automotive transportation, even as they recognized the dramatic benefits of mobility, productivity, and industrialization that the automobile brought with it. Elected government representatives of the people have consistently acknowledged and acted on their sworn responsibilities by assessing the public safety issues at stake and then regulating the technology accordingly.

Perhaps most analogous to the policy issues posed by encryption is the practice, begun by most states about a hundred years ago, of requiring cars to be registered and to bear license plates. More recently, federal law has required all vehicles to bear a vehicle identification number, or VIN. As you may recall, it was the VIN in the Oklahoma City bombing case that led the FBI to the truck rental office at which Timothy McVeigh rented the truck he used. We now recognize that license plates and VIN's afford victims of accidents, victims of car theft, and law enforcement officials with an essential means of identifying vehicles and obtaining information on the movements of criminals. Just as legislatures in the early 1900s acted to manage the risks posed by automotive technology, government leaders today, as the 21st century approaches, must bring the same sensitivity to the need to preserve and advance public safety as encryption use expands in the information age. And such a regulatory scheme, if constructed properly, will, like license plates, have benefits for businesses and consumers as well.

Of course, no analogy is perfect. Computers are not cars, and plaintext recovery is not a speed limit. But the broader point is an important one: The Framers of our Constitution determined that individuals would not have an absolute right of privacy. The Constitution recognizes that there are certain circumstances in which it is appropriate for law enforcement to obtain information that an individual wants to keep private: for example, when a judge finds probable cause to believe that such information is *** evidence of a crime. Decisions as to where that line should be drawn are political and legal ones, not scientific or business ones; they should be made by the Congress, the Executive, and the courts, not by programmers or marketers. Policy should regulate technology; technology should not regulate policy. Just as in the first part of the twentieth century, when the law had to take account of the changes in society brought about by the automobile, the law will have to take account of the changes brought about by encryption.

Q: We lived without wiretaps for centuries — couldn't we do so again?

A: Court-authorized wiretaps have proven to be one of the most successful law-enforcement tools in preventing and prosecuting serious crimes, including terrorism. The inability of law enforcement to conduct effective wiretaps would have a tremendous impact, especially as the use of "traditional investigative techniques" is no substitute for wiretaps. In fact, under 18 U.S.C. §2518(1)(c), such techniques must have been tried, be expected to fail, or be too dangerous to use, before a wiretap order may be issued. In other words, wiretaps may only be used when necessary. As society has becoming increasingly reliant on wire communication, law enforcement's need to access the contents of those communications in appropriate circumstances has also increased.

It is also important to recognize that widespread use of unrecoverable encryption will not merely negate wiretaps: the effect of encryption on court-authorized searches and seizures of computer data will also be significant. As society becomes more dependent on computers, evidence (and the fruits) of crime increasingly will be found in stored computer data, which can be searched and seized pursuant to court authorized warrants. But if unbreakable encryption proliferates, this critical law enforcement tool could also be nullified. And this would affect not only our ability to prosecute cases of terrorism and drug trafficking, but any case that relies on documents, such as fraud and child pornography cases.

If American society is to be protected as it rightfully expects and demands, law enforcement agents must have investigative tools that work. To the extent society is unwilling to grant law enforcement such tools, it must be willing to accept fewer successful investigations, fewer successful prosecutions, and, consequently, more crime that goes unprosecuted.

Q: Aren't you overstating the threat?

A: Not at all. Law enforcement has already confronted encryption in high-profile espionage, terrorist, and criminal cases. For example:

- An international terrorist was plotting to blow up 11 U.S.-owned commercial airliners in the Far East. His laptop computer, which was seized during his arrest in Manila, contained encrypted files concerning this terrorist plot.
- A subject in a child pornography case used encryption in transmitting obscene and pornographic images of children over the Internet.
- A major international drug trafficking subject recently used a telephone encryption device to frustrate court-approved electronic surveillance.

And this is just the tip of the iceberg. Convicted spy Aldrich Ames, for example, was told by the Russian Intelligence Service to encrypt computer file information that was to be passed to it.

There have also been numerous other cases where law enforcement, through the use of electronic surveillance, has not only solved and successfully prosecuted serious crimes but has also been able to prevent life-threatening criminal acts. For example, terrorists in New York were plotting to bomb the United Nations building, the Lincoln and Holland Tunnels, and the main federal building in New York City as well as conduct assassinations of political figures. Court-authorized electronic surveillance enabled the FBI to disrupt the plot as explosives were being mixed. Ultimately, the evidence obtained was used to convict the conspirators. In another example, electronic surveillance was used to stop and then convict two men who intended to kidnap, molest, and kill a child. In all of these cases, the use of unrecoverable encryption might have seriously jeopardized public safety and resulted in the loss of life.

As encryption proliferates and becomes an ordinary component of mass market items, and as the prevalence of encryption products increases to the point of regularly denying law enforcement access to intercepted communications or physical evidence, the threat to public safety will increase greatly.

Q: Isn't the government's policy unworkable because strong unrecoverable encryption is widely available and, therefore, criminals will not use data recovery products even if they are widely available and commonly used?

A: No policy will guarantee that, in every case, law enforcement's needs are met — some criminals won't use recoverable encryption under any circumstances. However, many criminals will use encryption that permits access by law enforcement, if that is the type of encryption that is commonly used and included in over-the-counter software. Criminals use telephones today, even though they are aware that telephones can be tapped. What we want to avoid is a situation where common street-corner drug dealers regularly without thinking make their record books and notes utterly unreadable by law enforcement at the click of a mouse button. In this regard, we hope that the availability of highly reliable encryption that provides recovery systems will reduce the demand for other types of encryption, and increase the likelihood that criminals will use recoverable encryption.

Q: Shouldn't we solve this problem by equipping law enforcement with the resources necessary to break encryption in particularly important cases?

A: Additional resources alone will not solve this problem. It is not possible to build machines with any reasonable resources that would permit law enforcement to break even 56-bit DES encryption in the time necessary to be useful in real cases. Obviously, stronger encryption would be even more difficult to crack. In many cases, it might be difficult even to determine the type of encryption used.

This is especially significant in investigations, which can be extremely time-critical. Particularly in the case of wiretaps, decrypting messages weeks or months after interception will not protect the public. Wiretaps are used only in the most critical cases, and often provide crucial information just before a crime is to occur. Near real-time access is necessary, as days or weeks are too long to wait to find out that a terrorist attack is about to occur.

Even if the FBI were able to build a supercomputer that could periodically crack a single message encoded with 56-bit DES, each wiretap or search can result in thousands of messages or files to be decoded. Cracking all of those messages is unrealistic. And, obviously, it would be impossible to supply such a supercomputer to every state and local law enforcement agency around the country. It will always be easier and cheaper to devise stronger cryptographic methods than to build computers powerful enough to break these methods in a reasonable period of time.

Q: I heard about one group of Internet users that worked together to crack a 56-bit encrypted message. If they did it, why can't the federal government?

A: That example actually underscores the problems that accompany a "brute force" approach. The successful group actually used over 14,000 computers and took over four months — over ten million hours of computer time — to decrypt one single message. That is not practical for law enforcement, especially if, for example, we are trying to prevent a terrorist attack or find a kidnap victim. Significantly, the time needed to decrypt a message rises exponentially as the length of the encryption key increases. If the message had been encrypted with a 64-bit key, it would take 10,000 Pentium computers on average *58 years* to crack a single message.

And a new message would require law enforcement to start again from scratch because each message may be encrypted with a different key. During 1995, for example, federal and state courts authorized more than a thousand electronic surveillance court orders, resulting in over two million intercepted communications, each of which could require separate decryption. Given such numbers, brute force attacks are not a feasible solution. This commitment of time and resources is unavailable for every wiretap and every search and seizure executed at federal, state, and local levels.

Additionally, law enforcement agencies at the federal, state, and local level are finding that searches in routine cases now commonly result in the seizure of electronically stored information. Because storage devices have increased in capacity and decreased in price, the quantity of data seized in "ordinary" cases continues to increase dramatically. If all of these communications and stored files were encrypted with unrecoverable cryptographic systems, brute force attacks would not provide a meaningful and timely solution. Thus, even if tens of thousands of computers were obtained and coordinated (an expensive undertaking, to say the least), the approximately 17,000 federal, state, and local law enforcement agencies could not be given timely access to the evidence needed to prevent and solve crimes.

Q: Don't Americans have a right to privacy?

A: Privacy is an extremely important value to be protected, and people sometimes lose sight of the fact that law enforcement is responsible, in part, for protecting privacy in a variety of circumstances. For example, we prosecute violations of the wiretap statute, as well as cases where data confidentiality has been breached. *See, e.g.,* 18 U.S.C. § 1030(a)(2). But our society has never recognized an absolute right to privacy. Rather, the Fourth Amendment strikes a careful balance, permitting government invasion of privacy to protect public safety and to prosecute crimes, but only when law enforcement can make the necessary showing, such as demonstrating "probable cause" to a neutral and detached magistrate. For example, most people would think it was justifiable for the police to search a man's bedroom pursuant to a search warrant — normally one of the most private places in one's life — if there were probable cause to believe that he had murdered someone there. In the Information Age, unbreakable encryption would upset this delicate constitutional balance, which is one of the bedrock principles of our legal system, by effectively nullifying a court's issuance of a search warrant or wiretap order.

Q: **Why does law enforcement want to be able to snoop on everyone's private communications?**

A: Government should not be able to access *arbitrarily* the plaintext of encrypted communications of citizens or businesses. Law enforcement should obtain access pursuant to legal procedures such as those set out by 18 U.S.C. § 2518, i.e., *only as part of a legally authorized investigation*, and only after making the necessary legal showing. The same constitutional protections — such as the requirement that a search warrant or Title III order be obtained from a neutral judicial official, upon determination of probable cause — that preserve every American's privacy interests today will continue to prevent unauthorized intrusions in a key recovery regime.

Constitutional Issues

Q: **Wouldn't the use by law enforcement of recovery systems in encryption products violate the Fourth Amendment?**

A: It is difficult to understand how use of recovery systems under the present, voluntary regime might violate the Fourth Amendment. As with any kind of stored and transmitted data, it is axiomatic that the government may obtain both encrypted text and decryption keys pursuant to lawful process, which may include a wiretap order, a search warrant issued upon probable cause, a subpoena, or the consent of the party possessing the particular item. Each of these procedures comports with the Fourth Amendment, and voluntary data recovery products do not change this analysis. Additionally, if an individual's encryption key were stored with a third party, Congress could require by legislation that, to compel production of the key, law enforcement would have to meet a standard higher than that required by the Fourth Amendment, much as the Electronic Communications Privacy Act requires a court order to obtain transactional data.

Q: **What about a mandatory plaintext recovery regime? Wouldn't that violate the Fourth Amendment?**

A: The Administration does not advocate a mandatory approach, and believes that a voluntary solution is preferable. Nonetheless, many have asked about the constitutionality of hypothetical legislation prohibiting the manufacture, distribution and import of encryption products that do not contain plaintext recovery technologies, so that the capability to decrypt encrypted data and communications is available to law enforcement upon presentation of valid legal authority.

A discussion of the constitutionality of such hypothetical legislation must be prefaced with several caveats. First, the constitutional issues that such a regime would present are undoubtedly novel ones. Indeed, the spectacular growth of the digital world has created many confounding legal issues that the Congress, the courts, the Administration, and our society at large are wrestling with. If history is any guide, changes in technology can lead to changes in our understanding of applicable constitutional doctrine. Moreover, these issues are particularly difficult to address in the abstract, because mandatory plaintext recovery could take a variety of forms. Nonetheless, and with these caveats, it is the best judgment of the Department of Justice that a mandatory plaintext recovery regime, if appropriately structured, could comport with constitutional doctrine.

The Fourth Amendment does not provide an absolute right of privacy, but protects reasonable expectations of privacy by prohibiting unreasonable searches and requiring that a warrant issue only upon a finding of probable cause by a neutral and detached magistrate. A well-designed plaintext recovery regime would ensure that users' reasonable expectations of privacy were preserved. Any legislation in this area, whether or not it imposed plaintext recovery requirements, should not lessen the showing the government must make to obtain access to plaintext. If a search warrant for data was required before, it should be required under any new regime. By requiring the government to meet current constitutional thresholds to obtain plaintext, such a regime would, in our view, comply with the Fourth Amendment. Moreover, Congress could require under such a regime that even if law enforcement obtains a search warrant for data or communications, it would need additional authority, such as a court order, to obtain the key or other information necessary to perform any decryption if the information is encrypted.

Q: Would such a hypothetical mandatory plaintext recovery regime violate the Fifth Amendment's prohibition against compulsory self-incrimination?

A: Again, it must be clearly stated that the Administration does not advocate a mandatory plaintext recovery regime. The Administration believes that a voluntary solution is preferable.

However, in response to questions about the Fifth Amendment, we note that the Fifth Amendment generally prohibits only disclosures that are compelled, testimonial, and incriminating. If a manufacturer of an encryption product were required to maintain information sufficient to allow law enforcement access to plaintext, we believe that there would be no violation of the Fifth Amendment because no disclosure at all would be compelled from the user of the encryption product. If, on the other hand, a mandatory plaintext recovery regime required the user of an encryption product to store his key (or other information needed for recovery) with a third party in advance of using the product, we do not believe that such an arguably compelled disclosure would be testimonial as that term has been interpreted by the Supreme Court. In *Doe v. United States*, 489 U.S. 201 (1988), the Court held that an order compelling a person to execute a form consenting to disclosure of foreign bank accounts did not violate the Fifth Amendment because the form was not testimonial. The compelled disclosure of decryption information to a third party would not seem to be any more testimonial. Moreover, we doubt whether such a disclosure would be incriminating, because unless and until the encryption product is used in the commission of a crime, the key would pose no threat of incrimination against the user.

Q: What about the First Amendment? Doesn't the First Amendment protect the right of persons to speak in "code"? Wouldn't a restriction on encryption products be analogous to placing a restriction on the use of a foreign language? Wouldn't restriction of available encryption products "chill" free speech?

A: Again, the Administration prefers a voluntary solution. Nevertheless, many ask about whether a mandatory plaintext recovery regime would in some manner violate the First Amendment.

A First Amendment argument that encrypted speech is like a foreign language rests on the faulty premise that the creation or dissemination of ciphertext itself is constitutionally protected. But, unlike a foreign language, the ciphertext that is created by strong encryption products cannot be understood by the viewer or listener. When it is heard, such as on a wiretap of a telephone, ciphertext simply takes the form of unintelligible static. In written form, ciphertext may be in the form of letters, numerals and symbols, but no human being can read or "understand" it: it does not contain characters or words or symbols that represent or correspond to any other characters, words or symbols. Accordingly, ciphertext is not like a foreign language, the use of which can convey unique meaning and nuance to the listener or reader. Thus, ciphertext itself — as opposed to the underlying plaintext — has none of the properties of protected "speech" that the Supreme Court has traditionally identified, and, accordingly, the dissemination of ciphertext should not be entitled to First Amendment protection.

A second form of First Amendment argument focuses not on the ciphertext, but on the underlying plaintext. Under this theory, a prohibition on the manufacture or distribution of nonrecoverable encryption products would inhibit an alleged constitutional right of persons to *obscure* their communications in any manner they see fit. Even if legislation would impose such a practical limitation on the manner in which speakers may obscure their underlying communications, it could be drafted so as to pass muster as a permissible time, place and manner restriction — particularly since any such restriction on the "tools" of speech would be unrelated to any communicative impact of the underlying plaintext and the controls would leave open ample and robust alternative channels or methods for obscuring the underlying plaintext.

A related argument is that a communications infrastructure in which recoverable encryption is the *de facto* standard will impermissibly chill a significant quantum of speech because individuals' knowledge of law enforcement's ability to overhear and decipher communications and data will unduly deter them from communicating. But under such a system, the government would have no greater access to the content of private parties' communications than it currently has, and it is well-settled that the government's exercise of its established statutory powers to intercept and seize communications does not create such a "chilling" effect on speech as to transgress the First Amendment, so long as that power is exercised consistent with the Fourth Amendment, and for valid reasons authorized by statute, such as to discover evidence of criminal wrongdoing. *See*, e.g., *United States v. Ramsey*, 503 F.2d 524, 526 n.5 (7th Cir. 1974) (Stevens, J.) (rejecting argument that "the very existence of wiretapping authority has a chilling effect on free speech and, therefore, ... violates the First Amendment"); *accord United States v. Moody*, 977 F.2d 1425, 1432 (11th Cir. 1992).

A final type of First Amendment argument often heard is that a restriction on the manufacture and distribution of certain types of encryption products would impermissibly restrict the ability of cryptographers, and others, to disseminate the computer code that is used by computers to transform plaintext into ciphertext. But that argument is based on the mistaken premise that dissemination of the code embedded in encryption products itself is necessarily a form of expression protected by the First Amendment. Most such code is in the form of "object code." Object code is simply an immense string of "0"s and "1"s, representing a bewildering concatenation of thousands or millions of high and low voltage electrical impulses. As such, machine-"readable" cryptographic object codes can reveal to possible "readers" neither the ideas they embody, nor the manner in which the ideas are expressed. And this is especially true where such object code is embedded in a product such as a semiconductor chip, so that even the "0"s and "1"s cannot be discerned. Therefore, a restriction on the dissemination of encryption products containing object code would not violate the First Amendment.

Somewhat more complicated questions might be raised if such legislation were to reach encryption products in the form of source code — i.e., the instructions to the computer that human beings write and revise. Some persons do disseminate source code for communicative purposes. Nevertheless, we believe that a restriction on the dissemination of certain encryption products could be constitutional even as applied to those relatively infrequent cases in which such products are in the form of software that is disseminated for communicative reasons, because such a restriction could satisfy the "intermediate" scrutiny that the First Amendment provides for incidental restrictions on communicative conduct. As we have argued in litigation in the export-control context, such intermediate scrutiny would be appropriate because the government's reason for regulating source-code software would not be based on any informational value that its dissemination might have. (Indeed, such legislation would not restrict the publication of any ideas reflected in such source code.) Instead, regulation would be premised on the fact that such software — like all of the "encryption products" that would be regulated —

has *physical*, functional properties that can cause a computer to encrypt information and thereby place plaintext beyond the technical capabilities of law enforcement to recover.

Interagency and State and Federal Law Enforcement Cooperation

On Monday, September 20, 1999, Attorney General Janet Reno addressed the High Technology Crime Investigation Association 1999 International Training Conference in San Diego, California. Her speech focused on the importance of interagency and state and federal law enforcement cooperation, as well as on the Department of Justice's policy position on encryption regulation. [http://www.cybercrime.gov/agsandie.htm]

Law Enforcement's Concerns Related to Encryption

On July 18, 1997, Attorney General Janet Reno and others sent a letter to Members of Congress outlining law enforcement's concerns about the public safety and national security threats posed by unbridled availability of strong encryption. It urged legislators to support a balanced approach that supports commercial and privacy interest while maintaining law enforcement's ability to investigate and prosecute serious crime. This letter was co-signed by:

- Louis Freeh, Director, Federal Bureau of Investigation
- Barry McCaffrey, Director, Office of National Drug Control Policy
- Thomas A. Constantine, Director, Drug Enforcement Administration
- Lewis C. Merletti, Director, United States Secret Service
- Raymond W. Kelly, Undersecretary for Enforcement, U.S. Department of Treasury
- George J. Weise, Commissioner, United States Customs Service
- John W. Magaw, Director, Bureau of Alcohol, Tobacco and Firearms

[The text of the letter is available at http://www.cybercrime.gove/aglet.htm.]

Privacy in a Digital Age: Encryption and Mandatory Access

Robert S. Litt, Principal Associate Deputy Attorney General, Department of Justice, testified before the Subcommittee on the Constitution, Federalism, and Property Rights, of the Committee on the Judiciary of the United States Senate on March 17, 1998. His testimony addressed legal issues, constitutional issues, and law enforcement issues related to encryption. His testimony is listed below.

Thank you, Mr. Chairman and members of the Committee, for this opportunity to discuss with you the important and complex issue of encryption. Encryption holds the promise of providing all of us with the ability to protect data and communications from unlawful and unauthorized access, disclosure, and alteration.

Moreover, encryption can help prevent crime by protecting a wide range of data as we and our valued information become more and more connected to each other and to potential adversaries through the spread of information networks. As a result, the law enforcement community supports the development and widespread use of strong encryption products and services.

At the same time, however, the widespread use of unbreakable encryption presents a tremendous potential threat to public safety and national security. Criminals and terrorists have already begun using encryption to conceal their illegal activities and to defeat important law enforcement and national security objectives. In developing our Nation's encryption policy, we must carefully balance the many different interests that the policy will affect. In seeking that balance, it is essential to understand both the promise and the peril that this technology holds, and to identify responsible ways forward that advance all of the competing interests.

I want to begin, Mr. Chairman, by clarifying the Clinton Administration's recent initiatives regarding encryption. For some time, the Administration's position has been to encourage the design, manufacture, and use of encryption products and services that allow for the plaintext of encrypted data to be recovered. The Administration's approach has in fact found support in the marketplace, in part because businesses and individuals need a routinely available method to recover encrypted information. For example, a company might find that one of its employees lost his encryption key, thus accidentally depriving the business of critically important and time-sensitive data. Or a business may find that a disgruntled employee has encrypted confidential information and then absconded with the key. In this type of case, a data recovery system promotes important private sector interests. Indeed, as the Government implements encryption in our own information technology systems, it also has a business need for plaintext recovery to assure that data and information that we are statutorily required to maintain are in fact available at all times. For these reasons, as well as to protect public safety, the Administration has been affirmatively encouraging the development of data recovery products, recognizing that only their widespread, ubiquitous use will both provide greater protection for data and protect public safety.

In further support of this goal, two weeks ago we set in motion a process of pursuing an intensive dialogue between industry and law enforcement. Our goal in this process is to bring the creative genius of America's technology leaders to bear in developing technical, market-savvy solutions that will enable Americans to realize the benefits of strong encryption while continuing to protect public safety and national security. We do not harbor any illusions that there is one magic technology, a silver bullet that addresses all the needs of the marketplace. But we think constructive dialogue in a variety of areas and fora is far preferable to a stalemate that arises from a battle of wills and rhetoric; working together is better than fighting legislative battles.

The Administration is not advocating any single product, technology, or even technical approach. Rather, we are flexible — provided that the resulting solutions and arrangements preserve the Nation's ability to protect the public safety and defend our national security. These are public interests of the highest order, shared by the Congress and by all of our law-abiding citizens. Industry has the technical know-how to develop commercially viable mechanisms that maintain the government's ability to safeguard its citizens, while protecting our citizens from unwarranted intrusions from any source.

Now let me describe in a little more detail the important law enforcement and national security interests that are at stake in the encryption debate. First, I want to reiterate that the Department of Justice supports the use of strong encryption. Law enforcement's responsibilities and concerns include protecting privacy and promoting secure commerce over our nation's information infrastructure. For example, we prosecute those who violate the privacy of others by illegal eavesdropping, hacking, or stealing confidential information. In the National Information Infrastructure Protection Act of 1996, at the request of the Administration, Congress provided further protection to the confidentiality of stored data. And the Department of Justice helps promote the growth of electronic commerce by enforcing the laws, including those that protect intellectual property rights and that combat computer and communications fraud.

Moreover, the Department of Justice, like other government agencies, realizes that our own information technology systems will increasingly require the use of strong encryption to provide appropriate security for the valuable and sensitive information that we hold on behalf of the American people. The Department, both as an enforcer of the law and as a consumer of encryption technologies, thus has a keen interest in the success of American industry in this area.

However, I don't think that it can reasonably be disputed that the unchecked spread of non-recoverable encryption will also endanger the public safety and our national security. People think of encryption primarily in the context of transmitted communications such as phone calls, and its effect on wiretaps. Indeed, it is absolutely essential that law enforcement preserve the ability to obtain the plaintext of information from lawfully authorized wiretaps and to authenticate this information in court. Court-ordered wiretaps are an essential tool for law enforcement in investigating and prosecuting some of our most important matters involving narcotics dealing, terrorism and organized crime.

But I'd like to focus for a moment on a slightly different aspect here: data stored on computers. It's very common, for example, for drug dealers or terrorists, or any other criminals for that matter, to keep records of their activities in notebooks or other written form. When I was an Assistant United States Attorney, I prosecuted several cases in which we arrested drug dealers and seized their "little black books" pursuant to search warrants or other valid legal authority. These notebooks provided invaluable evidence against the defendant and helped us identify and prosecute other members of the drug ring.

Today, however, we might find that the defendant is using one of the increasingly popular electronic organizers or personal information manager software programs to keep his records instead of a notebook. Or we might find that a swindler running a telemarketing scam has his records on a computer instead of in file cabinets. The switch from written to digital records does not undermine law enforcement interests — as long as the defendant hasn't encrypted the data. But if strong encryption becomes a standard feature, law enforcement will lose its ability to obtain and use this evidence. In fact, commonly available encryption products are already so strong that we cannot break them.

The same problem exists with respect to other types of criminals also. Ramzi Yousef, the mastermind of the World Trade Center bombing, used a laptop computer. Pedophiles who exchange child pornography via computer are already actively using encryption. White collar criminals and economic spies often use computers to steal our businesses' valuable intellectual property. I can't emphasize too strongly the danger that unbreakable, non-recoverable encryption poses: as we move further into the digital age, as more and more data is stored electronically rather than on paper, as very strong encryption becomes built into more and more applications, and as it becomes easier and easier to use this encryption as a matter of routine, our national security and public safety will be endangered — unless we act responsibly.

Some people have suggested that this is a mere resource problem for law enforcement. They believe that law enforcement agencies should simply focus their resources on cracking strong encryption codes, using high-speed computers to try every possible key when we need lawful access to the plaintext of data or communications that is evidence of a crime. But that idea is simply unworkable, because this kind of brute force decryption takes too long to be useful to protect the public safety. For example, decrypting one single message that had been encrypted with a 56-bit key took 14,000 Pentium-level computers over four months; obviously, these kinds of resources are not available to the FBI, let alone the Jefferson City Police Department. Moreover, it is far easier to extend key lengths than to increase computer power. Indeed, 128-bit encryption is already becoming commonplace. In this environment, no one has been able to explain how brute force decryption will permit law enforcement to fulfill its public safety responsibilities.

We believe that the most responsible solution is the development and widespread use of encryption systems that, through a variety of technologies, permit timely access to plaintext by law enforcement authorities acting under lawful authority. I will refer to these systems, collectively, as plaintext recovery systems, although they can encompass a variety of technical approaches. The concept of key recovery, where the key to encryption is held by a trusted third party, is one such approach, but it is by no means the only one that would meet law enforcement's goals.

Some have suggested that law enforcement's access to the plaintext of encrypted data and communications that is evidence of a crime would violate constitutional rights. Although I will discuss in a moment the constitutionality of a mandatory recovery regime, let me begin by reiterating that no such mandatory regime exists, nor does the Administration seek one. Rather, the Administration's efforts have been to encourage the voluntary use of data recovery products. In this context, there is no doubt that the government's efforts are constitutional.

It is certainly difficult to understand how a voluntary regime might violate the Fourth Amendment. As with any kind of stored and transmitted data, it is axiomatic that the government may obtain both encrypted text and decryption keys pursuant to lawful process, which may include a wiretap order, a search warrant issued upon probable cause, a subpoena, or the consent of the party possessing the particular item. Each of these comports with the Fourth Amendment, and voluntary data recovery products do not change this analysis. Additionally, if an individual's encryption key were stored with a third party, Congress could require by legislation that, to compel production of the key, law enforcement would have to meet a standard higher than that required by the Fourth Amendment, much as the Electronic Communications Privacy Act requires a court order to obtain transactional data. If Congress were to address this issue, we would be pleased to work with you to determine the appropriate standard and mechanisms for obtaining keys.

The Committee has requested that I address the legal issues that might be associated with a mandatory plaintext recovery regime. Again, let me restate that the Administration does not advocate such an approach, and believes that a voluntary solution is preferable. Nonetheless, I am prepared to discuss hypothetical legislation prohibiting the manufacture, distribution and import of encryption products that do not contain plaintext recovery technologies, so that the capability to decrypt encrypted data and communications is available to law enforcement upon presentation of valid legal authority.

In considering the Department's views on these issues, I would urge you to keep several caveats in mind. First, the constitutional issues that such a regime would present are undoubtedly novel ones. Indeed, the spectacular growth of the digital world has created many confounding legal issues that the Congress, the courts, the Administration, and our society at large are wrestling with. If history is any guide, changes in technology can lead to changes in our understanding of applicable constitutional doctrine. Moreover, these issues are particularly difficult to address in the abstract, because mandatory plaintext recovery could take a variety of forms. Nonetheless, and with these caveats, it is the best judgment of the Department of Justice that a mandatory plaintext recovery regime, if appropriately structured, could comport with constitutional doctrine.

Let me turn first to the Fourth Amendment. It should be remembered at the outset that the Fourth Amendment does not provide an absolute right of privacy, but protects reasonable expectations of privacy by prohibiting unreasonable searches and requiring that a warrant issue only upon a finding of probable cause by a neutral and detached magistrate. A well-designed plaintext recovery regime would ensure that users' reasonable expectations of privacy were preserved. Any legislation in this area, whether or not it imposed plaintext recovery requirements, should not lessen the showing the government must make to obtain access to plaintext. If a search warrant for data was required before, it should be required under any new regime. By requiring the government to meet current constitutional thresholds to obtain plaintext, such a regime would, in our view, comply with the Fourth Amendment. Moreover, Congress could require under such a regime that even if law enforcement obtains a search warrant for data or communications, it would need additional authority, such as a court order, to obtain the key or other information necessary to perform any decryption if the information is encrypted.

Some have also argued that mandatory plaintext recovery regime would violate the Fifth Amendment's prohibition against compulsory self-incrimination. However, the Fifth Amendment generally prohibits only disclosures that are compelled, testimonial, and incriminating. If a manufacturer of an encryption product were required to maintain information sufficient to allow law enforcement access to plaintext, we believe that there would be no violation of the Fifth Amendment because no disclosure at all would be compelled from the user of the encryption product. If, on the other hand, a mandatory plaintext recovery regime required the user of an encryption product to store his key (or other information needed for recovery) with a third party in advance of using the product, we do not believe that such an arguably compelled disclosure would be testimonial as that term has been interpreted by the Supreme Court. In *Doe v. United States*, 489 U.S. 201 (1988), the Court held that an order compelling a person to execute a form consenting to disclosure of foreign bank accounts did not violate the Fifth

Amendment because the form was not testimonial. The compelled disclosure of decryption information to a third party would not seem to be any more testimonial. Moreover, we doubt whether such a disclosure would be incriminating, because unless and until the encryption product is used in the commission of a crime, the key would pose no threat of incrimination against the user.

Finally, it has been suggested that a statutory restriction on the manufacture, import, and distribution of certain types of encryption products would violate the First Amendment. Opponents of encryption restrictions sometimes argue that the First Amendment protects the right of persons to speak in "code" — i.e., to speak in ciphertext — and that a restriction on the distribution of products that make a particular coded communication possible would be analogous to placing a restriction on the use of a foreign language. This First Amendment argument rests on the faulty premise that the creation or dissemination of ciphertext itself is constitutionally protected. But, unlike a foreign language, the ciphertext that is created by strong encryption products cannot be understood by the viewer or listener. When it is heard, such as on a wiretap of a telephone, ciphertext simply takes the form of unintelligible static. In written form, ciphertext may be in the form of letters, numerals and symbols, but no human being can read or "understand" it: it does not contain characters or words or symbols that represent or correspond to any other characters, words or symbols. Accordingly, ciphertext is not like a foreign language, the use of which can convey unique meaning and nuance to the listener or reader. Thus, ciphertext itself — as opposed to the underlying plaintext — has none of the properties of protected "speech" that the Supreme Court has traditionally identified, and, accordingly, the dissemination of ciphertext should not be entitled to First Amendment protection.

A second form of First Amendment argument focuses not on the ciphertext, but on the underlying plaintext. Under this theory, a prohibition on the manufacture or distribution of nonrecoverable encryption products would inhibit an alleged constitutional right of persons to *obscure* their communications in any manner they see fit. Even if legislation would impose such a practical limitation on the manner in which speakers may obscure their underlying communications, it could be drafted so as to pass muster as a permissible time, place and manner restriction — particularly since any such restriction on the "tools" of speech would be unrelated to any communicative impact of the underlying plaintext and the controls would leave open ample and robust alternative channels or methods for obscuring the underlying plaintext.

A related argument is that a communications infrastructure in which recoverable encryption is the *de facto* standard will impermissibly chill a significant quantum of speech because individuals' knowledge of law enforcement's ability to overhear and decipher communications and data will unduly deter them from communicating. But under such a system, the government would have no greater access to the content of private parties' communications than it currently has, and it is well-settled that the government's exercise of its established statutory powers to intercept and seize communications does not create such a "chilling" effect on speech as to transgress the First Amendment, so long as that power is exercised consistent with the Fourth Amendment, and for valid reasons authorized by statute, such as to discover evidence of criminal wrongdoing. *See*, e.g., *United States v. Ramsey*, 503 F.2d 524, 526 n.5 (7th Cir. 1974) (Stevens, J.) (rejecting argument that "the very existence of wiretapping authority has a chilling effect on free speech and, therefore, ... violates the First Amendment"); *accord United States v. Moody*, 977 F.2d 1425, 1432 (11th Cir. 1992).

A final type of First Amendment argument often heard is that a restriction on the manufacture and distribution of certain types of encryption products would impermissibly restrict the ability of cryptographers, and others, to disseminate the computer code that is used by computers to transform plaintext into ciphertext. But that argument is based on the mistaken premise that dissemination of the code embedded in encryption products itself is necessarily a form of expression protected by the First Amendment. Most such code is in the form of "object code." Object code is simply an immense string of "0"s and "1"s, representing a bewildering concatenation of thousands or millions of high and low voltage electrical impulses. As such, machine-"readable" cryptographic object codes can reveal to possible "readers" neither the ideas they embody, nor the manner in which the ideas are expressed. And this is especially true where such object code is embedded in a product such as a semiconductor chip, so that even the "0"s and "1"s cannot be discerned. Therefore, a restriction on the dissemination of encryption products containing object code would not violate the First Amendment.

The question would be somewhat more complicated with respect to source code — i.e., the instructions to the computer that human beings write and revise. Some persons do disseminate source code for communicative purposes. Nevertheless, we believe that a restriction on the dissemination of certain encryption products could be constitutional even as applied to those relatively infrequent cases in which such products are in the form of software that is disseminated for communicative reasons, because such a restriction could satisfy the "intermediate" scrutiny that the First Amendment provides for incidental restrictions on communicative conduct. As we have argued in litigation in the export-control context, such intermediate scrutiny would be appropriate because the government's reason for regulating source-code software would not be based on any informational value that its dissemination might have. Instead, regulation would be premised on the fact that such software — like all of the "encryption products" that would be regulated — has *physical*, functional properties that can cause a computer to encrypt information and thereby place plaintext beyond the technical capabilities of law enforcement to recover.

Once again, I would like to emphasize that I have presented our constitutional analysis of a mandatory plaintext recovery system to respond to the Committee's request for our views on the legal issues associated with such systems. As I noted above, this constitutional analysis would depend significantly on the nature of the particular system Congress mandated and the findings which supported it; our analysis is entirely generic. Moreover, I would emphasize again here that it is not the policy of the Administration to seek mandatory plaintext recovery legislation; it is the Department of Justice's hope and expectation that the dialogue with industry that I spoke of earlier will yield outcomes that make sense from both a business and a public policy perspective.

Those who argue against preserving lawful government access to encrypted communications often say that the government should bow to the inevitable and accept, even embrace, the spread of unbreakable encryption, rather than trying to fight it. For example, one of my colleagues recently met with a representative of a large computer company which is critical of the Administration's encryption policy. This industry representative said that he recognized that encryption poses a problem for law enforcement, but that we should recognize that other technologies, such as cars, also create problems for law enforcement, yet we have managed. He said, "We don't ban cars, do we? Then why are you trying to ban encryption?"

Of course, I hope it is clear by now that the Government is not trying to ban encryption. Law enforcement supports the responsible spread of strong encryption. Use of strong encryption will help deter crime and promote a safe national information infrastructure.

But the more fundamental point raised by the analogy to the rise of the automobile is that society "managed" the automobile, not by letting it develop completely unfettered and without regard to public safety concerns, but first by recognizing that cars could cause substantial damage to the public safety, and then by regulating the design, manufacture, and use of cars to protect the public safety. Cars must be inspected for safety on a regular basis. Cars are subject to minimum gasoline mileage requirements and maximum pollutant emission requirements. Cars built today must include seat belts and air bags. Perhaps most closely analogous, the laws of every jurisdiction in the United States closely regulate every aspect of driving cars on the public streets and highways, from driver's licenses to regulation of speed to direction and flow of traffic. Congress and the state legislatures recognized the public safety and health threats posed by the technology of automotive transportation, even as they recognized the dramatic benefits of mobility, productivity, and industrialization that the automobile brought with it. Elected government representatives of the people have consistently acknowledged and acted on their sworn responsibilities by assessing the public safety issues at stake and then regulating the technology accordingly.

Perhaps most relevant to the policy issues posed by encryption is the practice, begun by most states about a hundred years ago, of requiring cars to be registered and to bear license plates. More recently, federal law has required all vehicles to bear a vehicle identification number, or VIN. As you may recall, it was the VIN in the Oklahoma City bombing case that led the FBI to the truck rental office at which Timothy McVeigh rented the truck he used. We now recognize that license plates and VIN's afford victims of accidents, victims of car theft, and law enforcement officials with an essential means of identifying vehicles and obtaining information on the movements of criminals. Just as legislatures in the early 1900s acted to manage the risks posed by automotive technology, government leaders today, as the 21st century approaches, must bring the same sensitivity to the need to preserve and advance public safety in the face of encryption in the information age. And such a regulatory scheme, if constructed properly, will, like license plates, have benefits for businesses and consumers as well.

Of course, no analogy is perfect. Computers are not cars, and plaintext recovery is not a speed limit. But my broader point is an important one. The Framers of our Constitution determined that individuals would not have an absolute right of privacy. The Constitution recognizes that there are certain circumstances in which it is appropriate for law enforcement to obtain information that the individual wants to keep private: for example, when a judge finds probable cause to believe that information is evidence of a crime. Decisions as to where that line should be drawn are political and legal ones, not scientific or business ones; they should be made by this Congress and the courts, not by programmers or marketers. Policy should regulate technology; technology should not regulate policy. Just as in the first part of the twentieth century, the law had to take account of the changes in society brought about by the automobile, the law will have to take account of the changes brought about by encryption.

We at the Department of Justice look forward to continuing the productive discussions we have had with this Committee and the Congress on encryption issues. We share the goal of arriving at a policy and marketplace that appropriately balance the competing public and private interests in the spread of strong encryption.

Modification of H.R. 695

Robert S. Litt, Deputy Assistant Attorney General, Criminal Division, Department of Justice, testified before the Subcommittee on Telecommunications, Trade and Consumer Protection, of the House Commerce Committee, on September 4, 1997. His testimony addressed encryption and one of the bills proposing to modify the United States' regulation of cryptography, H.R. 695. His testimony, and a summary of his testimony, is listed below.

The nation's policy on encryption must carefully balance important competing interests. The Department of Justice has a vital stake in the country's encryption policy because encryption may be used not only to protect lawful data against unauthorized intruders, it may also be used to conceal illegitimate materials from law enforcement. While we support the spread of strong encryption, we believe that the widespread dissemination of unbreakable encryption without any accommodation for law enforcement access is a serious threat to public safety and to the integrity of America's commercial infrastructure.

Public safety and national security must be protected against the threats posed by terrorists, organized crime, foreign intelligence agents, and others. If unbreakable encryption proliferates without accommodations for law enforcement, critical law enforcement tools, including wiretapping and execution of search warrants, would be nullified, and the potential harm to public safety could be devastating. U.S. law enforcement and intelligence agencies do not possess and cannot obtain the resources necessary to decrypt large numbers of encrypted communications and stored data. Our experiences demonstrate that this concern is not theoretical and not exaggerated.

Our goal is to encourage the use of strong encryption to protect privacy and commerce, but in a way that *preserves* (without extending) law enforcement's ability to protect public safety and national security. Accordingly, the Administration has promoted the manufacture and use of key recovery products, aided the development of a global key management infrastructure ("KMI"), and liberalized United States restrictions on the export of robust cryptographic products. We anticipate that market forces will make key recovery products a *de facto* industry standard and thus preserve the balance of privacy and public safety that our Constitution embodies.

Because of its support for key recovery, the Department of Justice cannot support H.R. 695 as it is presently drafted. The bill would discourage the development of a KMI. The bill would also eliminate all export controls on strong encryption and thus would undermine public safety and national security by encouraging the proliferation of unbreakable encryption. We believe it would be unwise simply to lift export controls on encryption for the sake of uncertain commercial benefits. This action would be particularly imprudent when there is the possibility of balancing individual privacy, public safety, and commercial needs through global adoption of a key recovery system. As we have learned through extensive international discussions in the last year, a consensus is now emerging throughout much of the world that the most suitable approach is the use of a "key recovery" or "trusted third party" system.

We look forward to working with this Subcommittee as we continue to develop and implement the Administration's approach.

Security and Freedom Through Encryption Act

Ronald D. Lee, Associate Deputy Attorney General, Department of Justice, testified before the Subcommittee on Courts and Intellectual Property, of the House Committee on the Judiciary, on March 4, 1999. His testimony addressed law enforcement policy regarding encryption, and, more particularly, H.R. 850, the proposed Security and Freedom through Encryption Act. His testimony is as follows.

Mr. Chairman, thank you for the opportunity to testify about the Department of Justice's views on export controls on encryption, and particularly the proposed Security and Freedom through Encryption (SAFE) Act, recently introduced by Mr. Goodlatte as H.R. 850. As you are aware, export controls on encryption is a complex and difficult issue that we are attempting to address with our colleagues throughout the Administration. In my testimony, I will first outline the basic perspective and recent initiatives of the Department of Justice on encryption issues, and will then discuss some specific concerns with the SAFE Act.

The Department of Justice supports the spread of strong, recoverable encryption. Law enforcement's responsibilities and concerns include protecting privacy and commerce over our nation's communications networks. For example, we prosecute under existing laws those who violate the privacy of others by illegal eavesdropping, hacking or theft of confidential information. Over the last few years, the Department has continually pressed for the protection of confidential information and the privacy of citizens. Furthermore, we help protect commerce by enforcing the laws, including those that protect intellectual property rights, and that combat computer and communications fraud. (In particular, we help to protect the confidentiality of business data through enforcement of the recently enacted Economic Espionage Act.) Our support for robust encryption is a natural outgrowth of our commitment to protecting privacy for personal and commercial interests.

But the Department of Justice protects more than just privacy. We also protect public safety and national security against the threats posed by terrorists, organized crime, foreign intelligence agents, and others. Moreover, we have the responsibility for preventing, investigating, and prosecuting serious criminal and terrorist acts when they are directed against the United States. We are gravely concerned that the proliferation and use of non-recoverable encryption by criminal elements would seriously undermine these duties to protect the American people, even while we favor the spread of strong encryption products that permit timely and legal law enforcement access and decryption.

The most easily understood example is electronic surveillance. Court-authorized wiretaps have proven to be one of the most successful law enforcement tools in preventing and prosecuting serious crimes, including drug trafficking and terrorism. We have used legal wiretaps to bring down entire narcotics trafficking organizations, to rescue young children kidnapped and held hostage, and to assist in a variety of matters affecting our public safety and national security. In addition, as society becomes more dependent on computers, evidence of crimes is increasingly found in stored computer data, which can be searched and seized pursuant to court-authorized warrants. But if non-recoverable encryption proliferates, these critical law enforcement tools would be nullified. Thus, for example, even if the government satisfies the rigorous legal and procedural requirements for obtaining a wiretap order, the wiretap would be worthless if the intercepted communications of the targeted criminals amount to an unintelligible jumble of noises or symbols. Or we might legally seize the computer of a terrorist and be unable to read the data identifying his or her targets, plans and co-conspirators. The potential harm to public safety, law enforcement, and to the nation's domestic security could be devastating.

I want to emphasize that this concern is not theoretical, nor is it exaggerated. Although use of encryption is still not universal, we have already begun to encounter its harmful effects. For example, in an investigation of a multi-national child pornography ring, investigators discovered sophisticated encryption used to protect thousands of images of child pornography that were exchanged among members. Similarly, in several major hacker cases, the subjects have encrypted computer files, thereby concealing evidence of serious crimes. In one such case, the government was unable to determine the full scope of the hacker's activity because of the use of encryption. The lessons learned from these investigations are clear: criminals are beginning to learn that encryption is a powerful tool for keeping their crimes from coming to light. Moreover, as encryption proliferates and becomes an ordinary component of mass market items, and as the strength of encryption products increases, the threat to public safety will increase proportionately.

Export controls on encryption products have been in place for years and exist primarily to protect national security and foreign policy interests. The nation's intelligence gathering efforts often provide valuable information to law enforcement agencies relating to criminal or terrorist acts, and we believe that this capability cannot be lost. Nonetheless, U.S. law enforcement has much greater concerns about the use of non-recoverable encryption products by criminal elements within the United States that prevent timely law enforcement decryption of lawfully-seized encrypted data and communications relating to criminal or terrorist activity.

The Department of Justice, and the law enforcement community as a whole, supports the use of encryption technology to protect data and communications from unlawful and unauthorized access, disclosure, and alteration. Additionally, encryption helps to prevent crime by protecting a range of valuable information over increasingly widespread and interconnected computer and information networks. At the same time, we believe that the widespread use of unbreakable encryption by criminal elements presents a tremendous potential threat to both public safety and national security. Accordingly, the law enforcement community supports the development and widespread use of strong, recoverable encryption products and services.

The Department believes that encouraging the use of recoverable encryption products is an important part of protecting business and personal data as well as protecting public safety. In addition, this approach continues to find support among businesses and individuals that foresee a need to recover information that has been encrypted. For example, a company might find that one of its employees lost his encryption key, thus accidentally depriving the business of important and time-sensitive business data. Similarly, a business may find that a disgruntled employee has encrypted confidential information and then absconded with the key. In these cases, a plaintext recovery system promotes important private sector interests. Indeed, as the Government implements encryption in our own information technology systems, it also has a business need for plaintext recovery to assure that data and information that we are statutorily required to maintain are in fact available at all times. For these reasons, as well as to protect public safety, the Department has been affirmatively encouraging the voluntary development of data recovery products, recognizing that only their ubiquitous use will both provide both protection for data and protection of public safety.

Because we remain concerned with the impact of encryption on the ability of law enforcement at all levels of government to protect the public safety, the Department and the FBI are engaged in continuing discussions with industry in a number of different fora. These ongoing, productive discussions seek to find creative solutions, in addition to key recovery, to the dual needs for strong encryption to protect privacy and plaintext recovery to protect public safety and business interests. While we still have work to do, these dialogues have been useful because we have discovered areas of agreement and consensus, and have found promising areas for seeking compromise solutions to these difficult issues. While we do not think that there is one magic technology or solution to all the needs of industry, consumers, and law enforcement, we believe that by working with those in industry who create and market encryption products, we can benefit from the accumulated expertise of industry to gain a better understanding of technology trends and develop advanced tools that balance privacy and security.

We believe that a constructive dialogue on these issues is the best way to make progress, rather than seeking export control legislation. Largely as a result of the dialogue the Administration has had with industry, significant progress was made on export controls. Recent updates were announced by Vice President Gore on September 16, 1998, and implemented in an interim rule, which was issued on December 31, 1998. The Department of Justice supports these updates to export controls, which liberalized controls on products that have a bit length of 56-bits or less, and permits the export of unlimited-strength encryption to certain industry sectors, including banks, financial institutions, insurance companies, and medical facilities. These changes allow these sectors, which possess large amounts of highly personal information, to use products that will protect the privacy of their clients. We also expanded our policy to permit recoverable exports, such as systems managed by network administrators, to foreign commercial firms. We learned about these systems through our dialogue with industry, and they are largely consistent with the needs of law enforcement. In addition, the Department, in conjunction with the rest of the Administration, intends to continue our dialogue with industry, and will evaluate the export control process on an ongoing basis in order to ensure that the balance of interests remains fair to all concerned.

At the same time, the Department of Justice is also trying to address the threat to public safety from the widespread use of encryption by enhancing the ability of the Federal Bureau of Investigation and other law enforcement entities to obtain the plaintext of encrypted communications. Among the initiatives is the funding of a centralized technical resource within the FBI. This resource, when fully established, will support federal, state, and local law enforcement in developing a broad range of expertise, technologies, tools, and techniques to respond directly to the threat to public safety posed by the widespread use of encryption by criminals and terrorists. It will also allow law enforcement to stay abreast of rapid changes in technology. Finally, it will enhance the ability of law enforcement to fully execute the wiretap orders, search warrants, and other lawful process issued by courts to obtain evidence in criminal investigations when encryption is encountered.

The proposed Security and Freedom through Encryption Act raises several concerns from the perspective of the Department of Justice. First, we share the deep concern of the National Security Agency that the proposed SAFE Act would harm national security and public safety interests through the liberalization of export controls far beyond our current policy, and contrary to our international export control obligations. We are similarly concerned that a decontrol of unbreakable encryption will cause the further spread encryption products to terrorist organizations and international criminals and frustrate the ability of law enforcement to combat these problems internationally.

The second problem is that the Act may impede the development of products that could assist law enforcement to access plaintext even when also demanded by the marketplace. The Administration believes that the development of such products is important for a safe society. Unfortunately, to the extent that this provision would actually prohibit government from encouraging development of key management infrastructures and other similar technologies, the provision could preclude U.S. government agencies from complying with statutory requirements and would put public safety and national security at risk. For example, it might preclude the United States government from utilizing useful and appropriate incentives to use key recovery techniques. The government might not be able to require its own contractors to use key recovery or demand its use in the legally required storage of records regarding such matters as sales of controlled substances or firearms.

It is also important to consider that our allies concur that unrestricted export of encryption poses significant risk to national security, especially to regions of concern. As recently as December 1998, the thirty-three members of the Wassenaar Arrangement reaffirmed the importance of export controls on encryption for national security and public safety purposes and adopted agreements to enable governments to review exports of hardware and software with a 56-bit key length and above and mass-market products above 64 bits, consistent with national export control procedures. Thus, the elimination of U.S. export controls, as provided by the proposed Act, would severely hamper the international community's efforts to combat such international public safety concerns as terrorism, narcotics trafficking, and organized crime. In light of these factors, we believe that the Administration's more cautious balanced approach is the best way to protect our national interests, including a strong U.S. industry and promoting electronic commerce, while simultaneously protecting law enforcement and national security interests. We believe that legislation that eliminates all export controls on encryption could upset that delicate balance and is contrary to our national interests.

We as government leaders should embark upon the course of action that best preserves the balance long ago set by the Framers of the Constitution, preserving both individual privacy and society's interest in effective law enforcement. We should promote encryption products which contain robust cryptography but that also provide for timely and legal law enforcement plaintext access to encrypted evidence of criminal activity. We should also find ways to support secure electronic commerce while minimizing risk to national security and public safety. This is the Administration's approach. We look forward to working with this Subcommittee as it enters the markup phase of this bill.

OECD Guidelines for Cryptography Policy

In early 1996 the Organization for Economic Cooperation and Development (OECD) initiated a project on cryptography policy by forming the Ad hoc Group of Experts on Cryptography Policy Guidelines. The Ad hoc Group was charged with drafting Guidelines for Cryptography Policy ("Guidelines") to identify the issues which should be taken into consideration in the formulation of cryptography policies at the national and international level. The Ad hoc Group had a one year mandate to accomplish this task and it completed its work in December 1996. Thereafter, the Guidelines were adopted as a Recommendation of the Council of the OECD on 27 March 1997. [See http://www.cybercrime.gov/oeguide.htm.]

Recommended Reading

Speech by Attorney General Janet Reno before the High Technology Crime Investigation Association 1999 International Training Conference, www.usdoj.gov/criminal/cybercrime/agsandie.htm.

Chapter 16

Intellectual Property

Prosecuting Intellectual Property Crimes Guidance

The Department of Justice continually provides informal guidance to prosecutors and investigators as they work through complex substantive, procedural and practical elements of intellectual property crime cases. While this guidance does not provide any legal rights or obligations, it is helpful to law enforcement as they address challenging questions of law, policy or practice. For example, the manual, *Prosecuting Intellectual Property Crimes,* written by the Computer Crime and Intellectual Property Section, provides guidance to law enforcement on the investigation and prosecution of violations of federal intellectual property laws.

Deciding Whether to Prosecute an Intellectual Property Case

David Goldstone, U.S.A. Bulletin (March 2001)

Federal prosecutors know that deciding whether to prosecute a particular case requires the exercise of judgment and discretion, which can take years of experience to develop. But what if you are presented with an intellectual property ("IP") case and you have not done many of them before, if any? How should you decide whether a particular case of counterfeit computer chips, pirated music or software sold (or given away for free) over the Internet, or stolen satellite signals should be charged, even if an investigator provides evidence to prove all the elements? What special considerations, if any, come into play?

Government Reproduction of Copyrighted Materials

OLC Memorandum on Whether Government Reproduction of Copyrighted Materials Invariably is a "Fair Use" under Section 107 of the Copyright Act of 1976 (April 30, 1999)

There is no *per se* rule that government reproduction of copyrighted material — including, in particular, government photocopying of copyrighted materials for internal government use — automatically qualifies as a fair use under Section 107 of the Copyright Act of 1976. However, government photocopying would in many contexts be noninfringing because it would be a "fair use"; and there are good reasons that, if an agency decides to negotiate photocopying licensing agreements, it should seek to limit the scope of any such arrangement to cover only those government photocopying practices that otherwise would, in fact, be infringing.

Federal Statutes Protecting Intellectual Property Rights

The following is a list of criminal statutes that protect intellectual property rights.

- Copyright Offenses
  - 17 U.S.C. 506
  - 18 U.S.C. 2319
  - 18 U.S.C. 2318
  - Copyright Felony Act Legislative History
- Copyright Management Offenses — Digital Millennium Copyright Act (DMCA)
  - 17 U.S.C. 1201
  - 17 U.S.C. 1202
  - 17 U.S.C. 1203
  - 17 U.S.C. 1204
  - 17 U.S.C. 1205
- Bootlegging Offenses
  - 18 U.S.C. 2319A
- Trademark Offenses
  - 18 U.S.C. 2320
- Trade Secret Offenses
  - 18 U.S.C. 1831
  - 18 U.S.C. 1832
  - 18 U.S.C. 1833
  - 18 U.S.C. 1834
  - 18 U.S.C. 1835
  - 18 U.S.C. 1836
  - 18 U.S.C. 1837
  - 18 U.S.C. 1838
  - 18 U.S.C. 1839
- Offenses Relating to the Integrity of IP Systems
  - 17 U.S.C. 506(c-d)
  - 17 U.S.C. 506(e)
  - 18 U.S.C. 497
  - 35 U.S.C. 292
- Offenses Relating to the Misuse of Dissemination Systems
  - 18 U.S.C. 1341
  - 18 U.S.C. 1343
  - 18 U.S.C. 2512
  - 47 U.S.C. 553
  - 47 U.S.C. 605

The No Electronic Theft (NET) Act

Software Pirate Guilty of Copyright Infringement in First NET Act Trial

On May 11, 2001, a federal jury in the Northern District of Illinois found Christian Morley of Salem, Massachusetts, guilty of conspiracy to infringe software copyrights. Morley was indicted last year along with 16 other defendants from across the United States and Europe for conspiring to infringe the copyright of more than 5,000 computer software programs available through a hidden Internet site located at a university in Quebec, Canada.

Nine Indicted in Chicago in $1 Million "Fastlane" Software Piracy Conspiracy

A former North Carolina man who was arrested last fall and eight new defendants across the United States who allegedly were associated with the underground software piracy group known as "Fastlane" were indicted on February 15, 2001, for pirating more than $1 million of copyrighted computer software, games, and movies through non-public Internet sites. All nine defendants were charged in a nine-count indictment that was returned by a federal grand jury in Chicago, where the investigation was conducted, Scott R. Lassar, United States Attorney for the Northern District of Illinois, and Kathleen McChesney, Special Agent-in-Charge of the Chicago Field Division of the Federal Bureau of Investigation, announced on February 16, 2001.

Man Sentenced in Michigan for Offering Software Programs for Free Downloading on "Hacker Hurricane" Web Site

Brian Baltutat was sentenced on January 30, 2001, to 3 years probation, 180 days home confinement, restitution to software manufacturers, and 40 hours of community service. On October 12, 2000, Baltutat pleaded guilty to software copyright infringement. He had offered approximately 142 software programs for free downloading on a Web site called "Hacker Hurricane."

Man Pleads Guilty to Internet Piracy of Star Wars Film

On December 15, 2000, the United States Attorney for the Northern District of California announced that Jason Spatafore pled guilty to a one count information charging criminal copyright infringement in violation of 17 U.S.C. § 506(a)(2) and 18 U.S.C. § 2319(c)(3). The defendant willfully infringed a copyright by reproducing and distributing by electronic means copies of parts of the film Star Wars Episode I: The Phantom Menace. He did this by posting copies of parts of the film on various Web sites so others could download copies of the film from the Internet. He also encouraged others to download copies of the film from those sites.

U.S. Indicts 17 in Alleged International Software Piracy Conspiracy

On May 4, 2000, Scott R. Lassar, United States Attorney for the Northern District of Illinois, and Kathleen McChesney, Special Agent-in-Charge of the Chicago Field

Division of the Federal Bureau of Investigation announced the indictment of seventeen defendants from across the United States and Europe. The defendants allegedly conspired to infringe the copyright of more than 5,000 computer software programs. If convicted, conspiracy to infringe a copyright carries a maximum penalty of five years in prison and a $250,000 fine, or, as an alternative, the Court may impose a fine totaling twice the gross gain to any defendant or twice the gross loss to any victim, whichever is greater. Restitution is mandatory.

Eric Thornton Pleads Guilty to Charges Filed under the NET Act for Unlawful Distribution of Software on the Internet

On December 22, 1999, the Department of Justice, United States Attorney for the District of Columbia Wilma A. Lewis, and Assistant Director in Charge of the Federal Bureau of Investigation's Washington Field Office Jimmy C. Carter announced the guilty plea of Eric John Thornton to a charge of criminal infringement of a copyright. Mr. Thornton pleaded guilty to a violation of the NET Act. Mr. Thornton faces up to one year in jail and a fine of up to $100,000.00. He is scheduled to be sentenced on March 3, 2000.

Eric Thornton Pleads Guilty to Charges Filed under the NET Act for Unlawful Distribution of Software on the Internet

First Felony Conviction and Sentencing Under NET Act — The Justice Department and the United States Attorney for the District of Oregon announced the first conviction under the NET Act on August 20, 1999. Jeffrey Levy, a 22 year old University of Oregon senior, pled guilty to illegally posting computer software programs, musical recordings, entertainment software programs, and digitally-recorded movies on his Internet Web site, allowing the general public to download these copyrighted products. On November 23, 1999, Levy was sentenced to a two year period of probation with conditions. Since December, 1997, The NET Act punishes Internet piracy as a felony, even if the activity is not for profit. Assistant Attorney General for the Criminal Division, James K. Robinson said at the time of the plea, "This is theft, pure and simple."

President Clinton Signs into Law H.R. 2265, the NET Act

The NET Act provides for enhanced protection of copyrights and trademarks by amending provisions in titles 17 and 18 of the U.S. Code. Most notably, the NET Act permits federal prosecution of large-scale, willful copyright infringement even where the infringer does not act for a commercial purpose or for private financial gain. This amendment closes the gap in statutory protection discussed in *United States v. LaMacchia*, 871 F. Supp. 535 (D. Mass. 1994). Computers are changing the way that copyrighted goods are being illegally copied and distributed, creating new challenges for copyright owners and for law enforcement.

Law Enforcement Addresses NET Act

The Statement of Kevin V. DiGregory, Deputy Assistant Attorney General of the Criminal Division before the Subcommittee on Courts and Intellectual Property of the House Committee on the Judiciary, presented September 11, 1997, describes how law enforcement is addressing this challenge and expresses the Department's support for the goals of H.R. 2265, The NET Act.

The Economic Espionage Act

The Computer Crime and Intellectual Property Section is also charged with evaluating all requests for approval of charges under the Economic Espionage Act and making a recommendation regarding the approval of such requests to the Attorney General, Deputy Attorney General, or Assistant Attorney General. In addition, the Section also prosecutes certain Economic Espionage cases directly.

Federal Sentencing Guidelines for Intellectual Property Infringement

In May 2000, the United States Sentencing Commission amended the sentencing guidelines for certain IP crimes, including trademark and copyright infringement.

IP Sentencing Guidelines

United States Sentencing Commission Supplement to the 1998 Guidelines Manual (May 1, 2000)

§2B5.3. Criminal Infringement of Copyright or Trademark

a. Base Offense Level: **8**
b. Specific Offense Characteristics
   i. If the infringement amount exceeded $2,000, increase by the number of levels from the table in §2F1.1 (Fraud and Deceit) corresponding to that amount.
   ii. If the offense involved the manufacture, importation, or uploading of infringing items, increase by **2** levels. If the resulting offense level is less than level **12**, increase to level **12**.
   iii. If the offense was not committed for commercial advantage or private financial gain, decrease by **2** levels, but not less than level 8.
   iv. If the offense involved (A) the conscious or reckless risk of serious bodily injury; or (B) possession of a dangerous weapon (including a firearm) in connection with the offense, increase by 2 levels. If the resulting offense level is less than level **13**, increase to level **13**.

Commentary

Statutory Provisions: 17 U.S.C. § 506(a); 18 U.S.C. §§ 2318-2320, 2511. For additional statutory provision(s), see Appendix A (Statutory Index).

Application Notes

1. Definitions. — For purposes of this guideline:
   A. "Commercial advantage or private financial gain" means the receipt, or expectation of receipt, of anything of value, including other protected works.
   B. "Infringed item" means the copyrighted or trademarked item with respect to which the crime against intellectual property was committed.
   C. "Infringing item" means the item that violates the copyright or trademark laws.
   D. "Uploading" means making an infringing item available on the Internet or a similar electronic bulletin board with the intent to enable other persons to download or otherwise copy, or have access to, the infringing item.

2. Determination of Infringement Amount. — This note applies to the determination of the infringement amount for purposes of subsection (b)(1).
   A. Use of Retail Value of Infringed Item. — The infringement amount is the retail value of the infringed item, multiplied by the number of infringing items, in a case involving any of the following:
      i. The infringing item
         (I) is, or appears to a reasonably informed purchaser to be, identical or substantially equivalent to the infringed item; or
         (II) isa digital or electronic reproduction of the infringed item.
      ii. The retail price of the infringing item is not less than 75 percent of the retail price of the infringed item.
      iii. The retail value of the infringing item is difficult or impossible to determine without unduly complicating or prolonging the sentencing proceeding.
      iv. The offense involves the illegal interception of a satellite cable transmission in violation of 18 U.S.C. § 2511. (In a case involving such an offense, the "retail value of the infringed item" is the price the user of the transmission would have paid to lawfully receive that transmission, and the "infringed item" is the satellite transmission rather than the intercepting device.)
      v. The retail value of the infringed item provides a more accurate assessment of the pecuniary harm to the copyright or trademark owner than does the retail value of the infringing item.
   B. Use of Retail Value of Infringing Item. — The infringement amount is the retail value of the infringing item, multiplied by the number of infringing items, in any case not covered by subdivision (A) of this Application Note, including a case involving the unlawful recording of a musical performance in violation of 18 U.S.C. § 2319A.
   C. Retail Value Defined. — For purposes of this Application Note, the "retail value" of an infringed item or an infringing item is the retail price of that item in the market in which it is sold.
   D. Determination of Infringement Amount in Cases Involving a Variety of Infringing Items. — In a case involving a variety of infringing items, the infringement amount is the sum of all calculations made for those

items under subdivisions (A) and (B) of this Application Note. For example, if the defendant sold both counterfeit videotapes that are identical in quality to the infringed videotapes and obviously inferior counterfeit handbags, the infringement amount, for purposes of sub-section (b)(1), is the sum of the infringement amount calculated with respect to the counterfeit videotapes under subdivision (A)(i) (i.e., the quantity of the infringing videotapes multiplied by the retail value of the infringed videotapes) and the infringement amount calculated with respect to the counterfeit handbags under subdivision (B) (i.e., the quantity of the infringing handbags multiplied by the retail value of the infringing handbags).

3. Manufacturing, Importing, and Uploading Enhancement. — With respect to uploading, subsection (b)(2) applies only to uploading with the intent to enable other persons to download or otherwise copy, or have access to, the infringing item. For example, this subsection applies in the case of illegally uploading copyrighted software to an Internet site, but it does not apply in the case of downloading or installing that software on a hard drive on the defendant's personal computer.

4. Application of §3B1.3. — If the defendant de-encrypted or otherwise cir-cumvented a technological security measure to gain initial access to an infringed item, an adjustment under §3B1.3 (Abuse of Position of Trust or Use of Special Skill) will apply.

5. Upward Departure Considerations. — If the offense level determined under this guideline substantially understates the seriousness of the offense, an upward departure may be warranted. The following is a non-exhaustive list of factors that the court may consider in determining whether an upward departure may be warranted:

A. The offense involved substantial harm to the reputation of the copyright or trademark owner.

B. The offense was committed in connection with, or in furtherance of, the criminal activities of a national, or international, organized criminal enterprise.

Background

This guideline treats copyright and trademark violations much like theft and fraud. Similar to the sentences for theft and fraud offenses, the sentences for defendants convicted of intellectual property offenses should reflect the nature and magnitude of the pecuniary harm caused by their crimes. Accordingly, similar to the loss enhancement in the theft and fraud guidelines, the infringement amount in subsection (b)(1) serves as a principal factor in determining the offense level for intellectual property offenses.

Subsection (b)(1) implements Section 2(g) of the No Electronic Theft (NET) Act by using the retail value of the infringed item, multiplied by the number of infringing items, to determine the pecuniary harm for cases in which use of the retail value of the infringed item is a reasonable estimate of that harm. For cases referred to in Application Note 2(B), the Commission determined that use of the retail value of the infringed item would overstate the pecuniary harm or otherwise be inappropriate. In these types of cases, use of the retail value of the infringing item, multiplied by the number of those items, is a more reasonable estimate of the resulting pecuniary harm.

Section 2511 of title 18, United States Code, as amended by the Electronic Communications Act of 1986, prohibits the interception of satellite transmission for purposes of direct or indirect commercial advantage or private financial gain. Such violations are similar to copyright offenses and are therefore covered by this guideline.

Intellectual Property Policy and Programs

Joint Anti-Piracy Initiative

On July 23, 1999, the Department of Justice, the Federal Bureau of Investigation, and the U.S. Customs service announced the establishment of a law enforcement initiative aimed at combating the growing challenge of piracy and counterfeiting of intellectual property, both domestically and internationally. "At the same time that our information economy is soaring, so is intellectual property theft," said Deputy Attorney General Eric Holder. "We are here to send the message that those who steal our intellectual property will be prosecuted. This is theft, pure and simple." Mr. Holder's remarks and a press release describing the announcement of the initiative may be accessed via the links below:

> www.cybercrime.gov/dagipini.htm
> www.cybercrime.gov/ipinitia.htm

DOJ Speaks out on Intellectual Property Rights

On December 25, 2000, Attorney General Reno's article on "The Threat of Digital Theft: Intellectual property theft is faster, costlier and more dangerous than ever" appeared in theStandard.com. In the article, Ms. Reno discussed law enforcement concerns about intellectual property theft, and discussed recent law enforcement efforts to combat the problem, including the Intellectual Property Initiative, launched in July 1999.

The Threat of Digital Theft: Intellectual Property Theft Is Faster, Costlier and More Dangerous Than Ever

In December, the White House released an interagency International Crime Threat Assessment, a big report with some stark conclusions: Intellectual property theft today is faster, costlier and more dangerous than ever. These trends will continue unless law enforcement and rights holders recognize that the threat crosses national borders — and resolve to work collectively to defeat the increasingly more organized efforts of the perpetrators.

Products and methods protected by intellectual property laws are critical to our national defense and economic security. Intellectual property laws provide core protections for this economic engine. Anti-counterfeiting laws also safeguard the reliability of products that affect public health and safety, covering everything from aircraft parts to infant formula.

But economic espionage — unlawful practices engaged in by private companies and sometimes by foreign governments aimed at stealing assets such as formulas, blueprints or marketing strategies — is on the rise. The FBI estimates that a significant number of countries are targeting U.S. firms, with high-tech companies the most frequent targets. For developing nations, the stakes are higher still. Countries that fail to protect intellectual property will witness the exodus of their best talent, a loss of jobs and tax revenues, a nutrient environment for official corruption and an increase in crimes financed by intellectual property theft. With so much at stake, law enforcement officials are deeply disturbed by an explosion in piracy and counterfeiting.

Among our concerns are the following:

- Criminal organizations appear to be using the proceeds of IP-infringing products to facilitate a variety of enterprises, including guns, drugs, pornography and even terrorism. Invariably, when there is intellectual property crime, there is tax evasion and money laundering.
- The Internet, while promoting knowledge-based industries and commerce, also makes it easier to steal, produce and distribute merchandise such as software, music, films, books and games. With the click of a mouse, identical copies can be reproduced and transferred immediately, cheaply, surreptitiously and repeatedly. (See www.cybercrime.gov)
- Small businesses — the lifeblood of modern economies — can be devastated by organized, commercial-scale piracy. In one Latin American country, local music producers were nearly wiped out recently by music pirates using well-organized transborder operations to saturate the country with illegal domestic and foreign music products.

To meet this challenge, in July 1999 the Justice Department, FBI and Customs Service announced the first interagency effort to boost domestic enforcement of Francisco/San Jose agreed to make such cases a priority, share information and work closely with industry to encourage quality referrals.

As a result, we are beginning to see more promising prosecutions, including the first convictions under the No Electronic Theft Act, a 1997 law that punishes the latest wave of piracy on the Internet. Further, we are pleased the U.S. Sentencing Commission toughened the guideline range for criminal counterfeiting and piracy offenses.

To combat transborder intellectual-property crime, law enforcement in the U.S. and around the world must be trained and equipped, and our efforts linked across national and virtual borders, to meet the challenge of highly organized groups trafficking in these products. We need to continue efforts within the G8, the EU and countries in Asia and Latin America to elevate these crimes on their agendas.

Our citizens, policymakers and law enforcement experts must understand that stealing intellectual property will be prosecuted for what it is: not an exotic, hard-to-prosecute diversion or hobby, but theft, pure and simple.

The Audio Home Recording Act and Napster

On September 11, 2000, the Department of Justice filed an *amicus curiae* brief in the case of *A & M Records, Inc. v. Napster, Inc.* solely on the issue of whether Section 1008 of the Audio Home Recording Act of 1992, 17 U.S.C. §1008, excuses Napster from liability for copyright infringement.

The Digital Millennium Copyright Act and DeCSS

On February 20, 2000, the Department of Justice filed [] a brief as an intervenor in the case of *Universal City Studios, Inc. v. Corely,* on appeal from Universal City Studios, Inc. v. Reimerdes, 82 F. Supp. 2d 211 (S.D.N.Y. 2000), on three issues:

1. Whether, as applied to defendants' dissemination of circumvention technology, the DMCA is consistent with the First Amendment as an appropriate conduct regulation.
2. Whether the district court's order enjoining defendants from committing specific violations of the DMCA is both content neutral and sufficiently tailored to satisfy constitutional requirements.
3. Whether the district court correctly rejected defendants' overbreadth challenge to the DMCA, where defendants did not violate the statutory provision at the core of their challenge, did not establish an adequate factual record, and where the alleged overbreadth was not substantial in any event.

[http://www.cybercrime.gov/DOJbrief_Univ_Corely.htm]

The Importation of Counterfeit Pharmaceuticals

On October 3, 2000, Deputy Assistant Attorney General for the Civil Division Patricia Maher testified before the House Subcommittee on Oversight and Investigations of the Committee on Commerce on the importation of counterfeit pharmaceutical products. Her testimony addresses the health and safety dangers of this practice and highlights some recent prosecutions. [www.cybercrime.gov/FDCAover.htm]

G8 Law Enforcement Experts Agree to Examine Transborder IP Crime

On September 18-19, 2000, the United States sponsored the first-ever meeting of law enforcement experts from G-8 countries to discuss trends in trafficking in counterfeiting and pirated merchandise. Read a summary of the meetings below.

On September 18-19, 2000, the United States sponsored the first-ever meeting of law enforcement experts from G-8 countries to discuss trends in trafficking in counterfeiting and pirated merchandise. The purpose of the meeting was to identify ways in which the G-8 countries might usefully collaborate in combating transnational intellectual property crimes.

The meeting was held in Washington, D.C. under the auspices of the G-8's Senior Law Enforcement Experts on Transnational Organized Crime (Lyon Group).

The Department of Justice, Customs Service, and FBI jointly hosted delegations from Canada, France, Germany, United Kingdom, Italy, Japan, Russian Federation, and the European Commission.

The meeting focused on the involvement of organized criminal groups in counterfeiting and piracy, and the threats to public health and safety posed by infringing merchandise (including counterfeit pharmaceuticals). Delegates also discussed the role of mutual legal assistance and extradition agreements and other arrangements for providing evidence and witnesses for investigations and prosecutions of these offenses in other countries.

The law enforcement experts forwarded their observations and proposal for future cooperative activity to the Lyon Group plenary, which met in Hiroshima, Japan in November, 2000. The Lyon Group endorsed the experts' recommendations. These include: (1) exploring the possibility of sharing strategic intelligence information concerning groups trafficking in counterfeit or pirated merchandise, assigning high priority to products affecting health and safety and/or which manifest organized criminal involvement or associations with other crimes, and (2) sponsoring an annual briefing on trends in IP crime and member countries' enforcement activities.

Copyrights, Trademarks and Trade Secrets

The Department of Justice and other agencies are continually working to improve protections for intellectual property rights and the enforcement of intellectual property laws. You can find information on DOJ initiatives, summits, and speeches in this section. This section also contains information on U.S. interagency efforts, such as NIPLECC, as well as international efforts to protect intellectual property rights.

Recommended Reading

- *Prosecuting Intellectual Property Crimes Manual,* www.usdoj.gov/criminal/cybercrime/ipmanual.htm
- Deciding Whether to Prosecute an Intellectual Property Case, www.usdoj.gov/criminal/cybercrime/usamarch2001_1.htm
- Government Reproduction of Copyrighted Materials, www.usdoj.gov/criminal/cybercrime/fairuse.htm
- *Joint Anti-Piracy Initiative,* www.usdoj.gov/criminal/cybercrime/dagipini.htm or: www.usdoj.gov/criminal/cybercrime/ipinitia.htm
- Protecting Intellectual Property Rights in the Digital Age, www.usdoj.gov/criminal/cybercrime/ipsymposium.htm
- Overview of the challenges that law enforcement faces in the Information Age and specific steps that the Department of Justice is taking to combat high-tech crime, particularly crime involving the theft of intellectual property, www.usdoj.gov/criminal/cybercrime/dag0112.htm
- DOJ Supports Law Enforcement Cooperation Within the Single Market to Combat Growing Intellectual Property Crime, www.usdoj.gov/criminal/cybercrime/ecfinal.htm

- DOJ Presents Challenges and Responses to the Threat of Digital Piracy, www.usdoj.gov/criminal/cybercrime/eurfinal.htm
- *The Audio Home Recording Act and Napster,* www.usdoj.gov/criminal/cybercrime/napsterbr.htm
- *The Digital Millennium Copyright Act and DeCSS,* www.usdoj.gov/criminal/cybercrime/DOJbreif_Univ_Corley.htm
- *The Importation of Counterfeit Pharmaceuticals,* www.usdoj.gov/criminal/cybercrime/FDCAover.htm
- *The Audio Home Recording Act and Napster,* www.usdoj.gov/criminal/cybercrime/napsterbr.htm
- *Copyrights, Trademarks and Trade Secrets,* www.usdoj.gov/criminal/cybercrime/ippolicy.htm
- *Intellectual Property Cases,* www.usdoj.gov/criminal/cybercrime/ipcases.htm
- *Criminal Intellectual Property Laws,* www.usdoj.gov/criminal/cybercrime/iplaws.htm
- *The Economic Espionage Act,* www.usdoj.gov/criminal/cybercrime/eea.htm
- *Intellectual Property Documents,* www.usdoj.gov/criminal/cybercrime/ipdocs.htm

FORENSICS TOOLS

Chapter 17

Forensic and Security Assessment Tools

This chapter is provided as an additional resource to the reader. It lists many of the companies offering software/utilities for use in computer forensics. The inclusion of any vendor in this chapter is not an endorsement by the authors of any particular product, vendor, or solution. This chapter cannot realistically list all vendors and all products — this is merely a sampling of the products available. The reader is advised to seek further advice and information for additional sources, as new vendors and new products are introduced almost daily.

Detection, Protection, and Analysis

In a perfect world, we would be able to protect against all possible vulnerability areas with the use of a tool, or tools. The world is not perfect, however, and neither are tools. Each tool has its strengths and weaknesses. Each tool has an appropriate use, and each tool has the ability to help you to the extent you know how to use it for its designed purpose.

Learn each tool as best you can. Make prodigious use of online help, hardcopy manuals, or whatever else may be available with a given product. Most of all, do not be afraid to ask for help. It is impossible for everyone to know absolutely everything about a complex tool at times, so do not be afraid to speak up. Call their support, if available. Do whatever you need to but do not operate in a vacuum. If you are called upon to testify in court, you will no doubt be asked some questions aimed at casting doubt upon your ability, thoroughness, or understanding of a given tool you employed. Remember that the defense in such a situation will try to find the weakness in your armor, and you should be prepared for such an eventuality.

Detection and Prevention Tools for the PC Desktop

Anti-Viral Products

One tool that is sometimes neglected, and can be one of your primary defense as well as detection tool is a good anti-virus package. There are many out there and, as you would expect, there are those that are better than others. Two industry leaders are the tools made by companies Symantec and McAfee Associates. Both put out highly effective products that are among the best in the industry. Other lesser-known companies put out some good products as well, and in the field today companies work hard to try to leapfrog their competition, so it is always a battle to get on top and stay there.

Regardless of which anti-virus product you use, make absolutely certain you keep it updated. Anti-virus packages today are excellent tools, but only if you are also vigilant. One area that needs your attention to keeping things updated is the anti-virus software's "signature files." Signature files are basically data files that tell the anti-virus software how to identify a given virus by certain characteristics of behavior, size, names, aliases, and other digital characteristics that comprise a given virus's signature (hence, the name). New viruses literally pop up daily, and are usually variants of known ones, but the occasional new threat appears fairly regularly too. These signature files help against the known variants, and that is why it is so critical that you work to keep them updated in your organization.

Another part of the anti-virus tools in use today is the actual virus detection tool itself. This part of the tool is sometimes called the "engine;" it contains the brains of the product that tells it how to make use of the signature files and how to otherwise scan for unknown viruses by detecting behavior patterns that are virus-like. These tools are improving and work is being done to make such behavior analysis more effective; thus, it is just as important to keep up with the updates to your software package itself as it is to the signature files that support it.

Remember: viruses can do more than just infect a spreadsheet. They can delete critical files, send out e-mail, disable a computer, and spread through your network if it is not protected. All sorts of viruses are out there. Keep your guard up, and make sure everyone in your company is aware of safe computing guidelines. Viruses can travel on any media that transports them. If a file can be stored on a device, a virus can piggyback its way into a computer, or worse, through your corporate network, and put resources at great risk. You certainly do not need to invite in a virus that e-mails out all your company-sensitive information to some hacker!

The better anti-virus products also usually provide a method of alerting not just the individual victim of a virus, but also can send out alerts to a network administrator. It is highly advisable that you configure your anti-virus package this way.

Audit Trails

If you are monitoring a suspect machine, make use of the audit feature of the operating system as discussed in Chapter 3 entitled "The Liturgical Forensic Examination: Tracing Activity on a Windows-Based Desktop." Take advantage of remote viewing options such as having an administrative share where the logs are located, or physically having the logs on a server you have access to by way of folder redirection, if that is an option for you.

Many security products that monitor program activities also provide audit trail options that you should take advantage of.

Firewalls

A firewall is a device or software program that monitors data flowing between one computer and another on the network. Aspects of a computer operating system will determine how a particular system can be attacked, and a firewall helps to stop would-be attackers cold. This, by the way, can run either way — attacks from the outside coming in, or people inside trying to do things to get information out can both be blocked.

Firewalls are also used to help control the amount of data flowing over your network. For example, it is possible to configure a firewall so that it will not let the kinds of communications run that would allow video or audio streaming feeds into or out of your network. Such "streaming data" can take up a lot of resources, and limiting who can use that sort of capability keeps resources available for other users. In a network where bandwidth resources are limited, it becomes even more critical.

Remember the previous discussion in this book regarding chat clients being a security risk? Well, this aspect can also be controlled via a firewall. You can block the protocols necessary to support chat clients for the most part via a firewall.

Among the leading manufacturers of firewalls for both corporate and personal use are companies such as ZoneLabs (www.zonelabs.com), Inc. and Network ICE Corporation (www.networkice.com). Network ICE was just purchased by Internet Security Systems as of this writing and thus may have additional resources for you (www.iss.net)

Firewalls provide alert messaging and management for attempted break-ins. Attacks happen with such frequency that you may not want to actually get all the alerts sent to you, or the network administrator. Some prime hacking sites can have hundreds, if not thousands, of attacks each and every day. Even a home computer on a dial-up connection is at risk, although most never even know it. The risk increases with "always-on" connections like DSL, cable modems, T1, T3, and other constant connections. The longer a computer is on the network with a specific IP address, the more vulnerable it is.

Strong Password Policies

Set up corporate-enforced password policies for your network and desktop environments. This means making sure that people change them often enough to keep any window of opportunity for an ex-employee to use the Id and password of someone they may know. It means keeping passwords to a minimum length (usually eight characters), and having at least one numeric and one alphabetic character. It also means having a lockout policy on failed logon attempts and auditing those events, regardless of suspicions about the employee's veracity.

Vulnerability Surveys

There is reluctance among companies at times to have something like this done. Why? Because it can dramatically illustrate just how vulnerable your systems, processes, and safeguards are, even when you have already devoted significant resources to making things secure. A good IT manager should seriously consider bringing in an outside firm to try to find the vulnerable areas in a computer infrastructure. A security audit of password policies, encryption policies, mobile computing tools, and firewall and system analysis may well turn up unexpected holes in the armor you think surround your company's computing environment. A thorough audit by a reputable computer security firm is possibly one of the most valuable prevention tools you can have. It is often helpful just to have another set of eyes looking at things without preconception as to what is already in place. When one knows too much about the way something is put together, it often blinds that person to areas of vulnerabilities not previously considered.

Analysis Tools

Microsoft Notepad and Microsoft Wordpad Programs

Although these are simple text viewers, they can be used to bring up everything from cookie files to Web pages and some logs.

Microsoft Windows Explorer

Make sure you know how to use Windows Explorer to search for files and examine properties of a file, including the various file attributes, security settings, file access/revision times, and ownership. All of the features of the program can be explored in the product's online help.

Low-Level File Editors

Having a product that can open a binary file in hexadecimal can still be invaluable. Products such as UltraEdit32 (www.ultraedit.com) and others like it allow you to take a detailed look at a file, search its contents, and more.

Checksum Generators

These are programs that can let you take a snapshot of a file and generate a unique check digit associated with that file. A checksum, as it is called, can be used to cross-check the integrity of a file and see if it has been modified by anyone. If you benchmark a file, and then check it later and the checksum is different, then you have reason to suspect something might be happening.

Tools to perform checksum generation are available from companies such as NTI (www.forensics-intl.com) and other firms.

Usage Mapping Tools

A usage mapping tool is designed to allow you to track how often a given program or file is accessed, for how long, and by whom. Such mapping tools have been put into place for things such as Internet abuse tracking and the like.

Tools for this are also available from NTI and other sources.

Slack Space and Swap Space Analysis Tools

These tools let you capture and examine the slack space in files and the swap file, which Microsoft Windows uses as a temporary memory extension. Although you can use low-level file editor viewers such as UltraEdit32 to examine these, the process of doing so can be expedited utilizing some of the more advanced tools that will allow wildcard and keyword searching. Again, companies such as NTI can provide such tools to authorized persons.

Packet Sniffer Programs and Equipment

These tools are normally only used by a network administrator or network consultant because they can be very involved to operate. One must know certain things about the network configuration to use the equipment versions; and the software version, while easier to use, should not be employed without some level of training. Windows NT and Windows 2000 do come with such packet analysis tools in the server edition of their software.

Remote Logon to Administrative Shares

This is a way in which you can log on to someone's computer from yours over the network. Be *extremely* careful when doing this. While it is possible to remotely log on to someone's PC by knowing the machine's network name, and using a user ID with administrative privileges, remember that at that point you are logging directly onto their machine and you do run the risk of possibly contaminating evidence by inadvertently changing file access dates and times, revealing your presence in the event log, which the user could see if they also had administrative rights, etc.

While a technical possibility for forensic use, especially in a potential criminal investigation, it should not be used without extreme caution. The use of covert monitoring programs and sniffing packets is far more advisable because it preserves the integrity of the system to a greater extent.

Covert Monitoring Programs

Programs such as SpectorSoft (www.spectorsoft.com) provide the capability to covertly record everything, including Web-based e-mail and online chat sessions. There are a number of vendors that market these kinds of systems, and more are becoming available in various price and capability ranges.

Applications

SafeBack

SafeBack (Mirror Image Backup Software; www.forensics-intl.com/safeback.html) is a sophisticated evidence preservation tool. It can be used covertly to duplicate all storage areas on a computer's hard disk drive.

SafeBack is used to create mirror-image backups of partitions on hard disk drives and also to make a mirror-image copy of an entire hard disk that may contain multiple partitions or operating systems. Backup image files, created by SafeBack, can be written to essentially any writeable magnetic storage device, including SCSI tape backup units. SafeBack preserves all of the data on a backed-up or copied hard disk, including inactive or "deleted" data. Cyclical redundancy checksums (CRCs) distributed throughout the backup process enforce the integrity of backup copies to ensure the accuracy of the process.

CRCMd5

Data Validation Tool (www.forensics-intl.com/crcmd5.html) is a program that mathematically creates a unique signature for the contents of one, multiple, or all files on a given storage device. Such signatures can be used to identify whether or not the contents of one or more computer files have changed. This forensics tool relies on 128-bit accuracy and can easily be run from a floppy diskette to benchmark the files on a specific storage device (e.g., floppy diskette, hard disk drive, or zip disk). CRCMd5 can be used as the first step in the implementation of a configuration management policy. Such a policy and related system benchmarking can help computer specialists isolate problems and deal with computer incidents after they occur. The program is also used to document that computer evidence has not been altered or modified during computer evidence processing.

DiskSig

DiskSig is a bitstream backup validation tool (www.forensics-intl.com/disksig.html) is a program used to mathematically create a unique signature for the content of a computer hard disk drive. Signatures can then be used to validate the accuracy of forensic bitstream image backups of computer hard disk drives.

DiskSig is used to verify the accuracy of forensic bitstream backups and related restorations of the content of computer hard disk drives. This program can also be used to validate the accuracy of restored output created by any mirror image bitstream backup utility.

Filter_I

Filter_I (www.forensics-intl.com/filter_i.html) is an enhanced, intelligent forensic filter utility used to quickly make sense of non-sense in the analysis of ambient computer data; for example, Windows swap file data, file slack data, and data associated with erased files.

Filter_I relies on preprogrammed artificial intelligence to identify fragments of word-processing communications, fragments of e-mail communications, fragments of Internet chat room communications, fragments of Internet news group posts, encryption passwords, network passwords, network logons, database entries, credit card numbers, social security numbers, and the first and last names of individuals who have been listed in communications involving the subject computer.

This unique computer forensic tool can also be used effectively in computer security reviews because it quickly reveals security leakage and violations of corporate policy that might not otherwise be uncovered. Be aware that the software does not rely on keywords entered by the computer specialist. It is a pattern recognition tool that recognizes patters of text, letter combinations, number patterns, potential passwords, potential network logons, and the names of individuals.

To avoid possible violation of privacy laws, this software should only be used with the approval of corporate legal counsel.

GetFree

GetFree (www.forensics-intl.com/getfree.html) is a forensic data capture tool. When files are "deleted" in DOS, Windows, Windows 95, or Windows 98, the data associated with the file is not actually eliminated. It is simply reassigned to unallocated storage space, where it may eventually be overwritten by the creation of new files over time. Such data can provide the computer forensics investigator with valuable leads and evidence. However, the same data can create a significant security risk when sensitive data has been erased using DOS, Windows, Windows 95, or Windows 98 file deletion procedures and commands.

GetFree software is used to capture all of the unallocated file space on DOS-, Windows-, Windows 95- and Windows 98-based computer systems. The program can be used to identify leads and evidence. It is also effectively used to validate the secure scrubbing of unallocated storage space.

GetSlack

GetSlack (www.forensics-intl.com/getslack.html) is a forensic data capture utility. It is used to capture all of the file slack contained on a logical hard disk drive or floppy diskette on DOS, Windows, Windows 95, and Windows 98 systems.

This tool is used in computer security risk assessments because memory dumps in file slack are cause for security-related concerns. Typically, network logons and passwords are found in file slack. It is also possible for passwords used in file encryption to be stored as memory dumps in file slack.

GetTime

GetTime (www.forensics-intl.com/gettime.html) is a forensic documentation tool. It is used to document the system date and system time settings of the subject computer. File dates and times associated with allocated files and previously deleted files can be important in cases involving computer evidence. The reliability of the file dates and times are directly tied to the accuracy of the system settings for date and time on the subject computer. Therefore, it is important to document the accuracy of the system clock as soon as possible. Low battery power or daylight savings time changes are likely sources of system clock inaccuracies. This program aids in the documentation of the system clock settings for time and date. When the dates and times that files were created, modified, or last accessed, this information is relevant.

NTI-DOC

NTI-DOC (www.forensics-intl.com/ntidoc.html) is a forensic tool. This program is essentially used to take an "electronic snapshot" of files and subdirectories that have previously been identified as having evidentiary value.

Seized

Seized (www.forensics-intl.com/seized.html) is an evidence protection tool. This program is designed to limit access to computers that have been seized as evidence. When the Seized program is operated, it locks the computer system and displays a message on the screen advising the computer user that the computer contains evidence and it should not be operated without authorization.

TextSearch Plus

TextSearch Plus software (www.forensics-intl.com/txtsrchp.html) is used to quickly search hard disk drives, zip disks, and floppy diskettes for keywords or specific patterns of text. It operates at either a logical or physical level at the option of the user.

AnaDisk Diskette Analysis Tool

AnaDisk (www.forensics-intl.com/anadisk.html) is a diskette analysis tool primarily used to identify data storage anomalies on floppy diskettes and generic hardware in the form of floppy disk controllers; BIOS are needed when using this software.

CopyQM Plus

CopyQM Plus (www.forensics-intl.com/copyqm.html) is diskette duplication software that turns your PC into a diskette duplicator. In a single pass, diskettes are formatted, copied, and verified. CopyQM Plus will also create self-extracting executable programs tied to specific diskette images. When the resulting program is run, the diskette image will be restored to diskette.

DiskScrub Data Overwrite Utility

DiskScrub (www.secure-data.com/diskscrb.html) is a simple data overwrite utility that is used to eliminate all traces of data from a disk drive. It can be optionally set for one, three, or seven overwrites, and the patterns used for the overwrites conform to requirements set by the U.S. government for secure destruction of data in nonclassified environments. Classified environments require the manual destruction of the drives through heat or mutilation. This program is ideal for the clean-up of data that has accidentally spilled over to the wrong hard disk drive or storage location.

DiskSearch Pro

DiskSearch Pro (www.forensics-intl.com/dspro.html) is used to quickly find and document the occurrence of strings of text stored on computer storage devices.

NTAView

NTAView (www.forensics-intl.com/ntaview.html) is an Internet usage analysis tool. NTAView software is intended for use with NTI's Net Threat Analyzer software (NTA). NTA is a computer forensics tool used to capture leads of Internet e-mail, Internet browsing, and Internet file downloads from an analysis of the Windows swap file and other sources of ambient data.

M-Sweep Data Scrubber

M-Sweep (www.secure-data.com/ms.html) is a data scrubber tool that was developed primarily for use on notebook computers that contain trade secrets and other forms of confidential data.

Sometimes, sensitive information "leaks" into file slack, the Windows swap file, and unallocated space without the knowledge of the computer user. Such information is easily recovered using computer forensic tools and methods. This is a potential security threat and M-Sweep eliminates this problem. This software eliminates potential evidence.

TeleDisk

TeleDisk (www.forensics-intl.com/teledisk.html) is disk duplication software. It was developed to assist in the processing of computer evidence tied to floppy diskettes. It turns any diskette into a compressed data file and reconstructs copies of the original diskette from the file. It is ideal for the sharing of floppy diskette images over the Internet among computer forensics experts. TeleDisk can also be used to archive evidence diskettes that involve unusual formatting.

Ptable

Ptable (www.forensics-intl.com/ptable.html) is a hard sisk partition table analysis tool. This software tool is used in computer forensics to review and analyze the partition table(s) assigned to a hard disk drive. This tool is essential concerning network forensics and when multiple operating systems are stored on one hard disk drive in multiple partitions. This software is also used to identify hidden data potentially stored in the partition gap or "unknown" partitions.

Byte Back

Byte Back (www.toolsthatwork.com/ttw-tools.shtml) is a data recovery and computer forensic tool for powerful, low-level cloning, imaging, and disk analysis. It clones/ images most drive formats, and supports drives up to four terabytes. Integrated MD5. It performs safe recoveries on hard disk, Zip, Jaz, floppy, and more.

Desktop Surveillance

Desktop Surveillance (www.toolsthatwork.com/odse.shtml) is a recording and access control application that contains computer monitoring and security utility software. It monitors and records all Windows desktop activity, including keystrokes, e-mail, chat, surfing, instant messaging, hacking, etc.

Detective

Detective (www.toolsthatwork.com/odet.shtml) is a PC data sleuth that investigates the history of the PC to determine what the system was used for (i.e., which Web sites were visited, what images were downloaded, etc.), looks for adult content, hacking, and anything else the user decides.

ErgoSense

ErgoSense (www.toolsthatwork.com/ergo.shtml) is a health and safety monitoring program that keeps track of time spent on a workstation, indicating to the user that it is time for a break. The program guides users through low-impact exercises that help reduce incidents of RSI (repetitive strain injury), carpal tunnel syndrome, headache, neck and back ache, etc.

DAT Disk Emulator

The DAT disk emulator (www.vogon-computer-evidence.com/evidential_systems-02e.htm) is a software that allows forensic processing and evidential investigation to be carried out quickly and efficiently. It boasts a very high-capacity hard drive (typically 36 GB) and allows any disk to be emulated and the files viewed when attached to a suitable host computer.

Mobile Forensic Workstation

A mobile forensic workstation (www.vogon-computer-evidence.com/mobile-station.htm) is a highly flexible and modular piece of equipment that provides the facilities and power of a well equipped computer forensic laboratory to be set up anywhere in the world in the time it takes to arrive there yourself. The system allows direct imaging using the special hosting options, network connectivity, tape duplication, processing, and investigation activities to be carried out.

Forensic Processing Station

A forensic processing station (www.vogon-computer-evidence.com/forensic-station.htm) is equipment designed to meet the needs of the serious professional processing laboratory. It comprises a high-capacity autoloader, combined with large amounts of online disk storage and high-performance processing power. Used in conjunction with Vogon processing software, this equipment allows vast amounts of data to be processed automatically, virtually without human intervention. It is scalable to take advantage of new technology.

Enterprise Imaging System

An enterprise imaging system (www.vogon-computer-evidence.com/enterprise.htm) is equipment designed specifically for the large-scale law enforcement organization tasked with evidential capture at the organizational level. It is highly configurable and modular. Storage capacities are virtually unlimited, and are scalable to meet the most demanding requirements.

Drive Image Pro 3.0

Drive Image Pro 3.0 is available from PowerQuest Corporation (800-379-2566, www.powerquest.com). Drive Image Pro 4.0 provides IT professionals with powerful cloning tools for fast, flawless system deployment, whether the need is to distribute a new operating system, update an application suite, or simply manage multiple workstation images.

EnCase 2.08

EnCase 2.08, from Guidance Software, Inc. (626-229-9191, www.guidancesoftware.com), features a graphical user interface that enables examiners to easily manage large volumes of computer evidence and view all relevant files, including "deleted" files, file slack, and unallocated data. The integrated functionality of EnCase allows the examiner to perform all functions of the computer forensic investigation process — the initial "previewing" of a target drive, the acquisition of the evidentiary images, the search and recovery of the data, and the final reporting of findings — within the same application.

Further, EnCase methodology allows the examiner to perform these processes in a noninvasive manner, meaning not one byte of data is changed on the original evidence.

FileCNVT

FileCNVT, a FileList conversion utility, is a forensic tool used to quickly catalog the contents of one or more computer hard disk drives. The FileList output is compressed so that the program and related output will normally fit on just one floppy diskette.

FileCNVT is used to convert the FileList output from its native compressed format into a database file. FileCNVT is a simple but specialized program that creates a dBASE III file from the output of the FileList program.

DM

DM, a database analysis tool, is easy to use and is compatible with the dBASE III file structure. This file format is an industry standard and can be imported into most other database file structures and spreadsheet applications. Unfortunately, the program is undocumented and some trial and error is required on the part of the user to use the program. The program has the capacity to sort and view up to 999,999 records.

Net Threat Analyzer

Net Threat Analyzer Internet threat identification software is software that was developed by NTI to assist law enforcement agencies in the identification of potential Internet-related threats to children. It is provided free of charge to law enforcement computer crime specialists and school police.

The software relies on computer artificial intelligence, fuzzy logic to identify patterns of text that may be tied to Internet transactions or file downloads from the Internet. Its features include:

- DOS-based for speed. The speed of operation and results are amazing. Can be operated from a single floppy diskette.
- Automatically identifies and processes the Windows swap file (when configured as a static file).
- Command line switches allow batch file operation of the program. Provides output in database format for easy analysis.
- Audible alert for identification of probable pornography.
- Options allow for automatic e-mail pattern identification and automatic Internet browsing identification.
- Options allow for automatic identification of file downloads made from the Internet.
- Automatically flags probable Internet-related communications involving pornography.
- Automatically flags probable Internet-related communications involving narcotics.
- Automatically flags probable Internet-related communications involving bomb-making.
- Automatically flags probable Internet-related communications involving sex crimes.
- Automatically flags probable Internet-related communications involving hate crimes.
- Provided free for legitimate law enforcement purposes.

ShowFL

ShowFL, a specialized computer timeline analysis tool, is ideal for the timeline analysis of computer usage. It is also helpful in the investigation of conspiracies when multiple computers and computer users are involved.

FILTER

FILTER, a binary data filtering tool, is used to remove binary (non-alphanumeric) characters from computer data. Once a file has been processed with this program, the contents can be printed and viewed with traditional computer applications (e.g., word processors).

This program is primarily a documentation tool and has limited features. However, it has proven to be a valuable tool in dealing with documentation issues tied to file slack, swap files, and evidence found in unallocated file space.

Spaces

Spaces is an encryption pattern review aid. This program is very simple. It creates one or more files that contain nothing but spaces. Every file created by this program will contain exactly 10,000 spaces. Files containing repeated patterns of the same data are helpful in evaluating the effectiveness of encryption.

This program aids in the evaluation of data distribution tied to encryption.

Additional Free Forensics Software Tools

Red Hat, Inc.

Red Hat, Inc. (800-454-5502, 919-547-0012, www.redhat.com) includes an MD5 mechanism to validate data. It writes images to hard drive, tape, and any other media available to the forensics platform.

The dd file utility is distributed with most versions of UNIX and Linux, is probably the most overlooked and underused imaging and copying utility, and is free. It was originally designed as a tool to copy, convert, and format text files in UNIX file systems, enabling a user to convert a file from the EBCDIC character set to the ASCII character set, from ASCII to EBCDIC, or from ASCII to alternate EBCDIC. The dd file utility can also change all lowercase letters in the file to uppercase or change all uppercase letters to lowercase.

Chapter 18

How to Report Internet-Related Crime

Internet-related crime, like any other crime, should be reported to appropriate law enforcement investigative authorities at the local, state, federal, or international levels, depending on the scope of the crime. Citizens who are aware of federal crimes should report them to local offices of federal law enforcement.

Some federal law enforcement agencies that investigate domestic crime on the Internet include the Federal Bureau of Investigation (FBI), the United States Secret Service, the United States Customs Service, the United States Postal Inspection Service, and the Bureau of Alcohol, Tobacco and Firearms (ATF). Each of these agencies has offices conveniently located in every state to which crimes may be reported. Contact information regarding these local offices can be found in local telephone directories. In general, a federal crime can be reported to the local office of an appropriate law enforcement agency by a telephone call and by requesting the "Duty Complaint Agent."

Each law enforcement agency also has a headquarters (HQ) in Washington, D.C., which has agents who specialize in particular areas. For example, the FBI and the U.S. Secret Service both have headquarters-based specialists in computer intrusion (i.e., computer hacker) cases. In fact, the FBI HQ hosts an interagency center, the National Infrastructure Protection Center (NIPC), created just to support investigations of computer intrusions. The NIPC Watch number for reporting computer crimes is 202-323-3205. The U.S. Secret Service's Electronic Crimes Branch can be contacted at 202-406-5850. The FBI and the Customs Service also have specialists in intellectual property crimes (i.e., copyright, software, movie, or recording piracy, trademark counterfeiting). Customs has a nationwide toll-free hotline for reporting at 800-BE-ALERT, or 800-232-2538.

The FBI generally investigates violations of federal criminal law. Certain law enforcement agencies focus on particular kinds of crime. Other federal agencies with investigative authority are the Federal Trade Commission and the U.S. Securities and Exchange Commission.

Exhibit 1.   Federal Investigative Law Enforcement Agencies

Type of Crime	Appropriate Federal Investigative Law Enforcement Agencies
Computer intrusion (i.e., hacking)	FBI local office; NIPC (202-323-3205); U.S. Secret Service local office
Password trafficking	FBI local office; NIPC (202-323-3205); U.S. Secret Service local office
Copyright (software, movie, sound recording) piracy	FBI local office; if imported, U.S. Customs Service local office (800-BE-ALERT, or 800-232-2538)
Theft of trade secrets	FBI local office
Trademark counterfeiting	FBI local office; if imported, U.S. Customs Service local office (800-BE-ALERT, or 800-232-2538)
Counterfeiting of currency	U.S. Secret Service local office; FBI local office
Child pornography or exploitation	FBI local office; if imported, U.S. Customs Service local office (800-BE-ALERT, or 800-232-2538)
Child exploitation and Internet fraud matters that have a mail nexus	U.S. Postal Inspection local office
Internet fraud	The Internet Fraud Complaint Center; FBI local office; U.S. Secret Service local office; Federal Trade Commission; if securities fraud, Securities and Exchange Commission
Internet harassment	FBI local office
Internet bomb threats	FBI local office; ATF local office
Trafficking in explosive or incendiary devices or firearms over the Internet	FBI local office; ATF local office

To determine some of the federal investigative law enforcement agencies that may be appropriate for reporting certain kinds of crime, refer to Exhibit 1.

The Internet Fraud Complaint Center (IFCC)

The IFCC is a partnership between the Federal Bureau of Investigation (FBI) and the National White Collar Crime Center (NW3C). Its Web site provides a mechanism for victims of Internet fraud to report online fraud to the appropriate law enforcement and regulatory authorities.

Chapter 19

Internet Security: An Auditor's Basic Checklist

Firewalls

- Does your company have a firewall? (If not, do not even think about getting on the Web until one is selected.)
- If it does, what kind is it? (Hardware based with software controls, or just software based)?
- Who administers it? (External company or your own personnel?)
- How is it administered? (Via software-based dialog, or physical reconfigurations?)
- Can it be administered remotely? (Possible security risk if administration inroad is not well secured)
- If it can be administered remotely, how is this done? (Dial-up direct, or via VPN or HTTPS page link?) Virtual private networking (VPN) is a very secure method for external access into your network. HTTPS is also a secure method. Make sure you have browsers with the high-level encryption capability on them. Internet Explorer or Netscape with the 128-bit encryption are standards of the industry. (Do a "Help," "About" on Internet Explorer to find out what cipher strength it is using. If it is an older version, it is probably a 56-bit one by default and should be upgraded.)
- Are dial-in lines for your employees available on the same network segment as the Internet? (Risky... someone could hack into your private network via the Internet if they can take over your Internet gateway server.)
- Is there only one primary corporate firewall? (Recent cases of bugs found in certain firewalls make it critical that firewall software be stringently monitored and security patches applied immediately.)
- Consider multi-level firewall protection. (Primary firewall with secondary firewalls on each desktop. This can also help prevent the accidental

propagation of scripting viruses because some firewalls, such as ZonaAlarm — see our Web site for the link — can intercept and quarantine harmful files like that.)

- Does the firewall(s) make the software ports on your network computers invisible on the Internet? If not, hackers will keep trying to ping known visible ports and attack them, possibly breaking in if the firewall is not secured against those types of attacks. A hacker cannot hack you if he cannot find you. Be careful in deciding which firewall to use. Some firewalls make great claims, but do not block all your ports from probes. One of the most effective is ZoneAlarm from ZoneLabs. Other good ones are BlackICE from NetworkICE, GuardDog by McAfee, and several Norton products.

- Do you allow Java applications or ActiveX controls to be enabled on your desktop Web clients? This poses a risk in that a poorly written ActiveX control could allow, via a bug and crash, a malicious program to get into that PC and do damage, or propagate to other machines. Java is a risk because it has the power to also move, delete, rename, and send back information to the requestor over the Internet.

- Do you block untrusted sites and domains on your firewall? Known hacker sites should be blocked so that people cannot download software that could be used against your corporate infrastructure. Other sites that are questionable might be put on the ban list. Domains from countries with a history of hacker activity might be desirable. Remember that this is your company network. You have the right to restrict access for business purposes. People can surf wherever they want at home with their own computers. You are not facilitating their recreational surfing.

- Do you block sites and domains with potentially illegal activities on them? Pornographic sites open the company to legal liability by not preventing the access of such material because the technology exists. There have been cases of people bringing up adult sites on corporate computers and having co-workers become offended. Many such cases result in harassment suits against the offending employee and the company. A zero-tolerance policy should be adopted for such sites. At some companies, if it is discovered that an employee has browsed to an adult site purposefully, it is grounds for immediate termination. Software such as Specter, or Netcop can be used to monitor browsing activity and evaluate a given employee's activities on the Web. These software tools can maintain logs. Sites that may not be currently blocked might be discovered and then blocked using this kind of software.

- Another thing you may want to consider blocking is the ability to do video streaming. Unless your company has a very high bandwidth network and Internet gateway, and very few users (that is, most companies will want to do this), blocking video streaming such as RealAudio files should be considered. The reason is not security, but rather capacity. You will quickly run out of bandwidth if you get a lot of folks suddenly trying to see the latest "Whazzup!" video clip from some server somewhere. A T1 line can bring data through at speeds up to 1.5 megabits per second, but that is quickly overtaken by streaming video on a group of systems. It will slow down your Internet access and your intra-network because the data eventually travels down over the same pipe to the desktop.

Supported Protocols

- Are protocols and ports that allow instant Web messaging disabled? (These pose a risk from the standpoint of unmonitored communications going out where corporate sensitive data could be easily given to people outside your firm. Even if the conversation is with someone the person knows, instant messaging is not a secure way to communicate because it is easily subject to eavesdropping. Some messaging clients also allow files to be transferred, which means corporate documents are not secured and documents with viruses in them could also be received via an unsecured gateway.)
- Are protocols allowing FTP (File Transfer Protocol) enabled without special precautions allowed? (These also need to be secured via the firewall and those with the need to FTP should do so via an isolated area that has extra security protection on it.)
- Do you have printer sharing or drive shares enabled, or peer-to-peer drive shares enabled on your computers? This kind of sharing of resources is fine if you are not connected to the Internet, but remember that you are opening the gateway to someone with a virus spreading it around quickly. Peer-to-peer networking should be disallowed because of the inherent problems with security (spoofing is made easier because it can appear as if someone running a program off a remotely shared computer is the computer owner's and not the real person on another computer). It is also a risk because if a hacker does make it to a machine that is hooked into other shares, they will have the same access to the other PC as someone using the share point legitimately.

Anti-Virus Updates

- Are your computers protected with a good anti-virus suite? Laptops are notorious for picking up viruses with people trading infected floppies around and the like. It is critical that all laptops, desktops, network servers, e-mail servers, and file servers be protected. More than that, it is absolutely critical that you stay on top of the virus signature updates. The mechanism to distribute these updates should be automatic and non-optional. (See Software Management Systems in the next section.)
- Make sure your network administrators and IS managers know what is in place with regard to anti-virus protection. Make sure that processes and procedures are in place and everyone in the firm is aware of who to contact in case of a virus emergency.
- Software downloads are difficult to restrict. People will need the ability to get to files on the Internet, so it is an area of exposure you should be aware of. You will want to make sure that there is an established policy regarding the installation of downloaded software on your company computers. People need to understand that in addition to licensing issues, the potential for introducing viruses this way is far greater than through a hacker's attack.

Software Management Systems

■ One of the things you need to consider when taking a company on the Internet is how you are going to protect your corporate assets. Protection from viruses, the ability to update Web browsers, and enabling the configuration and management of those browsers and the network are key points to watch out for. You want to make sure people can use the Internet safely, productively, and within the constraints of business purposes without them feeling like they are being too restricted. One of these tools is a software management system. The two most common are Microsoft Systems Management Software (SMS) and IBM's Tivoli product. Other utilities exist for UNIX/Linux-based systems as well. These software tools let you force the installation of software, including update patches, and are very valuable tools for the management of your computer assets. Careful planning and implementation of theses tools is critical for the safety and security of your corporate network.

■ Browser administration is also part of a complete software management plan. Browsers can normally be configured by a master copy and distributed after being set with the right settings. The trick is to make sure that your users do not change the critical settings once their desktop receives the software. One such tool is Microsoft's Internet Explorer Administration Kit. It lets you customize what proxy servers you will let people go through, what kinds of things they can and cannot do (such as shutting off their ability to enable Java applications), and even letting you put your company name in the title bar of the Web browser. Once administered with a tool like this, the configuration can be "locked down" and the settings cannot be changed without administrative authority.

Backup Processes and Procedures

■ Your company should make sure that backups are available of any browser configuration, firewall, and network settings. Either an electronic backup or a written backup should be used, depending on the nature of the information. Make sure the people responsible for emergency response know where this information and backups are kept.

Intra-Network Security

■ You may be wondering why this needs to be mentioned when getting on the Internet in your firm. Consider the Internet as a wide-area extension of your local company network. Once some Web site can see your company's computers, you run the risk of being hacked. One of the often-overlooked hacks is in intra-network security. Routers that direct traffic between areas of your company must be properly secured against remote administration without due authority. Make sure that passwords used are not easily guessed. Each router can be programmed with administrative security. Once configured, they normally do not need to be touched. If they have to be rebooted, a saved profile can be reloaded. The only time administration needs to be done to these routers is if the network needs to be reconfigured for growth. Routers, switches, bridges, servers, and hubs are all part of your network and need to be secured from unauthorized tampering. This security should be both physical and under software control. Make sure that wiring closets are kept locked and keys have limited distribution. Make sure that people doing the router configurations and server setups take security seriously. Your corporate data is on the line.

- Logging is also critical. Event logs should be maintained for all servers. Firewall security should be set to log all breach attempts. These logs will become critical if you need to prosecute a hacker. Make sure you are ready before you need it. It does no good to start taking log administration seriously only after a system is hacked. These electronic logs should be included in your daily backups and archived. Sometimes, hackers are not discovered until well after damage is done. You may need to go back in time to find the start of activity.

APPENDICES

Appendix A: Glossary of Terms

Absent Character: A character or character combination which is present in one body of writing but is not present (e.g., does not have a corresponding character) in another body of writing. *Character*: Any letter, numeral, punctuation mark, symbol, or ornament.

Accreditation: A program whereby a laboratory demonstrates that it is operating under accepted standards to ensure quality assurance.

Acquisition of Digital Evidence: Begins when information or physical items are collected or stored for examination purposes. The term "evidence" implies that the collector of evidence is recognized by the courts. The process of collecting is also assumed to be a legal process and appropriate for rules of evidence in that locality. A data object or physical item only becomes evidence when so deemed by a law enforcement official or designee.

ASCLD-LAB: The American Society of Crime Laboratory Directors-Laboratory Accreditation Board.

Ambient Data: Ambient data is a forensic term that describes, in general terms, data stored in non-traditional computer storage areas and formats. The term was coined in 1996 by NTI to help students understand NTI's computer evidence processing techniques that deal with evidence stored in other than standard computer files, formats, and storage areas. The term is now widely used in the computer forensics community and it generally describes data stored in the Windows swap file, unallocated space, and file slack.

Archive: After processing discovery materials, an archive is created for each case. Viruses found in processing are removed (a clean archive), program-related files are removed (per instruction — a purged archive), erased files are analyzed and recovered if possible, slack space is checked, files are grouped according to file classes, and metadata is added to the database.

Backup and Recovery: The ability to recreate current master files using appropriate prior master records and transactions.

Biological Evidence: Any type of biological fluid, including blood, urine, semen, feces, tissue, decomposition fluid, saliva, tears, mucus, perspiration, vomitus, and pus.

BIOS: Every computer has one. It is the part of the operating system that controls the basic functions of the computer. The BIOS is configured at the time the computer is assembled at the factory (although there are ways to update it). It stores the date, time, and configuration of the hardware. It is important to access the BIOS without impacting the hard drives.

Bookmark: *(v)* To mark a document or a specific place in a document for later retrieval. Nearly all Web browsers support a bookmarking feature that lets you save the address (URL) of a Web page so that you can easily revisit the page at a later time. *(n)* A marker or address that identifies a document or a specific place in a document.

Browser: Short for *Web browser,* a software application used to locate and display Web pages. The two most popular browsers are Netscape Navigator and Microsoft Internet Explorer. Both of these are *graphical browsers,* which means that they can display graphics as well as text. In addition, most modern browsers can present multimedia information, including sound and video, although they require plug-ins for some formats.

Buffer: *(n)* A temporary storage area, usually in RAM. The purpose of most buffers is to act as a holding area, enabling the CPU to manipulate data before transferring it to a device. Because the processes of reading and writing data to a disk are relatively slow, many programs keep track of data changes in a buffer and then copy the buffer to a disk.

For example, word processors employ a buffer to keep track of changes to files. Then when you *save* the file, the word processor updates the disk file with the contents of the buffer. This is much more efficient than accessing the file on the disk each time you make a change to the file. Note that because your changes are initially stored in a buffer, not on the disk, all of them will be lost if the computer fails during an editing session. For this reason, it is a good idea to save your file periodically. Most word processors automatically save files at regular intervals.

Another common use of buffers is for printing documents. When you enter a print command, the operating system copies your document to a print buffer (a free area in memory or on a disk) from which the printer can draw characters at its own pace. This frees the computer to perform other tasks while the printer is running in the background. Print buffering is called *spooling*.

Most keyboard drivers also contain a buffer so that you can edit typing mistakes before sending your command to a program. Many operating systems, including DOS, also use a *disk buffer* to temporarily hold data that they have read from a disk. The disk buffer is really a cache.

Burn Box: A device used to destroy computer data, it is usually a box with magnets or electrical current that will degauss disks and tapes.

Cache: Pronounced *cash*, a special high-speed storage mechanism. It can be either a reserved section of main memory or an independent high-speed storage device. Two types of caching are commonly used in personal computers: *memory caching* and *disk caching*. A memory cache, sometimes called a *cache store* or *RAM cache*, is a portion of memory made of high-speed static RAM (SRAM) instead of the slower and cheaper dynamic RAM (DRAM) used for main memory. Memory caching is effective because most programs access the same data or instructions repeatedly. By keeping as much of this information as possible in SRAM, the computer avoids accessing the slower DRAM.

Disk caching works under the same principle as memory caching, but instead of using high-speed SRAM, a disk cache uses conventional main memory. The most recently accessed data from the disk (as well as adjacent sectors) is stored in a memory buffer. When a program needs to access data from the disk, it first checks the disk cache to see if the data is there. Disk caching can dramatically improve the performance of applications, because accessing a byte of data in RAM can be thousands of times faster than accessing a byte on a hard disk. When data is found in the cache, it is called a *cache hit*, and the effectiveness of a cache is judged by its *hit rate*.

Chain of Custody: The identity of persons who handle evidence between the time of commission of the alleged offense and the ultimate disposition of the case. It is the responsibility of each transferee to ensure that the items are accounted for during the time that it is in his or her possession, that it is properly protected, and that there is a record of the names of the persons from whom they received it and to whom they delivered it, together with the time and date of such receipt and delivery.

Chain of Evidence: The "sequencing" of the chain of evidence follows this order:

- Collection and identification
- Analysis
- Storage
- Preservation
- Transportation
- Presentation in court
- Return to owner

The chain of evidence shows:

- Who obtained the evidence
- Where and when the evidence was obtained
- Who secured the evidence
- Who had control or possession of the evidence

Character: Any letter, numeral, punctuation mark, symbol, or ornament.

Characteristic: A feature, quality, attribute, or property of writing.

Check Digit: One digit, usually the last, of an identifying field is a mathematical function of all of the other digits in the field. This value can be calculated from the other digits in the field and compared with the check digit to verify the validity of the whole field.

Cloning: The term given to the operation of creating an exact duplicate of one media on another like media. This is also referred to as a *mirror image* or *physical sector copy*.

Clusters: All Microsoft operating systems rely on the storage of data in fixed-length blocks of bytes called clusters. The size of these blocks depends on the type of storage device and the size of the storage device. For Microsoft DOS, Windows, Windows 95, and Windows 98, a File Location Table (FAT) is used to track which clusters have been allocated to a specific file.

Comparability: The questioned writing and known writing embody the same type of writing and character or character combinations. Other issues of comparability might include, but are not limited to, the contemporaneousness of the questioned writing and the known writing, different writing instruments, and document format.

Computer Evidence: Computer evidence is a copy of a document stored in a computer file that is identical to the original. The legal "best evidence" rules change when it comes to the processing of computer evidence. Another unique aspect of computer evidence is the potential for unauthorized copies to be made of important computer files without leaving behind a trace that the copy was made. This situation creates problems concerning the investigation of the theft of trade secrets (e.g., client lists, research materials, computer-aided design files, formulas, and proprietary software).

Computer Forensics: The term "computer forensics" was coined in 1991 in the first training session held by the International Association of Computer Specialists (IACIS) in Portland, Oregon. Since then, computer forensics has become a popular topic in computer security circles and in the legal community. Like any other forensic science, computer forensics deals with the application of law to a science. In this case, the science involved is computer science and some refer to it as forensic computer science. Computer forensics has also been described as the autopsy of a computer hard disk drive because specialized software tools and techniques are required to analyze the various levels at which computer data is stored after the fact.

Computer Forensics deals with the preservation, identification, extraction, and documentation of computer evidence. The field is relatively new to the private sector but it has been the mainstay of technology-related investigations and intelligence gathering in law enforcement and military agencies since the mid-1980s. Like any other forensic science, computer forensics involves the use of sophisticated technology tools and procedures that must be followed to guarantee the accuracy of the preservation of evidence and the accuracy of results concerning computer evidence processing. Typically, computer forensic tools exist in the form of computer software.

Cookie: A message given to a Web browser by a Web server. The browser stores the message in a text file called *cookie.txt*. The message is then sent back to the server each time the browser requests a page from the server. The main purpose of cookies is to identify users and possibly prepare customized Web pages for them. When you enter a Web site using cookies, you may be asked to fill out a form providing such information as your name and interests.

This information is packaged into a cookie and sent to your Web browser, which stores it for later use. The next time you go to the same Web site, your browser will send the cookie to the Web server. The server can use this information to present you with custom Web pages. So, for example, instead of seeing just a generic welcome page, you might see a welcome page with your name on it. The term "cookie" derives from UNIX objects called *magic cookies*. These are tokens that are attached to a user or program and change, depending on the areas entered by the user or program. Cookies are also sometimes called *persistent cookies* because they typically stay in the browser for long periods of time.

Copy: An accurate reproduction of information contained on an original physical item, independent of the original physical item.

Cryptography: The art of protecting information by transforming it (*encrypting* it) into an unreadable format, called ciphertext. Only those who possess a secret *key* can decipher (or *decrypt*) the message into plaintext. Encrypted messages can sometimes be broken by cryptanalysis, also called *code breaking*, although modern cryptography techniques are virtually unbreakable.

Data Analysis: Provides access to tools allowing users to perform sophisticated data analyses of both native data content and metadata. Features include: (1) basic keyword and Boolean search functionality; (2) natural language and search query support; (3) fuzzy logic and thesaurus-based search; and (4) advanced data mining capabilities such as artificial intelligence, neural-network, and thematic data mapping search.

Database: A collection of common data maintained in a "common" area; accessible by one or more systems or users.

Data Definition Language (DDL): A data definition language (DDL) is used to describe the structure of a database.

Data Diagram: Data diagrams detail the relationships and interdependencies of the data elements. Data diagrams may look like very confusing flowcharts, but they are used by the designers and architects to determine what data is used where and how often.

Data Flow Diagram (DFD): DFDs are used to represent a flow of data. The objective of a data flow-oriented design is to transform information flow obtained from information domain analysis into a program structure.

Data Integrity: Refers to the validity of data. Data integrity can be compromised in a number of ways, including:

- Human errors when data is entered
- Errors that occur when data is transmitted from one computer to another
- Software bugs or viruses
- Hardware malfunctions, such as disk crashes
- Natural disasters, such as fires and floods

There are many ways to minimize these threats to data integrity, including:

- Backing up data on a regular basis
- Controlling access to data via security mechanisms
- Designing user interfaces that prevent the input of invalid data
- Using error detection and correction software when transmitting data

Data Mapping: Going beyond basic search capabilities, data mapping is also called *keyless searching*. It finds or suggests associations between files within a large body of data, which may not be apparent using other techniques.

Data Manipulation Language (DML): A data manipulation language (DML) provides the necessary commands for all database operations, including storing, retrieving, updating, and deleting database records.

Data Objects: Objects or information of potential probative value that are associated with physical items. Data objects may occur in different formats without altering the original information.

Data Structures: The logical relationships among data units and description of attributes or features of a piece of data (e.g., type, length).

Data Transfer Rate: The data transfer rate indicates how fast the data must be moved into or out of the system. It also deals with whether the data transfer is done using parallel or serial transmission or analog/digital signal.

Data Utilization and Knowledge Application: At a basic level, provides the ability to retrieve, view, display, and print relevant information. At an advanced level, provides the ability to add value to discovery information in the form of annotations, links, and coding. Additional features include automatic pagination and automatic document numbering.

Digital Evidence: Information of probative value stored or transmitted in digital form.

Discrepancy Reports: A listing of items that have violated some detective control and require further investigation.

Dissimilarity: A characteristic not in common between two or more handwritten items but which may fall within the range of variation of the writer.

Disk Caching: *See* Cache.

Disk Duplexing: This refers to the use of two controllers to drive a disk subsystem. Should one of the controllers fail, the other is still available for disk I/O. Software applications can take advantage of both controllers to simultaneously read and write to different drives.

Disk Mirroring: Disk mirroring protects data against hardware failure. In its simplest form, a two-disk subsystem would be attached to a host controller. One disk serves as the mirror image of the other. When data is written to it, it is also written to the other. Both disks will contain exactly the same information. If one fails, the other can supply the data to the user without problem.

Distorted Writing: Writing that does not appear to reflect normal writing habits, either intentionally (e.g., disguise, simulation) or unintentionally (e.g., physical condition of the writer, writing conditions).

Document(s): In its fullest meaning, any material that contains marks, symbols, or signs either visible, partially visible, or invisible that may ultimately convey a meaning or message to someone. Pencil or ink writing, typewriting, or printing on paper are the more usual forms of documents.

Duplicate Digital Evidence: An accurate digital reproduction of all data objects contained on an original physical item.

Dynamic Link Library (DLL): Dynamic Link Library, a dynamically loaded runtime library.

Dynamic RAM (DRAM): *See* RAM

Electronic Data Vaulting: Electronic vaulting protects information from loss by providing automatic and transparent backup of valuable data over high-speed phone lines to a secure facility.

Elimination: A definite conclusion that two or more handwritten items were not written by the same person.

Expiration: A limit check based on a comparison of current date with the date recorded on a transaction, record, or file.

External Cache Memory: *Internal caches* are often called *Level 1 (L1) caches*. Most modern PCs also come with *external cache memory*, called *Level 2 (L2) cache*. These caches sit between the CPU and the DRAM. Like L1 caches, L2 caches are composed of SRAM but are much larger.

Extrinsic Data: Information about the file such as file signature, author, size, name, path, and creation and modification dates. This data is the accumulation of what is in the file, on the media label, discovered by the operator, and contributed by the user. Collectively, it represents the real value of examining an electronic file as opposed to its printed version.

File Allocation Table (FAT): All Microsoft operating systems rely on the storage of data in fixed-length blocks of bytes called clusters. The size of these blocks depends on the type of storage device and the size of the storage device. For Microsoft DOS, Windows, Windows 95, and Windows 98, a File Location Table (FAT) is used to track which clusters have been allocated to a specific file. The FAT is relied upon by the operating system much like a road map to locate the data associated with a specific file. References in the FAT act as pointers and they point to clusters by numeric reference. The top four bits of the cluster number in FAT 32 are reserved and are not available for cluster enumeration.

Thus, FAT 32 systems can have at most $2^{**}28 - 1$ or 268,435,455 clusters. The same rule of thumb applies for FAT 12 and FAT 16 systems. FAT 12 systems can have up to 4079 clusters and FAT 16 systems can have up to 65,519 clusters. The four reserved bits are reserved to identify values meaning things like "empty," "bad sector," and "End of file" in the referenced cluster.

The FAT on a floppy diskette will typically rely on 12-bit numbers (FAT 12). When hard disk drives are involved, Microsoft Windows and Windows 95a rely upon a 16-bit FAT. Microsoft Windows 95b and Windows 98 were designed to deal with more data and huge hard disk drives. The FAT on these newer operating systems relies on 32-bit numbers.

File Analysis: Examines each discovered digital file and creates a database record of file-related information (*metadata*, or data about the data) consisting of, among other things, file signature (indicating true file type), author, size, name, and path, as well as creation, access, and modification dates.

File Conversion: Converts digital files into formats that users can analyze, retrieve, view, and share. Designed to convert a growing number of legacy and modern file classes, including e-mail, text, spreadsheet, graphic, map, presentation, audio, and video.

File Inventory: Provide clients with a detailed inventory of discovered digital data files, including the number of files by class (e.g., e-mail, word processing, spreadsheet, presentation, graphic, etc.) and type (e.g., Word, WordPerfect, Excel, Lotus 123, PowerPoint, etc.).

File Maintenance Activity: The activity of keeping a file up-to-date by adding, changing, or deleting data.

File Signature: Within the file, the file signature is the information about the true program-related origin of the file and, therefore, its type. Tools for reading file signatures identify the true program source even if the file extension has been changed.

File Slack: Files are created in varying lengths depending on their contents. DOS-, Windows-, and Windows NT-based computers store files in fixed-length blocks of data called clusters. Rarely do file sizes exactly match the size of one or multiple clusters. The data storage space that exists from the end of the file to the end of the last cluster assigned to the file is called "file slack."

Cluster sizes vary in length depending on the operating system involved and, in the case of Windows 95, the size of the logical partition involved. Larger cluster sizes mean more file slack and also the waste of storage space when Windows 95 systems are involved. However, this computer security weakness creates benefits for the computer forensics investigator because file slack is a significant source of evidence and leads.

File slack potentially contains randomly selected bytes of data from computer memory. This happens because DOS/Windows normally writes in 512-byte blocks called sectors. Clusters are made up of blocks of sectors. If there is not enough data in the file to fill the last sector in a file, DOS/Windows makes up the difference by padding the remaining space with data from the memory buffers of the operating system.

This randomly selected data from memory is called RAM slack because it comes from the memory of the computer. RAM slack can contain any information that may have been created, viewed, modified, downloaded, or copied during work sessions that have occurred since the computer was last booted. Thus, if the computer has not been shut down for several days, the data stored in file slack can come from work sessions that occurred in the past.

Firewall: A system designed to prevent unauthorized access to or from a private network. Firewalls can be implemented in both hardware and software, or a combination of both. Firewalls are frequently used to prevent unauthorized Internet users from accessing private networks connected to the Internet, especially *intranets.* All messages entering or leaving the intranet pass through the firewall, which examines each message and blocks those that do not meet the specified security criteria. There are several firewall techniques, including:

- **Packet filter:** Looks at each packet entering or leaving the network and accepts or rejects it based on user-defined rules. Packet filtering is fairly effective and transparent to users, but it is difficult to configure. In addition, it is susceptible to IP spoofing.
- **Application gateway:** Applies security mechanisms to specific applications, such as FTP and Telnet servers. This is very effective, but can impose performance degradation.
- **Circuit-level gateway:** Applies security mechanisms when a TCP or UDP connection is established. Once the connection has been made, packets can flow between the hosts without further checking.
- **Proxy server:** Intercepts all messages entering and leaving the network. The proxy server effectively hides the true network addresses.

In practice, many firewalls use two or more of these techniques in concert. A firewall is considered a first line of defense in protecting private information. For greater security, data can be encrypted.

Forensic Computing: The science of extracting data so that it can be presented as evidence in a court of law.

Forensic Document Examiner: The definition of a forensic document examiner is currently under development by the SWGDOC Training and Qualifications Subcommittee.

Free Space: Space on storage media that appears to contain no data, either because it is unused or because files that were intact and accessible at one time are now erased. The file data remains in the slack space until overwritten.

GOTS: Government-Off-the-Shelf (often used in reference to software).

Ghosting or Ghost Imaging: Ghost imaging, using ghosting software, is a method of converting the contents of a hard drive — including its configuration settings and applications — into an image, and then storing the image on a server or burning it onto a CD.

When contents of the hard drive are needed again, ghosting software converts the image back to original form.

Companies use ghost imaging when they want to create identical configurations and install the same software on numerous machines. For example, if a company needs to dole out 100 laptops to its employees, then instead of manually setting configurations and installing applications on each machine, ghosting software (usually contained on a floppy) will retrieve the ghost image from the server, convert it into its original form, and copy it onto the laptop.

Graphical User Interface (GUI): A graphical user interface uses graphics such as a window, box, and menu to allow the user to communicate with the system. Allows users to move in and out of programs and manipulate their commands by using a pointing device (usually a mouse). Synonymous with user interface.

Handwritten Item: An item containing something written by hand (e.g., cursive writing, hand printing, signatures).

Hash Total: A meaningless, but useful, total developed from the accumulated numerical amounts of nonmonetary information.

Hidden File: A file with a special *hidden attribute* turned on, so that the file is not normally visible to users. For example, hidden files are not listed when you execute the DOS DIR command. However, most file management utilities allow you to view hidden files.

DOS hides some files, such as MSDOS.SYS and IO.SYS, so that you will not accidentally corrupt them. You can also turn on the hidden attribute for any normal file, thereby making it invisible to casual snoopers. On a Macintosh, you can hide files with the ResEdit utility.

Hierarchical Database: In a hierarchical database, data is organized like a family tree or organization chart with branches of parent records and child records.

Highly Probable Did: A qualified opinion in which the evidence supports, with virtual certainty, that two or more handwritten items were written by the same person.

Highly Probable Did Not: A qualified opinion in which the evidence supports, with virtual certainty, that two or more handwritten items were not written by the same person.

History Buffer: The history buffer is dynamically allocated storage space that is used to accumulate history file data fields.

HWCI: Hardware Configuration Item.

Identification: A definite conclusion that two or more handwritten items were written by the same person.

Identifying Characteristics: Marks or properties that serve to individualize writing (e.g., formations, relative sizes and heights of letters).

Image: Sometimes called "mirror," a bit-by-bit copy of media. Images pick up the spaces at the end of files, deleted and not overwritten files, and hidden partitions. Sometimes called a *physical backup.*

Indications Did: A qualified opinion in which the evidence suggests that two or more handwritten items may have been written by the same person.

Indications Did Not: A qualified opinion in which the evidence suggests that two or more handwritten items may not have been written by the same person.

Imaging: The term given to creating a physical sector copy of a disk and compressing this image in the form of a file. This image file can then be stored on dissimilar media for archiving or later restoration.

Independence: Not influenced or controlled by others.

Internal Cache Memory: *Internal caches* are often called *Level 1 (L1) caches.* Most modern PCs also come with external cache memory, called *Level 2 (L2) cache.* These caches sit between the CPU and the DRAM. Like L1 caches, L2 caches are composed of SRAM but they are much larger.

Inspection: A visual examination to detect errors and standards violations in requirements, design, code, user documentation, test plans and cases, and other software development products.

Integrity: *See also* Data Integrity. A security service that allows verification that an unauthorized modification (including changes, insertions, deletions, and duplications) has not occurred either maliciously or accidentally.

Interface: The boundary between two programs, two pieces of hardware, or a computer and its user.

Item: An object or quantity of material on which a set of observations can be made.

Known: Of established origin.

Latent Prints: The most common type of biological contamination the document examiner will encounter, latent prints are composed of skin secretions and pose no safety hazard.

Memory Caching: *See* Cache.

Metadata: Electronic information about a file that travels with the electronic file (file properties and Microsoft software and OS metadata).

Mirror Image Backup: Mirror image backups (also referred to as *bit-stream backups*) involve the backup of all areas of a computer hard disk drive or another type of storage media (e.g., Zip disks, floppy disks, Jaz disks, etc.). Such mirror image backups exactly replicate all sectors on a given storage device. Thus, all files and ambient data storage areas are copied. Such backups are sometimes referred to as evidence-grade backups and they differ substantially from standard file backups and network server backups.

The making of a mirror image backup is simple in theory, but the accuracy of the backup must meet evidence standards. Accuracy is essential and to guarantee accuracy, mirror image backup programs typically rely on mathematical CRC computations in the validation process. These mathematical validation processes compare the original source data with the restored data. When computer evidence is involved, accuracy is extremely important and the making of a mirror image backup is typically described as the preservation of the "electronic crime scene."

Natural Writing: Any specimen of writing executed normally without an attempt to control or alter its usual quality of execution.

No Conclusion: No determination can be made if two or more handwritten items were written by the same person.

On-line System: Applications that allow direct interaction of the user with the computer (CPU) via a CRT, thus enabling the user to receive back an immediate response to data entered (e.g., an airline reservation system).

Original Digital Evidence: Physical items and the data objects associated with such items at the time of acquisition or seizure.

Overflow Checks: A limit check based on the capacity of a memory or file area to accept data.

Parallel Port: The computer's printer port, which in a pinch allows user access to notebooks and computers that cannot be opened.

Peer Review: Review by a peer of notes, data, and other documents that form the basis for a scientific conclusion.

Physical Items: Items on which data objects or information may be stored or through which data objects are transferred.

Platform: Foundation upon which processes and systems are built, which can include hardware, software, firmware, etc.

Probably Did: A qualified opinion in which the evidence points rather strongly toward two or more handwritten items as having been written by the same person; however, this opinion falls short of the virtually certain degree of confidence.

Probably Did Not: A qualified opinion in which the evidence points rather strongly against two or more handwritten items as having been written by the same person; however, this opinion falls short of the virtually certain degree of confidence.

Proficiency Tests: Tests to evaluate the competence of analysts and the quality performance of a laboratory. In open tests, the analysts are aware they are being tested. In blind tests, they are unaware they are being tested. Internal proficiency tests are conducted by the laboratory. External proficiency tests are conducted by an agency independent of the laboratory being tested.

Quality Assurance: Those planned and systematic actions necessary to provide sufficient confidence that a laboratory's product or service will satisfy given requirements for quality.

Quality Control: Internal activities or activities according to externally established standards used to monitor the quality of analytical data and to ensure that it satisfies specified criteria.

Questioned: Of disputed or uncertain origin.

Range of Variation: The combination of all occurrences of all characteristics found in a body of writing.

RAID: RAID is the acronym for "Redundant Array of Inexpensive Disks" Instead of using one large disk to store data, you use many smaller disks (because they are cheaper). *See* Disk Mirroring and Duplexing. An approach to using many low-cost drives as a group to improve performance, yet also provides a degree of redundancy that makes the chance of data loss remote.

RAM: An acronym for *random access memory*, a type of computer memory that can be randomly accessed; that is, any byte of memory can be accessed without touching the preceding bytes. RAM is the most common type of memory found in computers and other devices, such as printers.

There are two basic types of RAM: dynamic RAM (DRAM) and static RAM (SRAM). The two types differ in the technology they use to hold data, dynamic RAM being the more common type. Dynamic RAM needs to be refreshed thousands of times per second. Static RAM does not need to be refreshed, which makes it faster; but it is also more expensive than dynamic RAM. Both types of RAM are *volatile,* meaning that they lose their contents when the power is turned off.

In common usage, the term "RAM" is synonymous with *main memory,* the memory available to programs. For example, a computer with 8M RAM has approximately eight million bytes of memory that programs can use. In contrast, *ROM (read-only memory)* refers to special memory used to store programs that boot the computer and perform diagnostics. Most personal computers have a small amount of ROM (a few thousand bytes). In fact, both types of memory (ROM and RAM) allow random access. To be precise, therefore, RAM should be referred to as *read/write RAM* and ROM as *read-only RAM.*

Reconciliation: An identification and analysis of differences between the values contained in two substantially identical files, or between a detail file and a control total. Errors are identified according to the nature of the reconciling items rather than the existence of a difference between the balances.

Relational Database: In a relational database, data is organized in two-dimensional tables or relations.

Response time: The length of time it takes for the time-sharing device to respond to a user's request. For example, the time it takes an application to respond to a query or command via a GUI menu or screen. The ability of a system or component to respond to an inquiry or demand within a prescribed time frame.

Resolution: The quantity and quality of the detail that can be observed.

Sectors: Sectors are created and mapped when the computer storage device is low-level formatted. For modern computer hard disk drives, the manufacturer of the hard disk drive usually performs low-level formats at the factory. Computer specialists can also obtain special low-level format utilities, but they typically are tied to a specific hard drive brand and model. During the low-level format, sectors are created and are written consecutively to disk on tracks. As the sector is created and written to disk, the storage media is verified for accuracy.

The verification process involves writing 512 bytes (4096 bits) of data to disk. The data written is usually uniform and it is referred to as a format pattern. After the data is written, the write process is validated by comparing what is read back from disk with what was supposed to have been written. This comparison is done at the bit level. Bad sectors (those that do not pass the validation test) are noted as being unreliable and they are mapped by the hard disk controller so that attempts will not be made to write data to them in the future.

Clusters are defined during the high-level format, which is performed by the operating system. When floppy diskettes are involved, the low-level format and the high-level format take place at the same time and they are performed by the operating system.

If a bad sector is found during the high-level format, the entire cluster will be marked as bad by the operating system in the File Allocation Table (FAT). However, from a computer forensics standpoint, you should be aware that data could be stored in clusters that have been marked as bad.

Security Policy: What security means to the user; a statement of what is meant when claims of security are made. More formally, it is the set of rules and conditions governing the access and use of information. Typically, a security policy will refer to the conventional security services, such as confidentiality, integrity, availability, etc. and perhaps their underlying mechanisms and functions.

Sensitive Data: Data that is considered confidential or proprietary. The kind of data that if disclosed to a competitor might give away an advantage.

Sequence Checking: A verification of the alphanumeric sequence of the "key" field in items to be processed.

Sequential Module: Pertains to modules that must be constructed or performed in a given sequence.

Significant Dissimilarity: A repeated identifying characteristic that varies between two or more handwritten items and that is outside the range of variation of the writer.

Significant Similarity: An identifying characteristic in common between two or more handwritten items.

Similarity: A characteristic in common between two or more handwritten items.

Static RAM (SRAM): *See* RAM.

Sufficient Quantity: That amount of writing required to assess the writer's range of variation, on the basis of the content of the questioned writing.

System: A series of related procedures designed to perform a specific task.

Systems Flowchart: A series of symbols designed to graphically illustrate the procedural steps in a system.

SWAP: An area operating systems such as Windows uses to increase its RAM memory by writing to the disk "temporarily." Like other deleted files, the SWAP remains until overwritten. This is a great source of online e-mail, passwords, pre-encrypted files, and chat.

Technical Review: *See* Peer Review.

Timeline: The linear representation of project tasks based on calendar measurement. The timeline can be represented in days, weeks, months, quarters, or years.

Trace Evidence: Any type of nonbiological evidence that may adhere to the document surface, such as hair, fibers, soil, glue, or paint.

Transaction: A transaction is an activity or request to a computer. Purchase orders, changes, additions, and deletions are examples of transactions that are recorded in a business information environment.

Transaction Serializability: The requirement that whenever a series of transactions overlap one another in time, their effect on the database and their environment must be the same as it would have been if they had been executed one after the other in the sequence in which they were initiated.

Transaction Trail: The availability of a manual or machine-readable means for tracing the status and contents of an individual transaction record backward or forward, between output, processing, and source.

Transcription: The subsequent transcription of data from one medium to another; similar to recording.

Transmit: Data must be transmitted to the computer facility before it can be processed. This transmission could take many forms — by communication network, by mails, by internal mail, or by hand. Once received by the computer facility, movement takes place between the control group and other phases of the operation — keypunch, key verify, computer operations, library, output handling, etc. There is always an exposure to loss of data or insertion of improper data during the transmit stage.

Type of Writing: Refers to handprinting, cursive writing, numerals, or combinations thereof, and signatures.

Unallocated Storage Space: When files are erased or deleted in DOS, Windows, Windows 95, Windows 98, and Windows NT, the content of the file is not actually erased. Unless security-grade file deletion software is used, such as NTI's M-Sweep or DiskScrub, data from the "erased file" remains behind in an area called unallocated storage space. The same is true concerning file slack that may have been attached to the file before it was deleted. As a result, the data remains behind for discovery through the use of data recovery or computer forensics software utilities.

URL: *Uniform Resource Locator*, the global address of documents and other resources on the World Wide Web.

The first part of the address indicates what protocol to use, and the second part specifies the IP address or the domain name where the resource is located. For example, the two URLs below point to two different files at the domain *pcwebopedia.com*. The first specifies an executable file that should be fetched using FTP; the second specifies a Web page that should be fetched using HTTP.

Validity Check: The characters in a coded field are either matched to an acceptable set of values in a table or examined for a designed pattern or format, legitimate subcodes, or character values, using logic and arithmetic rather than tables.

Variation: The combination of all occurrences of the same characteristic found in a body of writing.

Web Browser: *See* Browser.

Web Server: A computer that delivers (*serves up*) Web pages. Every Web server has an IP address and possibly a domain name. For example, if you enter the URL *http://www.pcwebopedia.com/index.html* in your browser, this sends a request to the server whose domain name is *pcwebopedia.com*. The server then fetches the page named *index.html* and sends it to your browser.

Any computer can be turned into a Web server by installing server software and connecting the machine to the Internet. There are many Web server software applications, including public domain software from NCSA and Apache, and commercial packages from Microsoft, Netscape, and others.

Windows Swap File: Microsoft Windows-based computer operating systems utilize a special file as a "scratch pad" to write data when additional random access
memory is needed. In Windows, Windows 95, and Windows 98, these are called
Windows Swap Files. In Windows NT and Windows 2000, they are called Windows
Page Files and have essentially the same characteristics as Windows Swap Files.

Swap files are potentially huge and most computer users are unaware of their
existence. The size of these files can range from 20 million bytes to over 200
million bytes, and the potential exists for these huge files to contain remnants of
word processing, e-mail messages, Internet browsing activity, database entries,
and almost any other work that may have occurred during past Windows work
sessions. This situation creates a significant security problem because the potential
exists for data to be transparently stored within the Windows Swap File without
the knowledge of the computer user. This can occur even if the work product
was stored on a computer network server. The result is a significant computer
security weakness that can be of benefit to the computer forensics specialist.
Windows Swap Files can actually provide the computer forensics specialist with
investigative leads that might not otherwise be discovered.

Windows Swap Files are relied upon by Windows, Windows 95, and Windows
98 to create "virtual memory;" that is, using a portion of the hard disk drive for
memory operations.

Wipe: Slang term for deliberately overwriting a piece of media and removing any
trace of files or file fragments. (*Also called* Nuked)

Appendix B

Recommended Reading List

Books

Forensics

1. *Forensic Computing: A Practitioner's Guide (Practitioner Series)*, First Edition, Tony Sammes, A. J. Sammes, and Brian Jenkinson, Springer-Verlag, October 2000
2. *The Casebook of Forensic Detection: How Science Solved 100 of the World's Most Baffling Crimes*, Colin Evans, John Wiley & Sons, October 1998
3. *Criminal Profiling: An Introduction to Behavioral Evidence Analysis*, Brent E. Turvey, Ed., Academic Press, June 1999
4. *Digital Evidence and Computer Crime: Forensic Science, Computers, and the Internet*, Eoghan Casey, Academic Press, March 2000
5. *Criminalistics: An Introduction to Forensic Science*, Seventh Edition, Richard Saferstein, Prentice-Hall, July 2000
6. *Criminal Investigation*, Seventh Edition, Charles R. Swanson, Neil C. Chamelin, and Leonard Territo, McGraw-Hill, August 1999
7. *Investigating Computer-Related Crime: A Handbook for Corporate Investigators*, Peter Stephenson, CRC Press, September 1999
8. *Secret Software: Making the Most of Computer Resources for Data Protection, Information Recovery, Forensic Examination, Crime Investigation and More*, Norbert Zaenglein, Paladin Press, July 2000
9. *Disk Detective: Secrets You Must Know to Recover Information from a Computer*, Norbert Zaenglein, Paladin Press, September 1998
10. *Risky Business: Protect Your Business From Being Stalked, Conned, or Blackmailed on the Web*, Daniel S. Janal, John Wiley & Sons, March 1998
11. *Digital Evidence and Computer Crime: Forensic Science, Computers, and the Internet*, Eoghan Casey, Academic Press, March 2000
12. *High Technology Crime Investigator's Handbook*, Gerald L. Kovacich and William C. Boni, Butterworth-Heinemann, September 1999

Cybercrime

1. Cybercrime and Security, Alan E. Brill, Fletcher N. Baldwin, and Robert John Munro, Oceana Publications, September 1998
2. *The Transnational Dimension of Cybercrime and Terrorism,* Seymour F. Goodman and Abraham D. Sofaer, Hoover Institute Press, August 2001
3. *Cybercrime Cyberterrorism Cyberwarfare: Averting an Electronic Waterloo* (CSIS Task Force Report), S. Lanz, Ed., Peterson, Gallagher, Borchgraze, Cillusso, and Berkowitz, Center for Strategic and International Studies, June 1998
4. *Identity Theft: The Cybercrime of the Millennium,* John Q. Newman, Loompanics Unlimited, May 1999
5. *I-Way Robbery: Crime on the Internet,* William C. Boni, Gerald L. Kovacich, and John P. Kenney, Butterman-Heinemann, May 1999
6. *Tangled Web: Tales of Digital Crime from the Shadows of Cyberspace,* Richard Power, Que, August 2000
7. *Netspionage: The Global Threat to Information,* William C. Boni, Gerald L. Kovacich, and Perry G. Luzwick, Butterworth-Heinemann, September 2000

Law Enforcement and Legal Issues

1. Cybercrime: Law Enforcement, Security and Surveillance in the Information Age, Brian Loader and Douglas Thomas, Routledge, October 2000
2. *Transnational Criminal Organizations, Cybercrime, and Money Laundering: A Handbook for Law Enforcement Officers, Auditors, and Financial Investigators,* James R. Richards, CRC Press, December 1998
3. *Cybercrime: Appellate Court Interpretations,* Martin L. Forst, Montclair Enterprises, March 1999

Security

1. *Information Security Management Handbook,* Fourth Edition, Volume 3, Harold F. Tipton and Micki Krause, Auerbach Publications, October 2001
2. *Information Security Risk Analysis,* Thomas R. Peltier, Auerbach Publications, January 2001
3. *Computer Security Basics,* Deborah Russell and G. T. Gangemi, O'Reilly & Associates, August 1991
4. *The Internet Security Guidebook: From Planning to Deployment,* Juanita Ellis, Tim Speed, and William Crowell, Academic Press, February 2001
5. *Intrusion Signatures and Analysis,* Mark Cooper, Stephen Northcutt, Matt Fearnow, and Karen Frederick, New Riders, January 2001
6. *Information Security Architecture: An Integrated Approach to Security in the Organization,* Jan Killmeyer Tudor, Auerbach Publications, September 2000
7. *Network Intrusion Detection, Second Edition,* Stephen Northcutt, Donald McLachlan, and Judy Novak, New Riders, September 2000

8. *Building Internet Firewalls, Second Edition,* Elizabeth D. Zwicky, Deborah Russell, Simon Cooper, and D. Brent Chapman, O'Reilly & Associates, January 2000

9. *Web Security & Commerce* (O'Reilly Nutshell), Simson Garfinkel and Gene Spafford, O'Reilly & Associates, June 1997

10. *Integrity and Internal Control in Information Systems: Strategic Views on the Need for Control: Ifip Tc11 Wg11.5* Third Working Conference on Integrity, Leon Strous, Kluwer Academic, March 2000

Privacy

1. *E-mail Security: How to Keep Your Electronic Messages Private,* Bruce Schneier, John Wiley & Sons, June 1995

2. *The Electronic Privacy Papers: Documents on the Battle for Privacy in the Age of Surveillance,* Bruce Schneier and David Banisar, John Wiley & Sons, August 1997

3. *The Official PGP User's Guide,* Philip R. Zimmermann, MIT Press, April 1995

4. *PGP: Pretty Good Privacy,* Simson Garfinkel and Deborah Russell, O'Reilly & Associates, August 1996

Encryption

1. *The Twofish Encryption Algorithm: A 128-Bit Block Cipher,* Bruce Schneier, Doug Whiting, David Wagner, John Kelsey, Chris Hall, and Niels Ferguson, John Wiley & Sons, March 1999

2. *Crypto: How the Code Rebels Beat the Government, Saving Privacy in the Digital Age,* Steven Levy, Viking Penguin, January 2001

3. *Cryptography Decrypted: A Pictorial Introduction to Digital Security,* H. X. Mel, Steve Burnett, and Doris M. Baker, Addison-Wesley-Longman, December 2000

4. *Applied Cryptography: Protocols, Algorithms, and Source Code in C,* Second Edition, Bruce Schneier, John Wiley & Sons, October 1995

5. *Cryptography: Theory and Practice (Discrete Mathematics and Its Applications),* Douglas R. Stinson, CRC Press, March 1995

6. *Handbook of Applied Cryptography* (CRC Press Series on Discrete Mathematics and Its Applications), Alfred J. Menezes, Paul C. Van Oorschot, and Scott A. Vanstone, CRC Press, October 1996

7. *Internet Cryptography,* First Edition, Richard E. Smith, Addison-Wesley, January 1997

8. *Cryptography and Network Security: Principles and Practice,* William Stallings, Prentice Hall, July 1998

9. *Digital Certificates: Applied Internet Security,* Jalal Feghhi and Peter Williams, Addison-Wesley, October 1998

10. *ICSA Guide to Cryptography,* Randall K. Nichols, McGraw-Hill Professional Publishing, November 1998

Hacking and Viruses

1. *The Complete Hacker's Handbook: Everything You Need to Know About Hacking in the Age of the Web,* Dr. X, Carlton Books, October 2000
2. *The Hacker Ethic,* Pekka Himanen, Manuel Castells (Epilogue), and Linus Torvalds, Random House, January 2001
3. *Hackers: Heroes of the Computer Revolution,* Steven Levy, Penguin USA, January 2001
4. *Virus Within: A Coming Epidemic,* Nicholas Regush, Plume, March 2001

Networks and Systems

1. *Essential System Administration* (Nutshell Handbook), Aeleen Frisch, O'Reilly & Associates, Inc., December 1996
2. *Secrets and Lies: Digital Security in a Networked World,* Bruce Schneier, John Wiley & Sons, August 2000
3. *IPSec: The New Security Standard for the Internet, Intranets, and Virtual Private Networks,* First Edition, Naganand Doraswamy and Dan Harkins, Prentice Hall, August 1999
4. *LAN Times Guide to Security and Data Integrity,* Marc Farley, Tom Stearns, and Jeffrey Hsu, Osbourne McGraw-Hill, May 1996
5. *Novell's Guide to Network Security,* David J. Clarke, Sybex, January 1995
6. *Mastering Network Security,* Chris Brenton, Sybex, December 1998
7. *Open Source: The Unathorized White Papers,* First Edition, Donald K. Rosenberg, Hungry Minds, January 2000

Windows

1. *Securing Windows NT/2000 Servers for the Internet,* Stefan Norberg and Deborah Russell, O'Reilly & Associates, November 2000
2. *Windows 2000 Security,* Roberta Bragg, New Riders, October 2000
3. *Windows 2000 Security Handbook,* First Edition, Philip Cox and Tom Sheldon, McGraw-Hill Professional Publishing, November 2000
4. *Windows 2000 Administration in a Nutshell: A Desktop Quick Reference,* Mitch Tulloch, O'Reilly & Associates, February 2001
5. *Windows 2000: Quick Fixes,* Jim Boyce, O'Reilly & Associates, January 2001

UNIX and Linux

1. *Real World Linux Security: Intrusion Prevention, Detection and Recovery,* First Edition, Bob Toxen, Prentice Hall, November 2000
2. *Linux Security Toolkit,* David A. Bandel, Hungry Minds, May 2000
3. *Linux Apache Web Server Administration,* Charles Aulds, Sybex, November 2000

4. *Linux System Administration,* First Edition, Vicki Stanfield and Roderick W. Smith, Sybex, February 2001
5. *Practical Unix and Internet Security,* Simson Garfinkel and Gene Spafford, O'Reilly & Associates, April 1996
6. *Rebel Code: Linux and the Open Source Revolution,* Glyn Moody, Perseus Press, January 2001

Protocols

1. *A Technical Guide to IPSec Virtual Private Networks,* James S. Tiller, Auerbach Publications, December 2000
2. *SSH, the Secure Shell: The Definitive Guide,* Daniel J. Barrett and Richard Silverman, O'Reilly & Associates, February 2001
3. *Internet Core Protocols: The Definitive Guide,* Eric A. Hall, and Vinton G. Cerf, O'Reilly & Associates, March 2000
4. *TCP/IP Network Administration,* Craig Hunt and Gigi Estabrook, O'Reilly & Associates, Janaury 1998

Java and Smart Cards

1. *Smart Card Application Development Using Java,* Uwe Hansmann, Ed., et al, Springer-Verlag, October 1999
2. *Java Security* (Java Series), Scott Oaks, O'Reilly & Associates, May 1998
3. *Java Cryptography* (Java Series), Jonathan Knudsen, O'Reilly & Associates, May 1998
4. *Java Threads* (Java Series), Scott Oaks, Henry Wong, and Mike Loukides, O'Reilly & Associates, January 1999
5. *Java I/O* (O'Reilly Java), Elliotte Rusty Harold and Mike Loukides, O'Reilly & Associates,
6. *Java Network Programming,* Elliotte Rusty Harold, O'Reilly & Associates, August 2000
7. *Java Card Technology for Smart Cards: Architecture and Programmer's Guide* (The Java Series), Zhiqun Chen, Addison-Wesley, June 2000
8. *Smart Card Handbook,* W. Rankl and W. Effing (Translator), John Wiley & Sons, September 2000
9. *Smart Cards: Seizing Strategic Business Opportunities: The Smart Card Forum,* Catherine A. Allen, Ed., et al, McGraw-Hill Professional Publishing, 1997

Articles

1. John Patzakis, "Computer Forensics: From Cottage Industry to Standard Practice," *Information Systems Control Journal,* Volume 2, 2001, Page 25
2. Michael Tucker, "Computer Forensics," *SC Magazine,* October 1998
3. Illena Armstrong, "Computer Forensics: Tracking Down the Clues," *SC Magazine,* April 2001

Web Sites

U.S. Federal Government Sites

1. NIST Computer Security Clearinghouse, http://csrc.ncsl.nist.gov/
2. Information Technology Laboratory, http://www.itl.nist.gov/
3. NASA Incident Response Center, http://www-nasirc.nasa.gov/
4. General Accounting Office, http://www.gao.gov/
5. Computer Crime and Intellectual Property Section (CCIPS) of the Criminal Division of the U.S. Department of Justice, http://www.usdoj.gov/criminal/cybercrime/

Organizations

1. Organisation for Economic Co-operation and Development (OECD) Cryptography Policy Guidelines and the Report on Background and Issues of Cryptography Policy, http://www.oecd.org/dsti/sti/it/secur/
2. COAST (Computers, operations, audit, security and technology), http://www.cs.purdue.edu/coast/coast.html
3. Warinet IT audit, security and control, http://www.rain.org/~lonestar/index.html
4. CISSP certification, http://www.isc2.org/
5. Risks Forum, http://catless.ncl.ac.uk/Risks/VL.IS.html
6. American Society for Industrial Security, http://www.asisonline.org/
7. National Security Institute, http://nsi.org/compsec.html
8. Computer Security Group, http://www.cl.cam.ac.uk/Research/Security/index.html
9. Center for High Assurance Computer Systems, http://chacs.nrl.navy.mil/
10. IEEE Computer Society Technical Committee on Security and Privacy, http://www.ieee-security.org/index.html
11. International Federation for Information Processing, http://www.ifip.or.at/
12. Internet Society, http://www.isoc.org/
13. Information Systems Security Association, http://www.issa-intl.org/
14. American Society for Industrial Security, http://www.asisonline.org/

Resources

1. Computer crime research resources, http://mailer.fsu.edu/~btf1553/ccrr/states.htm
2. Firewalls Wizards, http://www.nfr.net/firewall-wizards/
3. Computer Crime Research Resources, http://mailer.fsu.edu/~btf1553/ccrr/welcome.htm
4. Security Focus, http://www.securityfocus.com/
5. Computer Science Laboratory, http://www.csl.sri.com/
6. Info Security News, http://www.infosecnews.com/

7. The University of Melbourne, Department of Computer Science and Software Engineering, http://www.cs.mu.oz.au/research/groups/netsec/overview.html
8. Security Nerdnet, http://security.nerdnet.com/index.php
9. The Information Security Policies / Computer Security Policies Directory, http://www.information-security-policies-and-standards.com/
10. The Risk Digest, http://catless.ncl.ac.uk/Risks/VL.IS.html
11. Computer Crime Research Resources, http://mailer.fsu.edu/~btf1553/ccrr/states.htm

New Technologies, Inc.

NTI posts information on various topics which are related to computer evidence, computer forensics, document discovery, computer incident response, and computer security risk management issues, available at http://www.forensics-intl.com/info.html. Articles on the following topics are available:

- Computer evidence documentation
- Computer evidence (electronic fingerprints)
- Data validation using the MD5 hash
- Electronic document discovery
- Forensic identification of Internet evidence
- Huge hard drives — the forensics dilemma
- Industrial espionage
- Internet security (firewalls vs. encryption)
- Law enforcement computer evidence seizure
- Law enforcement and the internet
- Law enforcement liabilities with computer evidence
- Preservation of computer evidence
- Shadow data

The following guidelines are also available at this site:

- Classified Agency Security Reviews
- Computer Evidence Processing
- Computer Incident Response

Commercial Sites

1. The World Wide Information Sharing and Analysis Center, http://www.wwisac.com/
2. Computer Security Institute, http://www.gocsi.com/
3. Antionline, http://www.antionline.com/
4. RSA Security, http://www.rsasecurity.com/

Specific Documents of Interest

1. "Draft Convention on Cyber-Crime," http://www.cyber-rights.org/documents/cybercrime24.htm
2. "Cyberstalking: A New Challenge for Law Enforcement and Industry" (Report from the Attorney General to the Vice President), http://www.usdoj.gov/criminal/cybercrime/cyberstalking.htm
3. "The Electronic Frontier: The Challenge of Unlawful Conduct Involving the Use of the Internet" (Report of the President's Working Group on Unlawful Conduct on the Internet), http://www.usdoj.gov/criminal/cybercrime/unlawful.htm
4. "Legal Considerations in Designing and Implementing Electronic Processes: A Guide for Federal Agencies," http://www.cybercrime.gov/eprocess.htm
5. "Combatting Child Pornography" on the Internet, www.usdoj.gov/criminal/cybercrime/dagceos.htm

Computer Facilitated Crime Cases

- "Two Men Plead Guilty in California to Mail and Wire Fraud in eBay Shill Bidding Scheme that Auctioned Fake Diebenkorn Painting for $135,805," www.usdoj.gov/criminal/cybercrime/ebayplea.htm
- "Portland, Oregon 18 year old Arrested for Sending Threatening Internet Communication Resulting in New York School Closing," www.usdoj.gov/criminal/cybercrime/BallardArrest.htm
- "Internet False ID Scam Defendants Sentenced in the District of Columbia," www.usdoj.gov/criminal/cybercrime/WrightSent.htm
- "Three Men Indicted in Sacramento for eBay Shill Bidding Ring That Auctioned Fake Diebenkorn Painting for $135,805," www.usdoj.gov/criminal/cybercrime/Fetterman_indict.htm
- "New York Father and Son Are Accused in Playstation 2 Internet Auction Scam," www.usdoj.gov/criminal/cybercrime/garay.htm
- "High-Tech Defendants Sentenced to Jail," www.usdoj.gov/criminal/cybercrime/Williams_Wilson.htm
- "Two Indicted and Arrested in South Carolina for Trafficking in Counterfeit Luxury Goods over www.fakegifts.com Web site," www.usdoj.gov/criminal/cybercrime/fakegifts.htm
- "Man Indicted for Engaging in Stock Hoax by Using Bogus Press Release," www.usdoj.gov/criminal/cybercrime/emulex.htm

Ways Computers Can Be Used In Crimes

- "Internet as the Scene of Crime," www.usdoj.gov/criminal/cybercrime/roboslo.htm
- "Cybercrime and The Internet Integrity and Critical Infrastructure Act," www.usdoj.gov/criminal/cybercrime/robtest.htm

- "The Federal Bureau of Investigation on Cybercrime," www.usdoj.gov/criminal/cybercrime/freeh328.htm
- "High-Tech Crime Summit in Washington, DC," www.usdoj.gov/criminal/cybercrime/dag0112.htm

Internet Gambling

- "Gambling on the Internet," www.usdoj.gov/criminal/cybercrime/kvd0600.htm
- "Internet Gambling and Indian Gaming," www.usdoj.gov/criminal/cybercrime/s692tst.htm
- S. 692, the Internet Gambling Prohibition Act of 1999, www.usdoj.gov/criminal/cybercrime/s692ltr.htm
- "Jay Cohen Convicted of Operating an Off-Shore Sports Betting Business that Accepted Bets from Americans Over the Internet," www.usdoj.gov/criminal/cybercrime/cohen.htm
- "Owners, Managers and Employees of Internet Sports Betting Companies Charged with Violating Federal Law," www.usdoj.gov/criminal/cybercrime/nypr.htm
- "Gambling Against Enforcement—Internet Sports Books and the Wire Wager Act," www.usdoj.gov/criminal/cybercrime/usamarch2001.htm

Cyberstalking and Harassing Speech

- "Maryland Man Pleads Guilty to "Cyber-Stalking" High School Administrator," www.usdoj.gov/criminal/cybercrime/gray.htm
- "Man Convicted of Threatening Federal Judges by Internet E-mail," www.usdoj.gov/criminal/cybercrime/johnson.htm
- "Man Sentenced to Thirty-Seven Months Imprisonment for Threatening Federal Judges by Internet E-mail," www.usdoj.gov/criminal/cybercrime/johnson2.htm
- "Individual pleaded guilty to felony for repeatedly causing e-mail to be transmitted over the Internet solely with the intent to harass another individual," www.usdoj.gov/criminal/cybercrime/ngo_pr.htm

Sale of Prescription Drugs Over the Internet

- "New Jersey Man Pleads Guilty to Selling Non-FDA Approved HIV Test Kits over the Internet," www.usdoj.gov/criminal/cybercrime/hivtest.htm
- "Online Pharmaceutical Drug Sales," www.usdoj.gov/criminal/cybercrime/posner.htm
- "Kent Aoki Lee Charged by Federal Grand Jury with Wire Fraud, Trademark Violations, and Selling Viagra over the Internet Without a Prescription," www.usdoj.gov/criminal/cybercrime/kaokilee.htm
- "Sale of Prescription Drugs over the Internet," www.usdoj.gov/criminal/cybercrime/fong9907.htm

Index